TRANSFORMATION 1

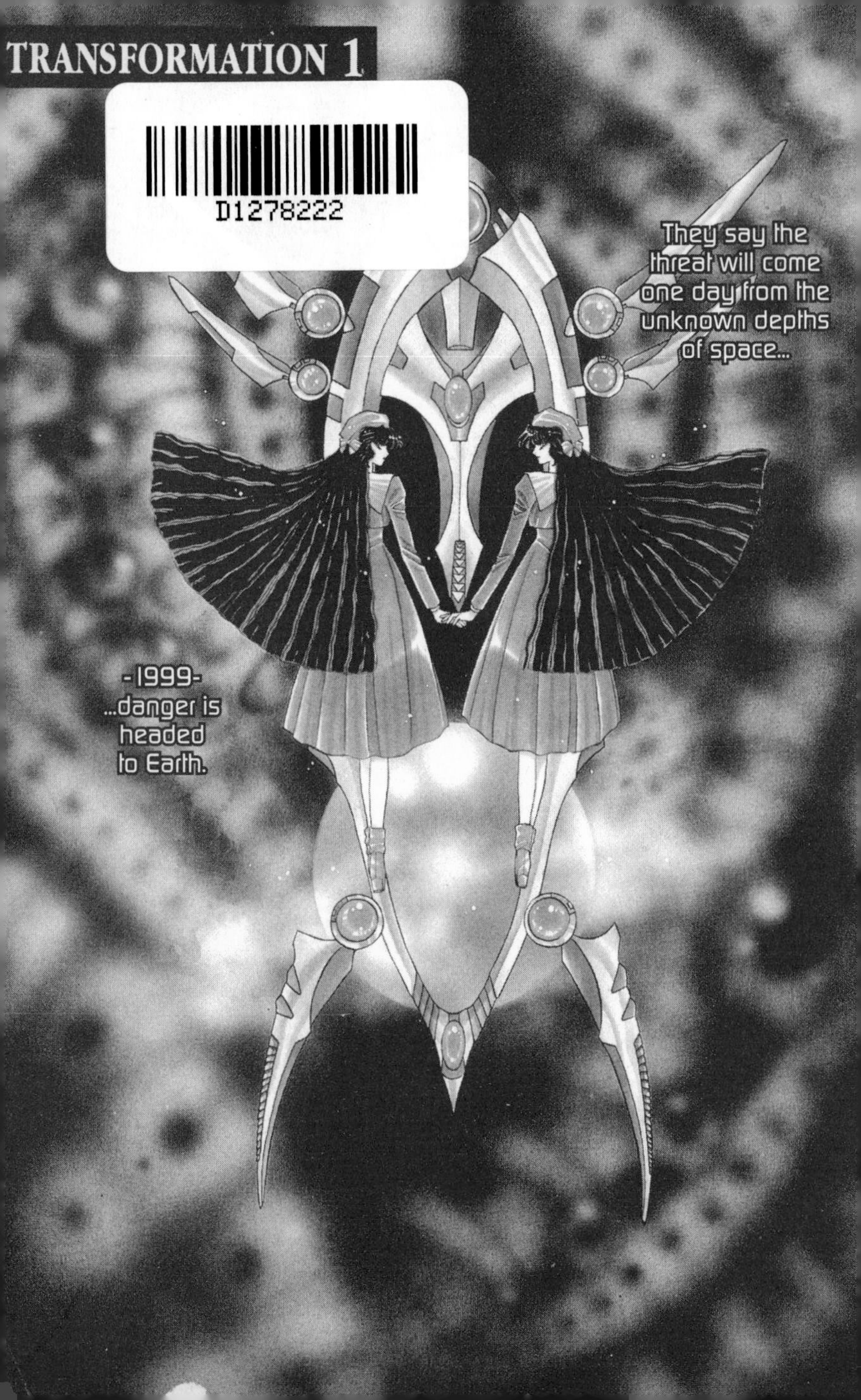
They say the threat will come one day from the unknown depths of space...
-1999- ...danger is headed to Earth.

Hyper Rune Vol. 1
Created by Tamayo Akiyama

Translation - Alexis Kirsch
Copy Editor - Carol Fox
Retouch and Lettering - Abelardo Bigting
Cover Design - Gary Shum

Editor - Jake Forbes
Digital Imaging Manager - Chris Buford
Pre-Press Manager - Antonio DePietro
Production Managers - Jennifer Miller and Mutsumi Miyazaki
Art Director - Matt Alford
Managing Editor - Jill Freshney
VP of Production - Ron Klamert
President and C.O.O. - John Parker
Publisher and C.E.O. - Stuart Levy

A  Manga

TOKYOPOP Inc.
5900 Wilshire Blvd. Suite 2000
Los Angeles, CA 90036

E-mail: info@TOKYOPOP.com
Come visit us online at www.TOKYOPOP.com

ISBN: 1-59532-241-8

First TOKYOPOP printing: November 2004
10 9 8 7 6 5 4 3 2 1
Printed in the USA

Hyper ☆ Rune

Volume I

By
Tamayo Akiyama

HAMBU

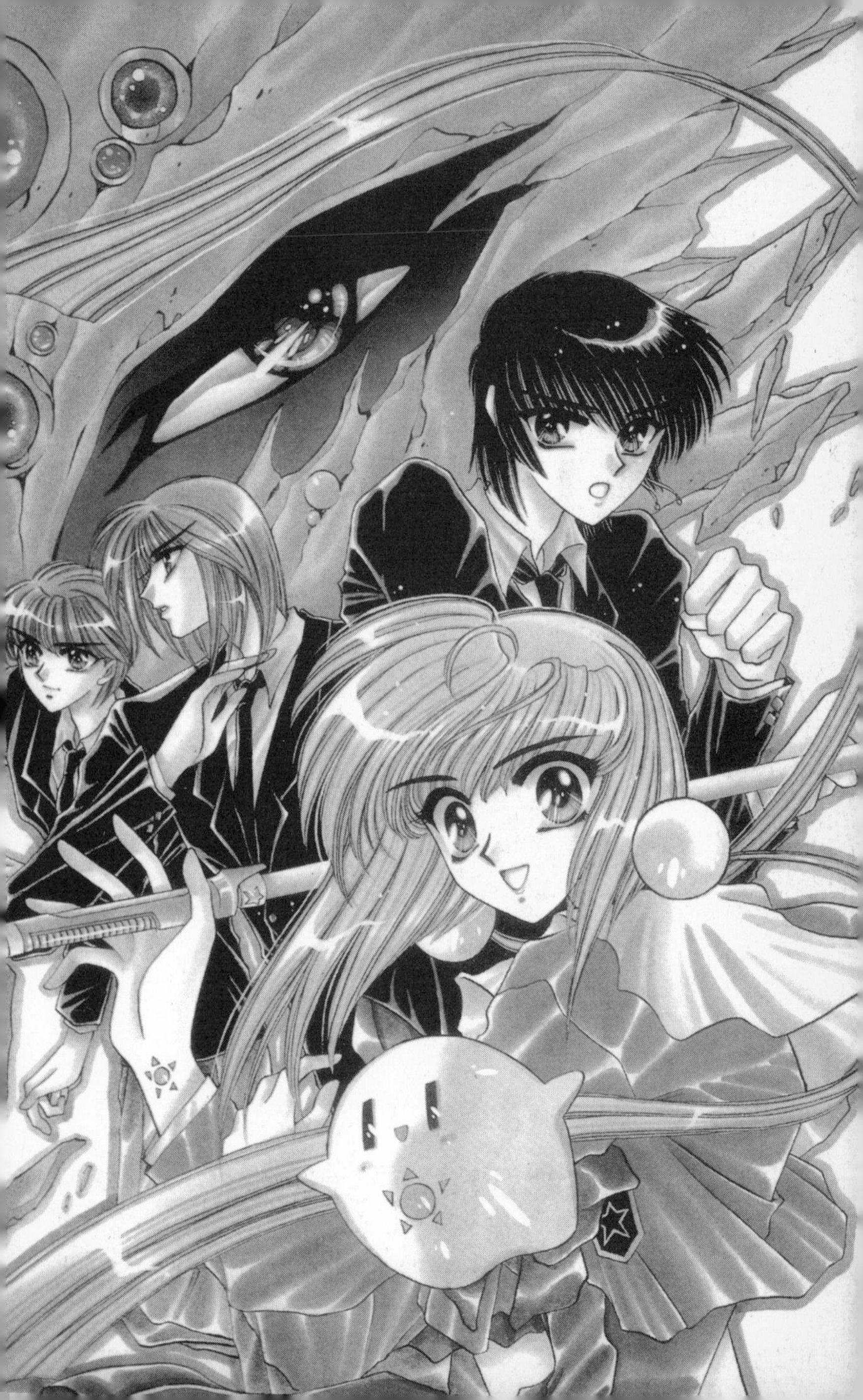

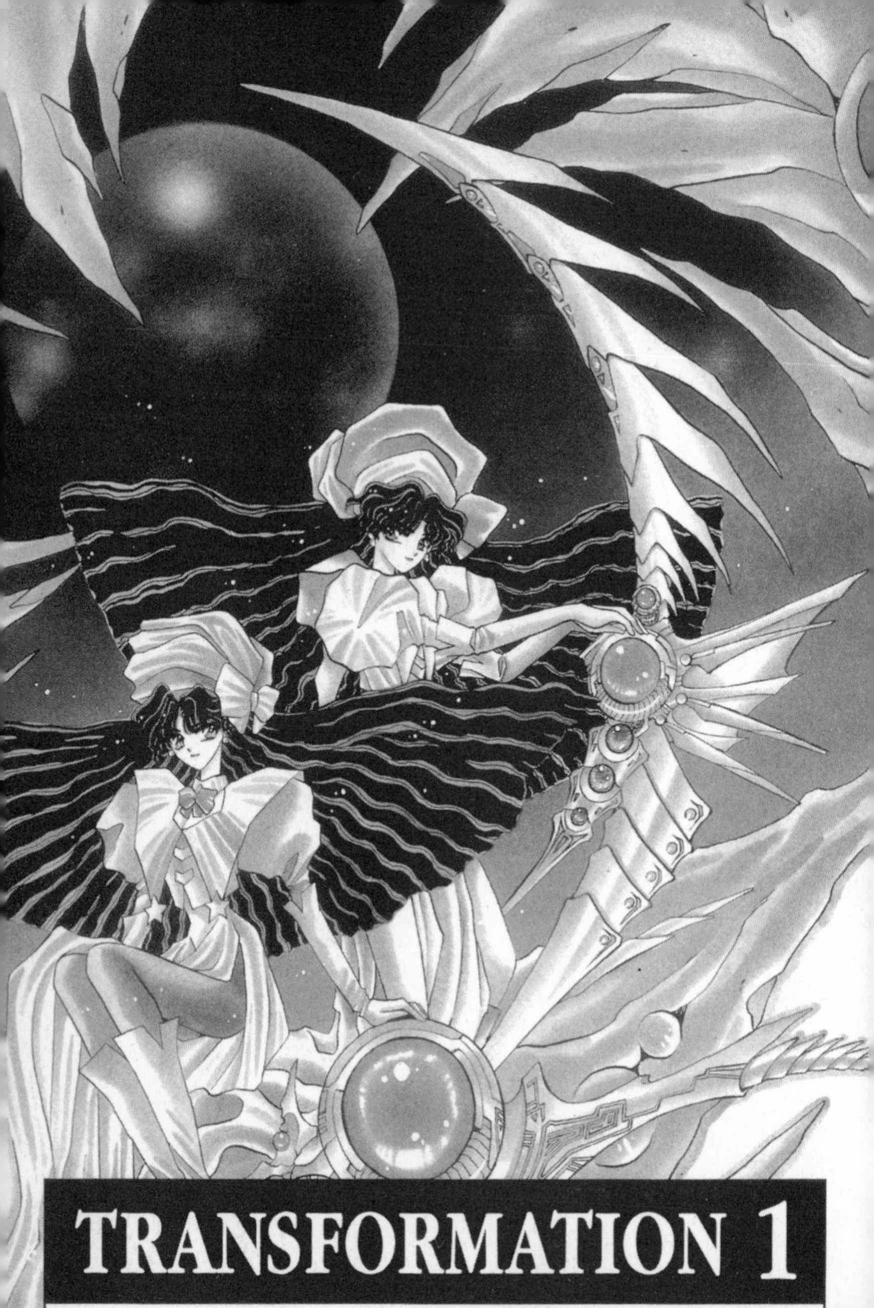

TRANSFORMATION 1

ACCESS RUN【出撃】

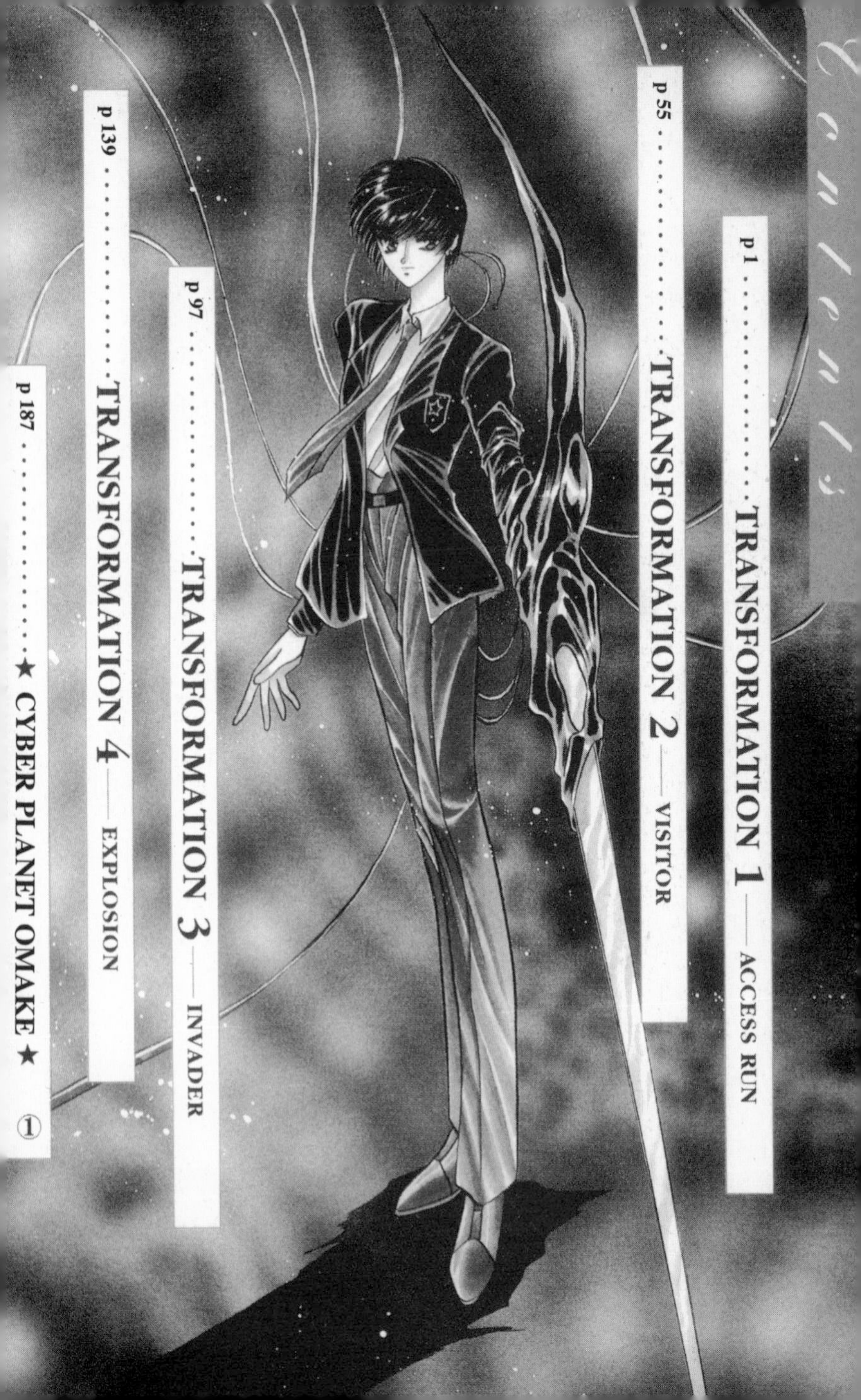

Contents

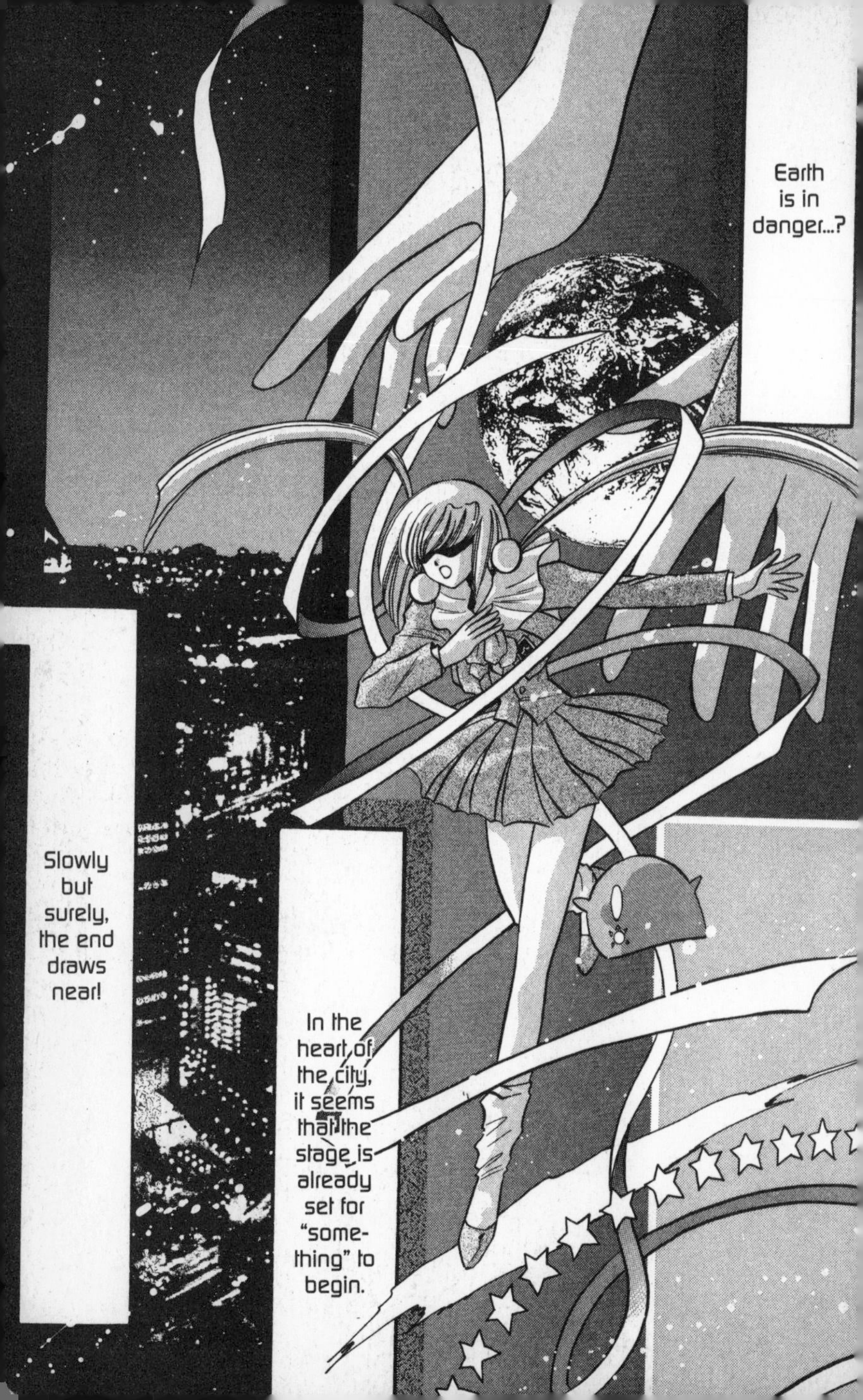
Earth is in danger...?
In the heart of the city, it seems that the stage is already set for "something" to begin.
Slowly but surely, the end draws near!

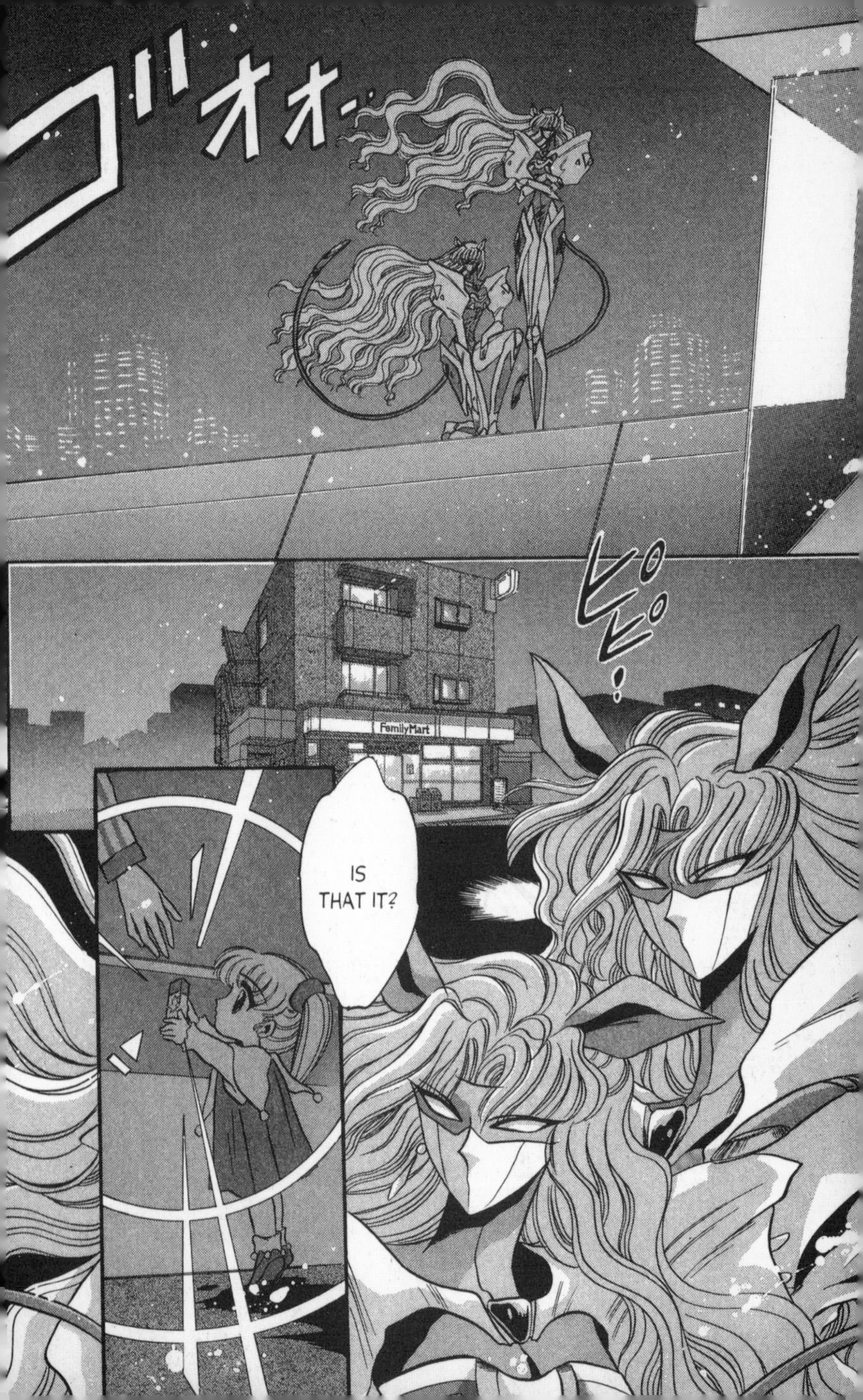
ゴオオー
ピピ!
FamilyMart
IS THAT IT?

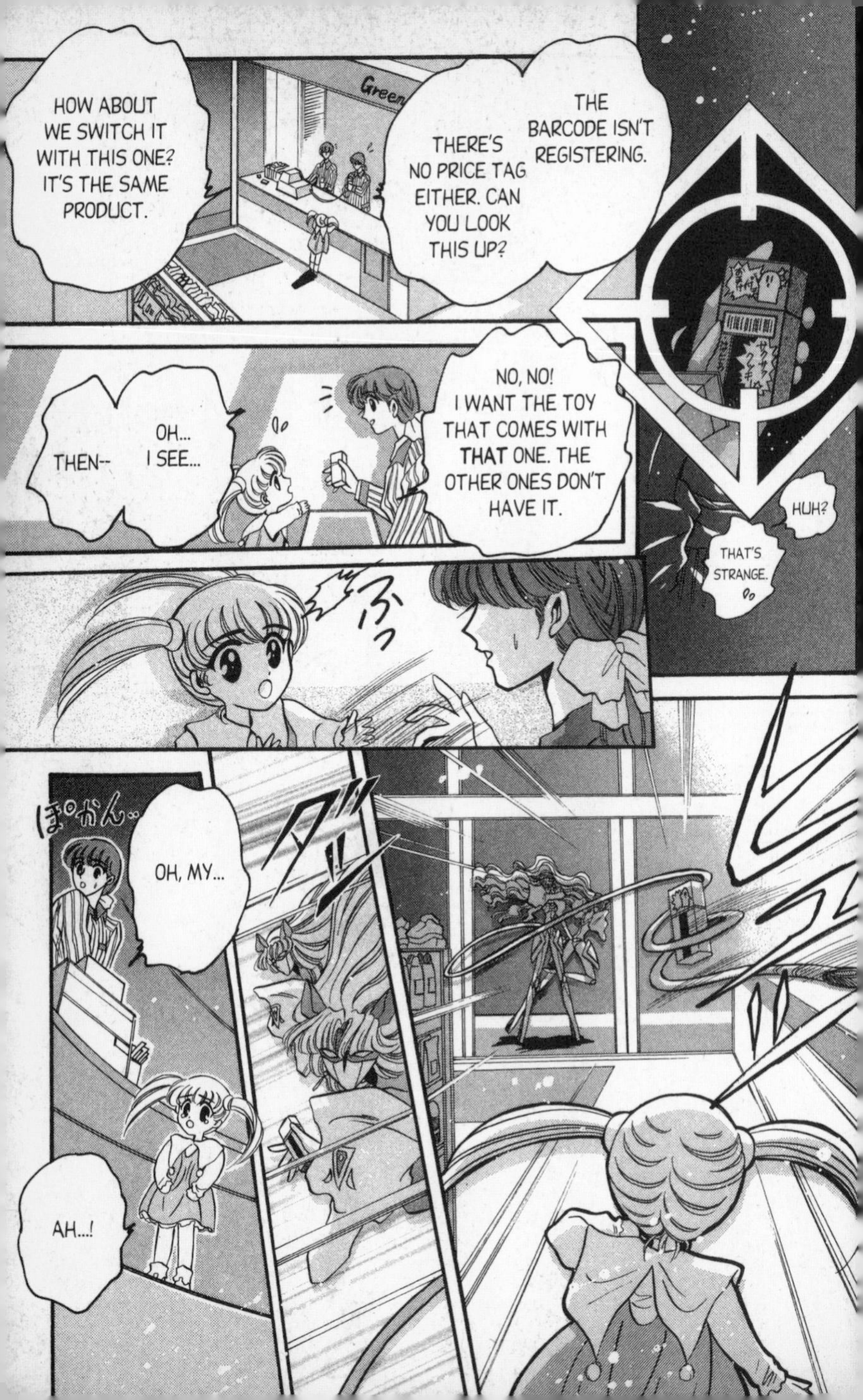
HUH?
THAT'S STRANGE.
THE BARCODE ISN'T REGISTERING.
THERE'S NO PRICE TAG EITHER. CAN YOU LOOK THIS UP?
Green
HOW ABOUT WE SWITCH IT WITH THIS ONE? IT'S THE SAME PRODUCT.
NO, NO! I WANT THE TOY THAT COMES WITH **THAT** ONE. THE OTHER ONES DON'T HAVE IT.
OH... I SEE...
THEN--
ふっ
ぽかん..
OH, MY...
AH...!

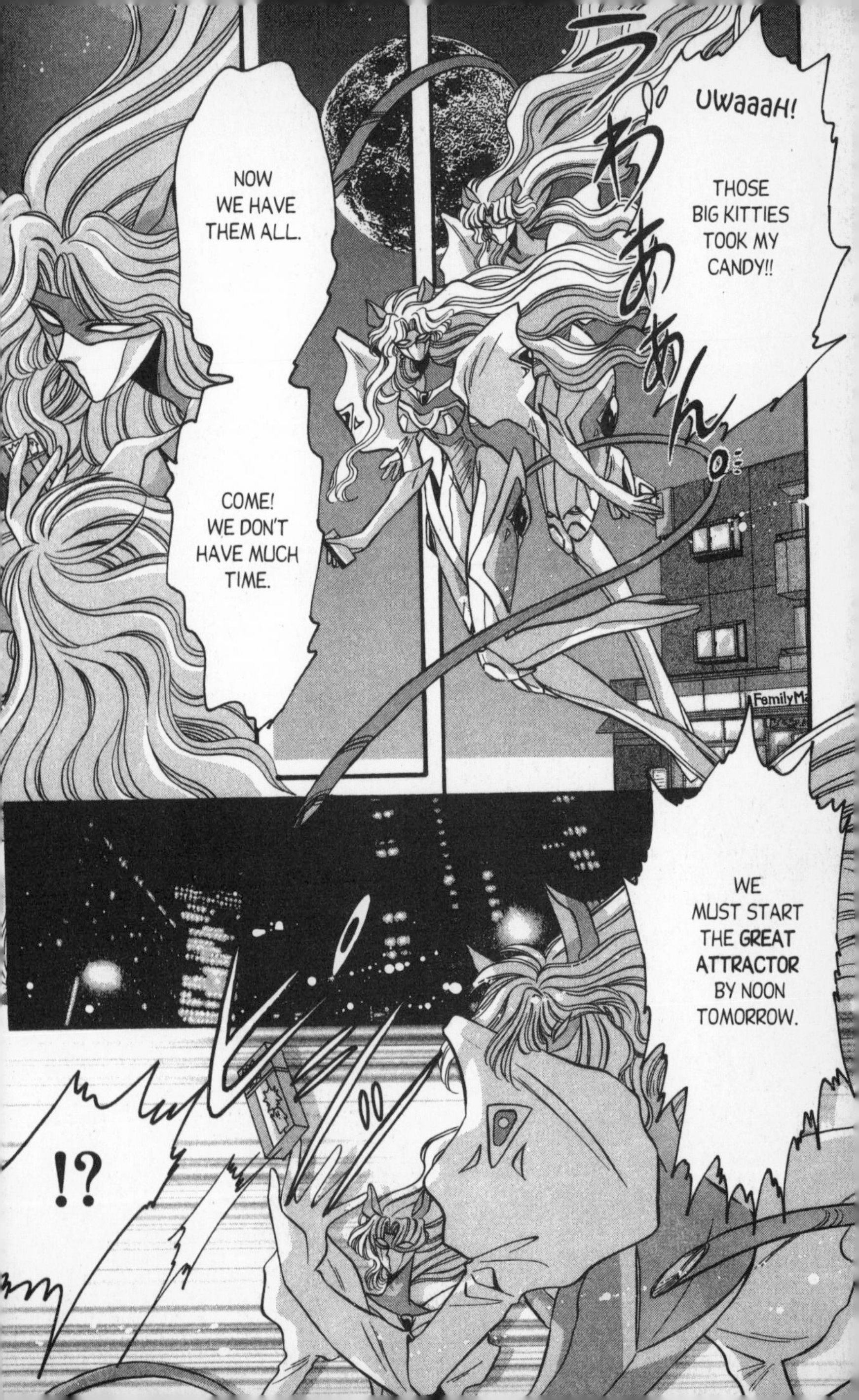
うわああん。
UWAAAH!
THOSE BIG KITTIES TOOK MY CANDY!!
NOW WE HAVE THEM ALL.
COME! WE DON'T HAVE MUCH TIME.
FamilyMa
WE MUST START THE **GREAT ATTRACTOR** BY NOON TOMORROW.
!?

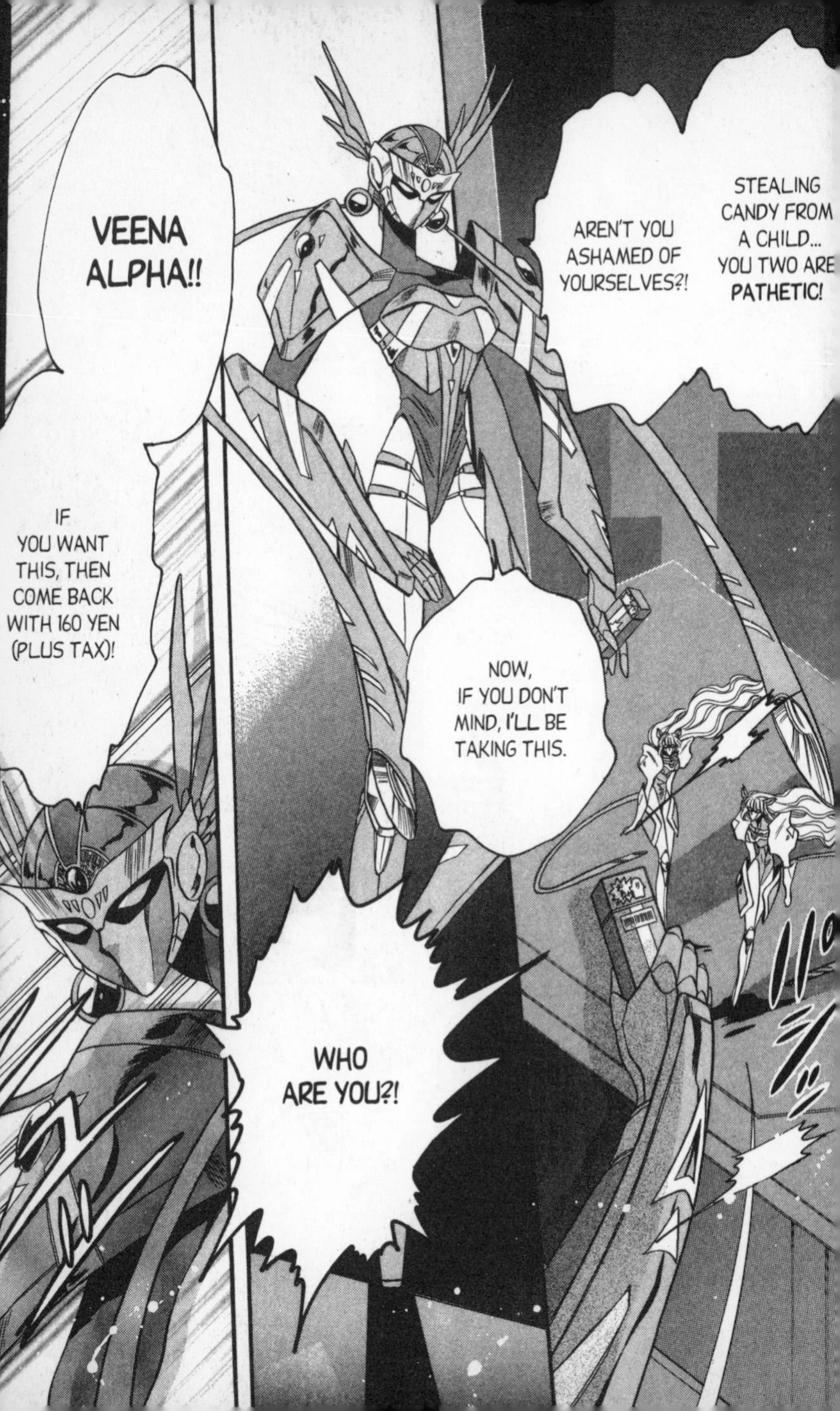
STEALING CANDY FROM A CHILD... YOU TWO ARE PATHETIC!
AREN'T YOU ASHAMED OF YOURSELVES?!
NOW, IF YOU DON'T MIND, I'LL BE TAKING THIS.
WHO ARE YOU?!
VEENA ALPHA!!
IF YOU WANT THIS, THEN COME BACK WITH 160 YEN (PLUS TAX)!

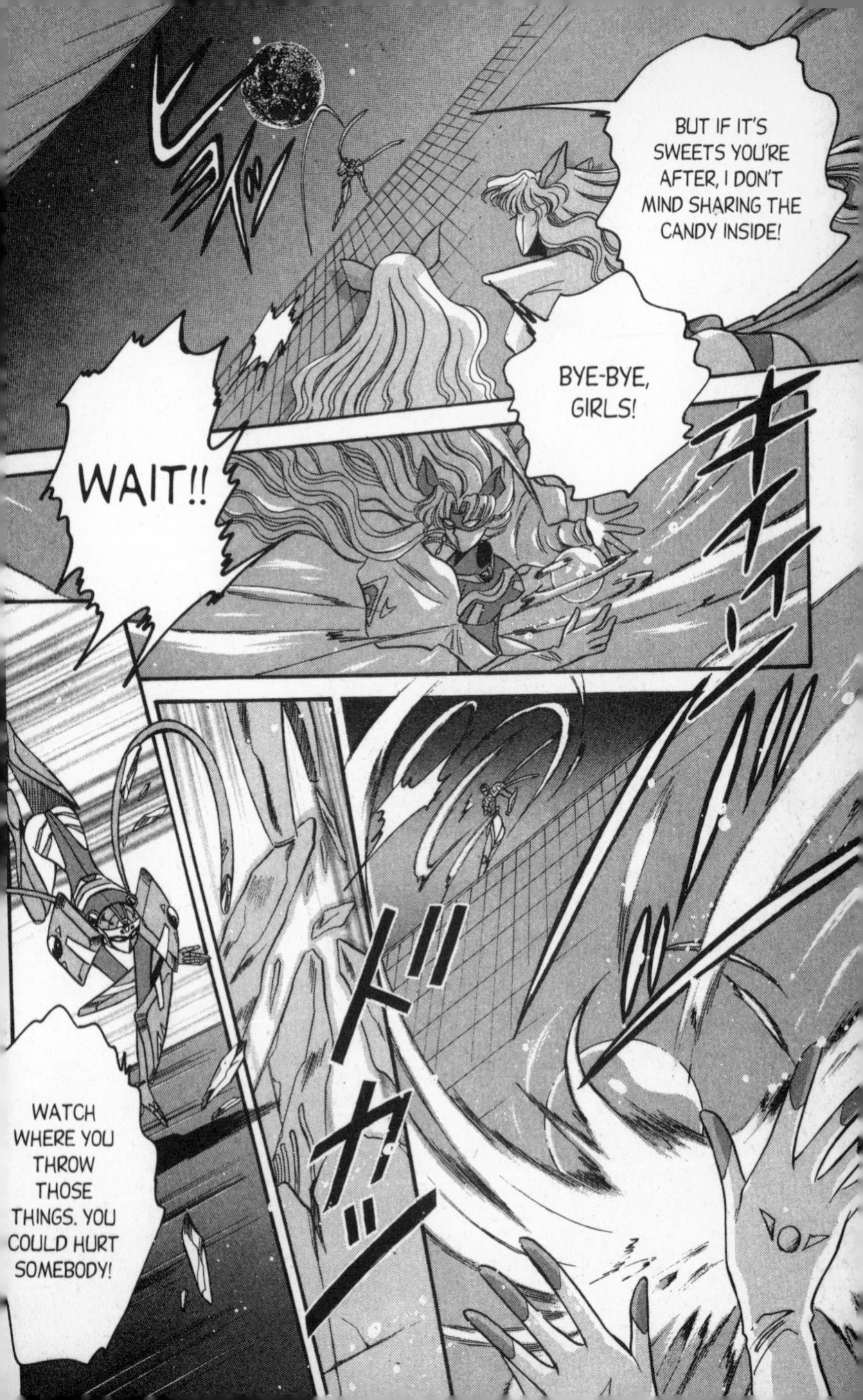
BUT IF IT'S SWEETS YOU'RE AFTER, I DON'T MIND SHARING THE CANDY INSIDE!
BYE-BYE, GIRLS!
WAIT!!
WATCH WHERE YOU THROW THOSE THINGS. YOU COULD HURT SOMEBODY!

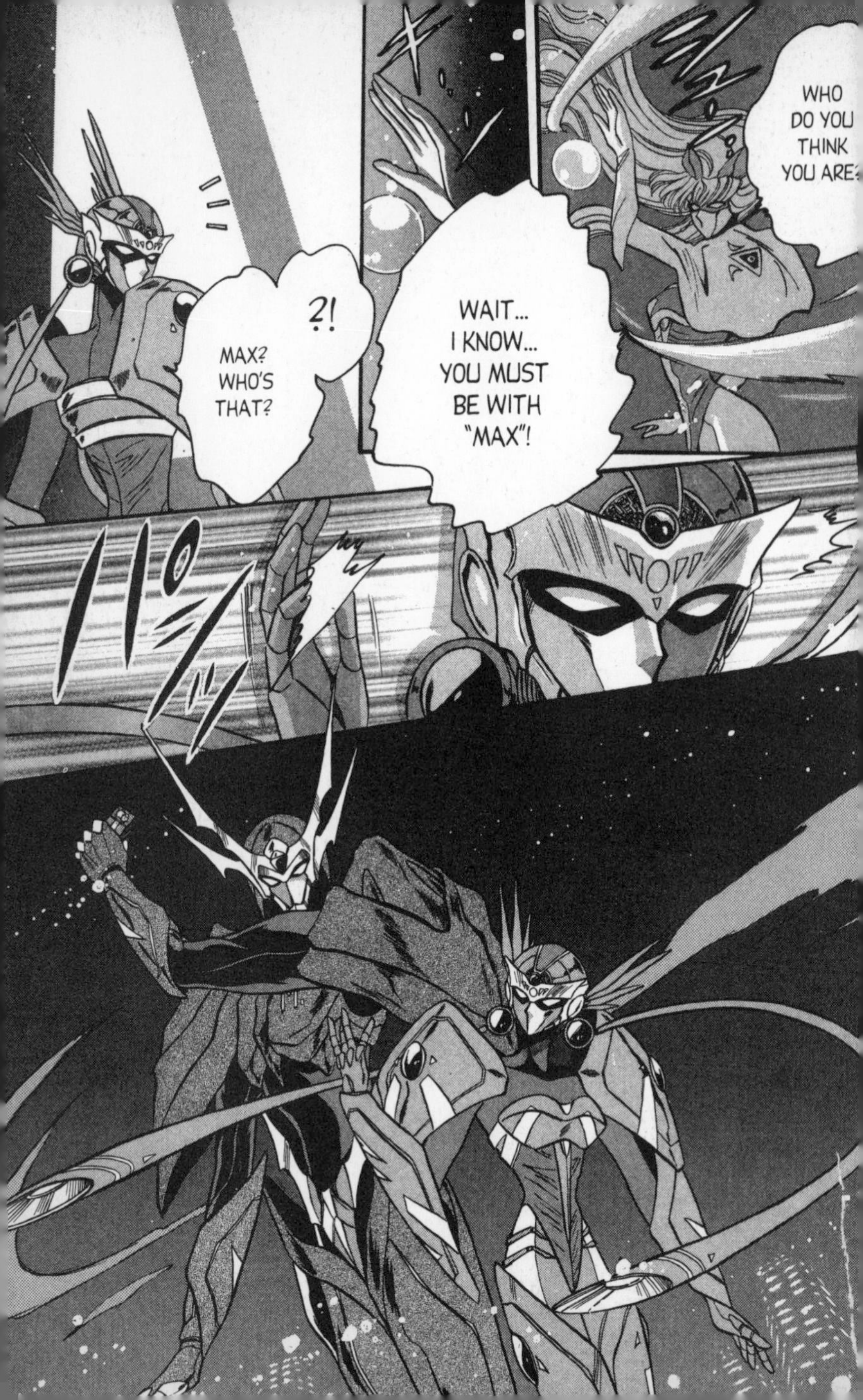
WHO DO YOU THINK YOU ARE?
WAIT... I KNOW... YOU MUST BE WITH "MAX"!
?!
MAX? WHO'S THAT?

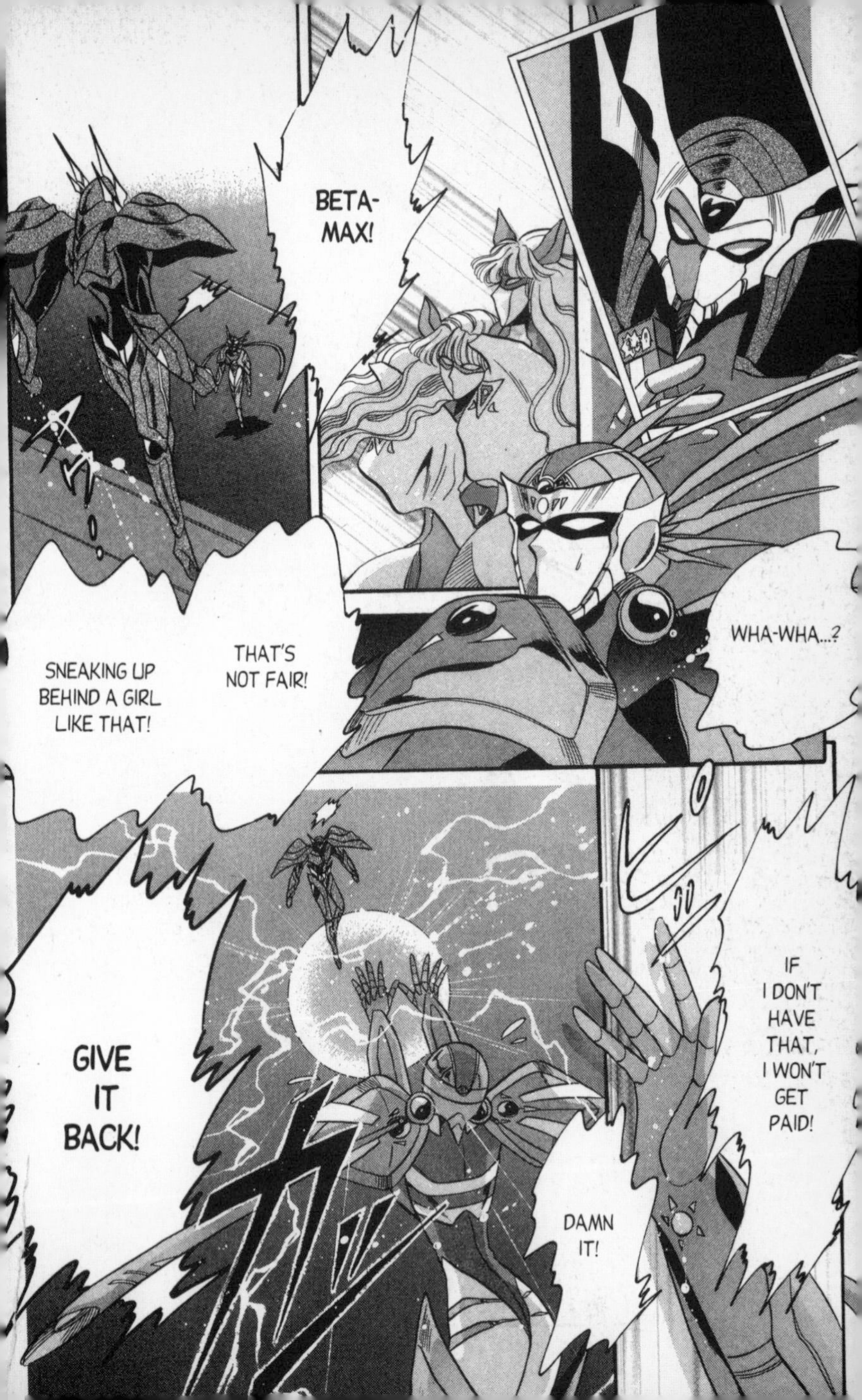
BETA-MAX!
WHA-WHA...?
THAT'S NOT FAIR!
SNEAKING UP BEHIND A GIRL LIKE THAT!
IF I DON'T HAVE THAT, I WON'T GET PAID!
DAMN IT!
GIVE IT BACK!

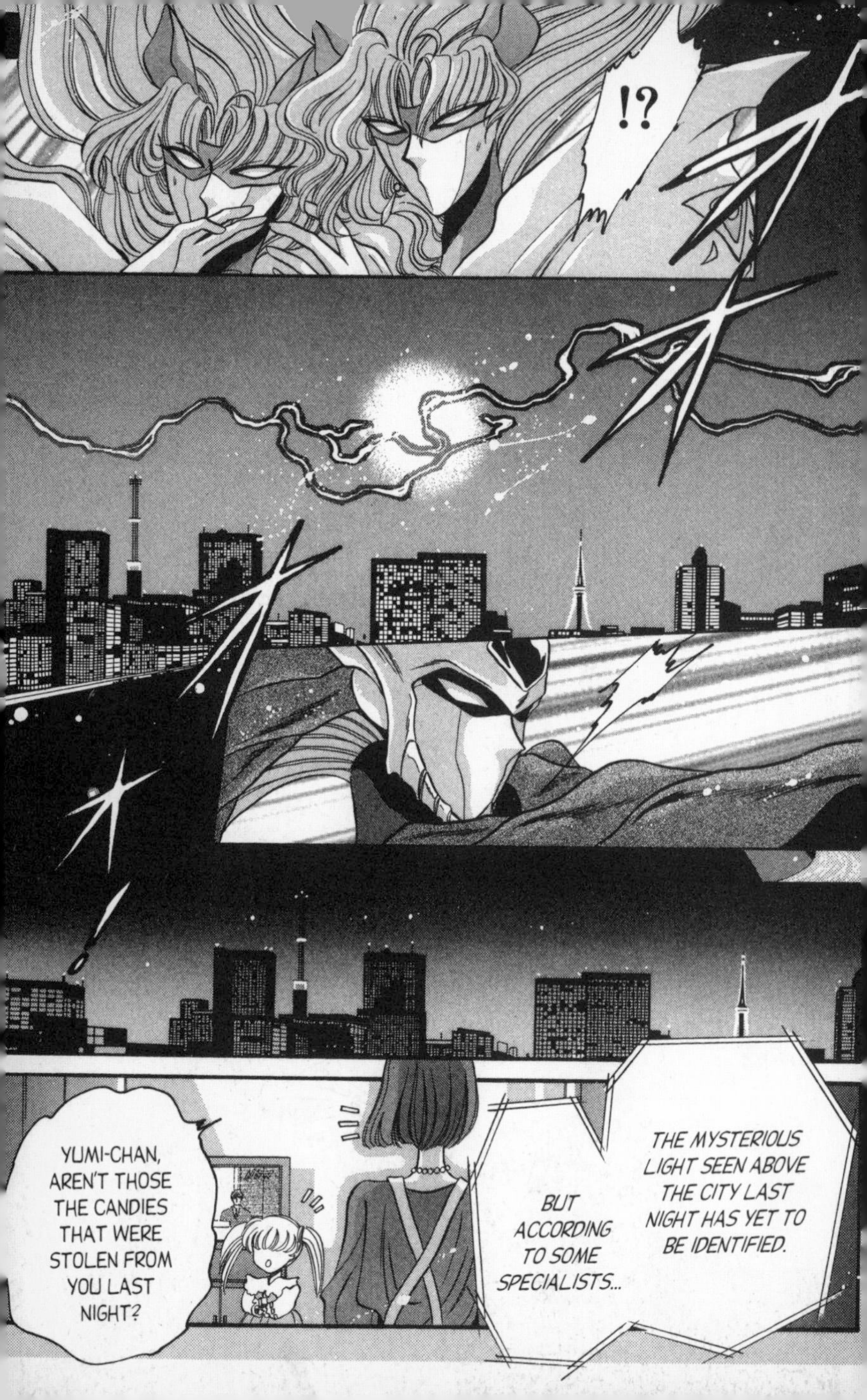
!?
THE MYSTERIOUS LIGHT SEEN ABOVE THE CITY LAST NIGHT HAS YET TO BE IDENTIFIED.
BUT ACCORDING TO SOME SPECIALISTS...
YUMI-CHAN, AREN'T THOSE THE CANDIES THAT WERE STOLEN FROM YOU LAST NIGHT?

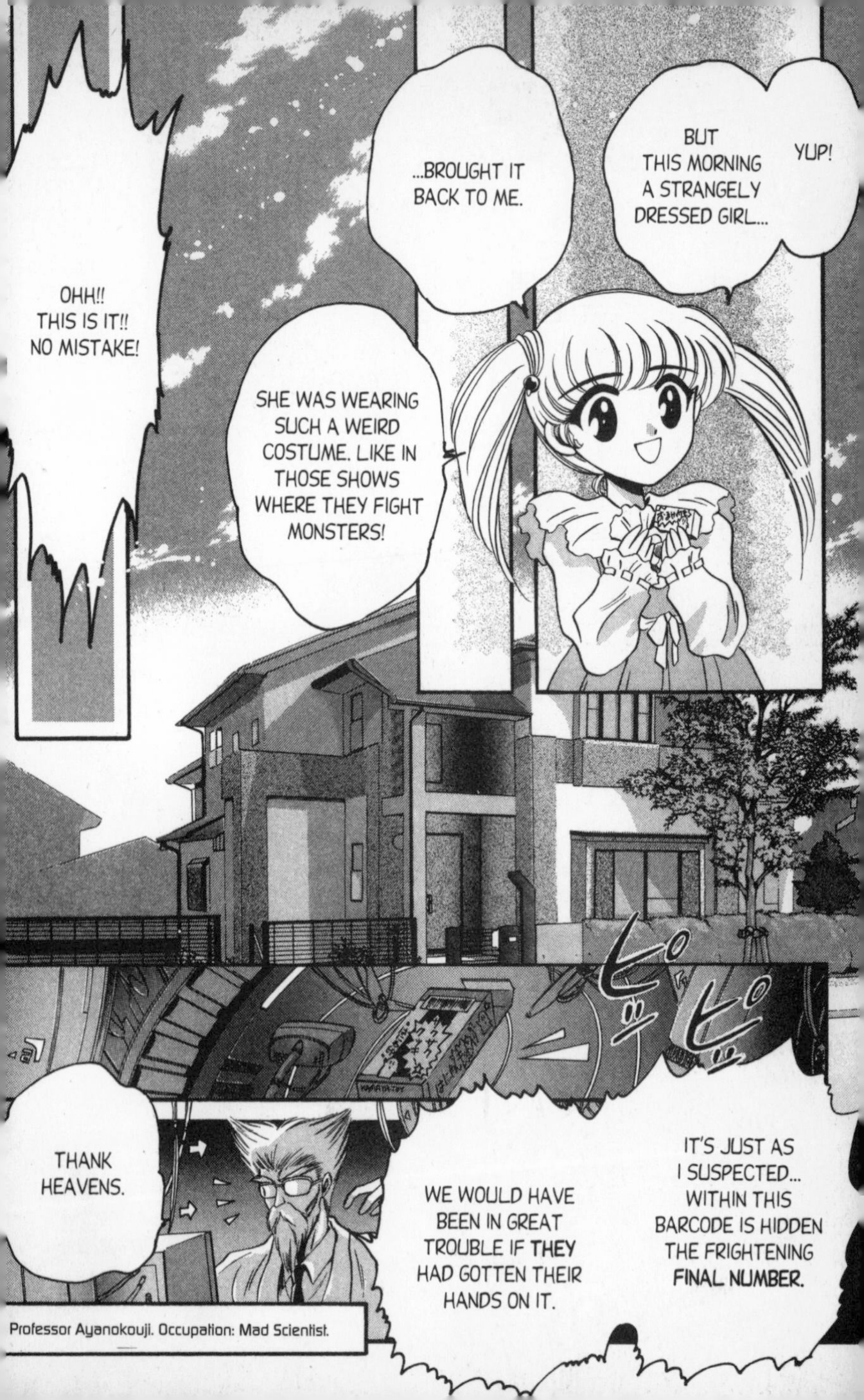

YUP!
BUT THIS MORNING A STRANGELY DRESSED GIRL...
...BROUGHT IT BACK TO ME.
SHE WAS WEARING SUCH A WEIRD COSTUME. LIKE IN THOSE SHOWS WHERE THEY FIGHT MONSTERS!
OHH!! THIS IS IT!! NO MISTAKE!
IT'S JUST AS I SUSPECTED... WITHIN THIS BARCODE IS HIDDEN THE FRIGHTENING **FINAL NUMBER.**
WE WOULD HAVE BEEN IN GREAT TROUBLE IF **THEY** HAD GOTTEN THEIR HANDS ON IT.
THANK HEAVENS.
Professor Ayanokouji. Occupation: Mad Scientist.

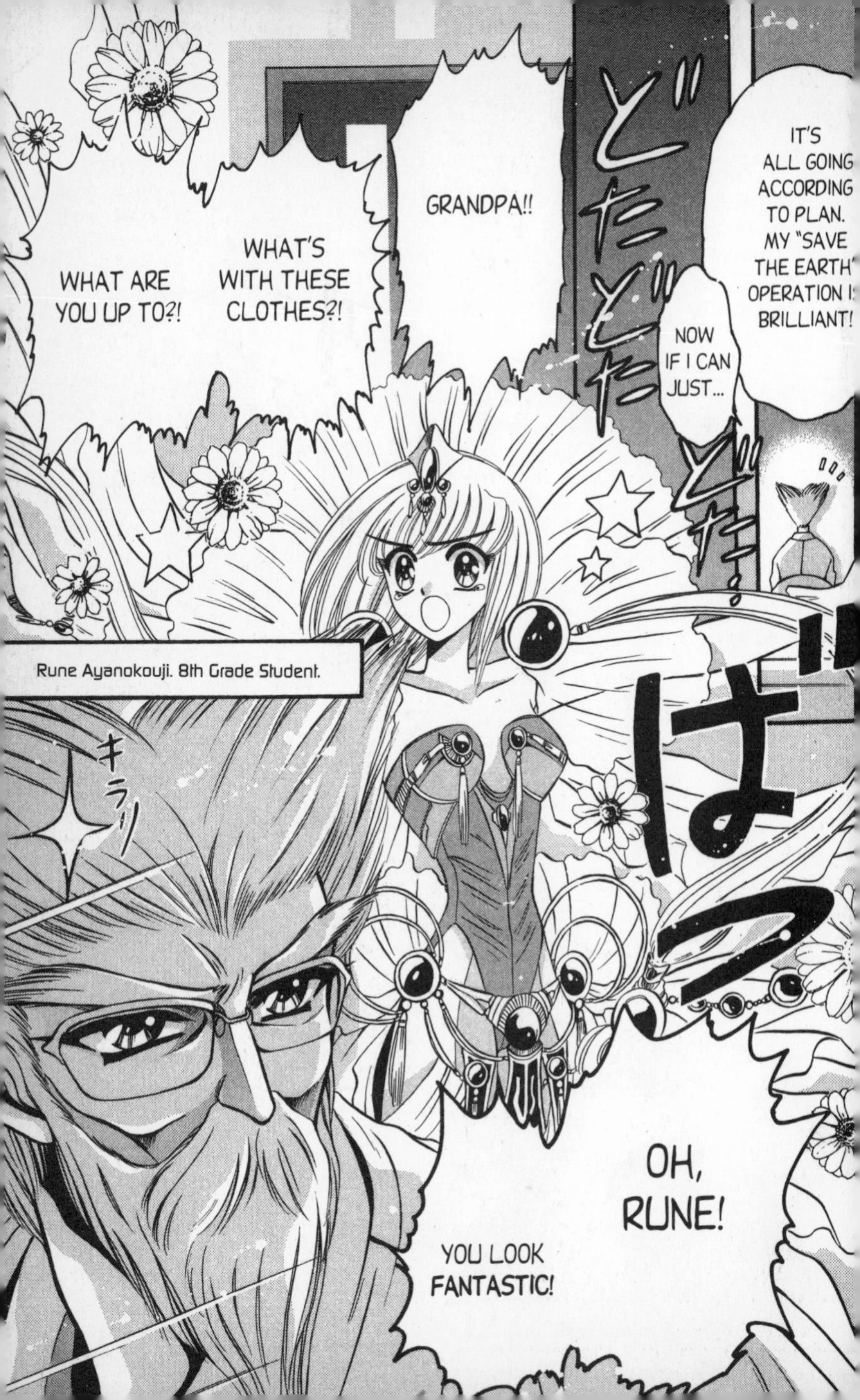
IT'S ALL GOING ACCORDING TO PLAN. MY "SAVE THE EARTH OPERATION I BRILLIANT!
NOW IF I CAN JUST...
どたどたどた
GRANDPA!!
WHAT'S WITH THESE CLOTHES?!
WHAT ARE YOU UP TO?!
ばっ
Rune Ayanokouji. 8th Grade Student.
OH, RUNE!
YOU LOOK FANTASTIC!
キラッ

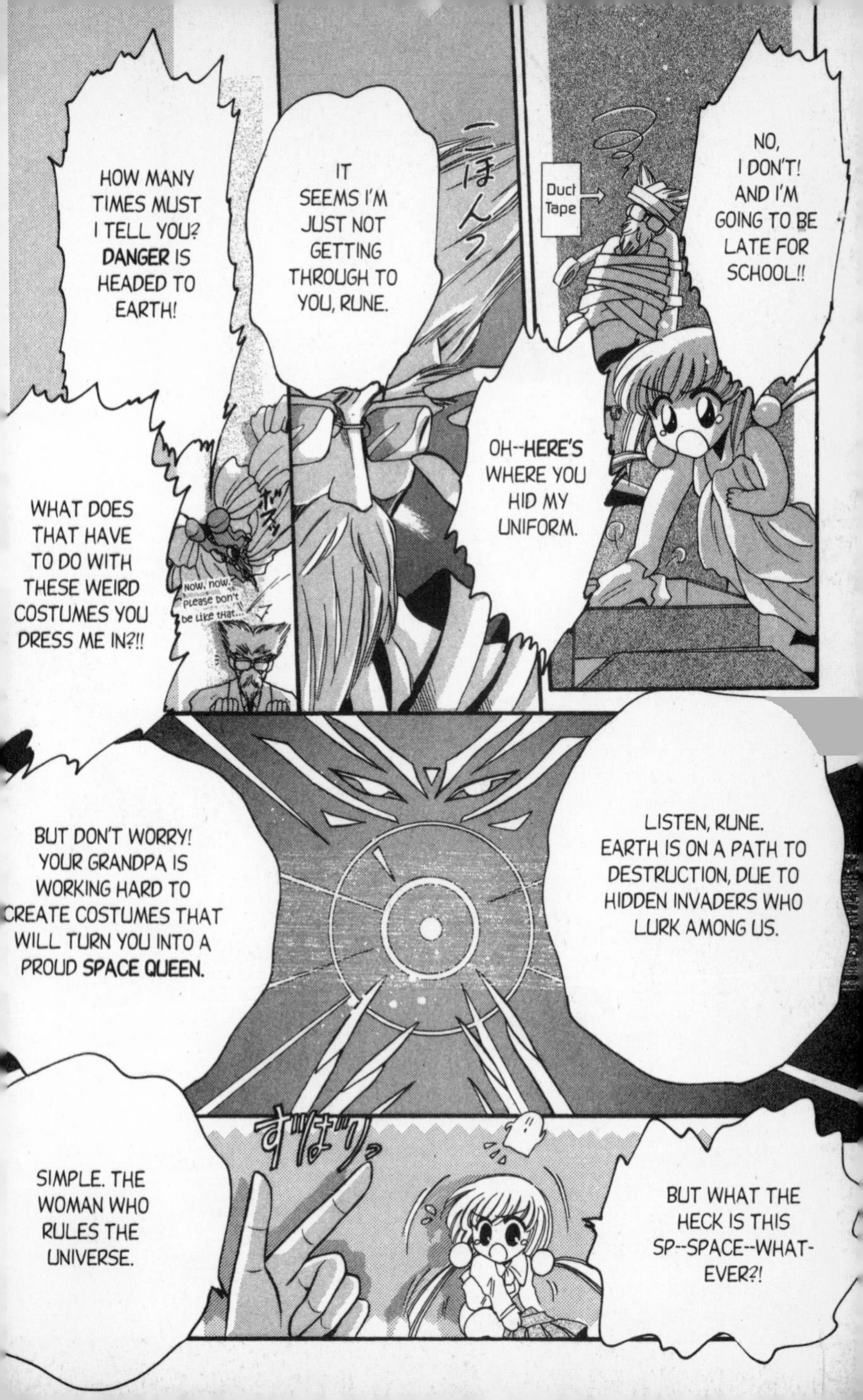
NO, I DON'T! AND I'M GOING TO BE LATE FOR SCHOOL!!
Duct Tape
OH--HERE'S WHERE YOU HID MY UNIFORM.
こほんっ
IT SEEMS I'M JUST NOT GETTING THROUGH TO YOU, RUNE.
HOW MANY TIMES MUST I TELL YOU? DANGER IS HEADED TO EARTH!
WHAT DOES THAT HAVE TO DO WITH THESE WEIRD COSTUMES YOU DRESS ME IN?!!
Now, now. Please don't be like that...
LISTEN, RUNE. EARTH IS ON A PATH TO DESTRUCTION, DUE TO HIDDEN INVADERS WHO LURK AMONG US.
BUT DON'T WORRY! YOUR GRANDPA IS WORKING HARD TO CREATE COSTUMES THAT WILL TURN YOU INTO A PROUD SPACE QUEEN.
BUT WHAT THE HECK IS THIS SP--SPACE--WHAT-EVER?!
SIMPLE. THE WOMAN WHO RULES THE UNIVERSE.

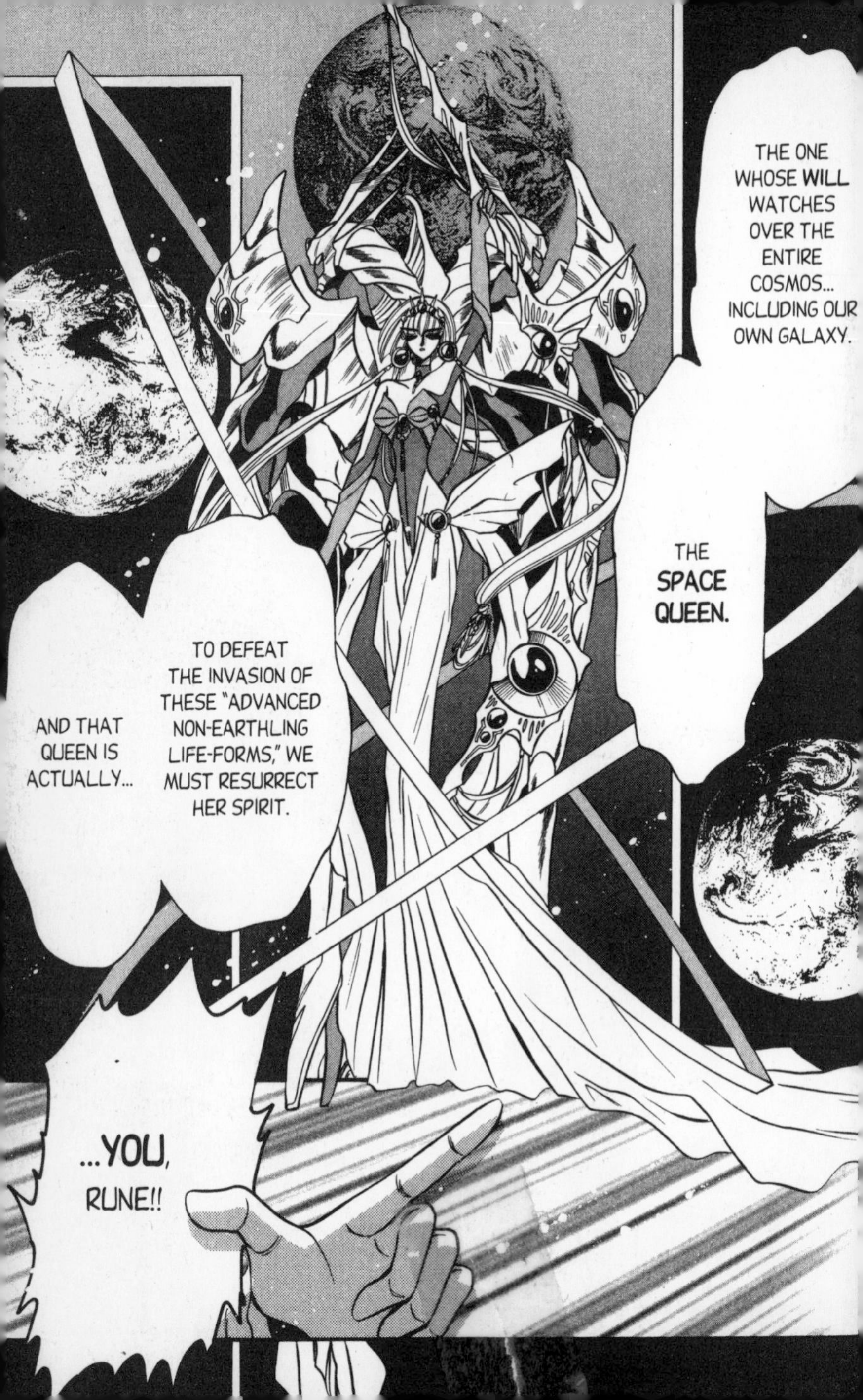
THE ONE WHOSE WILL WATCHES OVER THE ENTIRE COSMOS... INCLUDING OUR OWN GALAXY.
THE SPACE QUEEN.
TO DEFEAT THE INVASION OF THESE "ADVANCED NON-EARTHLING LIFE-FORMS," WE MUST RESURRECT HER SPIRIT.
AND THAT QUEEN IS ACTUALLY...
...YOU, RUNE!!

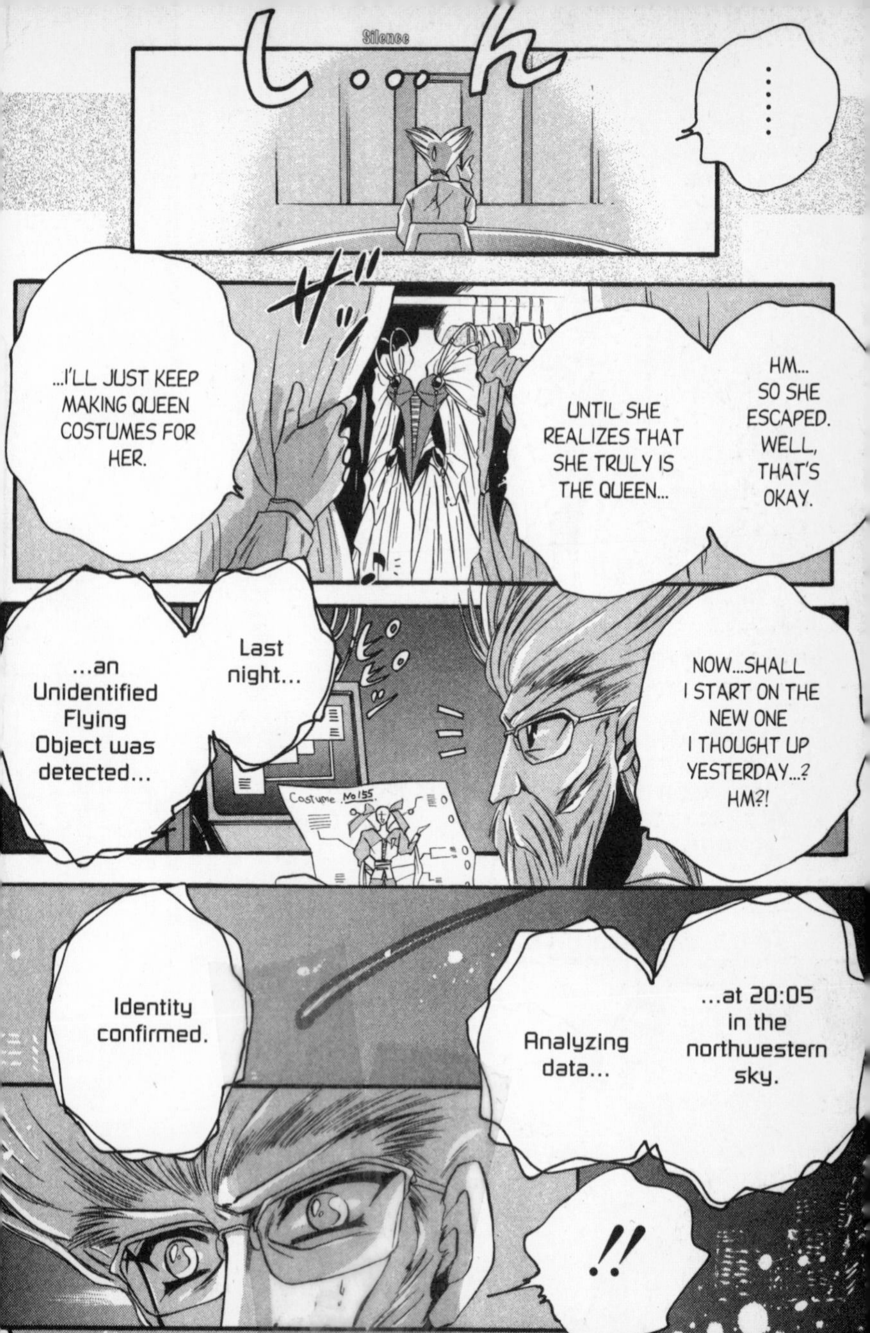
……
Silence
し…ん
ザッ
HM... SO SHE ESCAPED. WELL, THAT'S OKAY.
UNTIL SHE REALIZES THAT SHE TRULY IS THE QUEEN...
...I'LL JUST KEEP MAKING QUEEN COSTUMES FOR HER.
NOW...SHALL I START ON THE NEW ONE I THOUGHT UP YESTERDAY...? HM?!
Costume No155
Last night...
...an Unidentified Flying Object was detected...
...at 20:05 in the northwestern sky.
Analyzing data...
Identity confirmed.
!!

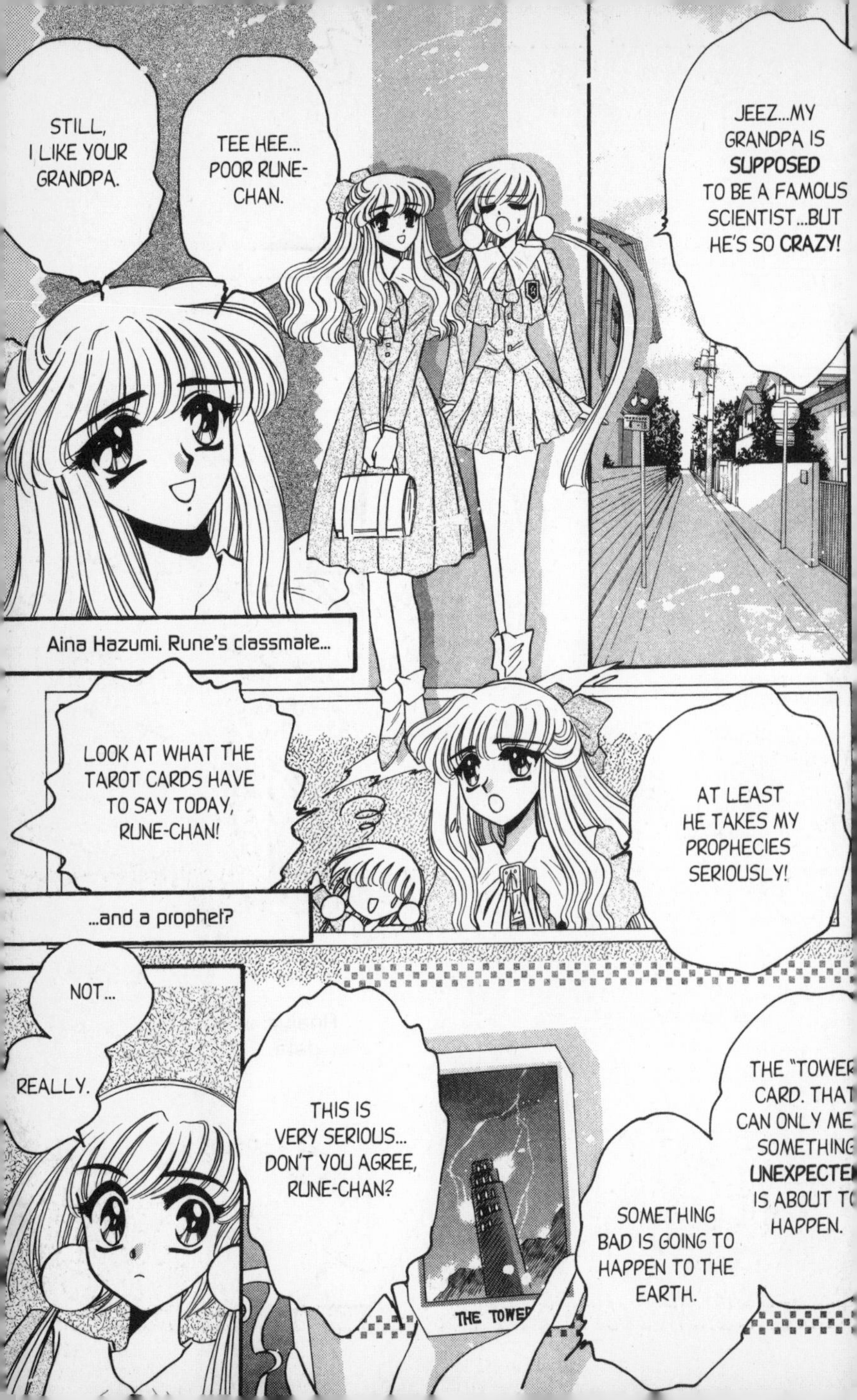
JEEZ...MY GRANDPA IS **SUPPOSED** TO BE A FAMOUS SCIENTIST...BUT HE'S SO **CRAZY!**
TEE HEE... POOR RUNE-CHAN.
STILL, I LIKE YOUR GRANDPA.
Aina Hazumi. Rune's classmate...
AT LEAST HE TAKES MY PROPHECIES SERIOUSLY!
LOOK AT WHAT THE TAROT CARDS HAVE TO SAY TODAY, RUNE-CHAN!
...and a prophet?
THE "TOWER CARD. THAT CAN ONLY ME SOMETHING **UNEXPECTE** IS ABOUT T HAPPEN.
SOMETHING BAD IS GOING TO HAPPEN TO THE EARTH.
THE TOWE
THIS IS VERY SERIOUS... DON'T YOU AGREE, RUNE-CHAN?
NOT...
REALLY.

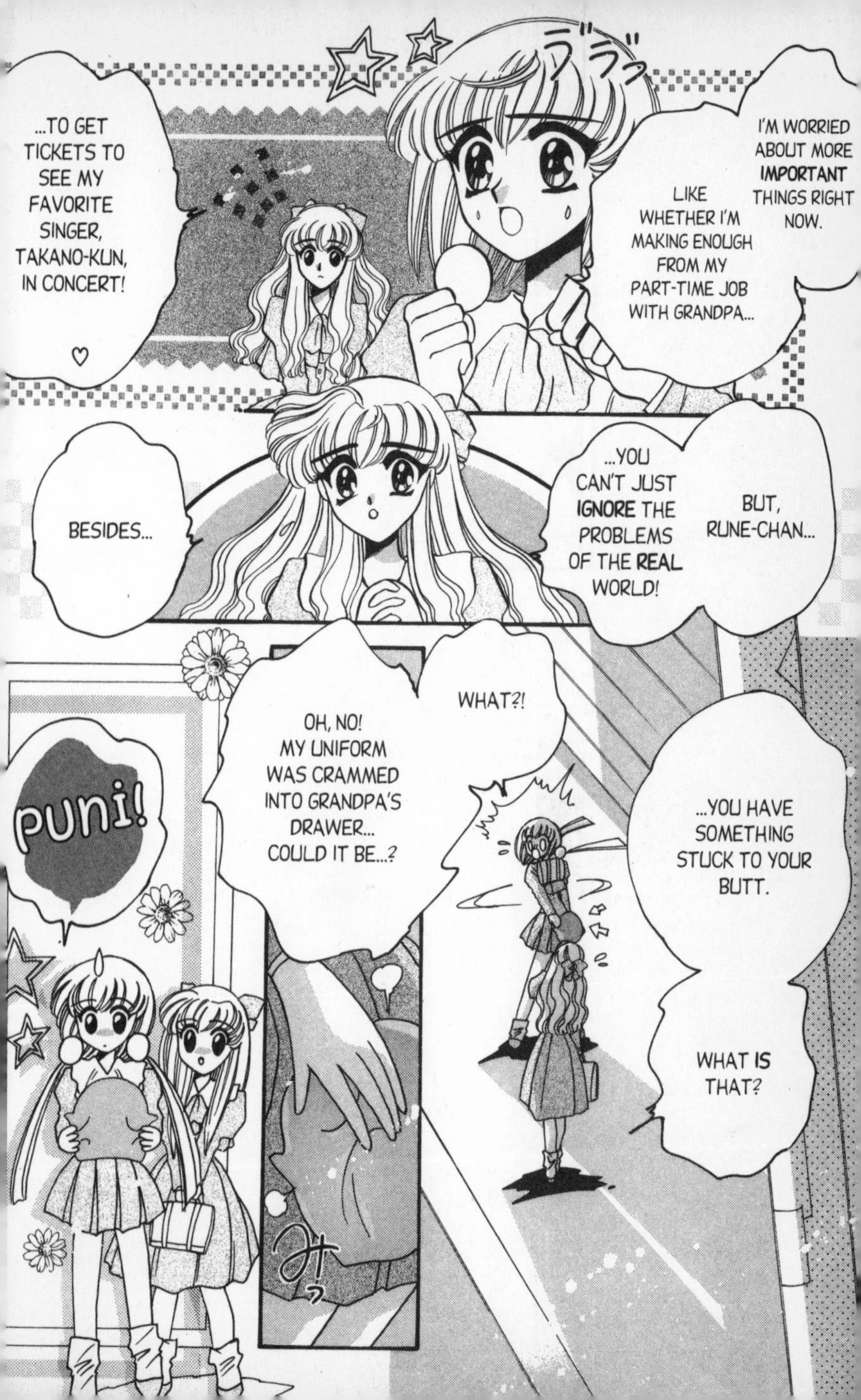
I'M WORRIED ABOUT MORE **IMPORTANT** THINGS RIGHT NOW.
LIKE WHETHER I'M MAKING ENOUGH FROM MY PART-TIME JOB WITH GRANDPA...
...TO GET TICKETS TO SEE MY FAVORITE SINGER, TAKANO-KUN, IN CONCERT! ♡
BUT, RUNE-CHAN...
...YOU CAN'T JUST **IGNORE** THE PROBLEMS OF THE **REAL** WORLD!
BESIDES...
...YOU HAVE SOMETHING STUCK TO YOUR BUTT.
WHAT **IS** THAT?
WHAT?!
OH, NO! MY UNIFORM WAS CRAMMED INTO GRANDPA'S DRAWER... COULD IT BE...?
puni!

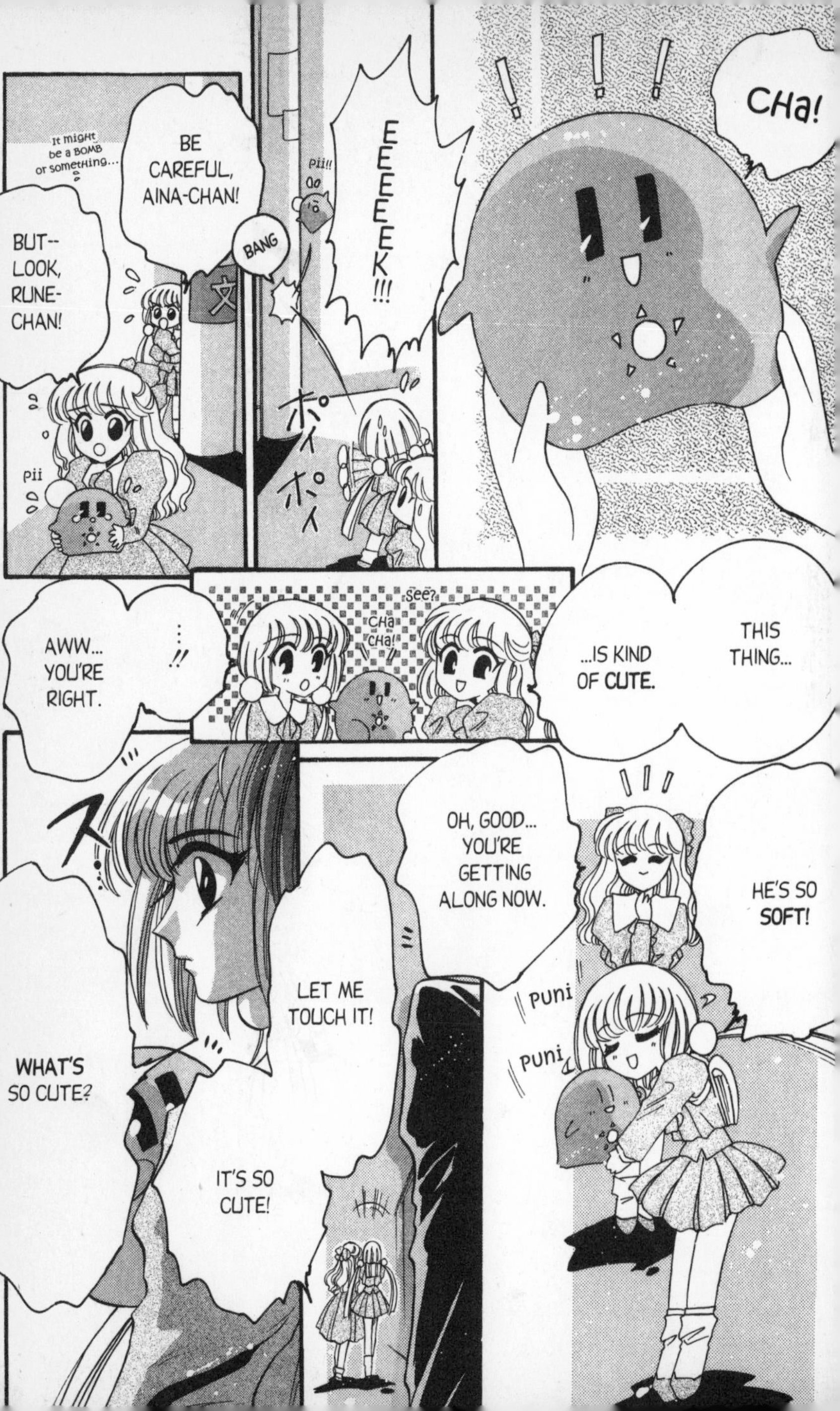
CHa!
EEEEEK!!!
Pii!!
BANG
ポイポイ
BE CAREFUL, AINA-CHAN!
It might be a BOMB or something...
BUT-- LOOK, RUNE-CHAN!
Pii
THIS THING...
...IS KIND OF CUTE.
see?
CHa CHa!
...!!
AWW... YOU'RE RIGHT.
HE'S SO SOFT!
OH, GOOD... YOU'RE GETTING ALONG NOW.
Puni
Puni
LET ME TOUCH IT!
IT'S SO CUTE!
WHAT'S SO CUTE?

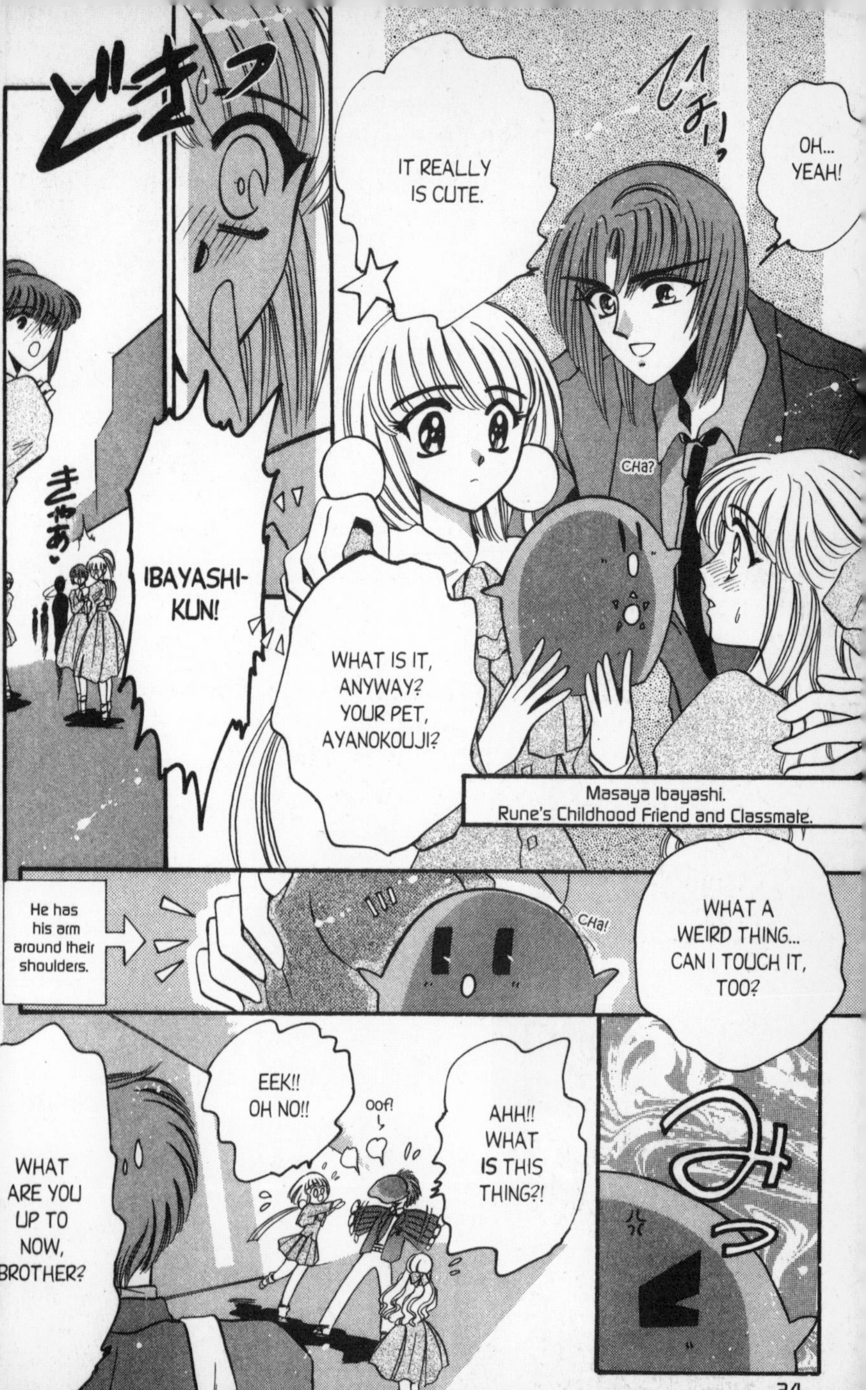
ひょい!
OH... YEAH!
IT REALLY IS CUTE.
CHa?
WHAT IS IT, ANYWAY? YOUR PET, AYANOKOUJI?
Masaya Ibayashi. Rune's Childhood Friend and Classmate.
どきっ
IBAYASHI-KUN!
きゃあ♥
WHAT A WEIRD THING... CAN I TOUCH IT, TOO?
CHa!
He has his arm around their shoulders.
みっ
AHH!! WHAT IS THIS THING?!
oof!
EEK!! OH NO!!
WHAT ARE YOU UP TO NOW, BROTHER?

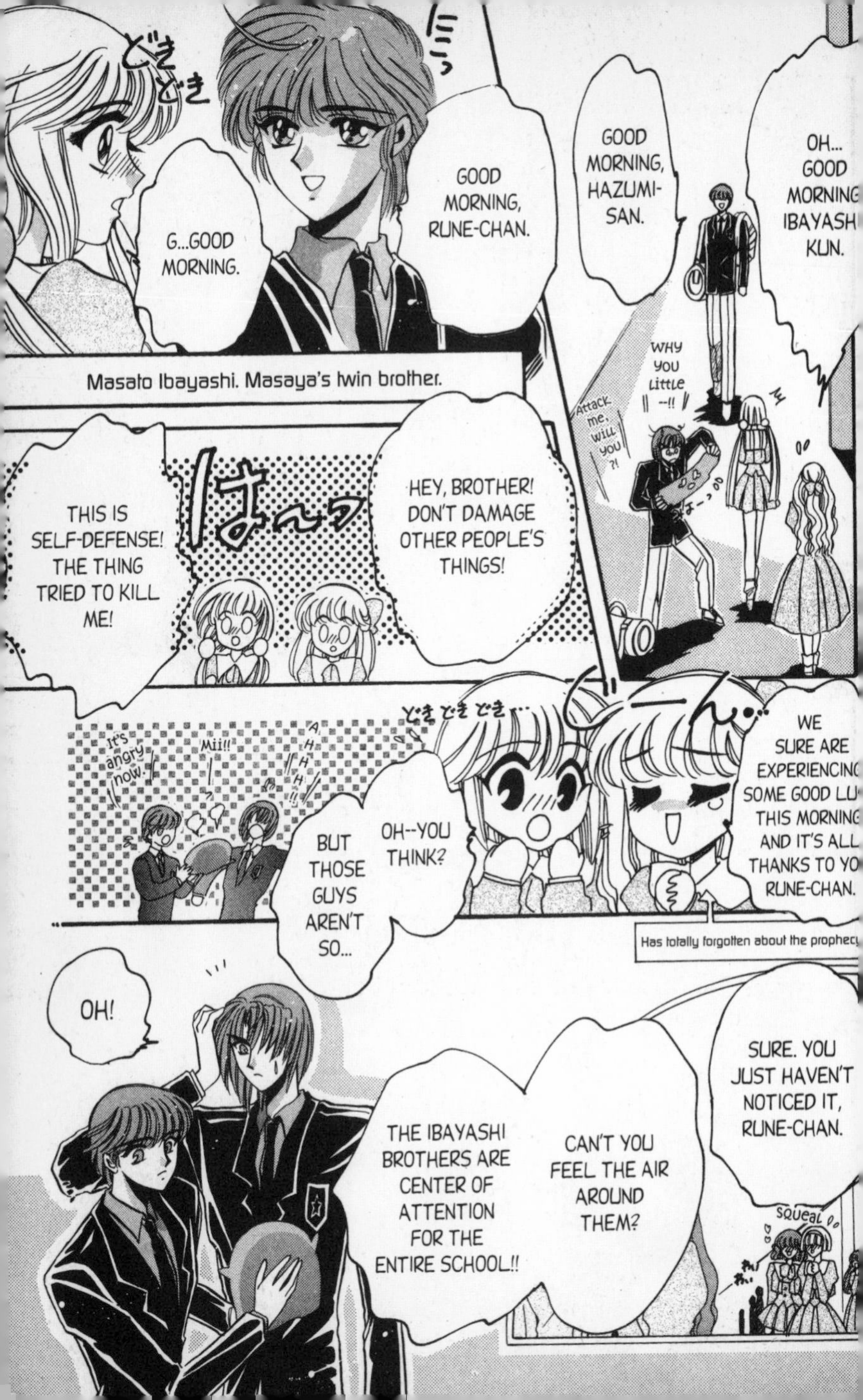
OH... GOOD MORNING IBAYASH KUN.
GOOD MORNING, HAZUMI-SAN.
にこっ
GOOD MORNING, RUNE-CHAN.
どきどき
G...GOOD MORNING.
Masato Ibayashi. Masaya's twin brother.
WHY YOU LITTLE --!!
Attack me, will you?!
HEY, BROTHER! DON'T DAMAGE OTHER PEOPLE'S THINGS!
はんっ
THIS IS SELF-DEFENSE! THE THING TRIED TO KILL ME!
WE SURE ARE EXPERIENCING SOME GOOD LU THIS MORNING AND IT'S ALL THANKS TO YO RUNE-CHAN.
Has totally forgotten about the prophecy
どきどきどき...
OH--YOU THINK?
BUT THOSE GUYS AREN'T SO...
AHHHH!!
Mii!!
It's angry now.
SURE. YOU JUST HAVEN'T NOTICED IT, RUNE-CHAN.
squeal
CAN'T YOU FEEL THE AIR AROUND THEM?
THE IBAYASHI BROTHERS ARE CENTER OF ATTENTION FOR THE ENTIRE SCHOOL!!
OH!

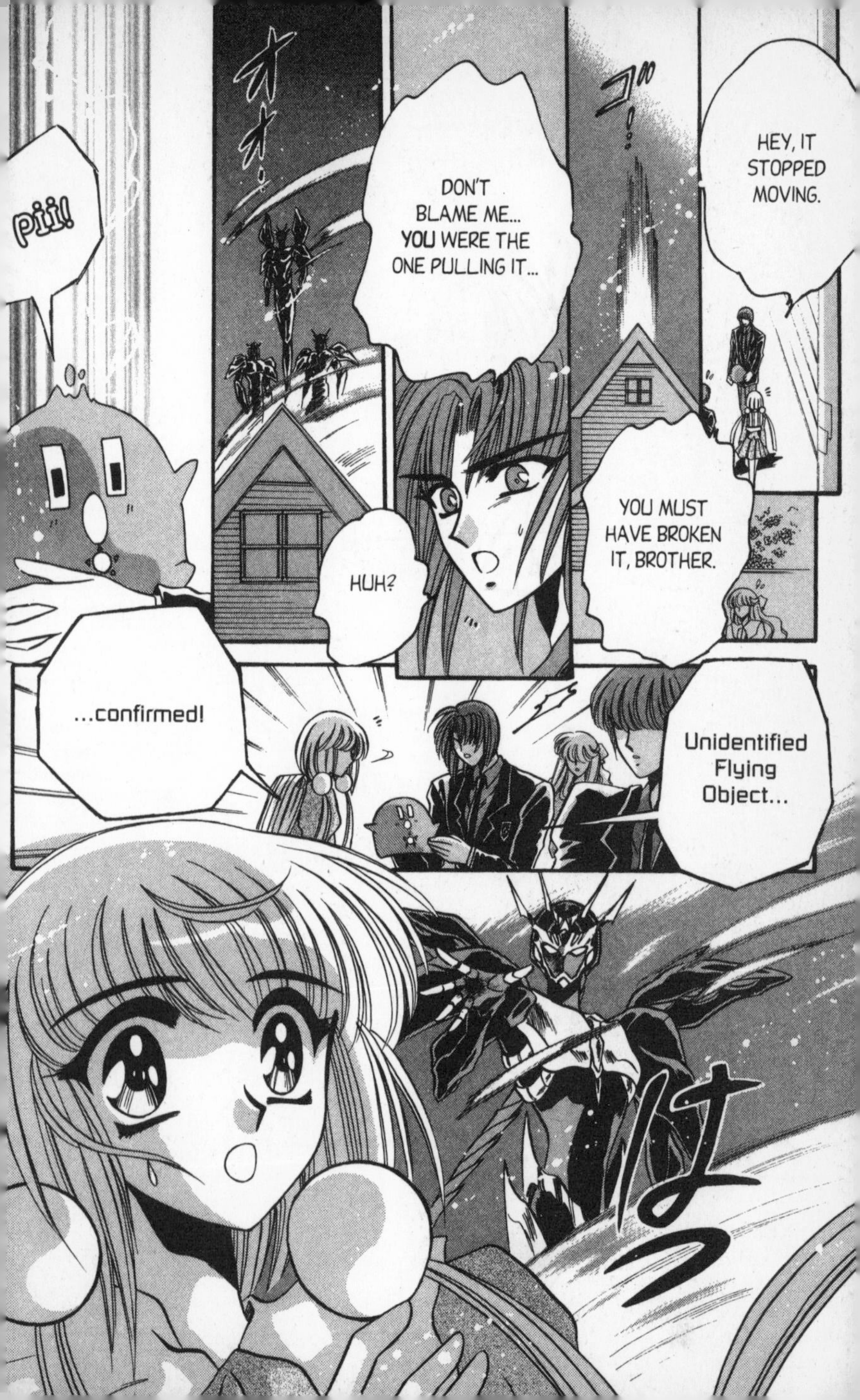
HEY, IT STOPPED MOVING.
YOU MUST HAVE BROKEN IT, BROTHER.
DON'T BLAME ME... YOU WERE THE ONE PULLING IT...
HUH?
pii!
Unidentified Flying Object...
...confirmed!

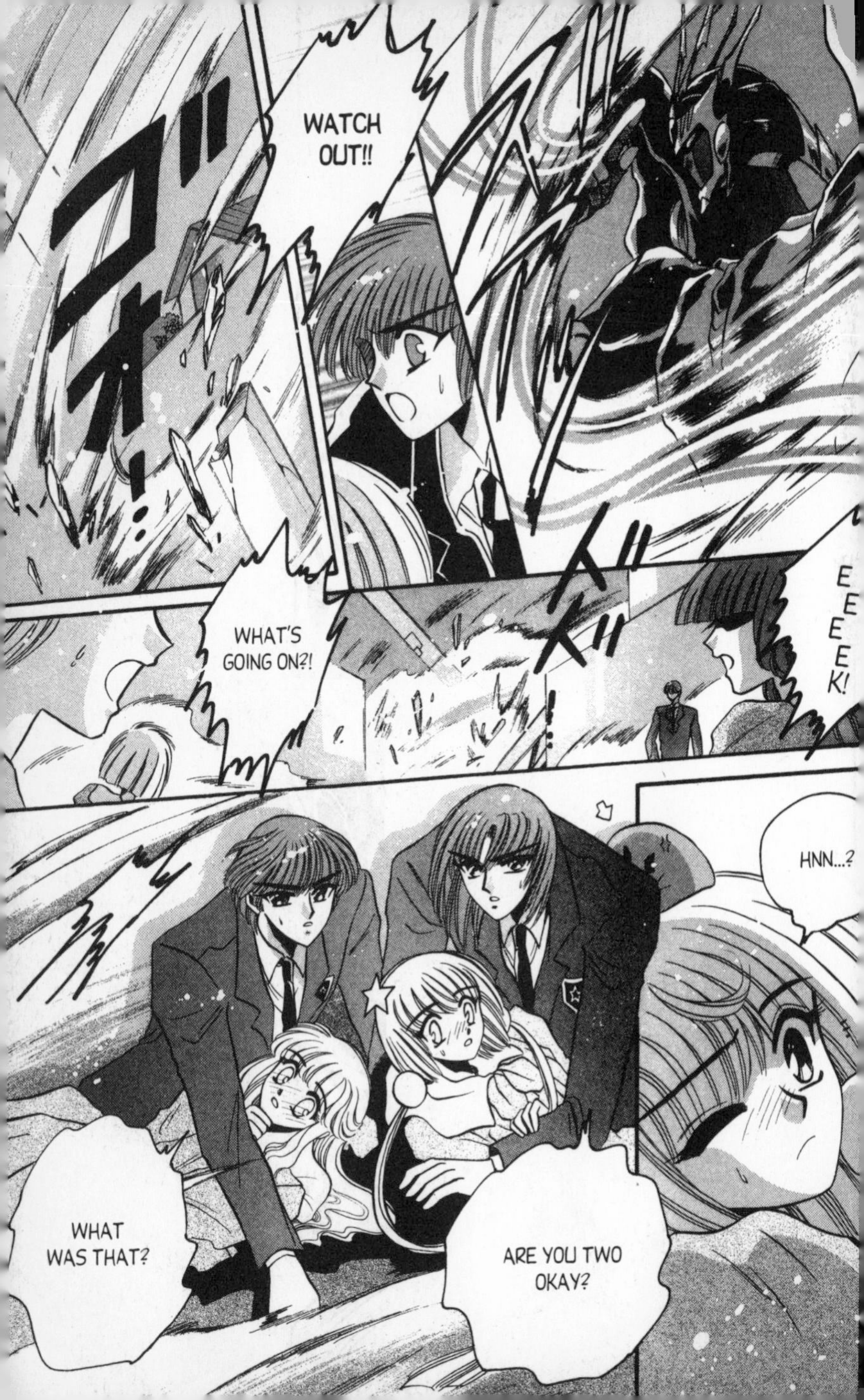
WATCH OUT!!
ゴォ
ドド
EEEEEK!
WHAT'S GOING ON?!
HNN...?
ARE YOU TWO OKAY?
WHAT WAS THAT?

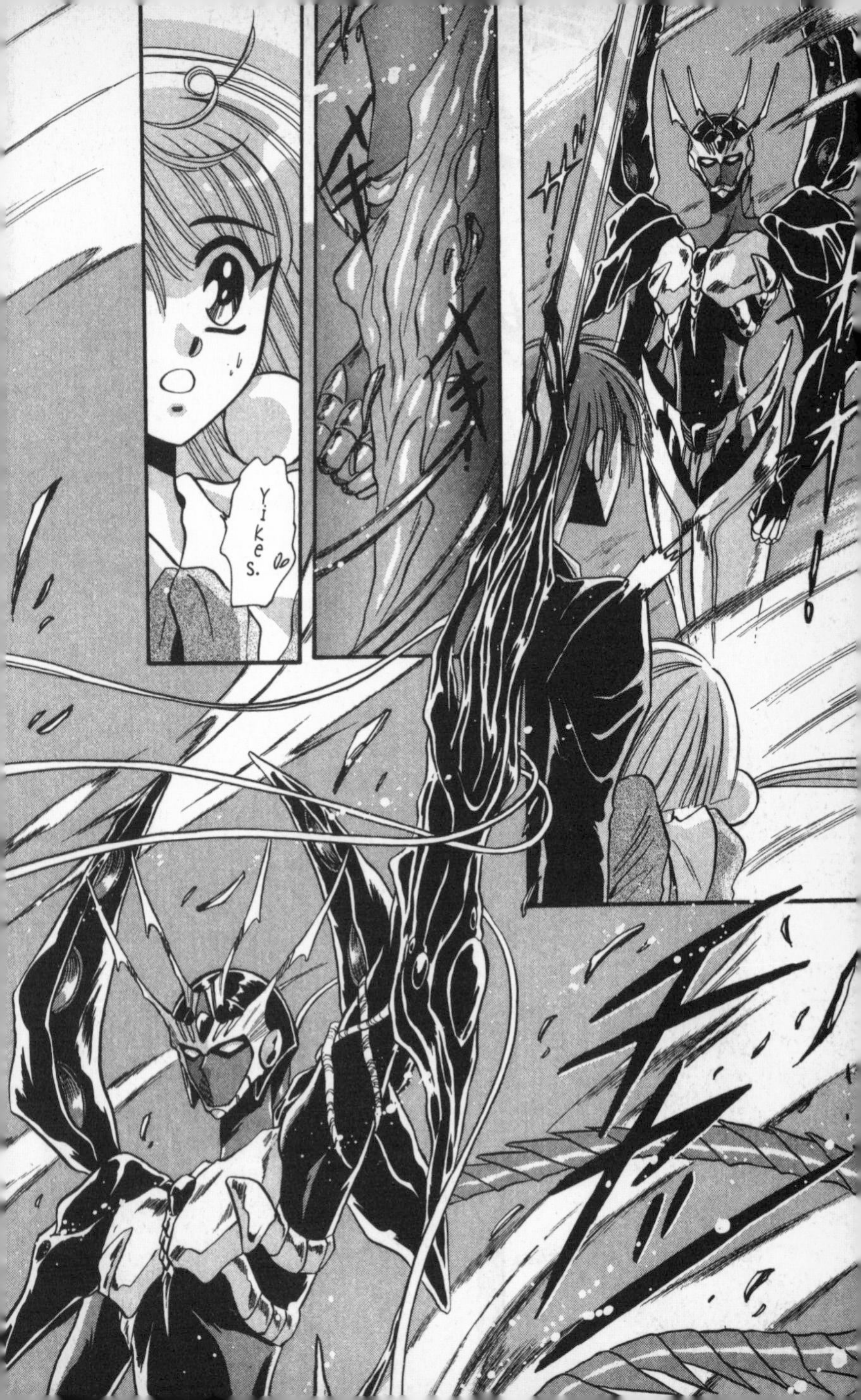
Yikes.

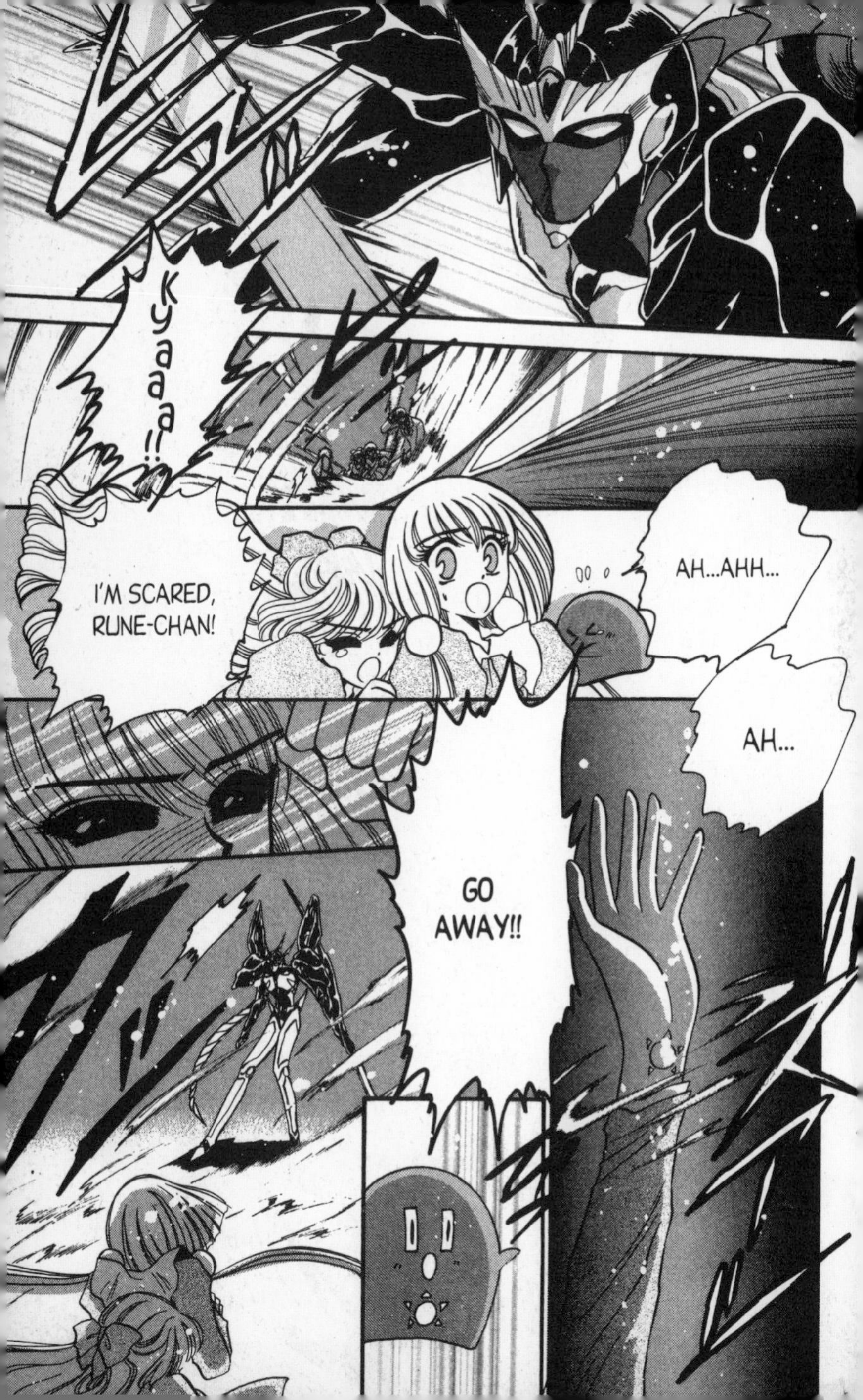
Kyaaaa!!
AH...AHH...
I'M SCARED, RUNE-CHAN!
AH...
GO AWAY!!

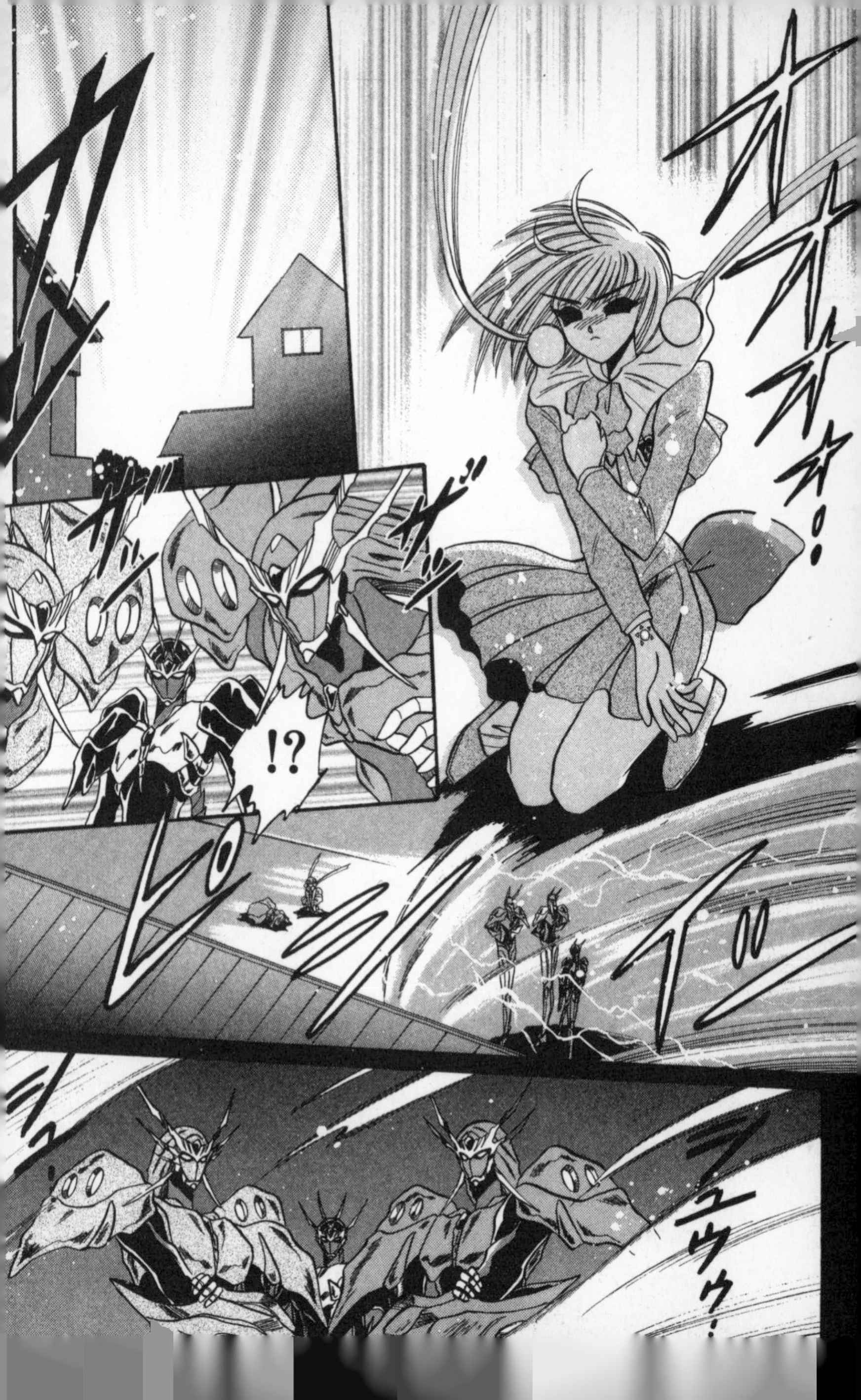
!?

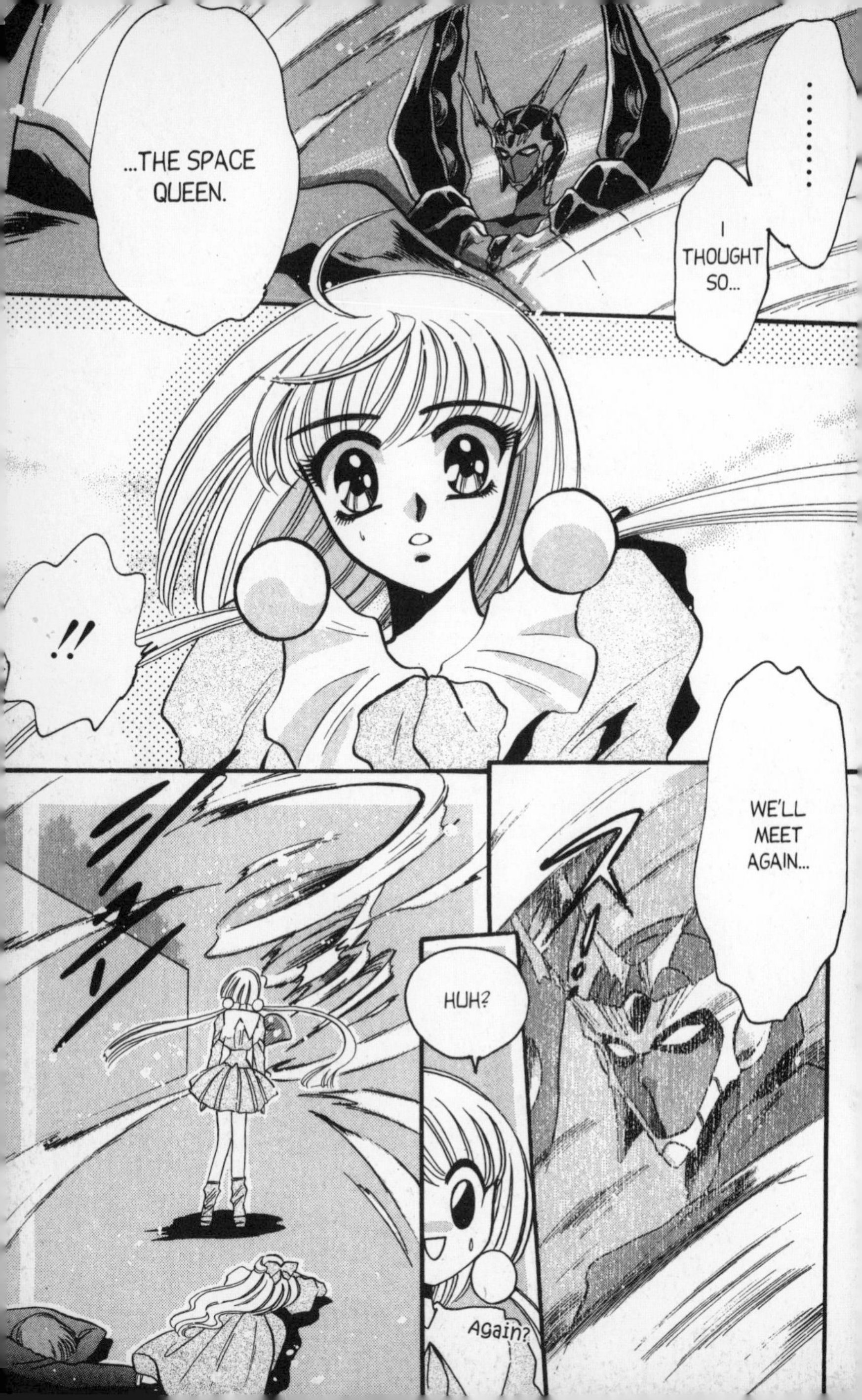

......
I THOUGHT SO...
...THE SPACE QUEEN.
!!
WE'LL MEET AGAIN...
HUH?
Again?

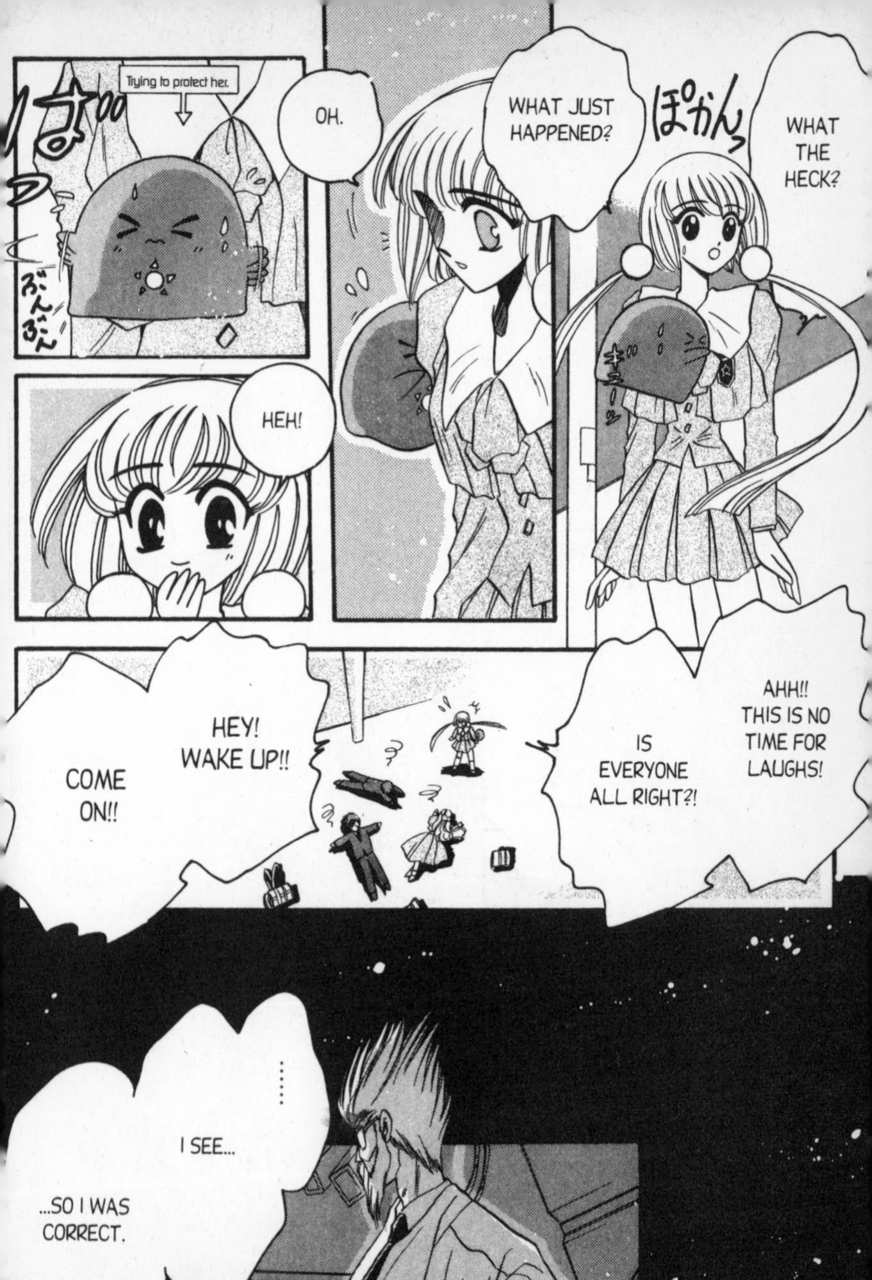
ぽかん
WHAT THE HECK?
WHAT JUST HAPPENED?
OH.
Trying to protect her.
はっ
ぶんぶん
HEH!
AHH!! THIS IS NO TIME FOR LAUGHS!
IS EVERYONE ALL RIGHT?!
HEY! WAKE UP!!
COME ON!!
......
I SEE...
...SO I WAS CORRECT.

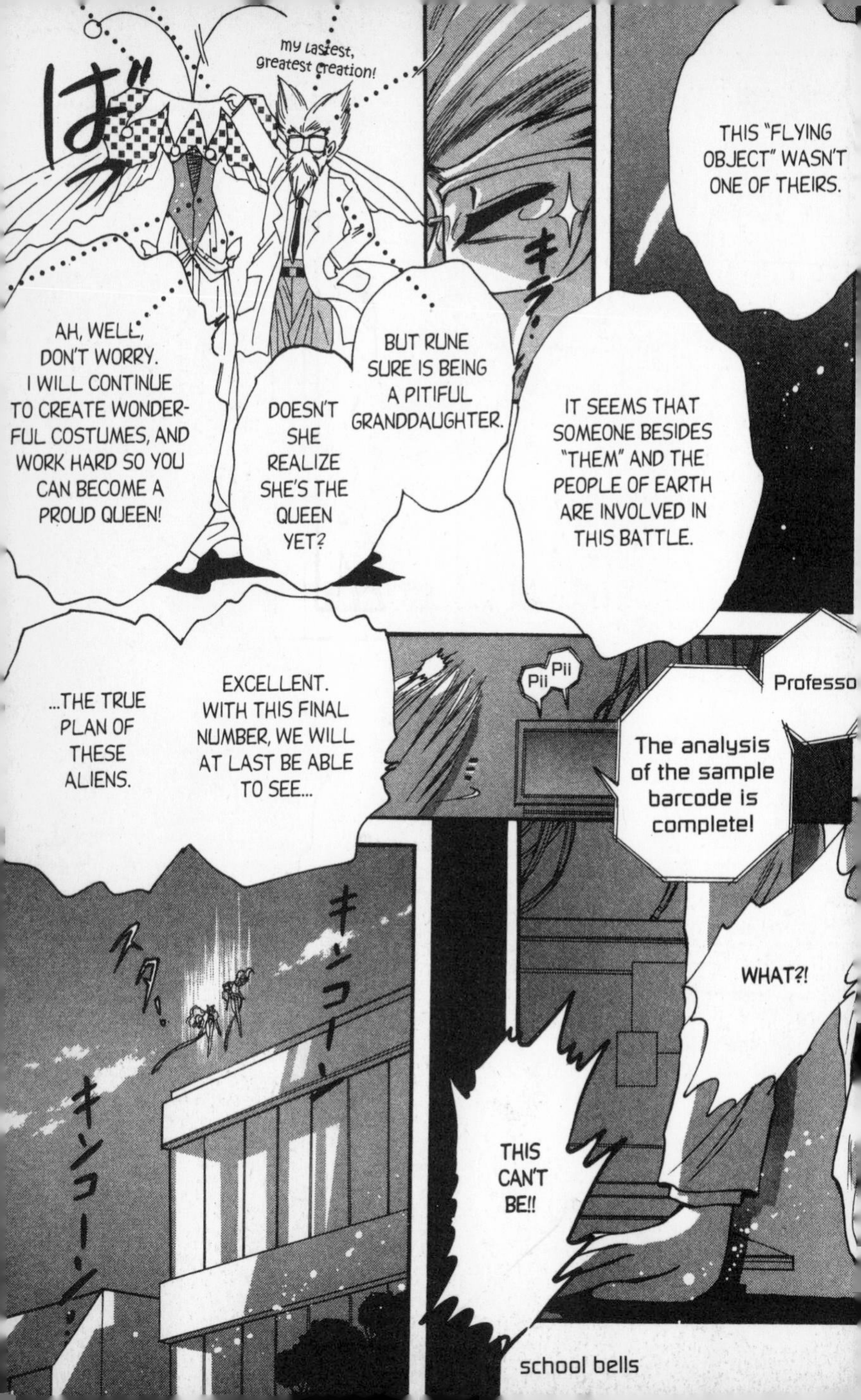
THIS "FLYING OBJECT" WASN'T ONE OF THEIRS.
IT SEEMS THAT SOMEONE BESIDES "THEM" AND THE PEOPLE OF EARTH ARE INVOLVED IN THIS BATTLE.
my lastest, greatest creation!
BUT RUNE SURE IS BEING A PITIFUL GRANDDAUGHTER.
DOESN'T SHE REALIZE SHE'S THE QUEEN YET?
AH, WELL, DON'T WORRY. I WILL CONTINUE TO CREATE WONDERFUL COSTUMES, AND WORK HARD SO YOU CAN BECOME A PROUD QUEEN!
Professo
Pii Pii
The analysis of the sample barcode is complete!
EXCELLENT. WITH THIS FINAL NUMBER, WE WILL AT LAST BE ABLE TO SEE...
...THE TRUE PLAN OF THESE ALIENS.
WHAT?!
THIS CAN'T BE!!
school bells

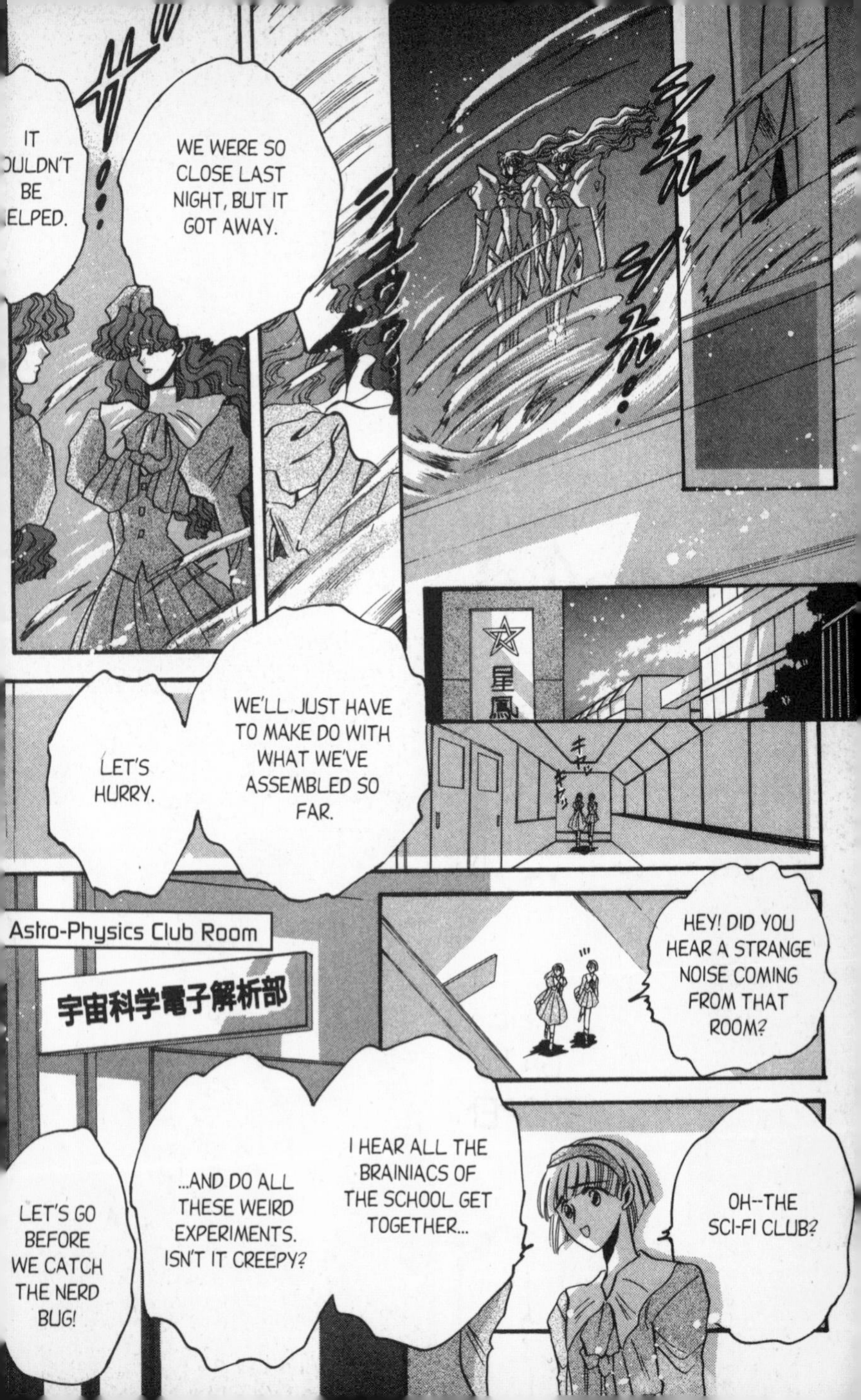
WE WERE SO CLOSE LAST NIGHT, BUT IT GOT AWAY.
IT OULDN'T BE ELPED.
星鳳
WE'LL JUST HAVE TO MAKE DO WITH WHAT WE'VE ASSEMBLED SO FAR.
LET'S HURRY.
HEY! DID YOU HEAR A STRANGE NOISE COMING FROM THAT ROOM?
Astro-Physics Club Room
宇宙科学電子解析部
OH--THE SCI-FI CLUB?
I HEAR ALL THE BRAINIACS OF THE SCHOOL GET TOGETHER...
...AND DO ALL THESE WEIRD EXPERIMENTS. ISN'T IT CREEPY?
LET'S GO BEFORE WE CATCH THE NERD BUG!

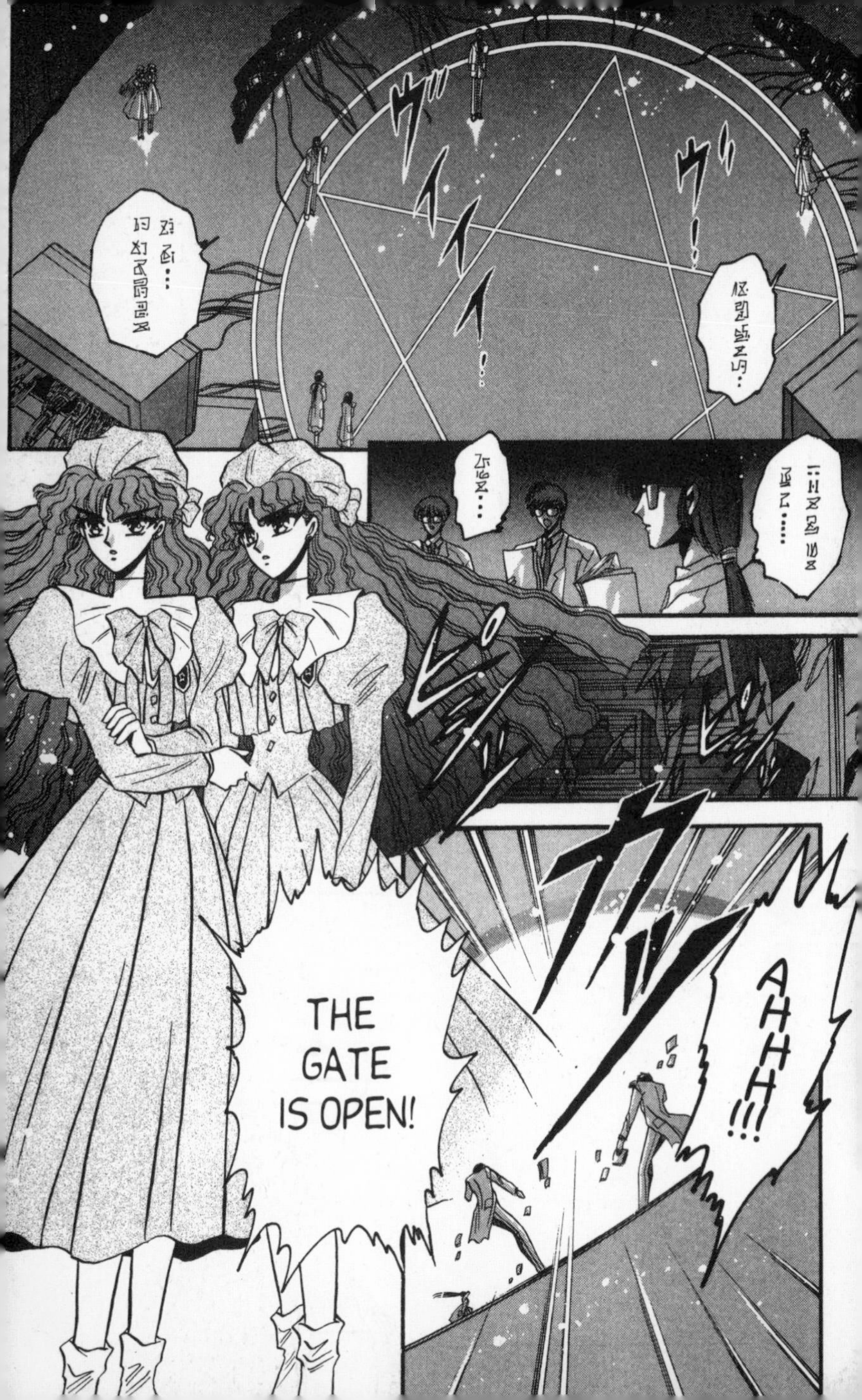
AHHH!!!
THE GATE IS OPEN!

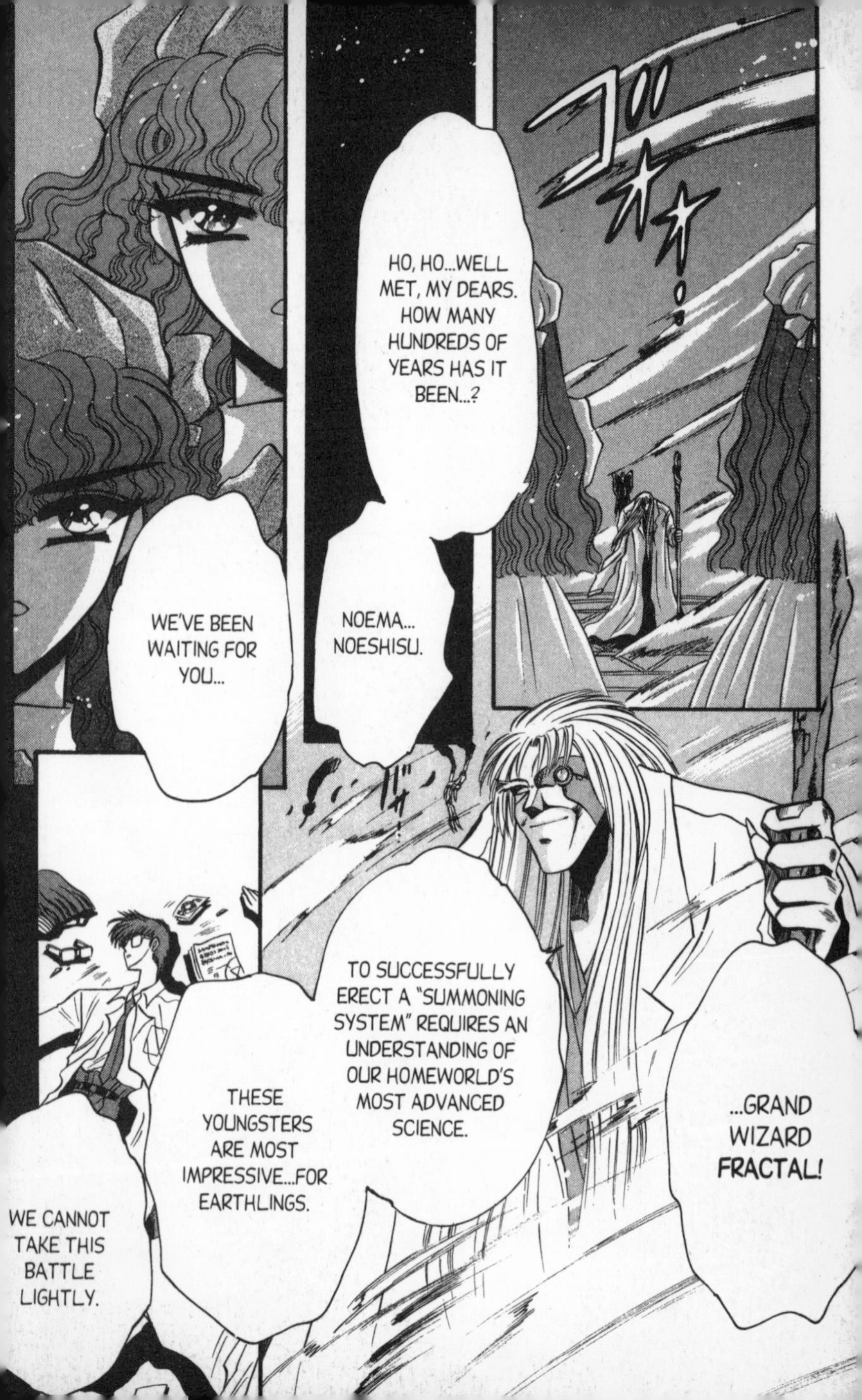
HO, HO...WELL MET, MY DEARS. HOW MANY HUNDREDS OF YEARS HAS IT BEEN...?
NOEMA... NOESHISU.
WE'VE BEEN WAITING FOR YOU...
...GRAND WIZARD FRACTAL!
TO SUCCESSFULLY ERECT A "SUMMONING SYSTEM" REQUIRES AN UNDERSTANDING OF OUR HOMEWORLD'S MOST ADVANCED SCIENCE.
THESE YOUNGSTERS ARE MOST IMPRESSIVE...FOR EARTHLINGS.
WE CANNOT TAKE THIS BATTLE LIGHTLY.

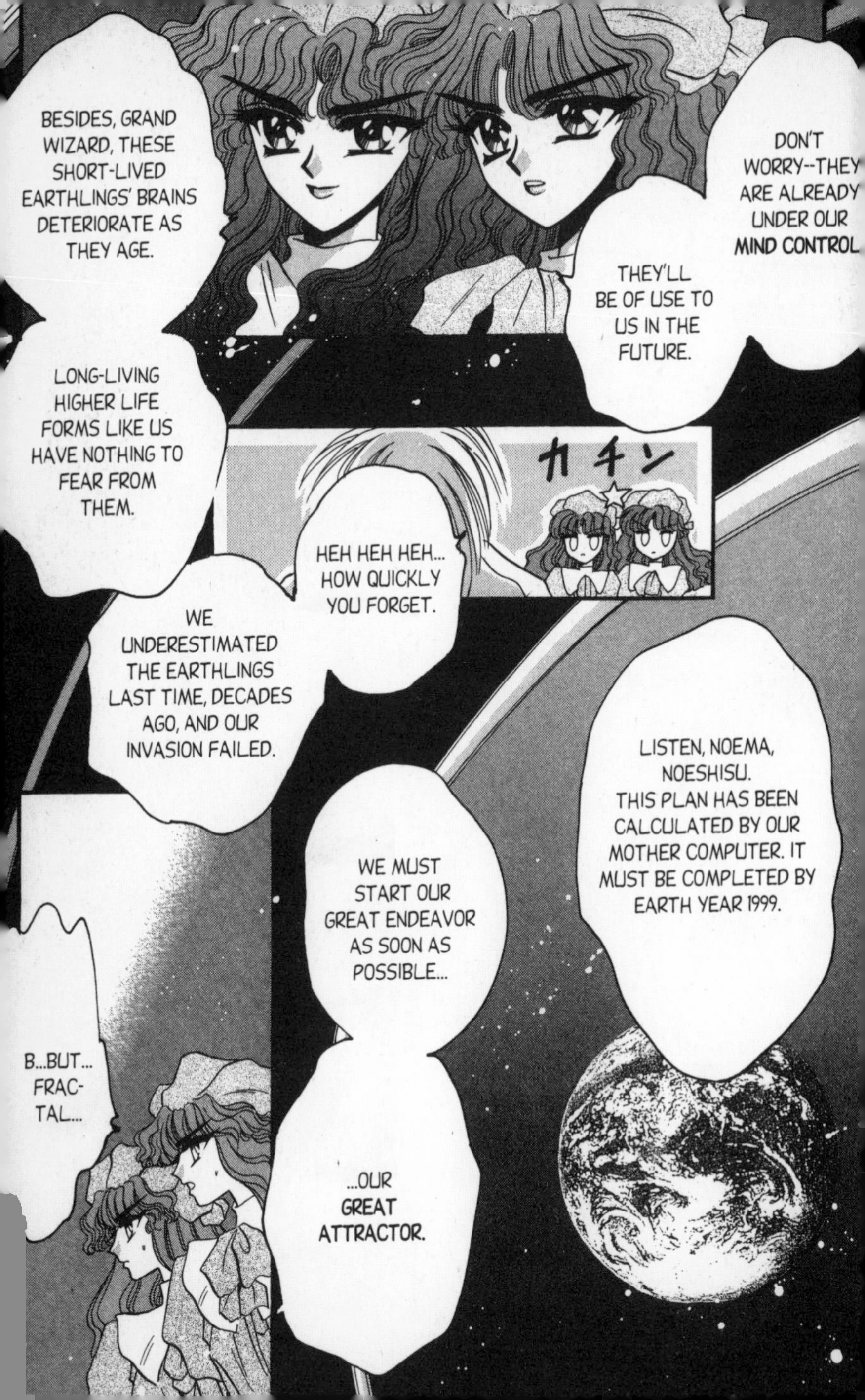
DON'T WORRY--THEY ARE ALREADY UNDER OUR **MIND CONTROL**
THEY'LL BE OF USE TO US IN THE FUTURE.
BESIDES, GRAND WIZARD, THESE SHORT-LIVED EARTHLINGS' BRAINS DETERIORATE AS THEY AGE.
LONG-LIVING HIGHER LIFE FORMS LIKE US HAVE NOTHING TO FEAR FROM THEM.
カチン
HEH HEH HEH... HOW QUICKLY YOU FORGET.
WE UNDERESTIMATED THE EARTHLINGS LAST TIME, DECADES AGO, AND OUR INVASION FAILED.
LISTEN, NOEMA, NOESHISU. THIS PLAN HAS BEEN CALCULATED BY OUR MOTHER COMPUTER. IT MUST BE COMPLETED BY EARTH YEAR 1999.
WE MUST START OUR GREAT ENDEAVOR AS SOON AS POSSIBLE...
...OUR **GREAT** ATTRACTOR.
B...BUT... FRAC-TAL...

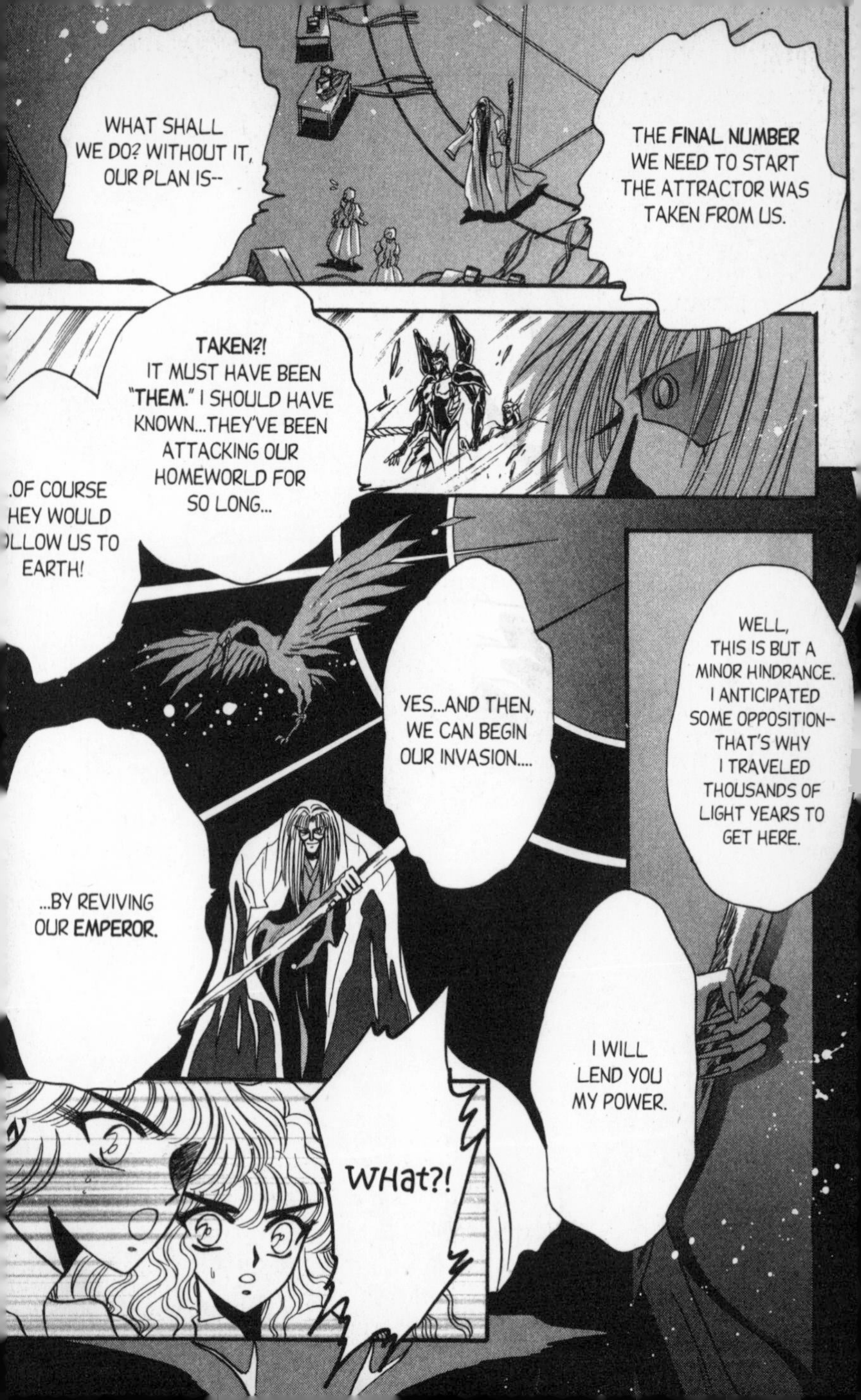

THE FINAL NUMBER WE NEED TO START THE ATTRACTOR WAS TAKEN FROM US.
WHAT SHALL WE DO? WITHOUT IT, OUR PLAN IS--
TAKEN?! IT MUST HAVE BEEN "THEM." I SHOULD HAVE KNOWN...THEY'VE BEEN ATTACKING OUR HOMEWORLD FOR SO LONG...
.OF COURSE HEY WOULD LLOW US TO EARTH!
WELL, THIS IS BUT A MINOR HINDRANCE. I ANTICIPATED SOME OPPOSITION-- THAT'S WHY I TRAVELED THOUSANDS OF LIGHT YEARS TO GET HERE.
YES...AND THEN, WE CAN BEGIN OUR INVASION....
...BY REVIVING OUR EMPEROR.
I WILL LEND YOU MY POWER.
WHAT?!

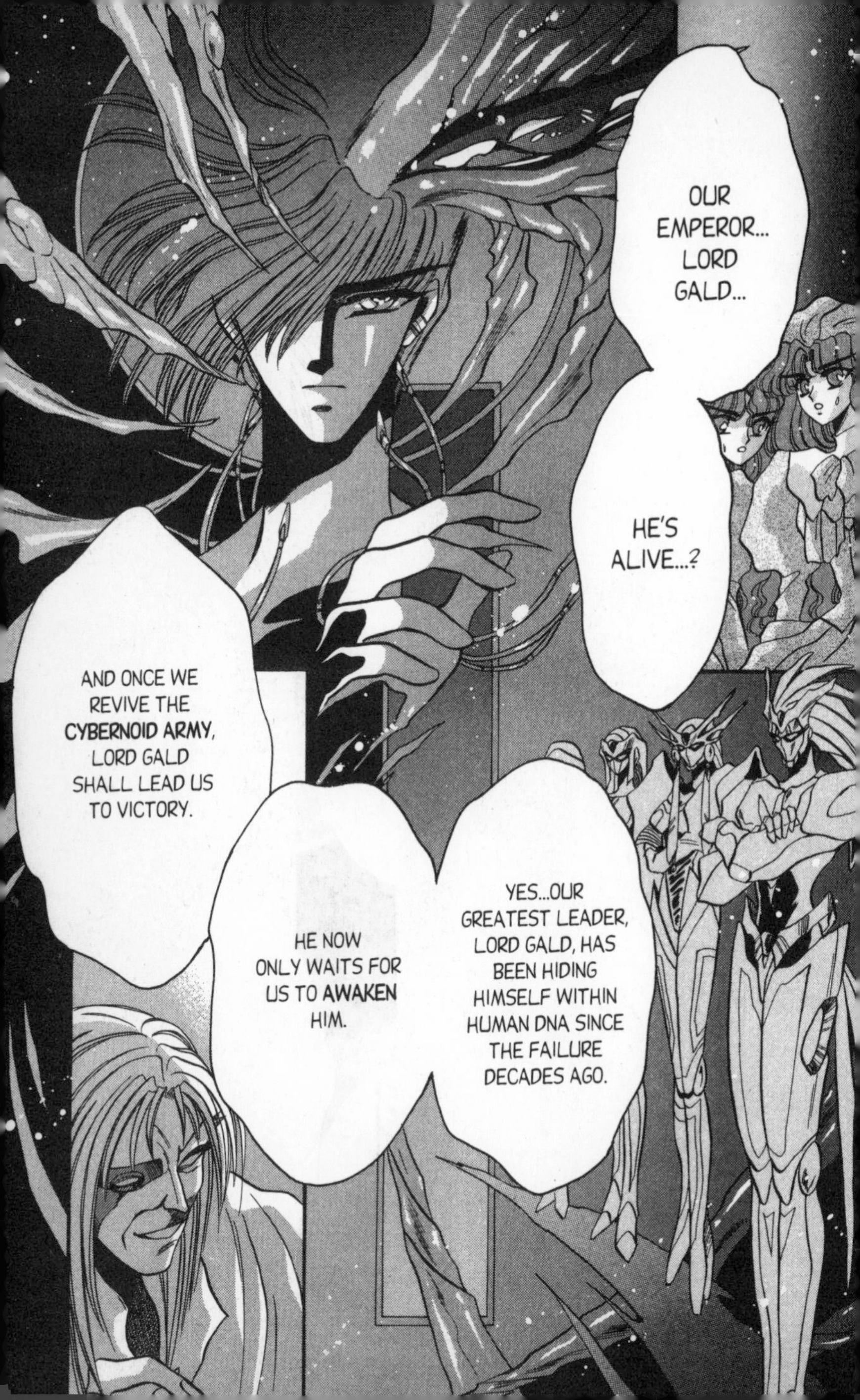
OUR EMPEROR... LORD GALD...
HE'S ALIVE...?
AND ONCE WE REVIVE THE **CYBERNOID ARMY**, LORD GALD SHALL LEAD US TO VICTORY.
YES...OUR GREATEST LEADER, LORD GALD, HAS BEEN HIDING HIMSELF WITHIN HUMAN DNA SINCE THE FAILURE DECADES AGO.
HE NOW ONLY WAITS FOR US TO **AWAKEN** HIM.

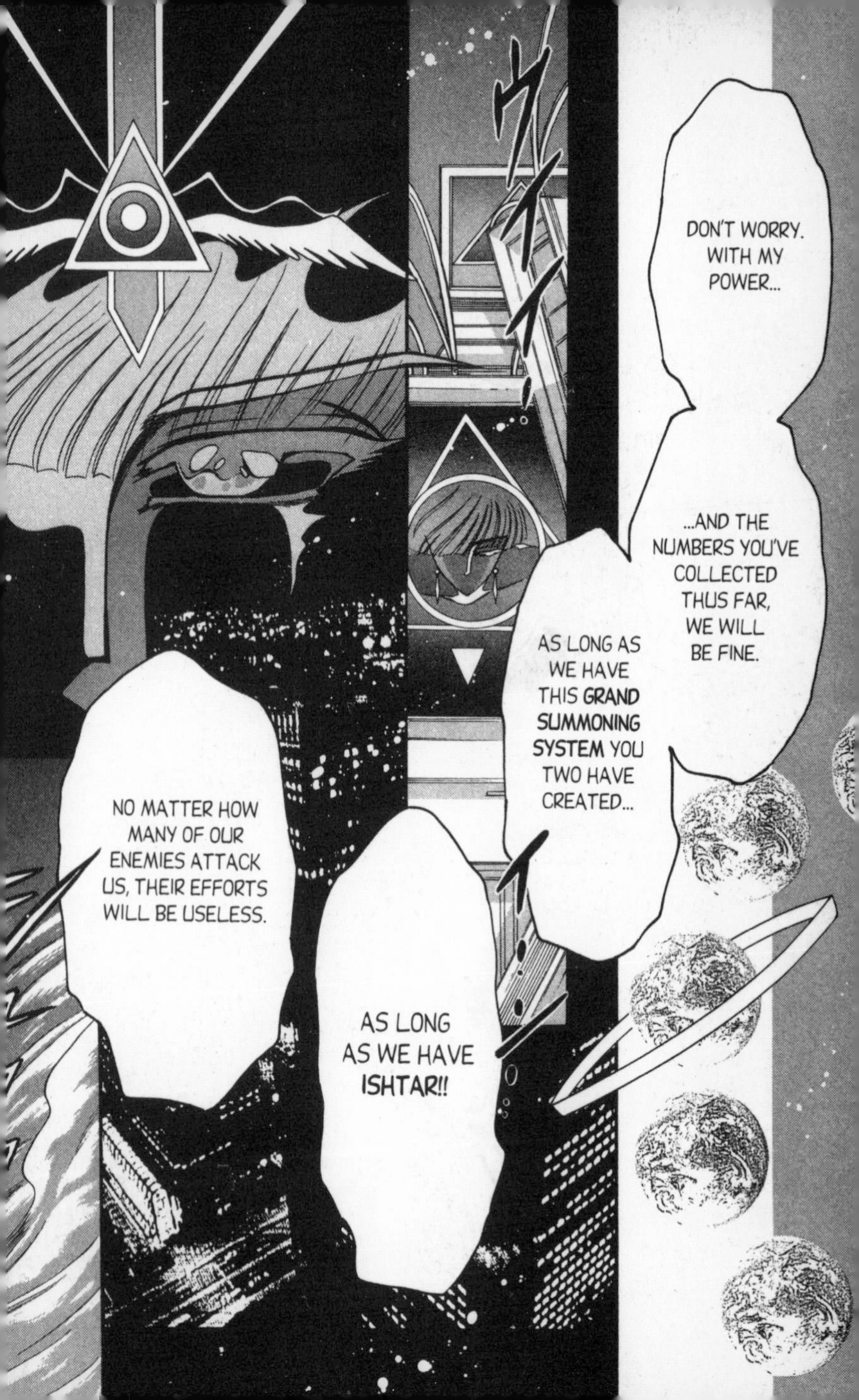
DON'T WORRY. WITH MY POWER...
...AND THE NUMBERS YOU'VE COLLECTED THUS FAR, WE WILL BE FINE.
AS LONG AS WE HAVE THIS GRAND SUMMONING SYSTEM YOU TWO HAVE CREATED...
NO MATTER HOW MANY OF OUR ENEMIES ATTACK US, THEIR EFFORTS WILL BE USELESS.
AS LONG AS WE HAVE ISHTAR!!

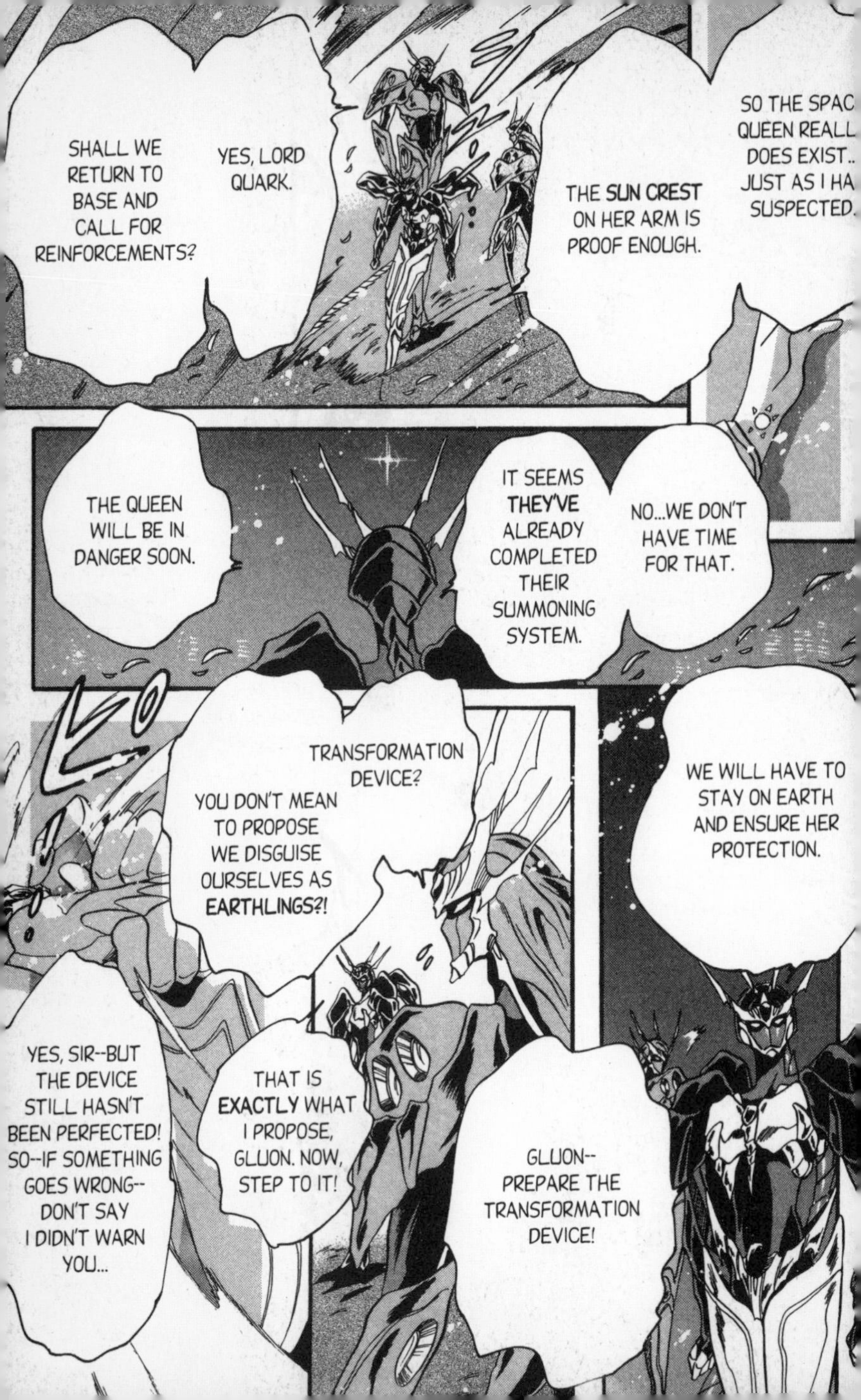

SO THE SPAC QUEEN REALL DOES EXIST.. JUST AS I HA SUSPECTED.
THE SUN CREST ON HER ARM IS PROOF ENOUGH.
YES, LORD QUARK.
SHALL WE RETURN TO BASE AND CALL FOR REINFORCEMENTS?
NO...WE DON'T HAVE TIME FOR THAT.
IT SEEMS THEY'VE ALREADY COMPLETED THEIR SUMMONING SYSTEM.
THE QUEEN WILL BE IN DANGER SOON.
WE WILL HAVE TO STAY ON EARTH AND ENSURE HER PROTECTION.
GLUON-- PREPARE THE TRANSFORMATION DEVICE!
TRANSFORMATION DEVICE?
YOU DON'T MEAN TO PROPOSE WE DISGUISE OURSELVES AS EARTHLINGS?!
THAT IS EXACTLY WHAT I PROPOSE, GLUON. NOW, STEP TO IT!
YES, SIR--BUT THE DEVICE STILL HASN'T BEEN PERFECTED! SO--IF SOMETHING GOES WRONG-- DON'T SAY I DIDN'T WARN YOU...

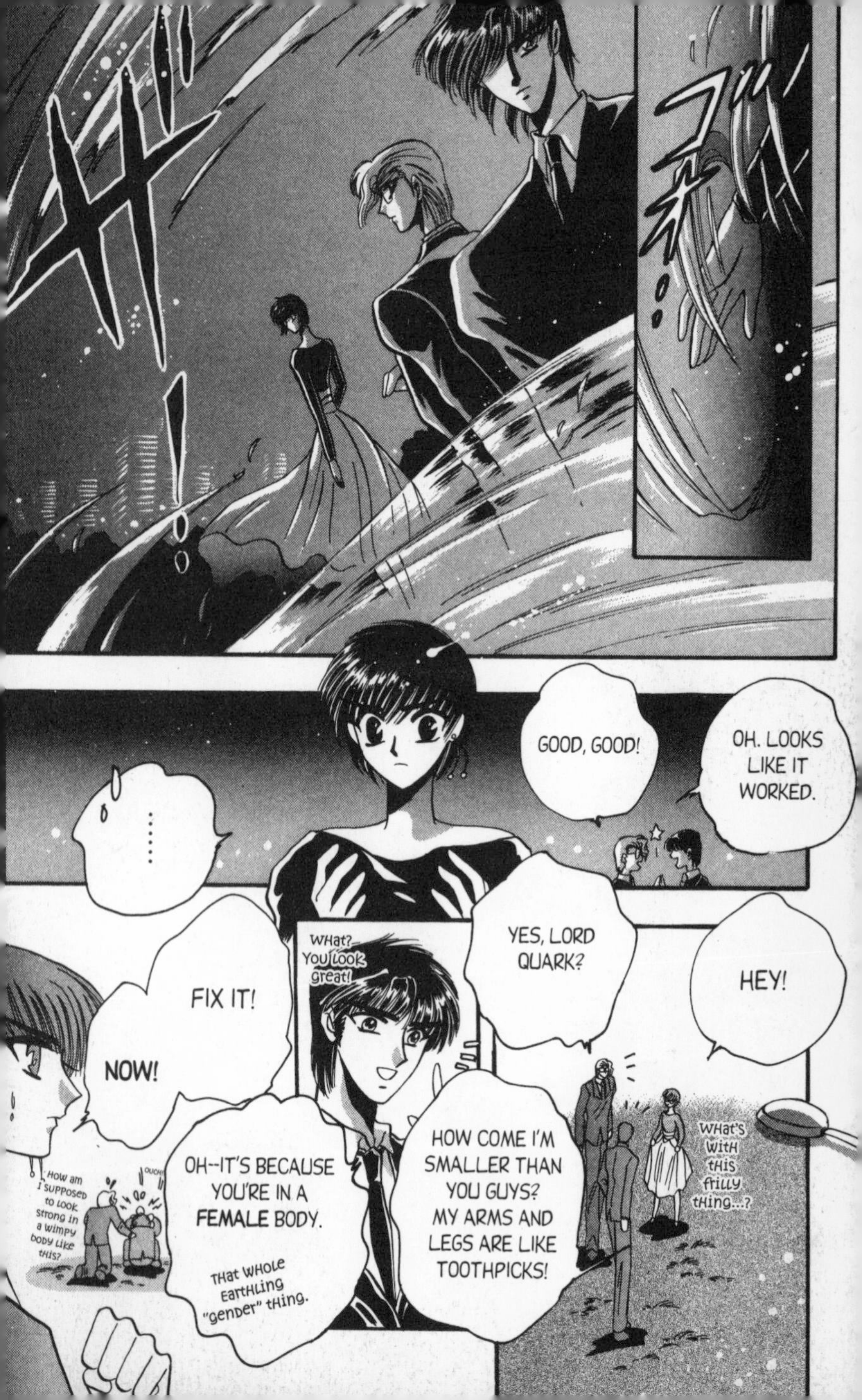
OH. LOOKS LIKE IT WORKED.
GOOD, GOOD!
......
HEY!
YES, LORD QUARK?
What's with this frilly thing...?
What? You look great!
HOW COME I'M SMALLER THAN YOU GUYS? MY ARMS AND LEGS ARE LIKE TOOTHPICKS!
OH--IT'S BECAUSE YOU'RE IN A **FEMALE** BODY.
That whole Earthling "gender" thing.
FIX IT!
NOW!
How am I supposed to look strong in a wimpy body like this?
OUCH!

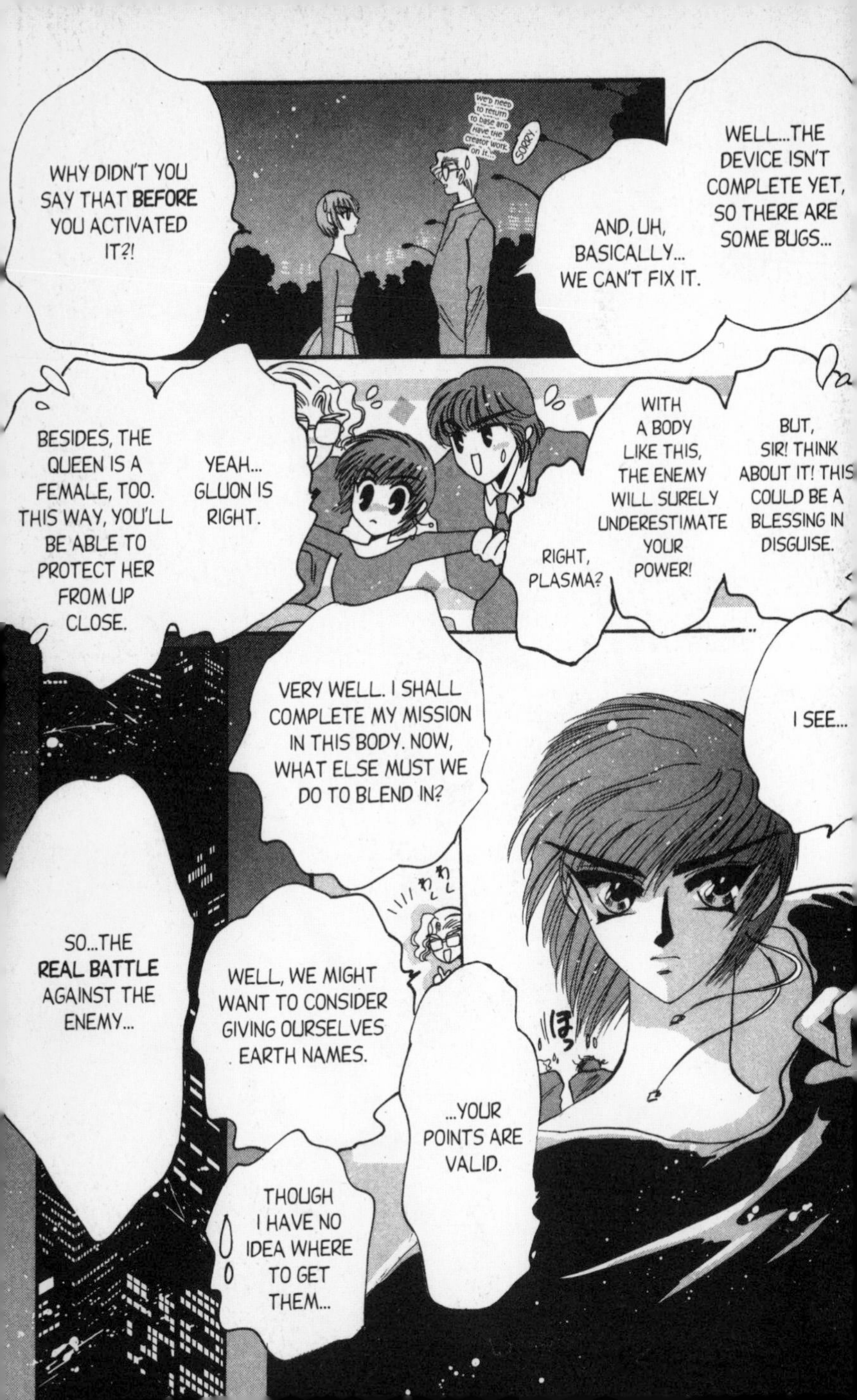

WELL...THE DEVICE ISN'T COMPLETE YET, SO THERE ARE SOME BUGS...
AND, UH, BASICALLY... WE CAN'T FIX IT.
SORRY.
We'd need to return to base and have the creator work on it...
WHY DIDN'T YOU SAY THAT BEFORE YOU ACTIVATED IT?!
BUT, SIR! THINK ABOUT IT! THIS COULD BE A BLESSING IN DISGUISE.
WITH A BODY LIKE THIS, THE ENEMY WILL SURELY UNDERESTIMATE YOUR POWER!
RIGHT, PLASMA?
YEAH... GLUON IS RIGHT.
BESIDES, THE QUEEN IS A FEMALE, TOO. THIS WAY, YOU'LL BE ABLE TO PROTECT HER FROM UP CLOSE.
I SEE...
...YOUR POINTS ARE VALID.
ほっ
VERY WELL. I SHALL COMPLETE MY MISSION IN THIS BODY. NOW, WHAT ELSE MUST WE DO TO BLEND IN?
WELL, WE MIGHT WANT TO CONSIDER GIVING OURSELVES EARTH NAMES.
THOUGH I HAVE NO IDEA WHERE TO GET THEM...
SO...THE REAL BATTLE AGAINST THE ENEMY...

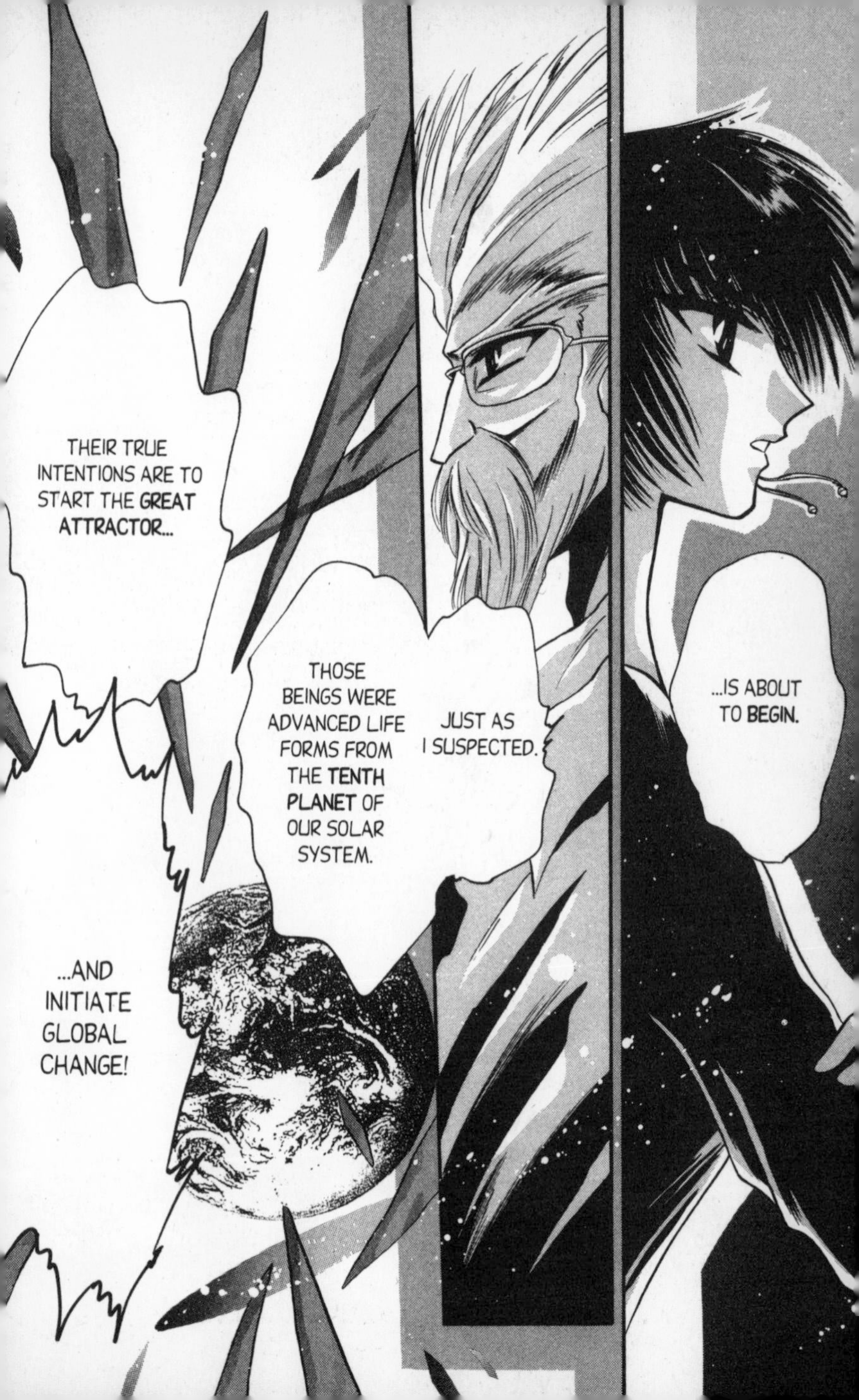
...IS ABOUT TO BEGIN.
JUST AS I SUSPECTED.
THOSE BEINGS WERE ADVANCED LIFE FORMS FROM THE TENTH PLANET OF OUR SOLAR SYSTEM.
THEIR TRUE INTENTIONS ARE TO START THE GREAT ATTRACTOR...
...AND INITIATE GLOBAL CHANGE!

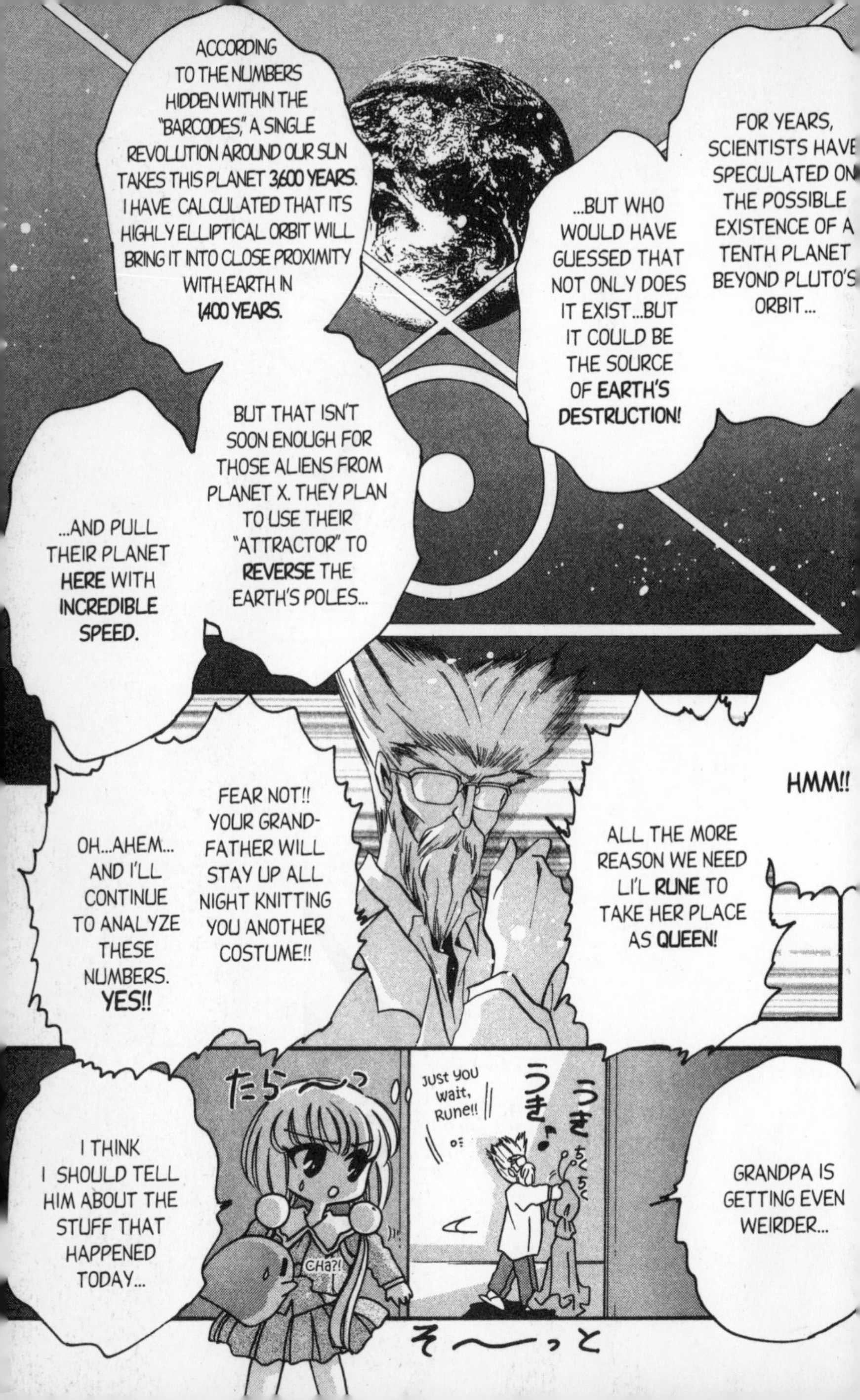
FOR YEARS, SCIENTISTS HAVE SPECULATED ON THE POSSIBLE EXISTENCE OF A TENTH PLANET BEYOND PLUTO'S ORBIT...
...BUT WHO WOULD HAVE GUESSED THAT NOT ONLY DOES IT EXIST...BUT IT COULD BE THE SOURCE OF **EARTH'S DESTRUCTION!**
ACCORDING TO THE NUMBERS HIDDEN WITHIN THE "BARCODES," A SINGLE REVOLUTION AROUND OUR SUN TAKES THIS PLANET **3,600 YEARS.** I HAVE CALCULATED THAT ITS HIGHLY ELLIPTICAL ORBIT WILL BRING IT INTO CLOSE PROXIMITY WITH EARTH IN **1,400 YEARS.**
BUT THAT ISN'T SOON ENOUGH FOR THOSE ALIENS FROM PLANET X. THEY PLAN TO USE THEIR "ATTRACTOR" TO **REVERSE** THE EARTH'S POLES...
...AND PULL THEIR PLANET **HERE** WITH **INCREDIBLE SPEED.**
HMM!!
ALL THE MORE REASON WE NEED LI'L **RUNE** TO TAKE HER PLACE AS **QUEEN!**
FEAR NOT!! YOUR GRAND-FATHER WILL STAY UP ALL NIGHT KNITTING YOU ANOTHER COSTUME!!
OH...AHEM... AND I'LL CONTINUE TO ANALYZE THESE NUMBERS. **YES!!**
GRANDPA IS GETTING EVEN WEIRDER...
うき うき♪
ちくちく
Just you wait, Rune!!
たら〜っ
CHA?!
I THINK I SHOULD TELL HIM ABOUT THE STUFF THAT HAPPENED TODAY...
そ〜っと

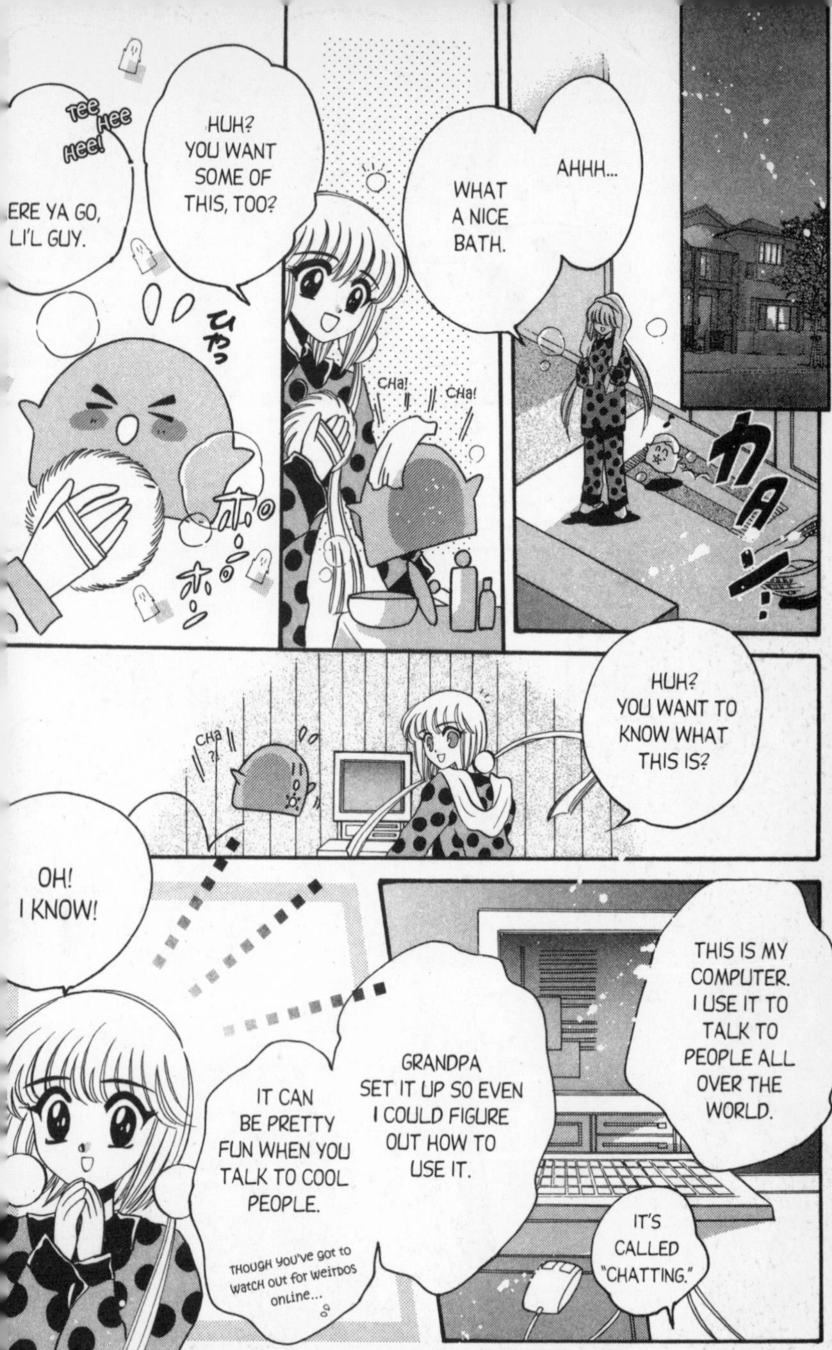
AHHH...
WHAT A NICE BATH.
カタン!
HUH? YOU WANT SOME OF THIS, TOO?
CHA!
CHA!
TEE HEE HEE!
ERE YA GO, LI'L GUY.
ひゃっ
ホッ
ホッ
HUH? YOU WANT TO KNOW WHAT THIS IS?
CHA?
THIS IS MY COMPUTER. I USE IT TO TALK TO PEOPLE ALL OVER THE WORLD.
IT'S CALLED "CHATTING."
OH! I KNOW!
GRANDPA SET IT UP SO EVEN I COULD FIGURE OUT HOW TO USE IT.
IT CAN BE PRETTY FUN WHEN YOU TALK TO COOL PEOPLE.
THOUGH you've got to watch out for weirdos online...

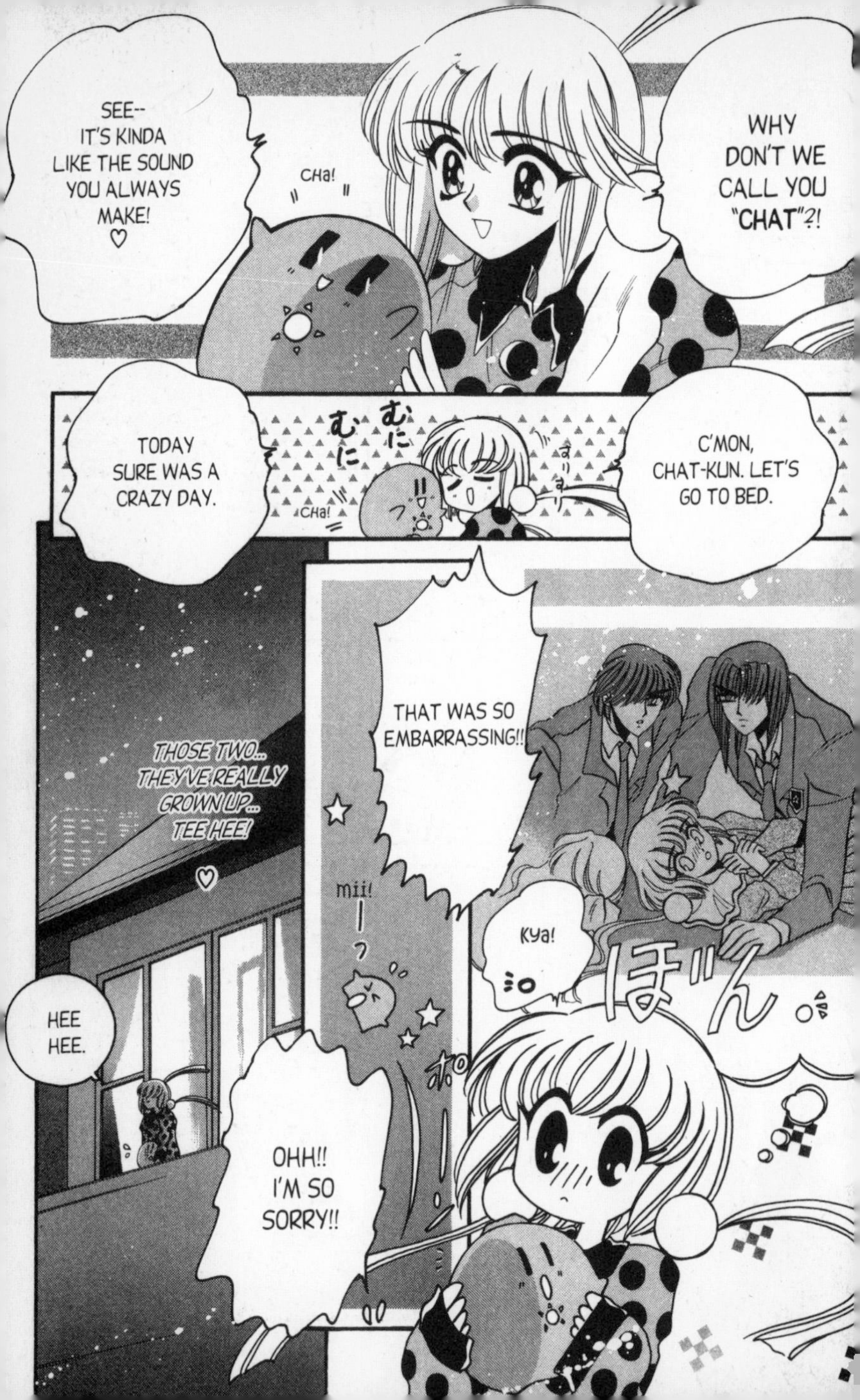
WHY DON'T WE CALL YOU "CHAT"?!
CHA!
SEE-- IT'S KINDA LIKE THE SOUND YOU ALWAYS MAKE! ♡
C'MON, CHAT-KUN. LET'S GO TO BED.
すりすり
むにむに
CHA!
TODAY SURE WAS A CRAZY DAY.
ぼん
KYA!
THAT WAS SO EMBARRASSING!!
mii!
OHH!! I'M SO SORRY!!
THOSE TWO... THEY'VE REALLY GROWN UP... TEE HEE! ♡
HEE HEE.

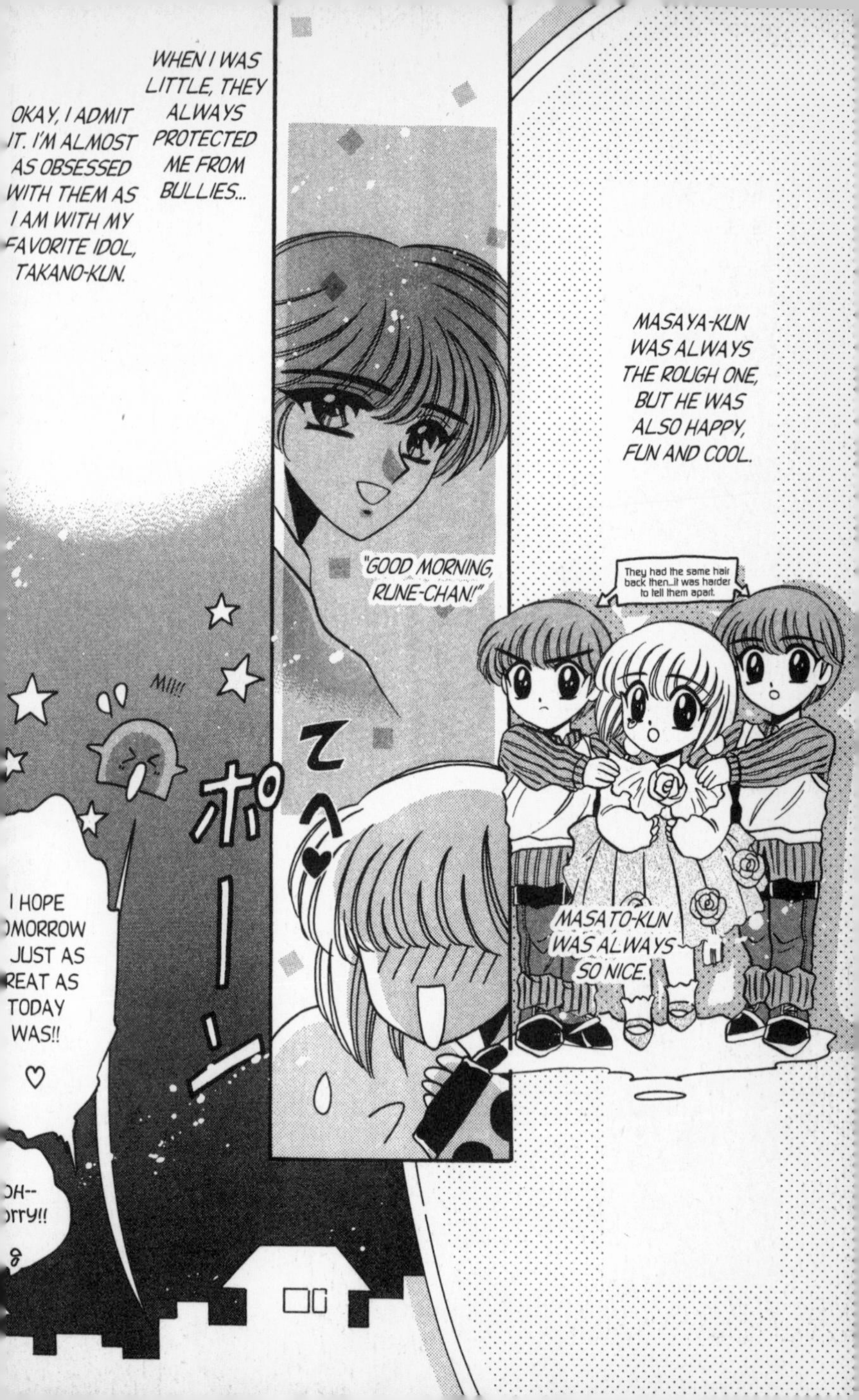
MASAYA-KUN WAS ALWAYS THE ROUGH ONE, BUT HE WAS ALSO HAPPY, FUN AND COOL.
They had the same hair back then...it was harder to tell them apart.
MASATO-KUN WAS ALWAYS SO NICE.
WHEN I WAS LITTLE, THEY ALWAYS PROTECTED ME FROM BULLIES...
"GOOD MORNING, RUNE-CHAN!"
OKAY, I ADMIT IT. I'M ALMOST AS OBSESSED WITH THEM AS I AM WITH MY FAVORITE IDOL, TAKANO-KUN.
MI!!
I HOPE MORROW JUST AS REAT AS TODAY WAS!! ♡
OH-- orry!!

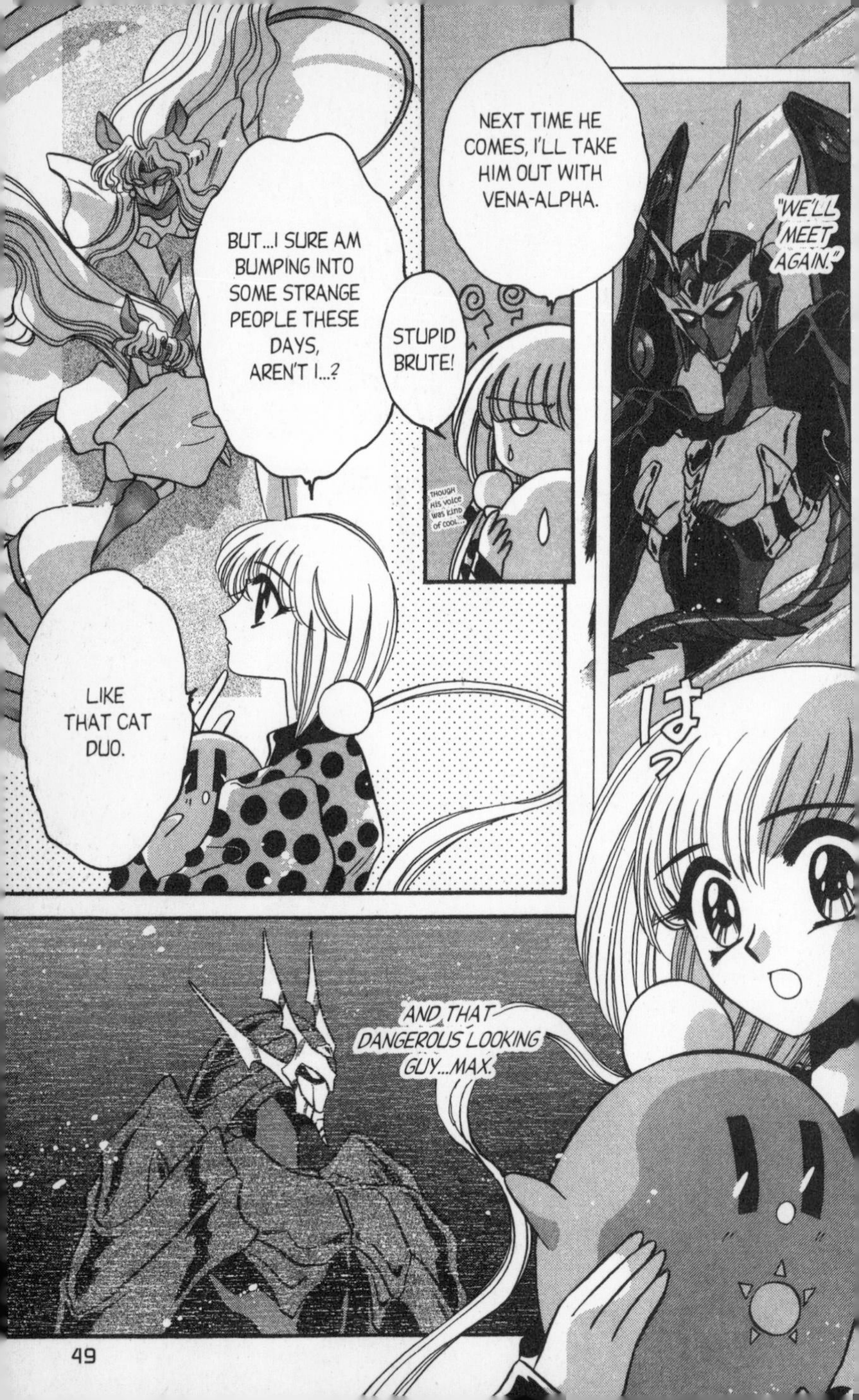
"WE'LL MEET AGAIN."
NEXT TIME HE COMES, I'LL TAKE HIM OUT WITH VENA-ALPHA.
STUPID BRUTE!
THOUGH HIS VOICE WAS KIND OF COOL...
BUT...I SURE AM BUMPING INTO SOME STRANGE PEOPLE THESE DAYS, AREN'T I...?
LIKE THAT CAT DUO.
はっ
AND THAT DANGEROUS LOOKING GUY...MAX.

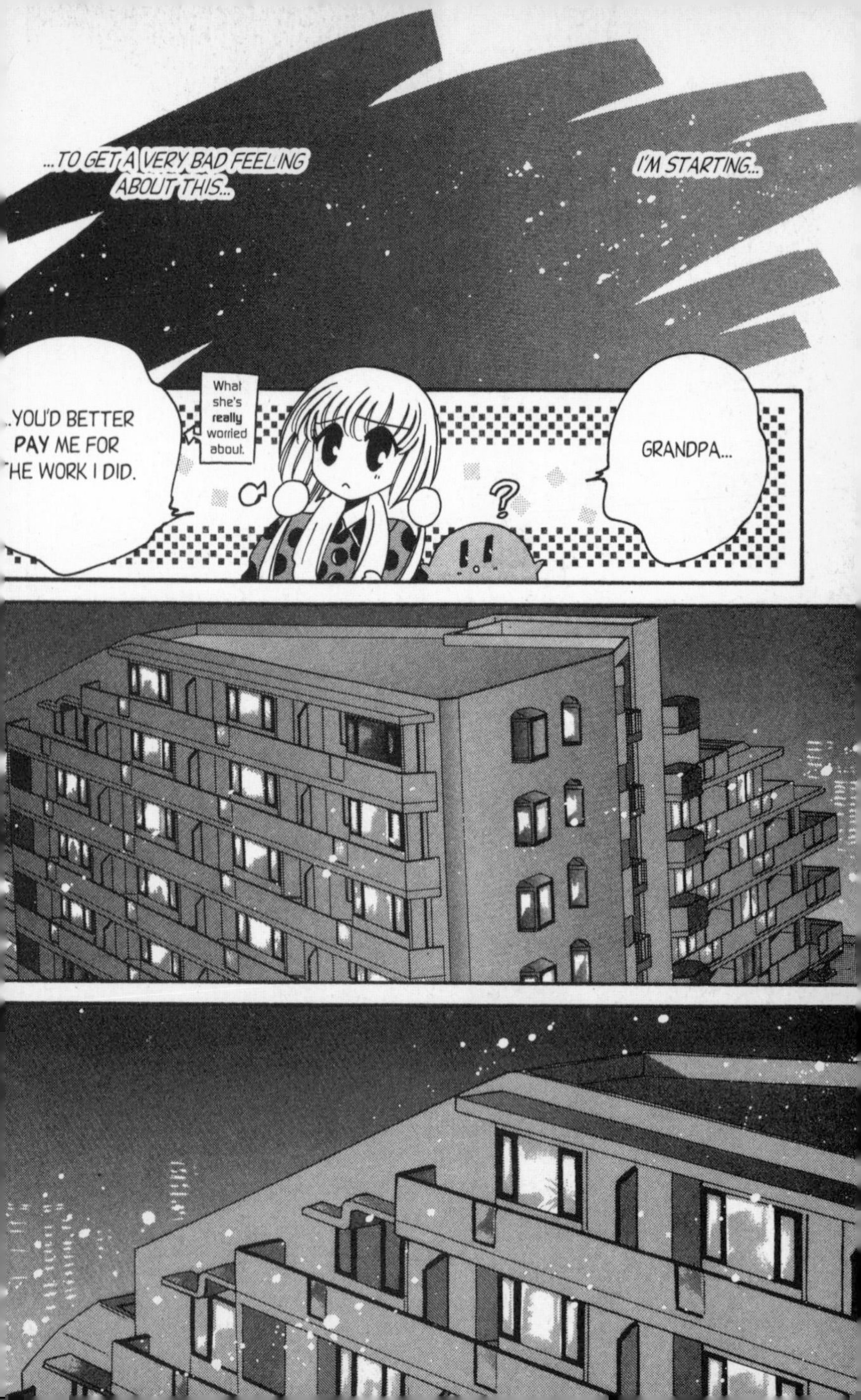
I'M STARTING...
...TO GET A VERY BAD FEELING ABOUT THIS...
GRANDPA...
What she's really worried about.
..YOU'D BETTER PAY ME FOR THE WORK I DID.

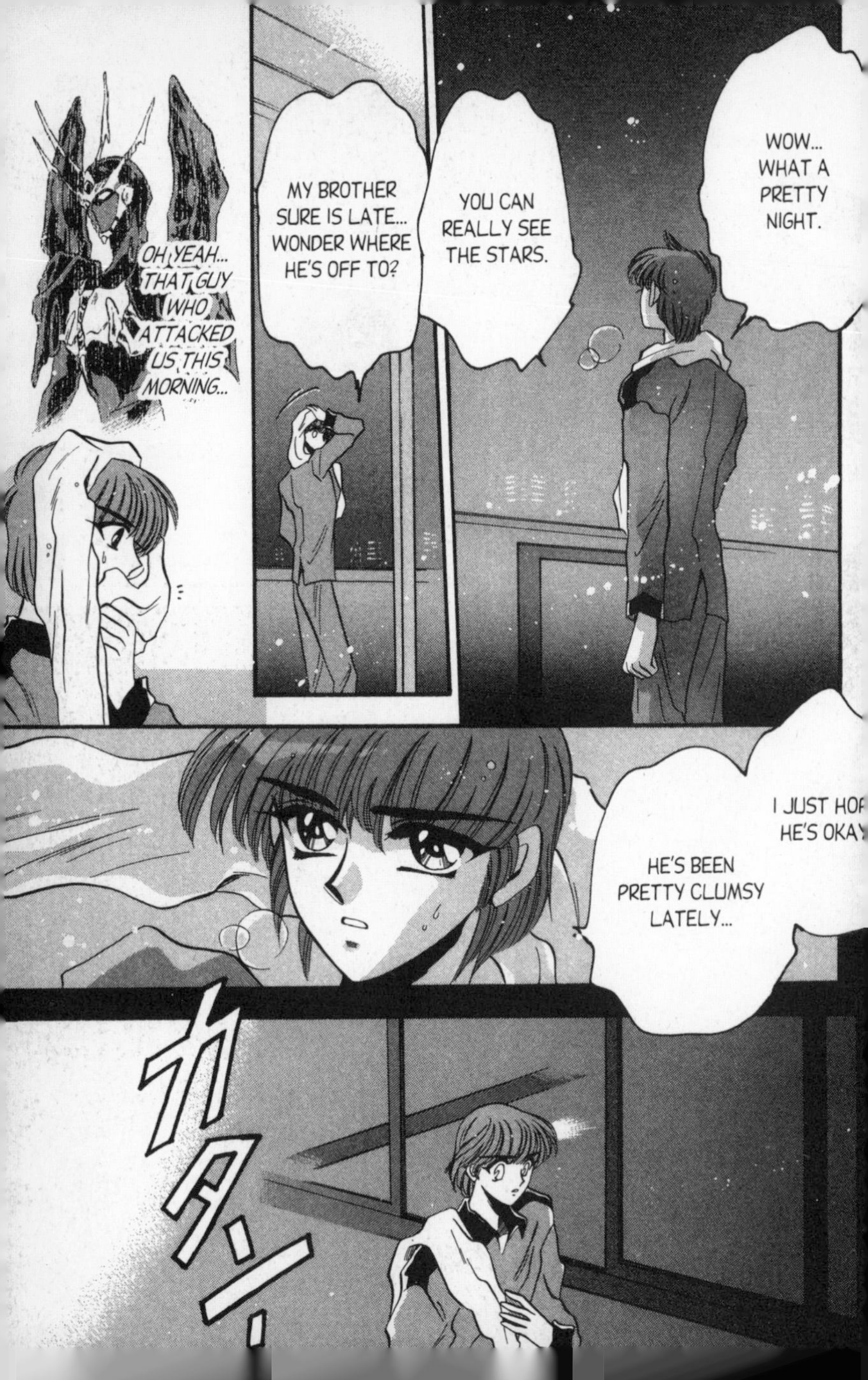
WOW... WHAT A PRETTY NIGHT.
YOU CAN REALLY SEE THE STARS.
MY BROTHER SURE IS LATE... WONDER WHERE HE'S OFF TO?
OH YEAH... THAT GUY WHO ATTACKED US THIS MORNING...
I JUST HOP HE'S OKA
HE'S BEEN PRETTY CLUMSY LATELY...
カタン

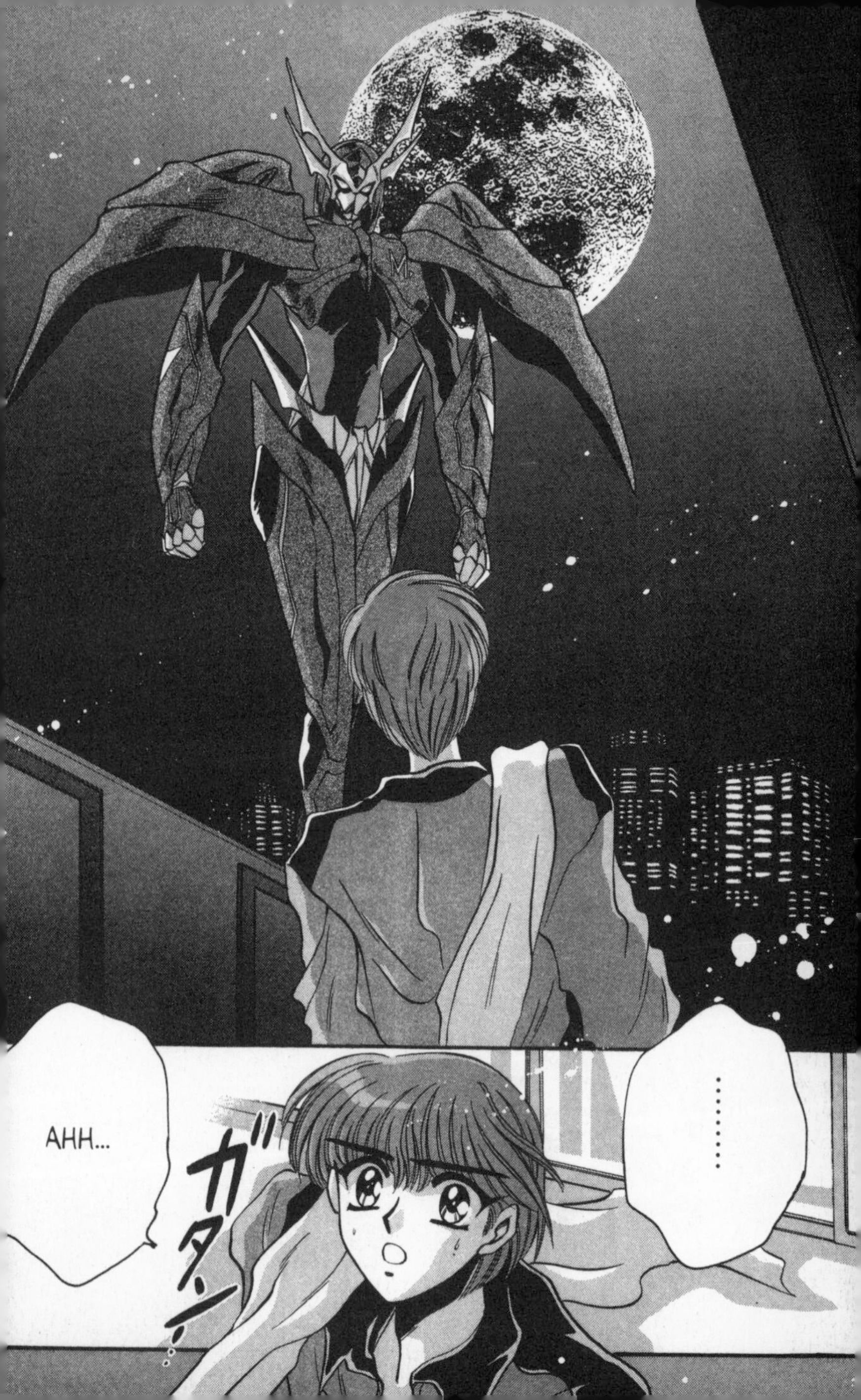

......
ガタン
AHH...

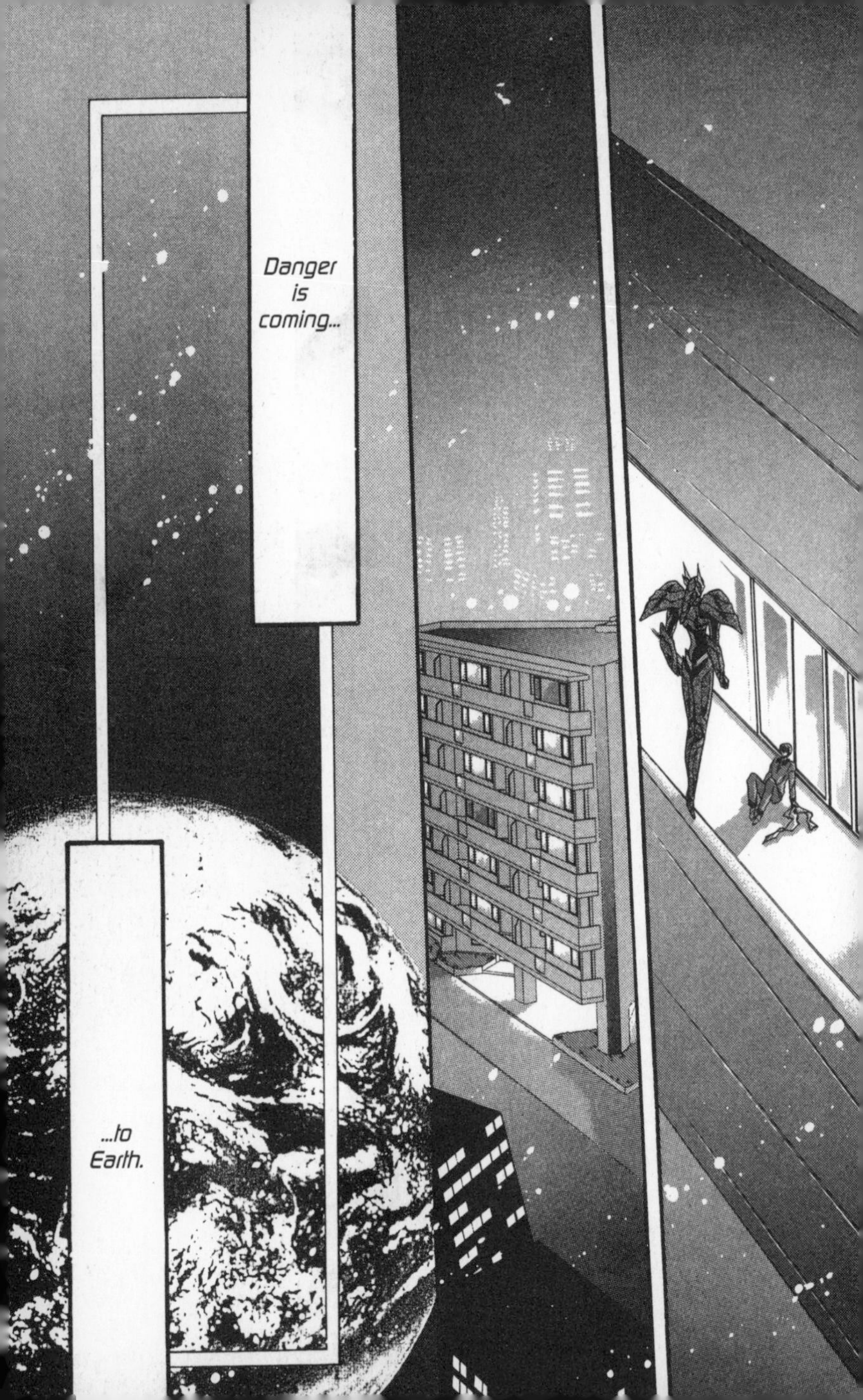
Danger is coming...
...to Earth.

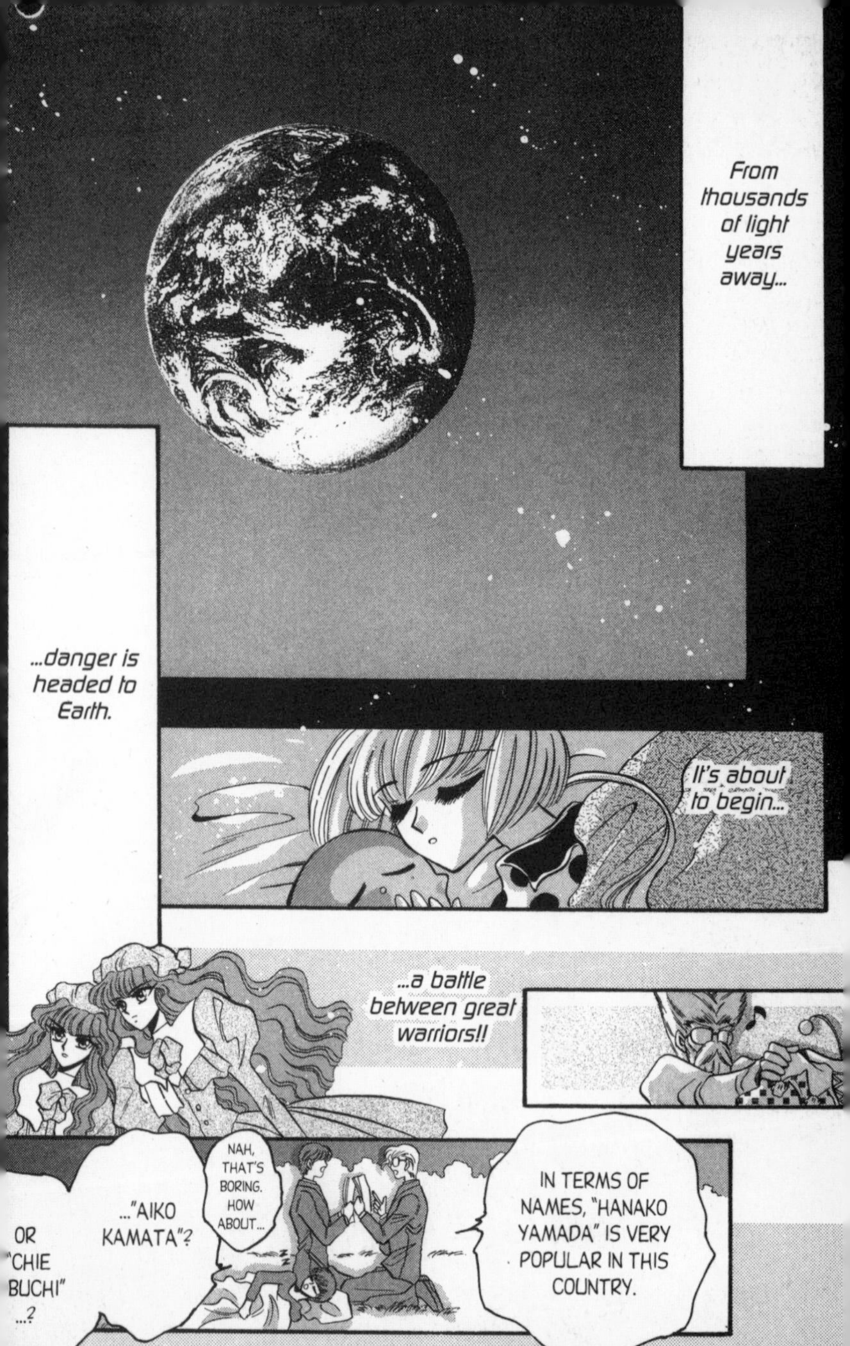
From thousands of light years away...
...danger is headed to Earth.
It's about to begin...
...a battle between great warriors!!
IN TERMS OF NAMES, "HANAKO YAMADA" IS VERY POPULAR IN THIS COUNTRY.
NAH, THAT'S BORING. HOW ABOUT...
..."AIKO KAMATA"?
OR "CHIE BUCHI" ...?

ese are all girls' names.

TRANSFORMATION 1 —— END

TRANSFORMATION 2

VISITOR【訪問者】

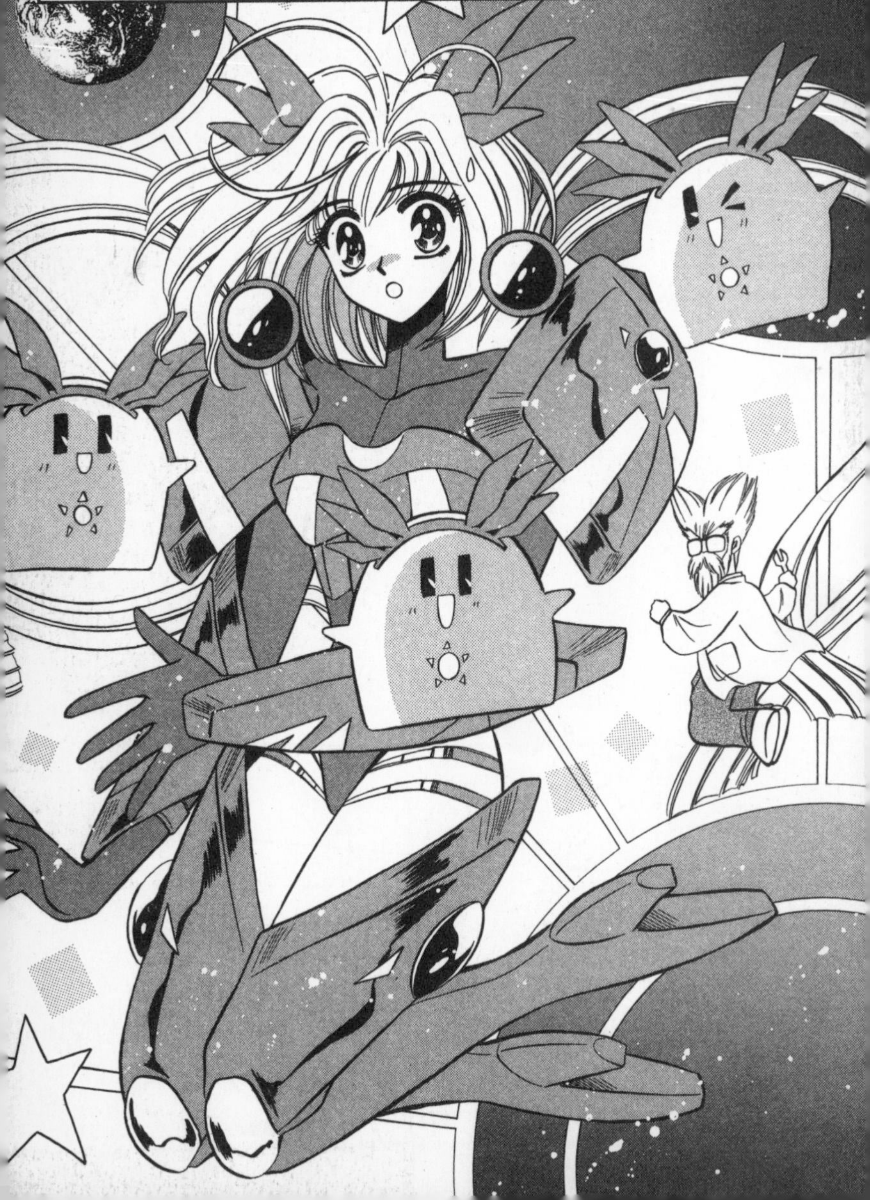

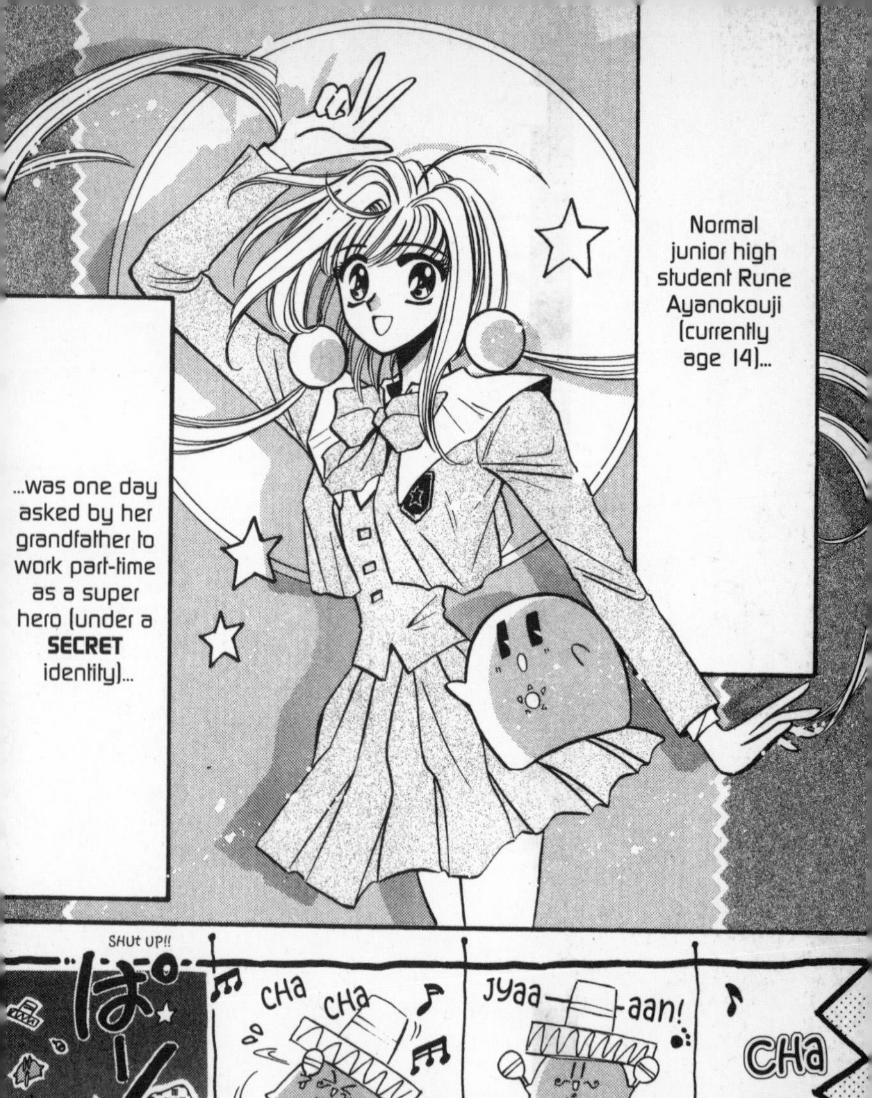
Normal junior high student Rune Ayanokouji (currently age 14)...
...was one day asked by her grandfather to work part-time as a super hero (under a **SECRET** identity)...

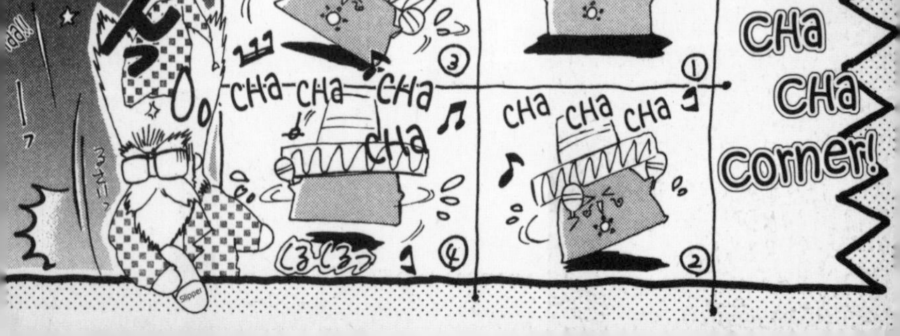
CHa CHa CHa Corner!
Jyaa—aan!
CHa CHa CHa
CHa CHa
CHa-CHa-CHa CHa
くるくるっ
SHUt UP!!
ぱーんっ
Slipper

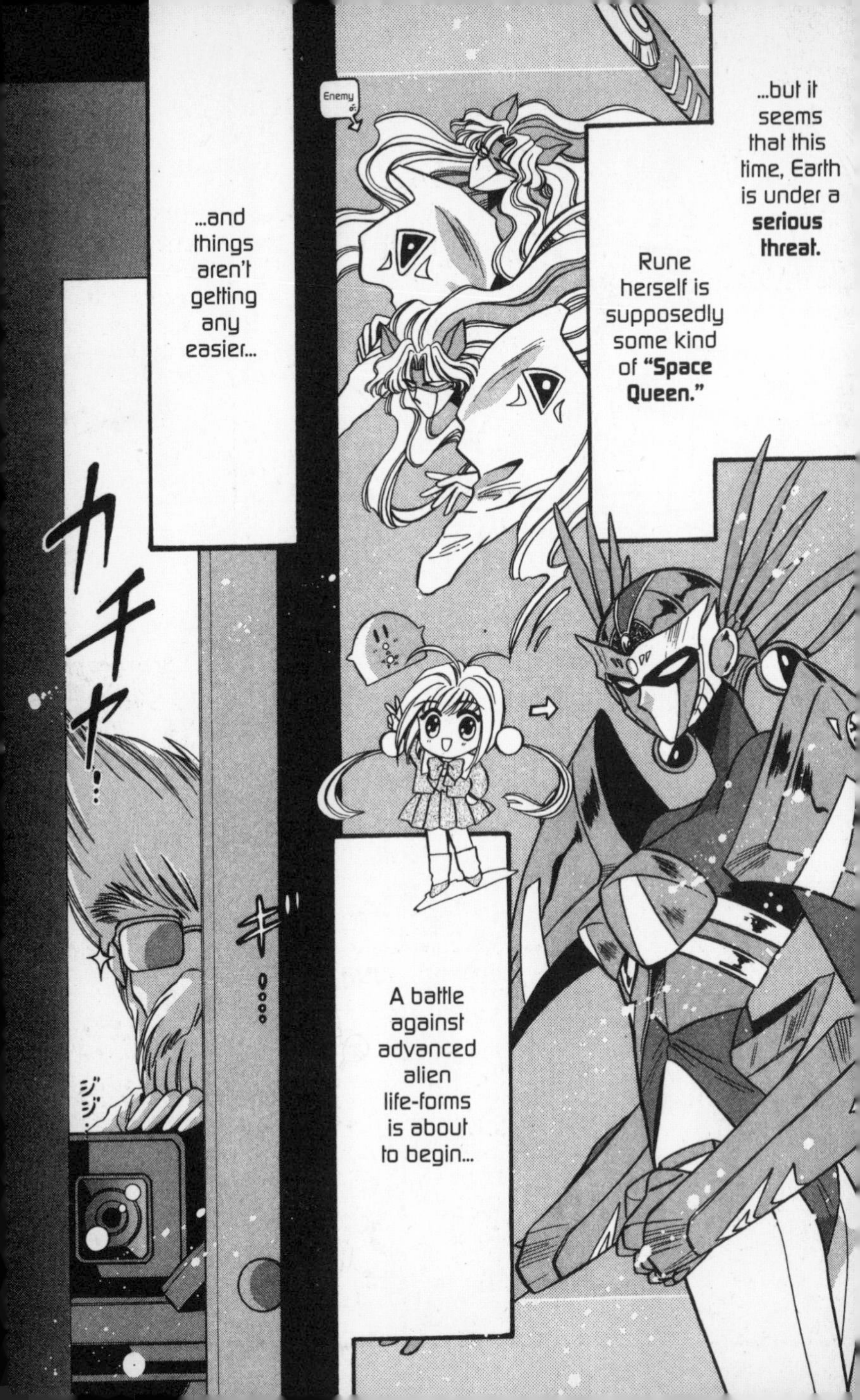

...but it seems that this time, Earth is under a **serious threat.**
Rune herself is supposedly some kind of **"Space Queen."**
Enemy
!!
A battle against advanced alien life-forms is about to begin...
...and things aren't getting any easier...
カチャ!!
キ…
ジジ…

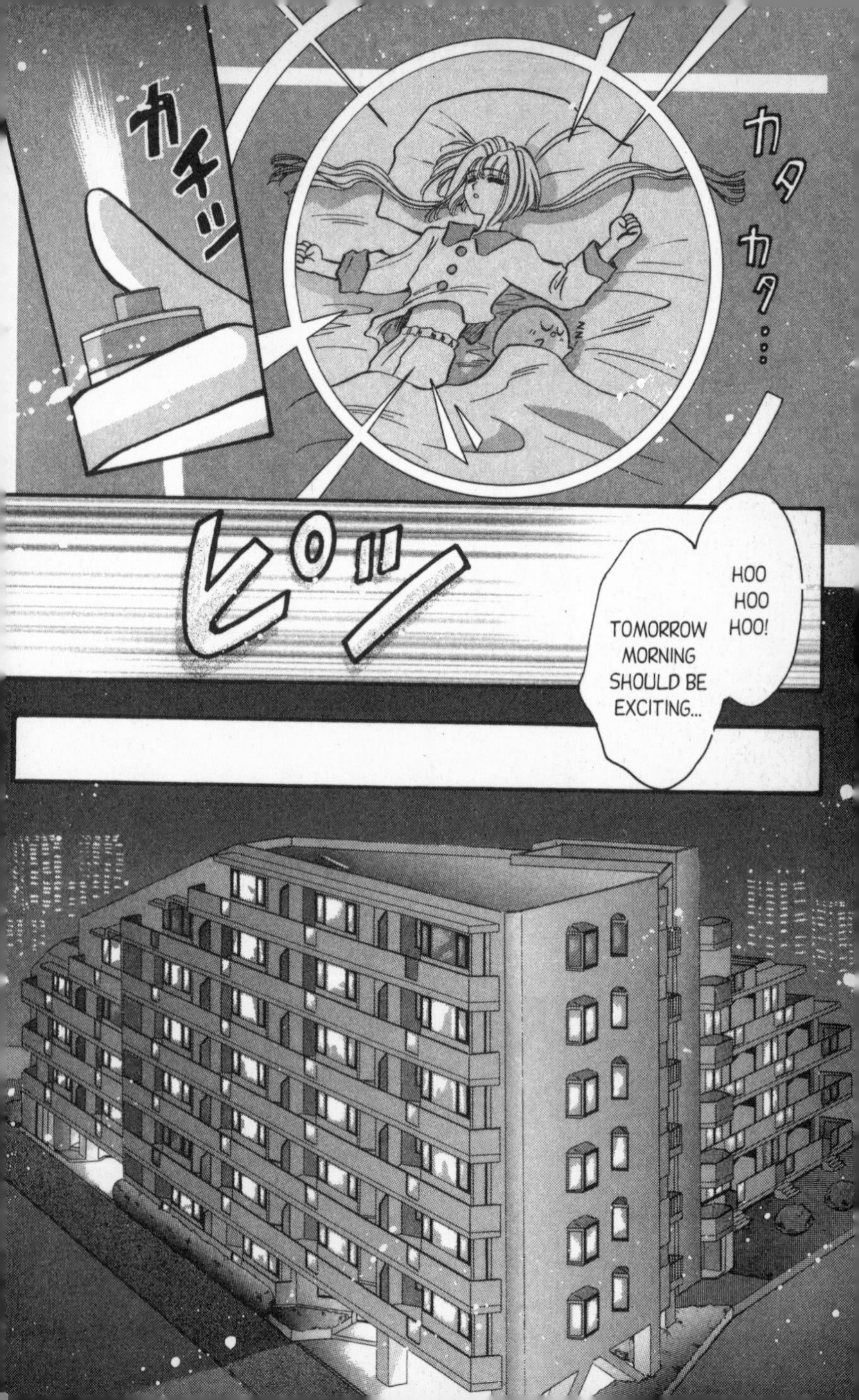
カタカタ…
カチッ
ピッ
HOO HOO HOO! TOMORROW MORNING SHOULD BE EXCITING...

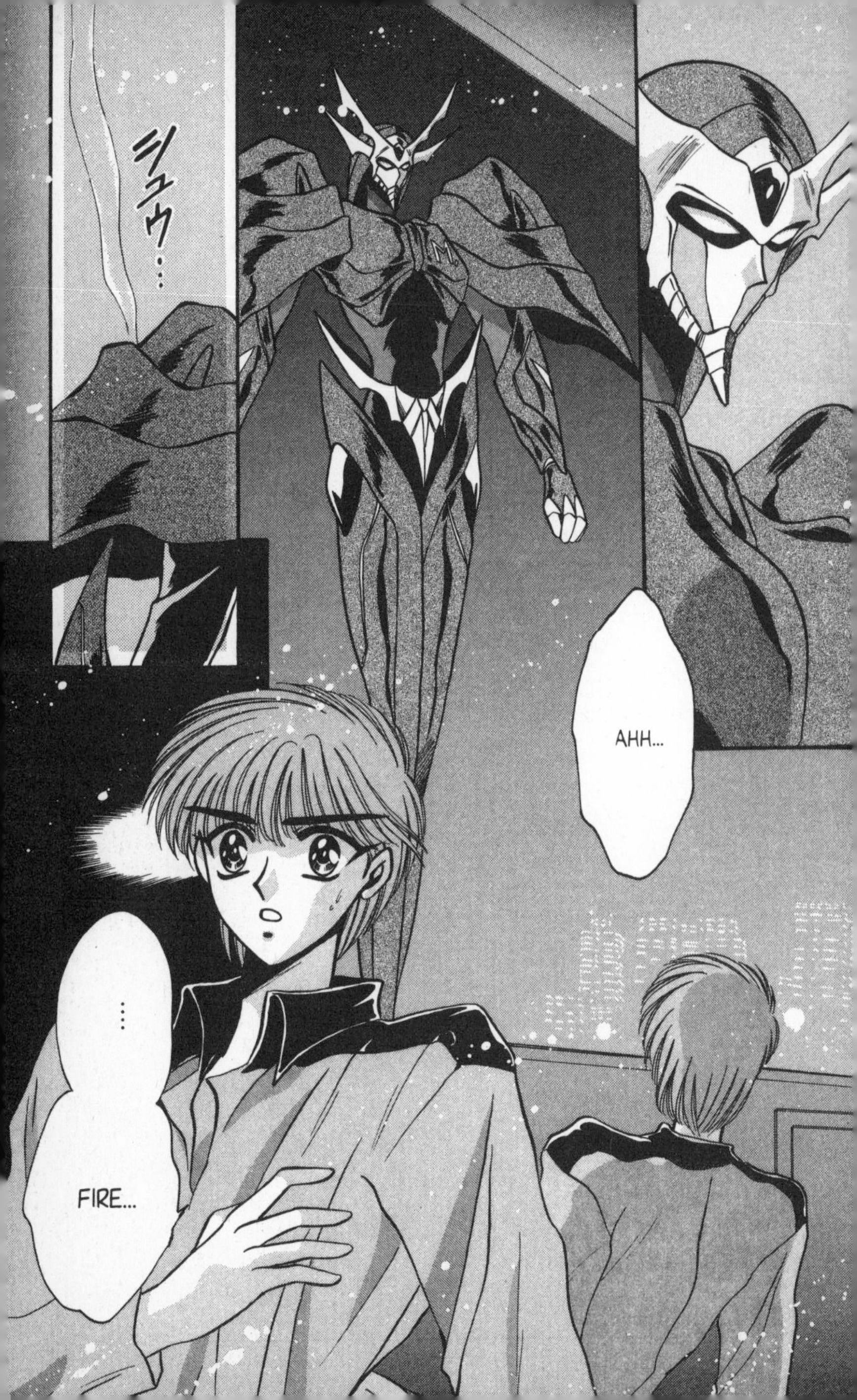
シュウ…
AHH...
...
FIRE...

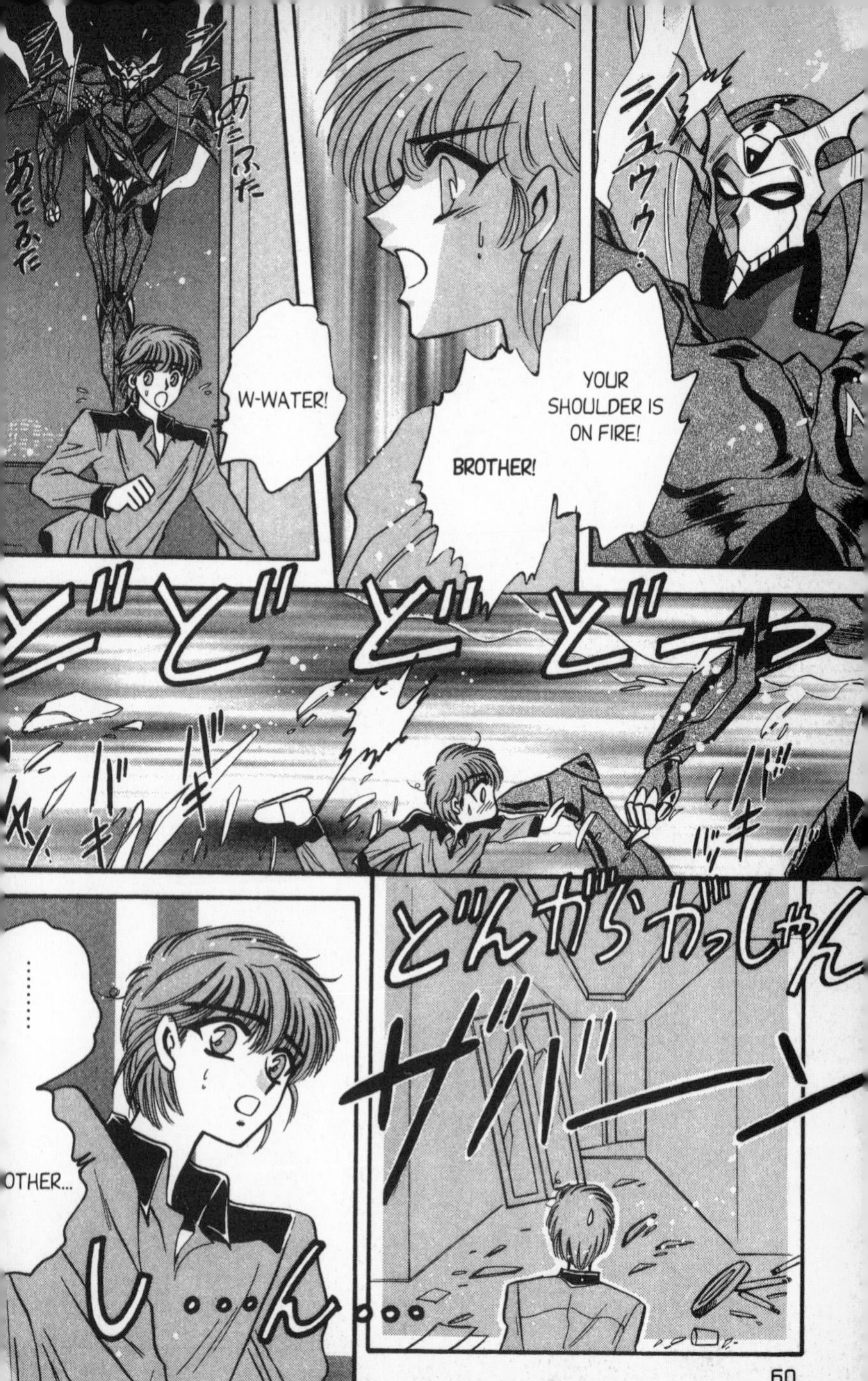
シュウウ…
YOUR SHOULDER IS ON FIRE!
BROTHER!
W-WATER!
あたふた
あたふた
どどどどどっ
バキ
バキッ
どんがらがっしゃん
ザバーン
……
OTHER...
し…ん…

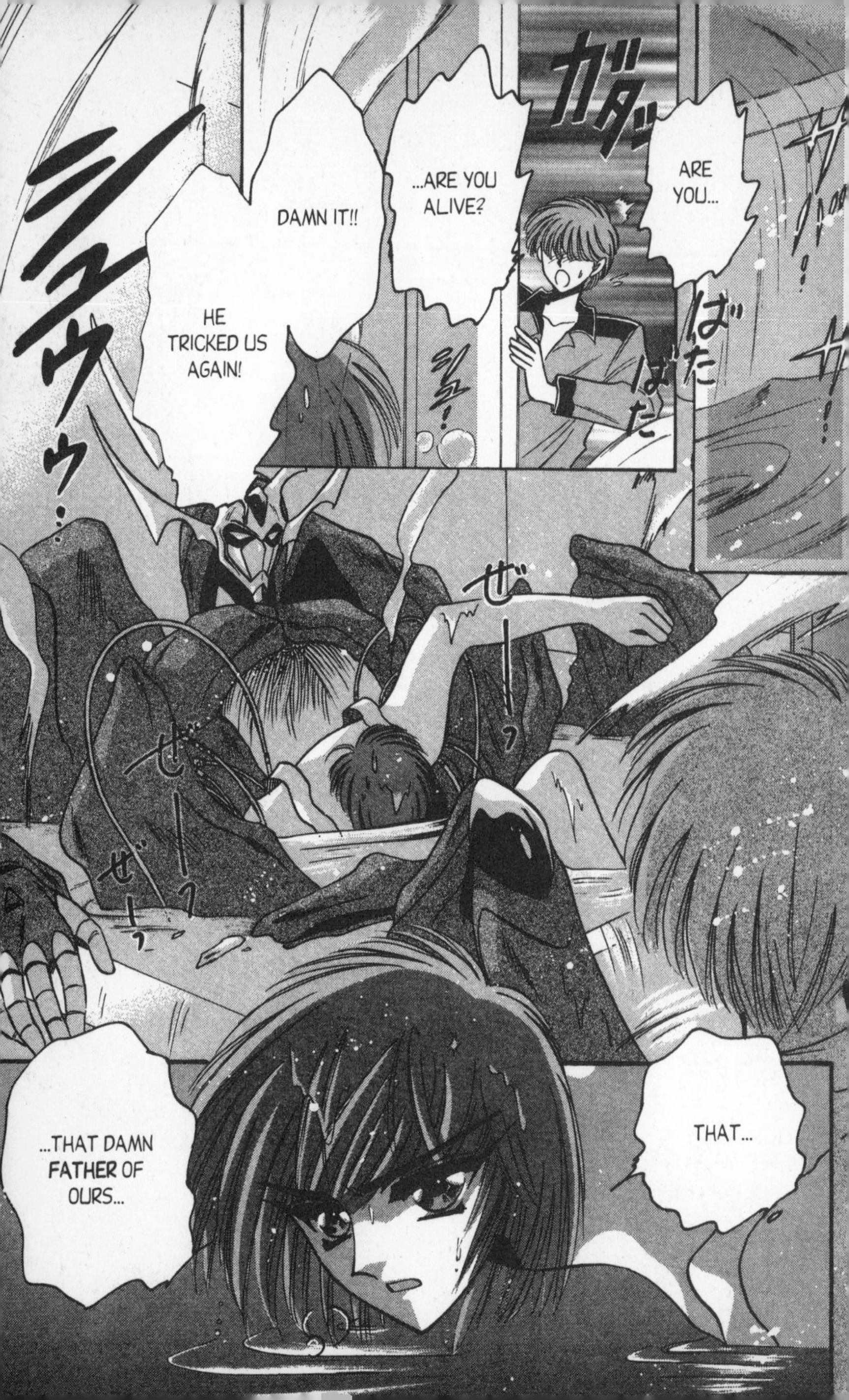
ガタッ
ARE YOU...
...ARE YOU ALIVE?
ばたばた
DAMN IT!!
HE TRICKED US AGAIN!
シュウゥ...
ぜーっ
THAT...
...THAT DAMN FATHER OF OURS...

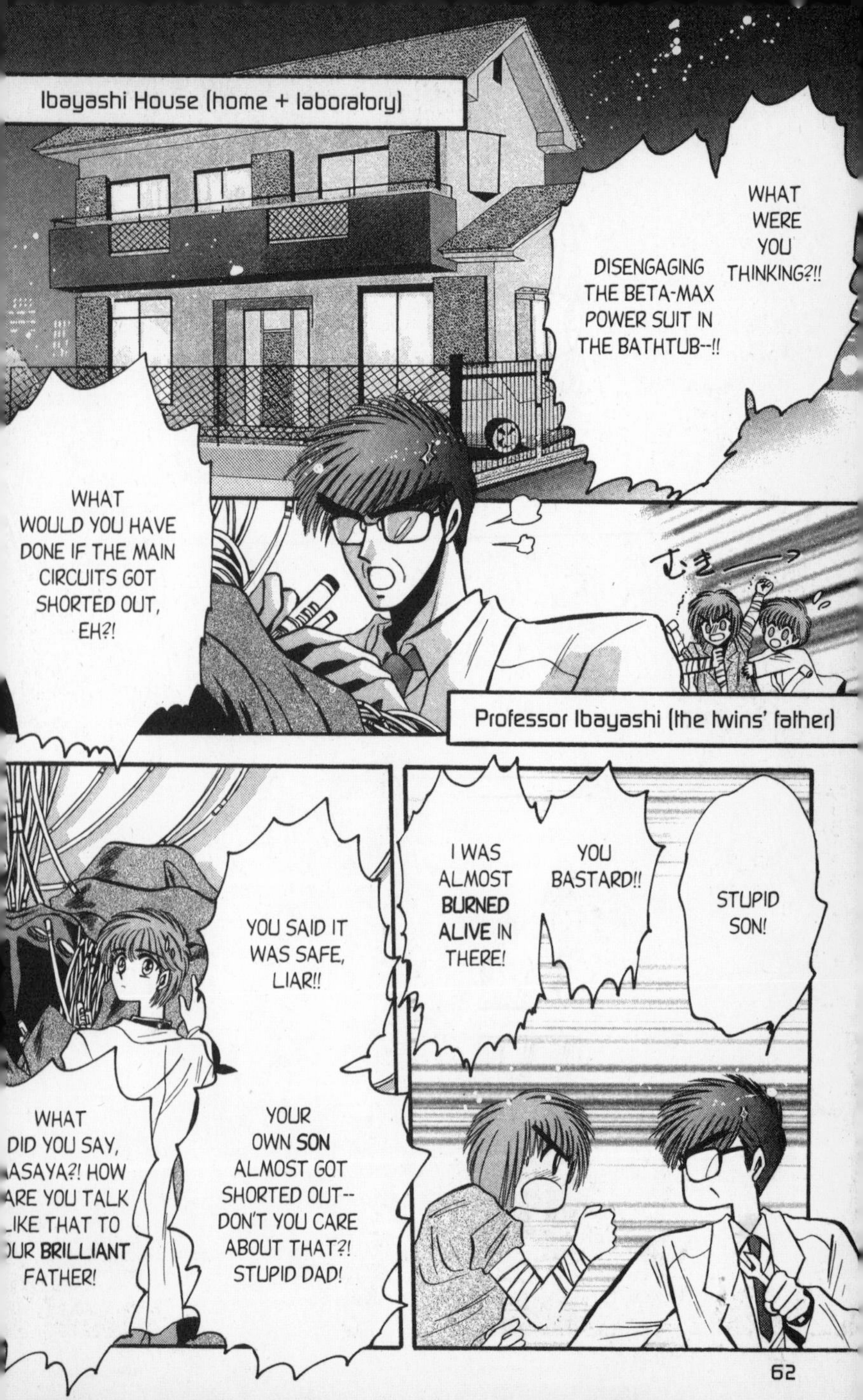
Ibayashi House (home + laboratory)
WHAT WERE YOU THINKING?!!
DISENGAGING THE BETA-MAX POWER SUIT IN THE BATHTUB--!!
WHAT WOULD YOU HAVE DONE IF THE MAIN CIRCUITS GOT SHORTED OUT, EH?!
むきーー
Professor Ibayashi (the twins' father)
STUPID SON!
YOU BASTARD!!
I WAS ALMOST **BURNED ALIVE** IN THERE!
YOU SAID IT WAS SAFE, LIAR!!
YOUR OWN **SON** ALMOST GOT SHORTED OUT-- DON'T YOU CARE ABOUT THAT?! STUPID DAD!
WHAT DID YOU SAY, ASAYA?! HOW ARE YOU TALK LIKE THAT TO OUR **BRILLIANT** FATHER!

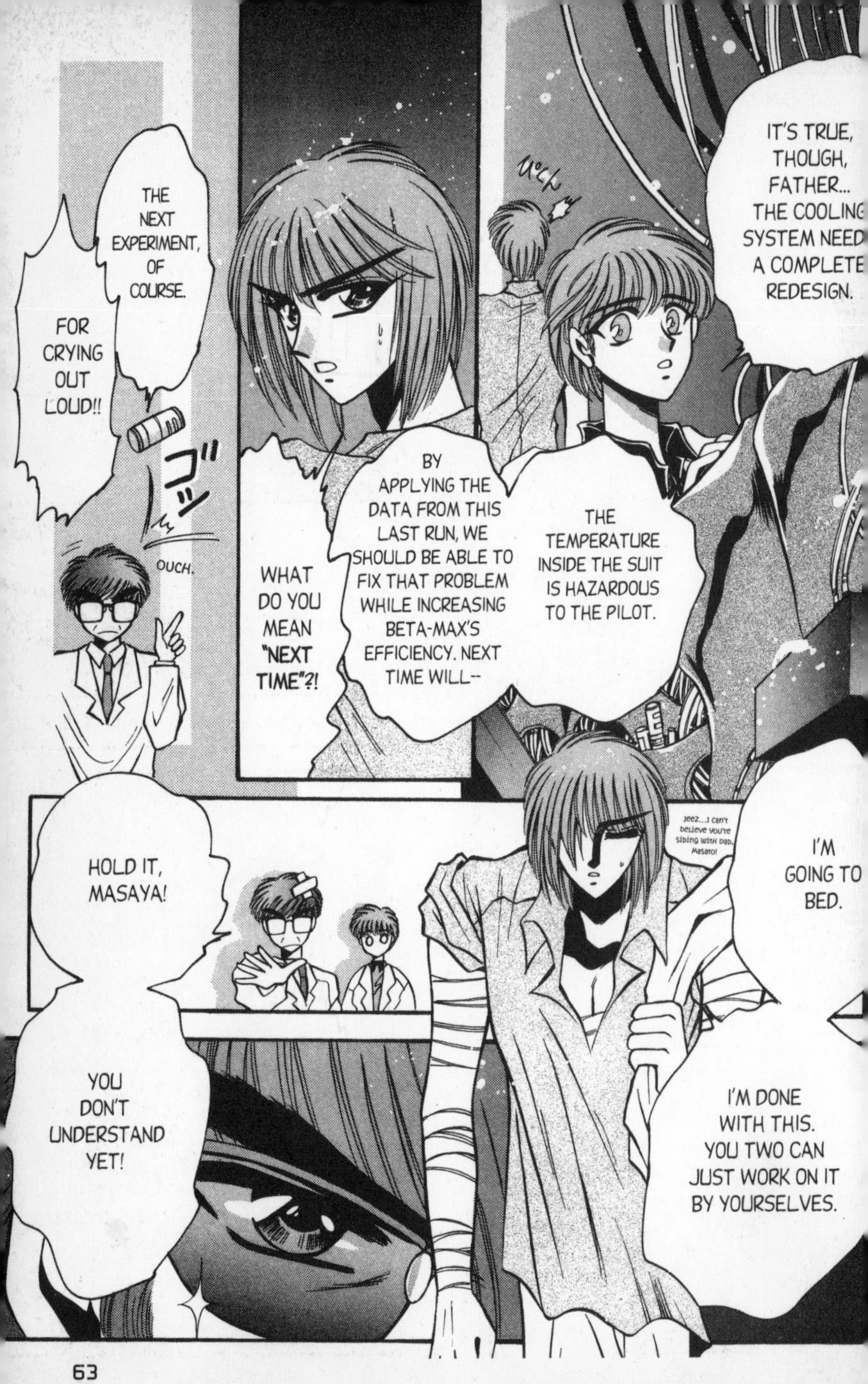
IT'S TRUE, THOUGH, FATHER... THE COOLING SYSTEM NEED A COMPLETE REDESIGN.
ぴくん
THE TEMPERATURE INSIDE THE SUIT IS HAZARDOUS TO THE PILOT.
BY APPLYING THE DATA FROM THIS LAST RUN, WE SHOULD BE ABLE TO FIX THAT PROBLEM WHILE INCREASING BETA-MAX'S EFFICIENCY. NEXT TIME WILL--
WHAT DO YOU MEAN **"NEXT TIME"**?!
THE NEXT EXPERIMENT, OF COURSE.
FOR CRYING OUT LOUD!!
ゴッ
OUCH.
I'M GOING TO BED.
Jeez...I can't believe you're siding with Dad, Masato!
I'M DONE WITH THIS. YOU TWO CAN JUST WORK ON IT BY YOURSELVES.
HOLD IT, MASAYA!
YOU DON'T UNDERSTAND YET!

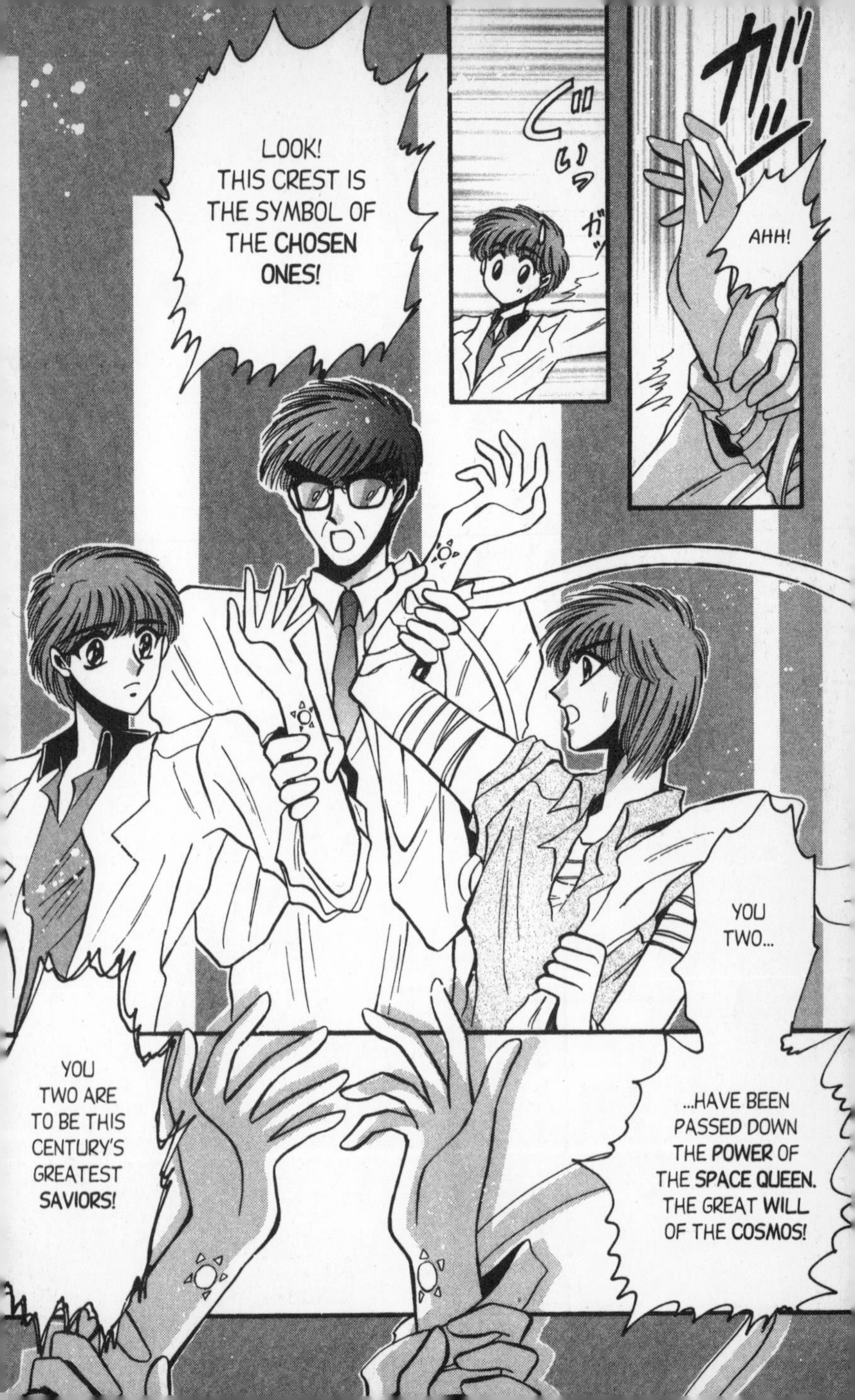

ガッ
AHH!
LOOK! THIS CREST IS THE SYMBOL OF THE CHOSEN ONES!
YOU TWO...
...HAVE BEEN PASSED DOWN THE POWER OF THE SPACE QUEEN. THE GREAT WILL OF THE COSMOS!
YOU TWO ARE TO BE THIS CENTURY'S GREATEST SAVIORS!

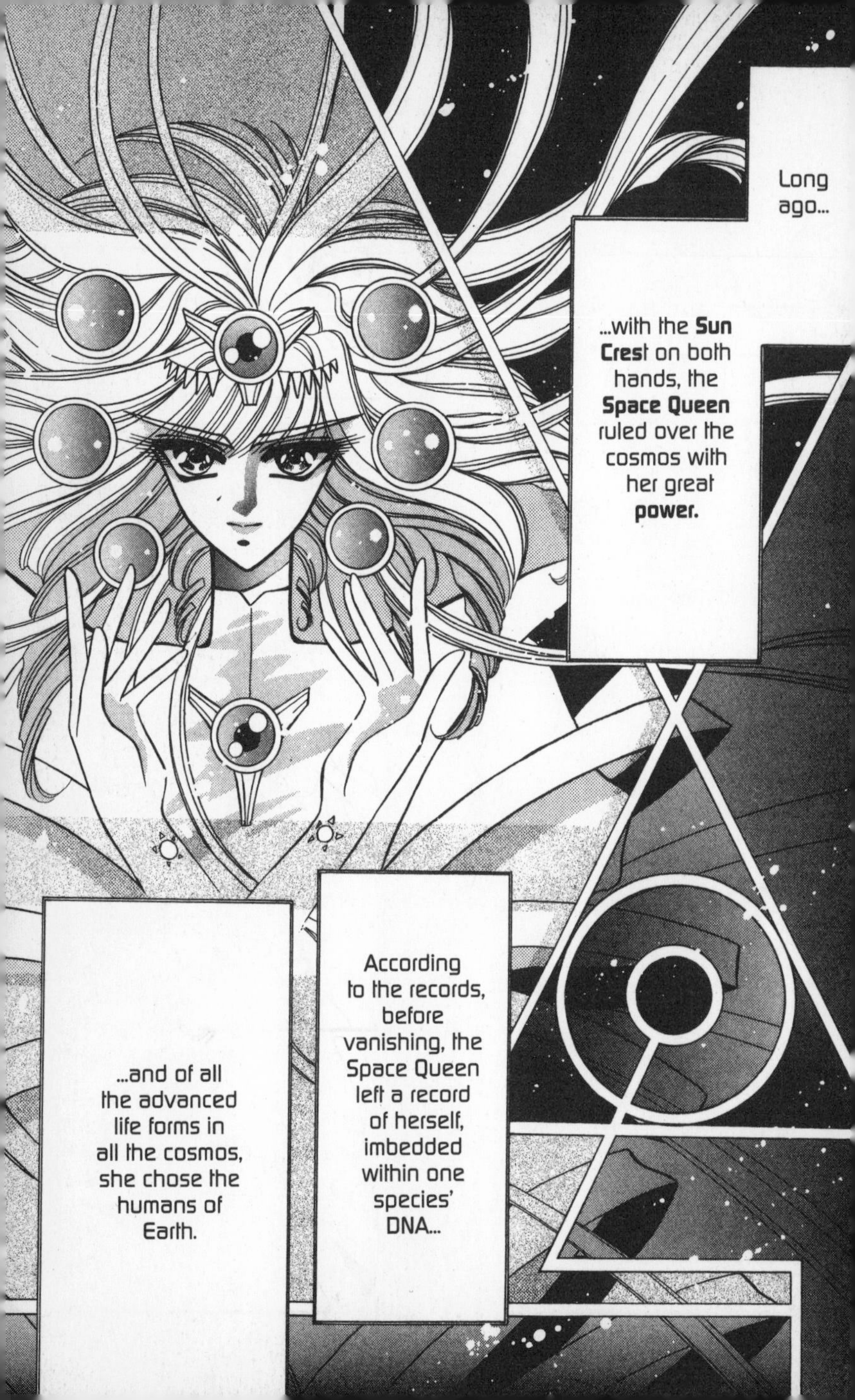
Long ago...
...with the Sun Crest on both hands, the Space Queen ruled over the cosmos with her great power.
According to the records, before vanishing, the Space Queen left a record of herself, imbedded within one species' DNA...
...and of all the advanced life forms in all the cosmos, she chose the humans of Earth.

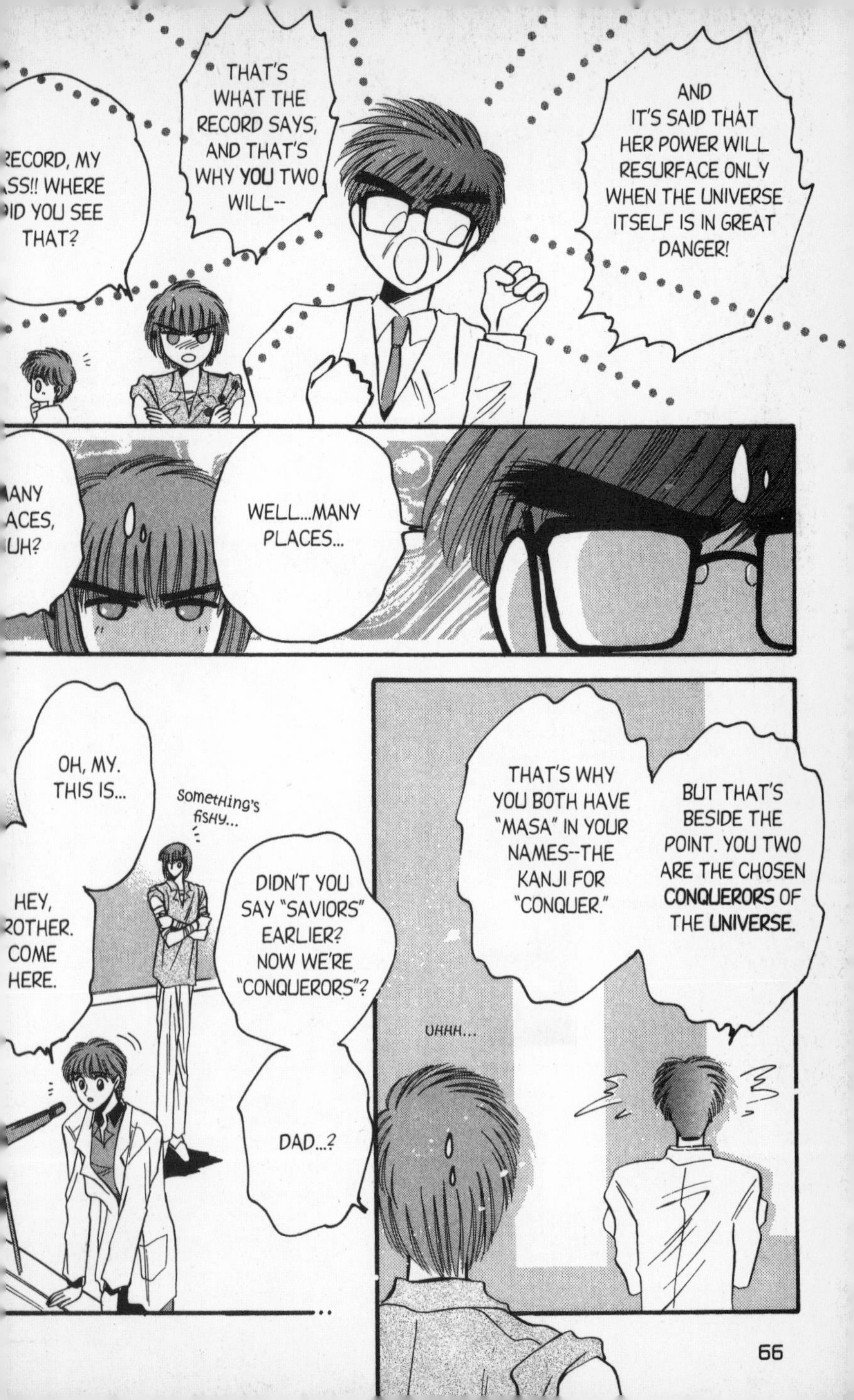
AND IT'S SAID THAT HER POWER WILL RESURFACE ONLY WHEN THE UNIVERSE ITSELF IS IN GREAT DANGER!
THAT'S WHAT THE RECORD SAYS, AND THAT'S WHY YOU TWO WILL--
RECORD, MY ASS!! WHERE DID YOU SEE THAT?
WELL...MANY PLACES...
MANY PLACES, HUH?
BUT THAT'S BESIDE THE POINT. YOU TWO ARE THE CHOSEN CONQUERORS OF THE UNIVERSE.
THAT'S WHY YOU BOTH HAVE "MASA" IN YOUR NAMES--THE KANJI FOR "CONQUER."
UHHH...
DIDN'T YOU SAY "SAVIORS" EARLIER? NOW WE'RE "CONQUERORS"?
OH, MY. THIS IS...
Something's fishy...
HEY, BROTHER. COME HERE.
DAD...?

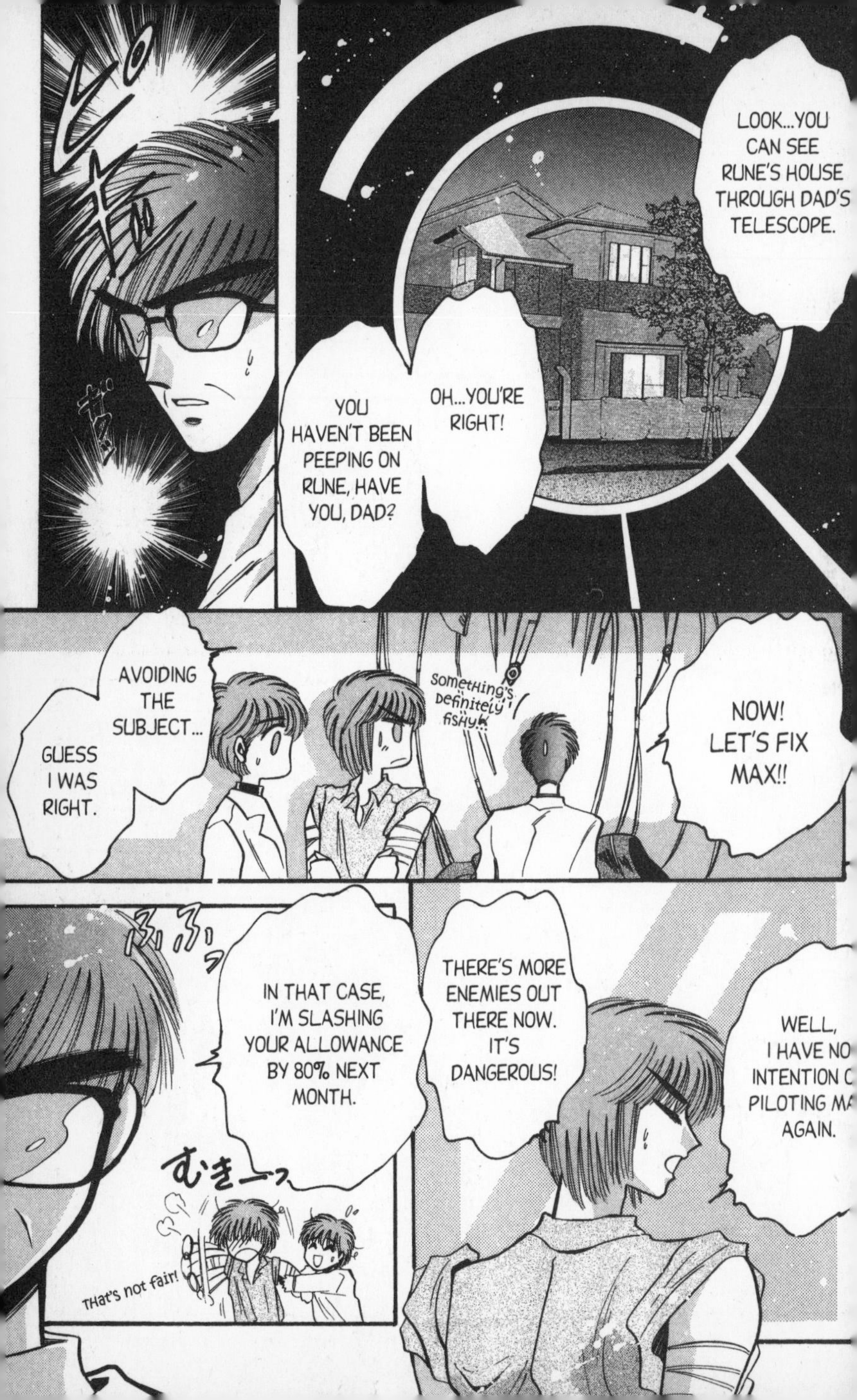

LOOK...YOU CAN SEE RUNE'S HOUSE THROUGH DAD'S TELESCOPE.
OH...YOU'RE RIGHT!
YOU HAVEN'T BEEN PEEPING ON RUNE, HAVE YOU, DAD?
NOW! LET'S FIX MAX!!
Something's definitely fishy...
AVOIDING THE SUBJECT...
GUESS I WAS RIGHT.
WELL, I HAVE NO INTENTION O PILOTING MA AGAIN.
THERE'S MORE ENEMIES OUT THERE NOW. IT'S DANGEROUS!
ふふっ
IN THAT CASE, I'M SLASHING YOUR ALLOWANCE BY 80% NEXT MONTH.
むきーっ
That's not fair!

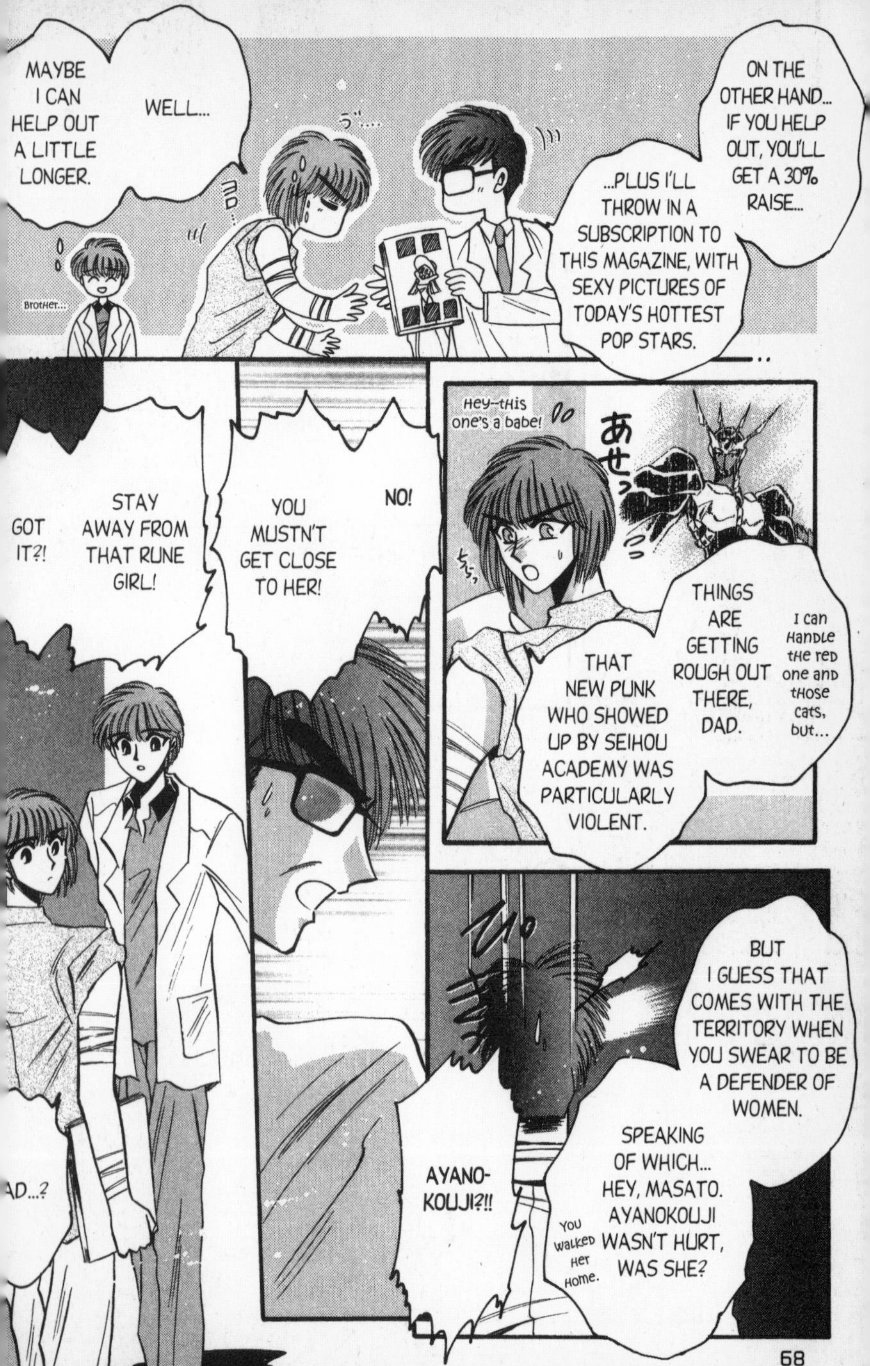
ON THE OTHER HAND... IF YOU HELP OUT, YOU'LL GET A 30% RAISE...
...PLUS I'LL THROW IN A SUBSCRIPTION TO THIS MAGAZINE, WITH SEXY PICTURES OF TODAY'S HOTTEST POP STARS.
WELL...
MAYBE I CAN HELP OUT A LITTLE LONGER.
Brother...
Hey--this one's a babe!
あせっ
THINGS ARE GETTING ROUGH OUT THERE, DAD.
I can handle the red one and those cats, but...
THAT NEW PUNK WHO SHOWED UP BY SEIHOU ACADEMY WAS PARTICULARLY VIOLENT.
BUT I GUESS THAT COMES WITH THE TERRITORY WHEN YOU SWEAR TO BE A DEFENDER OF WOMEN.
SPEAKING OF WHICH... HEY, MASATO. AYANOKOUJI WASN'T HURT, WAS SHE?
You walked her home.
AYANO-KOUJI?!!
NO!
YOU MUSTN'T GET CLOSE TO HER!
STAY AWAY FROM THAT RUNE GIRL!
GOT IT?!
AD...?

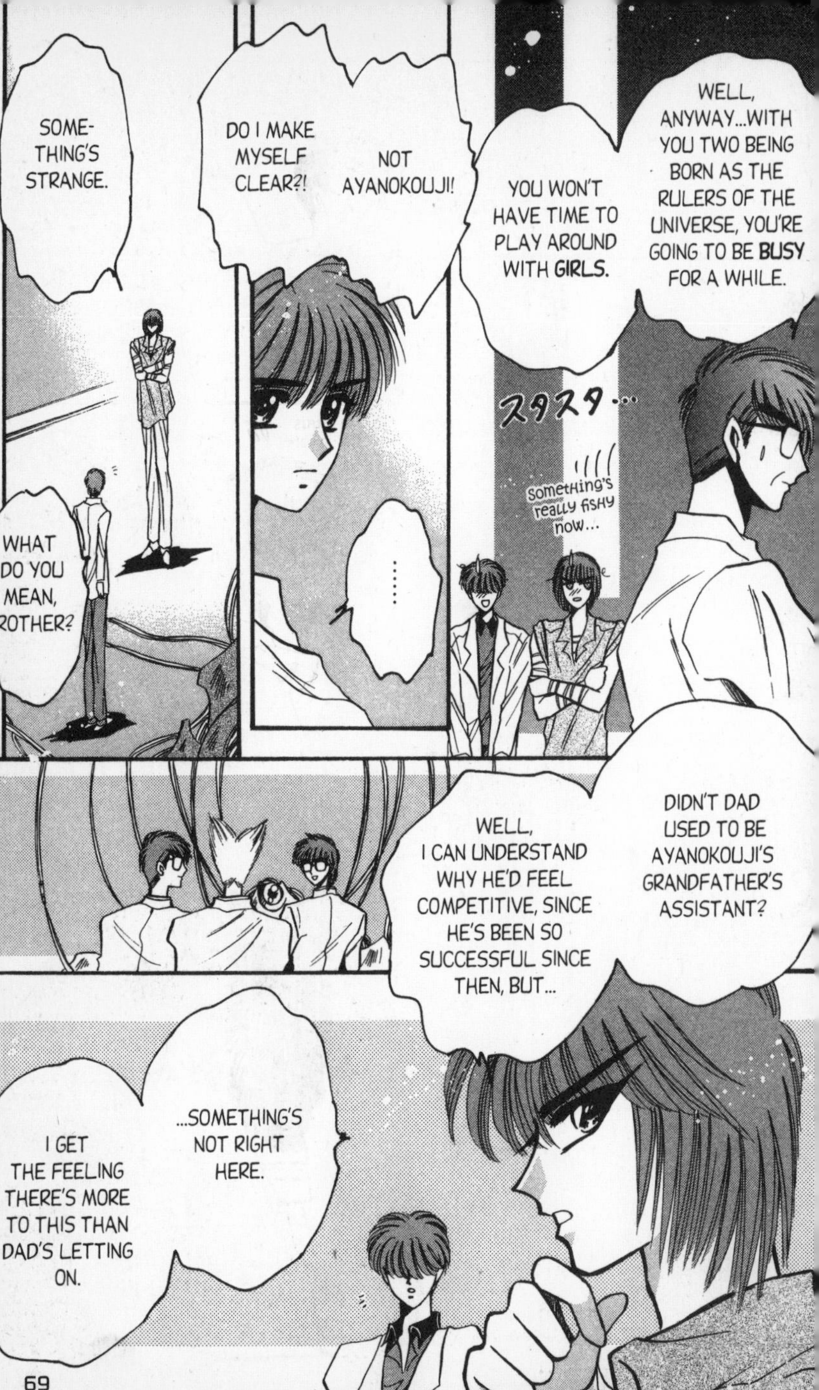
WELL, ANYWAY...WITH YOU TWO BEING BORN AS THE RULERS OF THE UNIVERSE, YOU'RE GOING TO BE **BUSY** FOR A WHILE.
YOU WON'T HAVE TIME TO PLAY AROUND WITH **GIRLS**.
スタスタ…
Something's really fishy now...
NOT AYANOKOUJI!
DO I MAKE MYSELF CLEAR?!
......
SOME-THING'S STRANGE.
WHAT DO YOU MEAN, BROTHER?
DIDN'T DAD USED TO BE AYANOKOUJI'S GRANDFATHER'S ASSISTANT?
WELL, I CAN UNDERSTAND WHY HE'D FEEL COMPETITIVE, SINCE HE'S BEEN SO SUCCESSFUL SINCE THEN, BUT...
...SOMETHING'S NOT RIGHT HERE.
I GET THE FEELING THERE'S MORE TO THIS THAN DAD'S LETTING ON.

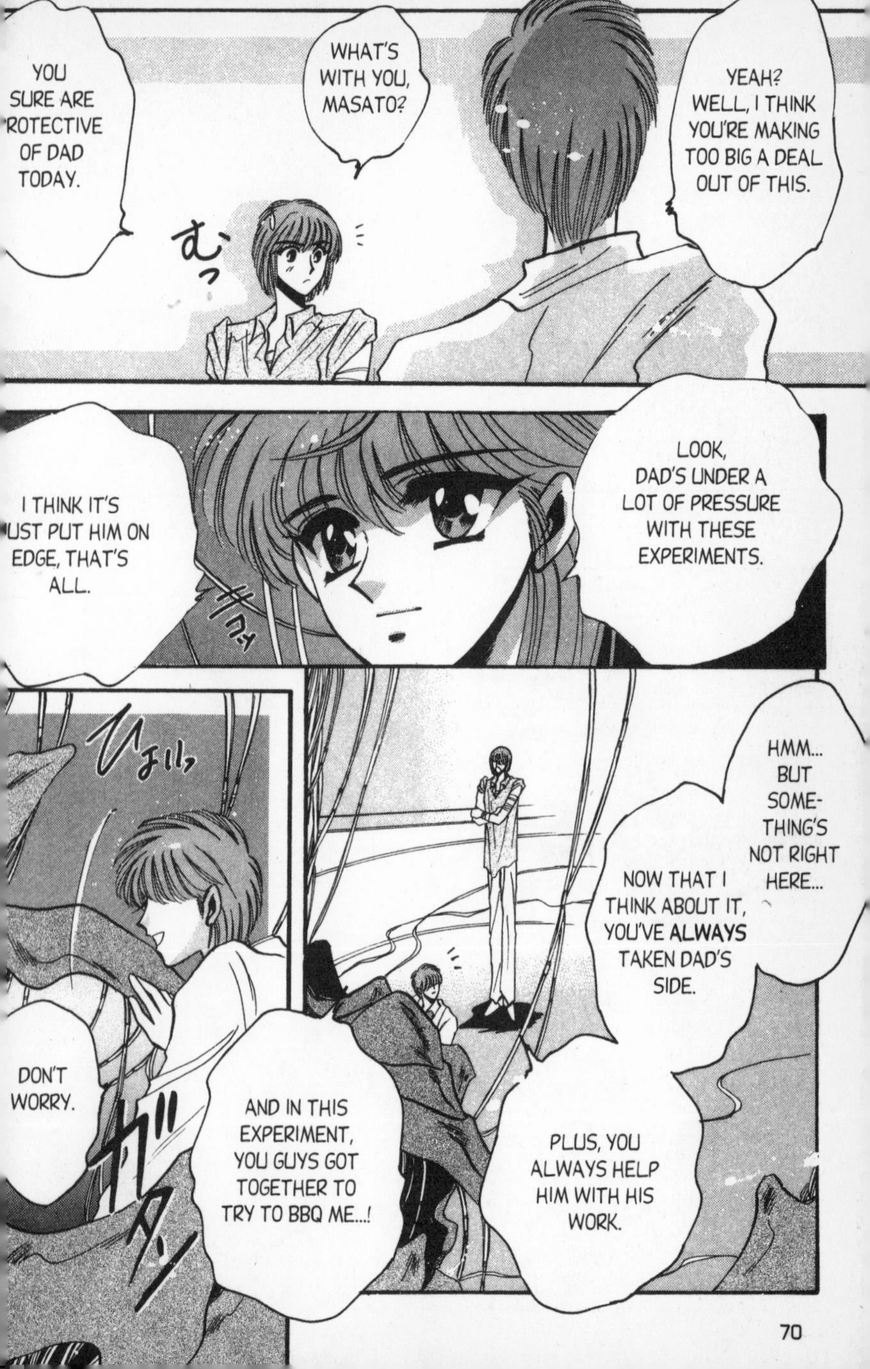
YEAH? WELL, I THINK YOU'RE MAKING TOO BIG A DEAL OUT OF THIS.
WHAT'S WITH YOU, MASATO?
YOU SURE ARE ROTECTIVE OF DAD TODAY.
むっ
LOOK, DAD'S UNDER A LOT OF PRESSURE WITH THESE EXPERIMENTS.
I THINK IT'S UST PUT HIM ON EDGE, THAT'S ALL.
HMM... BUT SOME-THING'S NOT RIGHT HERE...
NOW THAT I THINK ABOUT IT, YOU'VE **ALWAYS** TAKEN DAD'S SIDE.
PLUS, YOU ALWAYS HELP HIM WITH HIS WORK.
AND IN THIS EXPERIMENT, YOU GUYS GOT TOGETHER TO TRY TO BBQ ME...!
ひょいっ
DON'T WORRY.

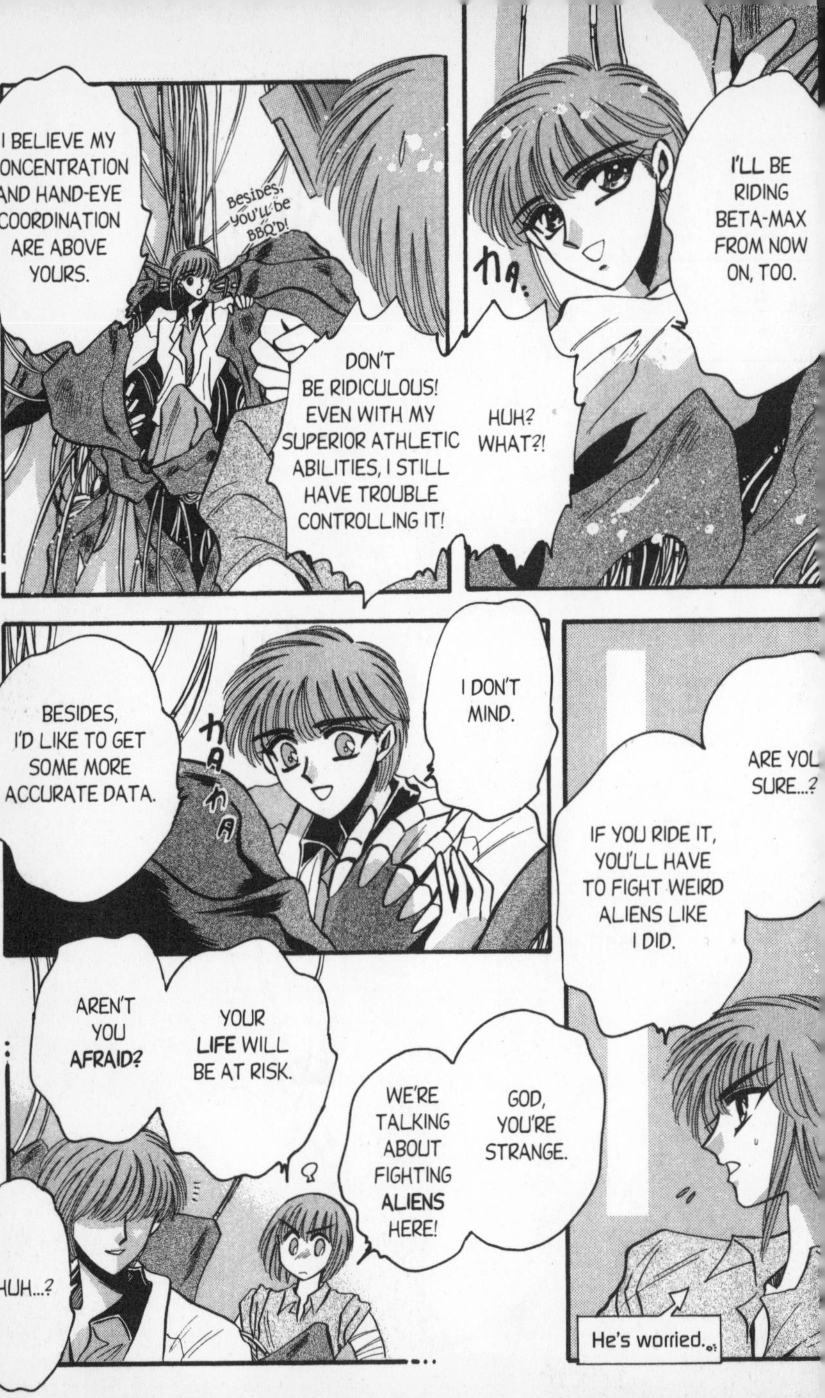
I'LL BE RIDING BETA-MAX FROM NOW ON, TOO.
HUH? WHAT?!
DON'T BE RIDICULOUS! EVEN WITH MY SUPERIOR ATHLETIC ABILITIES, I STILL HAVE TROUBLE CONTROLLING IT!
Besides, you'll be BBQ'd!
I BELIEVE MY CONCENTRATION AND HAND-EYE COORDINATION ARE ABOVE YOURS.
ARE YOU SURE...?
IF YOU RIDE IT, YOU'LL HAVE TO FIGHT WEIRD ALIENS LIKE I DID.
He's worried.
I DON'T MIND.
BESIDES, I'D LIKE TO GET SOME MORE ACCURATE DATA.
YOUR LIFE WILL BE AT RISK.
AREN'T YOU AFRAID?
GOD, YOU'RE STRANGE.
WE'RE TALKING ABOUT FIGHTING ALIENS HERE!
HUH...?

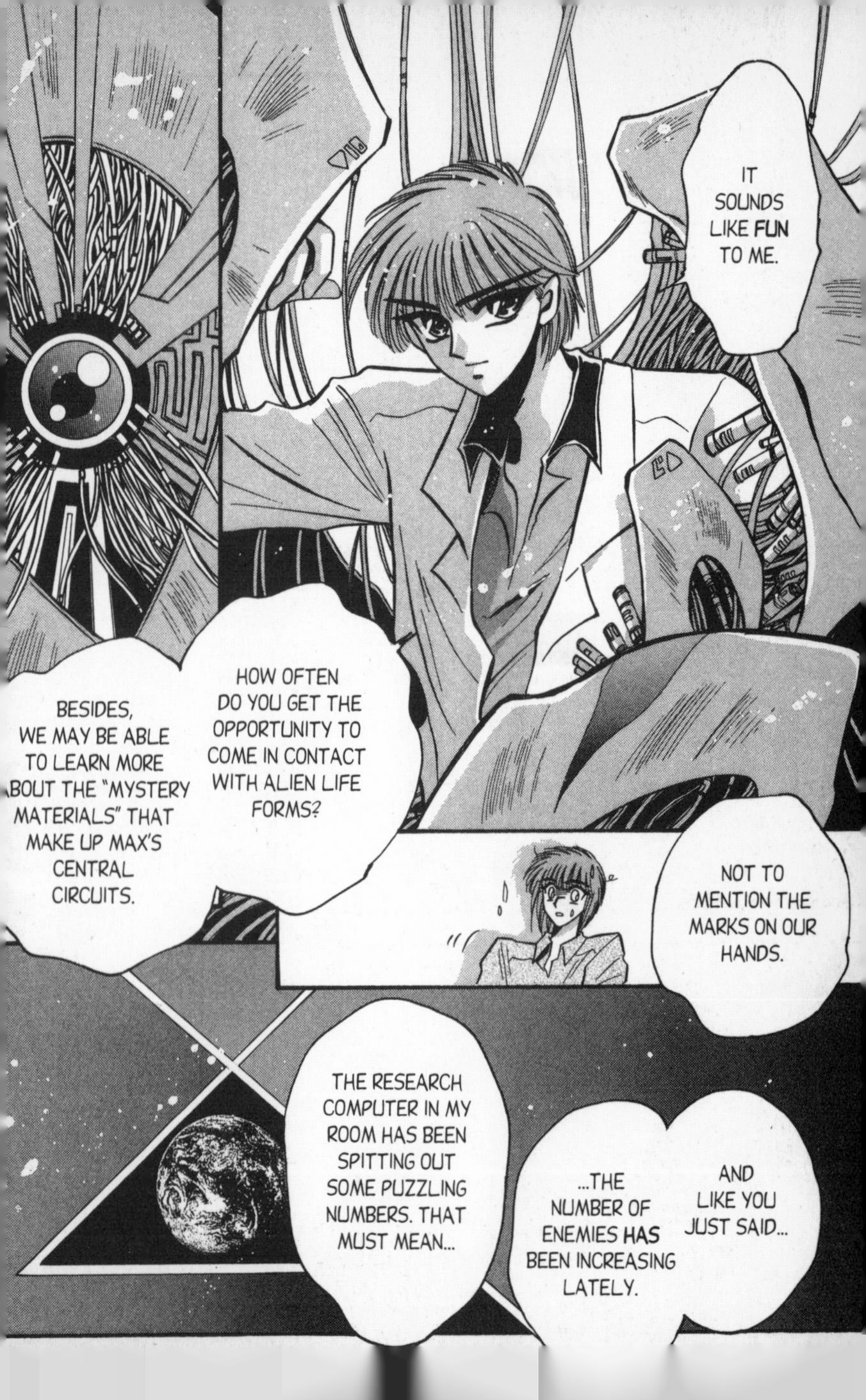
IT SOUNDS LIKE FUN TO ME.
HOW OFTEN DO YOU GET THE OPPORTUNITY TO COME IN CONTACT WITH ALIEN LIFE FORMS?
BESIDES, WE MAY BE ABLE TO LEARN MORE ABOUT THE "MYSTERY MATERIALS" THAT MAKE UP MAX'S CENTRAL CIRCUITS.
NOT TO MENTION THE MARKS ON OUR HANDS.
AND LIKE YOU JUST SAID...
...THE NUMBER OF ENEMIES HAS BEEN INCREASING LATELY.
THE RESEARCH COMPUTER IN MY ROOM HAS BEEN SPITTING OUT SOME PUZZLING NUMBERS. THAT MUST MEAN...

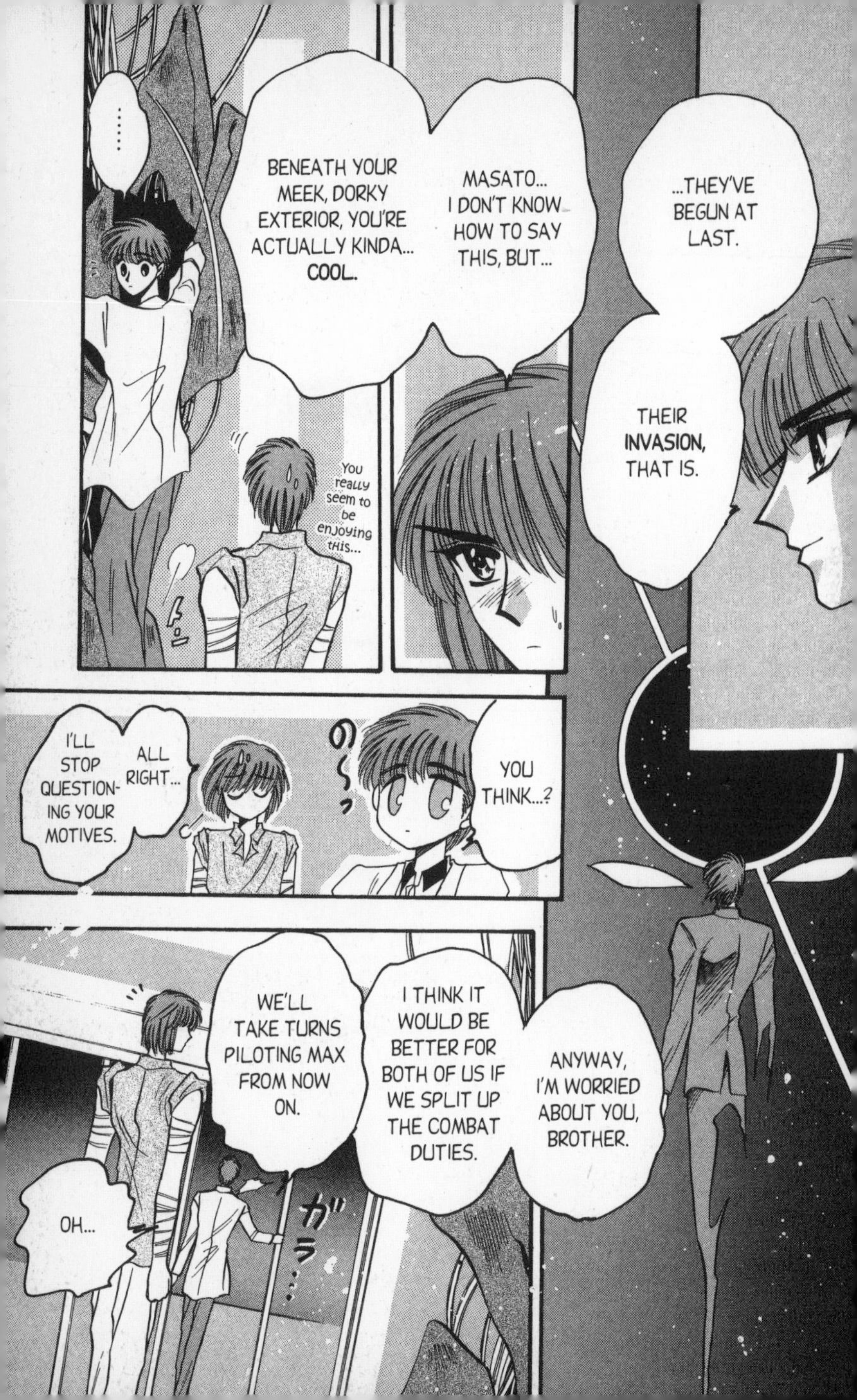
...THEY'VE BEGUN AT LAST.
THEIR INVASION, THAT IS.
MASATO... I DON'T KNOW HOW TO SAY THIS, BUT...
BENEATH YOUR MEEK, DORKY EXTERIOR, YOU'RE ACTUALLY KINDA... COOL.
……
You really seem to be enjoying this...
YOU THINK...?
ALL RIGHT...
I'LL STOP QUESTIONING YOUR MOTIVES.
ANYWAY, I'M WORRIED ABOUT YOU, BROTHER.
I THINK IT WOULD BE BETTER FOR BOTH OF US IF WE SPLIT UP THE COMBAT DUTIES.
WE'LL TAKE TURNS PILOTING MAX FROM NOW ON.
ガラ…
OH...

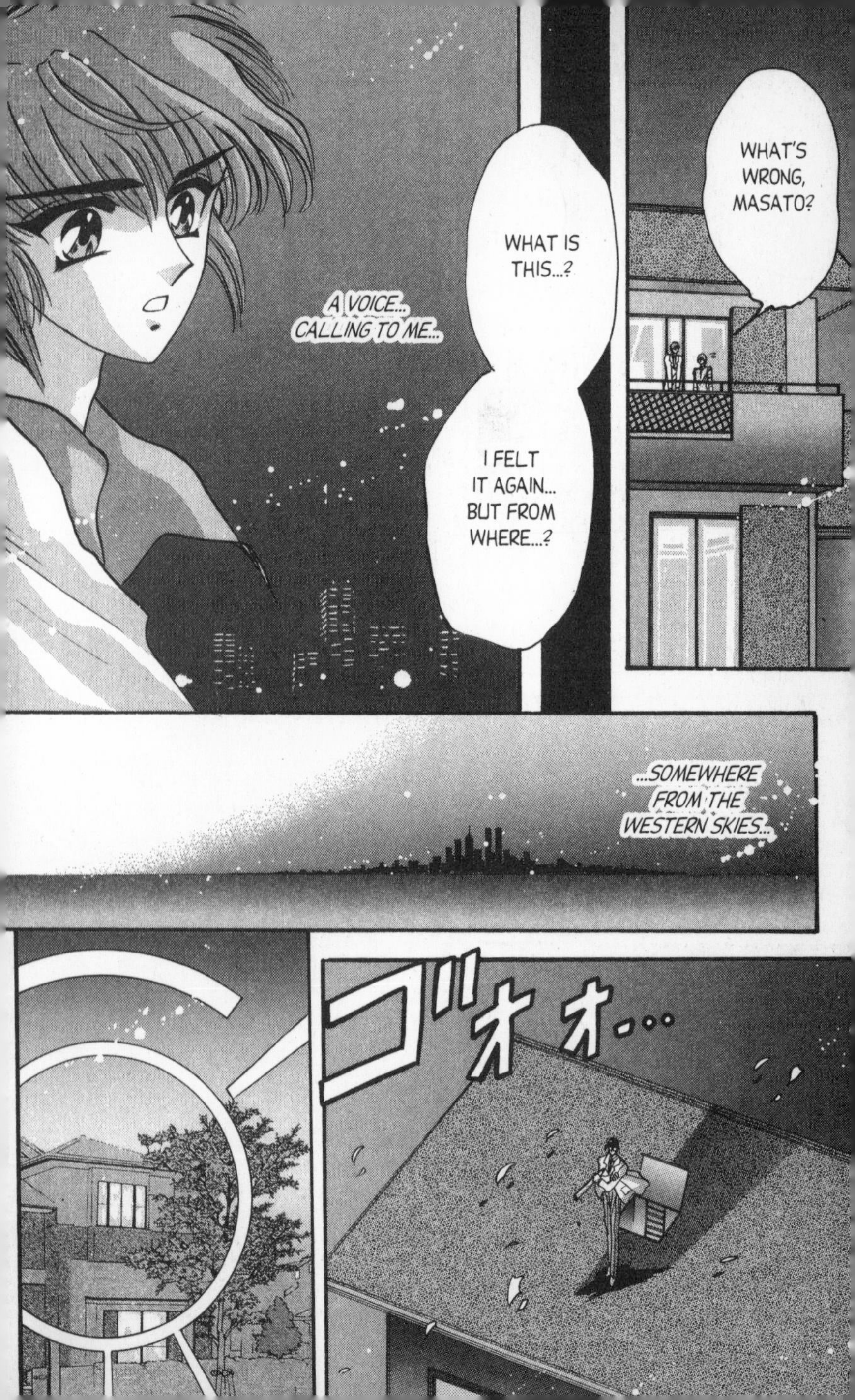
WHAT'S WRONG, MASATO?
WHAT IS THIS...?
A VOICE... CALLING TO ME...
I FELT IT AGAIN... BUT FROM WHERE...?
...SOMEWHERE FROM THE WESTERN SKIES...
ゴオオ…

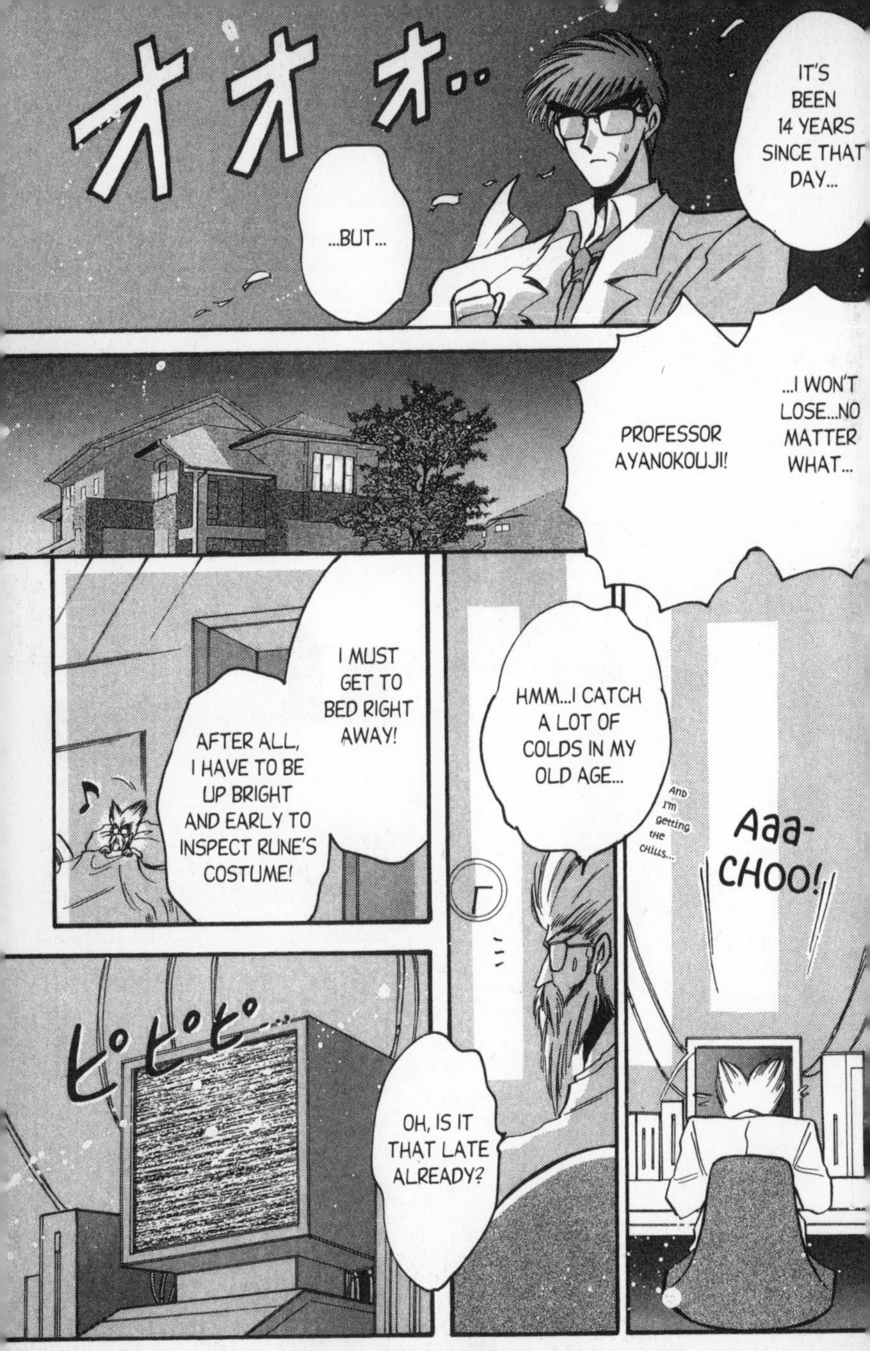
IT'S BEEN 14 YEARS SINCE THAT DAY...
オオオ..
...BUT...
...I WON'T LOSE...NO MATTER WHAT...
PROFESSOR AYANOKOUJI!
Aaa-CHOO!
And I'm getting the chills...
HMM...I CATCH A LOT OF COLDS IN MY OLD AGE...
OH, IS IT THAT LATE ALREADY?
I MUST GET TO BED RIGHT AWAY!
AFTER ALL, I HAVE TO BE UP BRIGHT AND EARLY TO INSPECT RUNE'S COSTUME!
ピピピ...

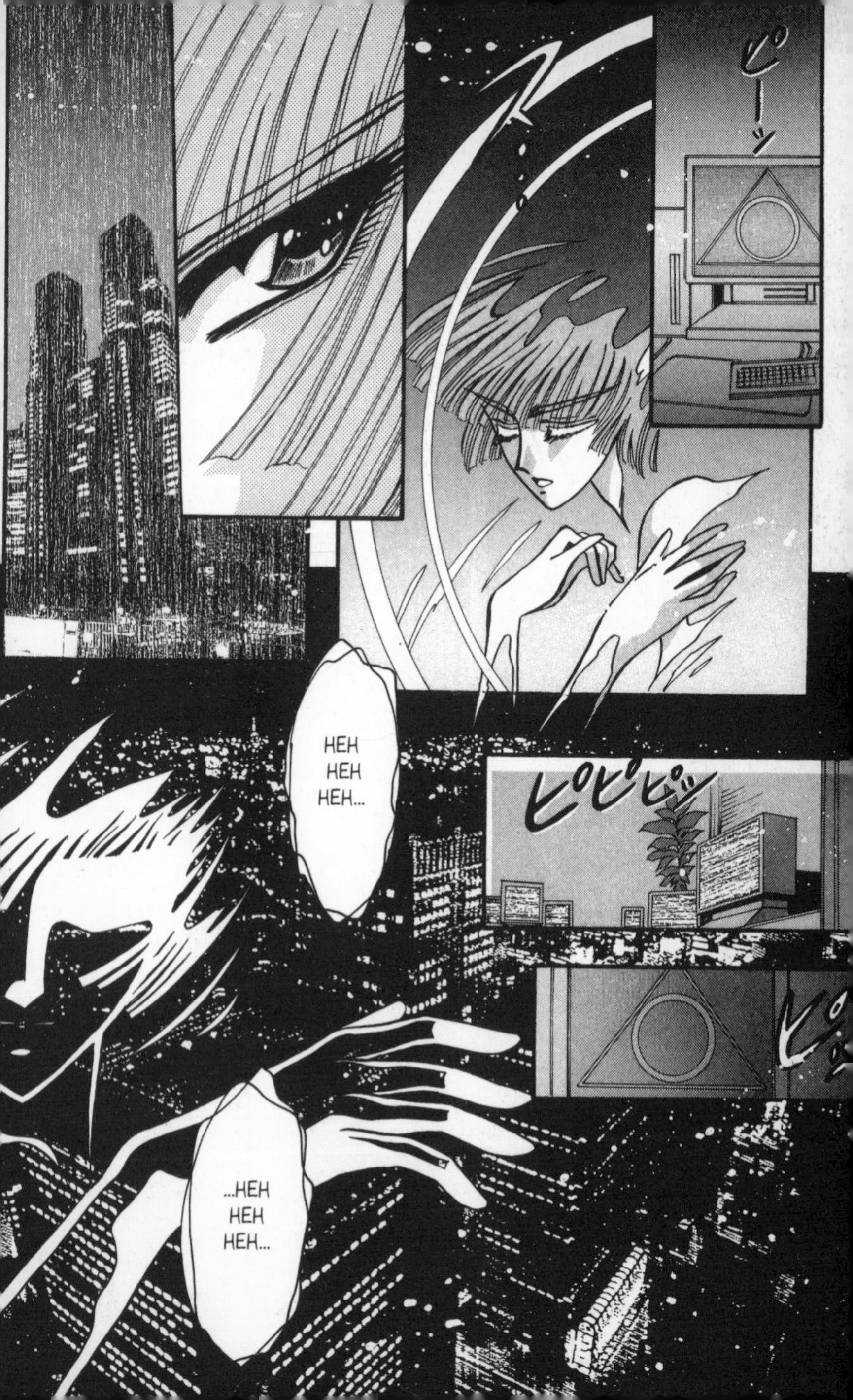
ピーッ
HEH HEH HEH...
ピピピッ
ピッ
...HEH HEH HEH...

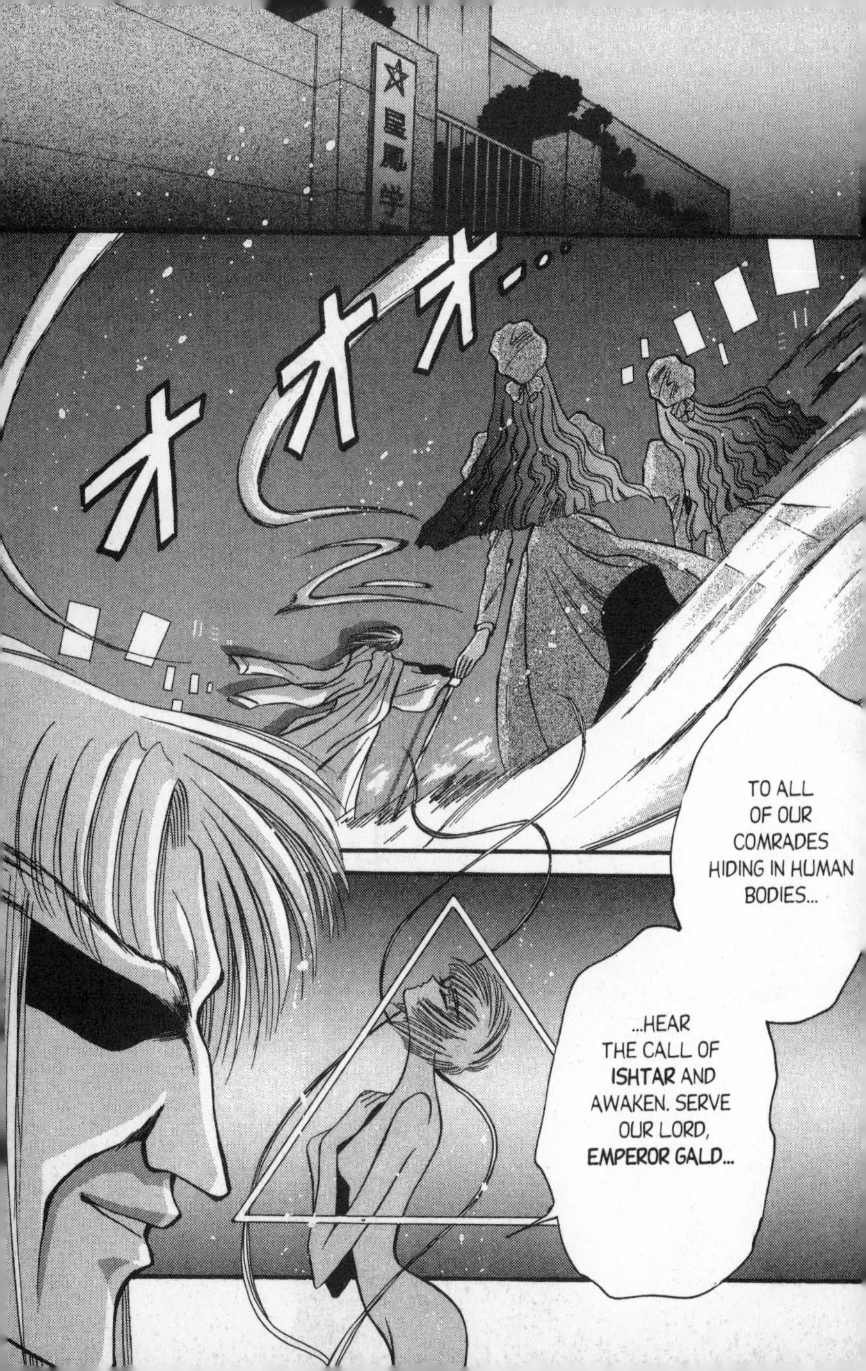
オオオー・・・
TO ALL OF OUR COMRADES HIDING IN HUMAN BODIES...
...HEAR THE CALL OF **ISHTAR** AND AWAKEN. SERVE OUR LORD, **EMPEROR GALD**...

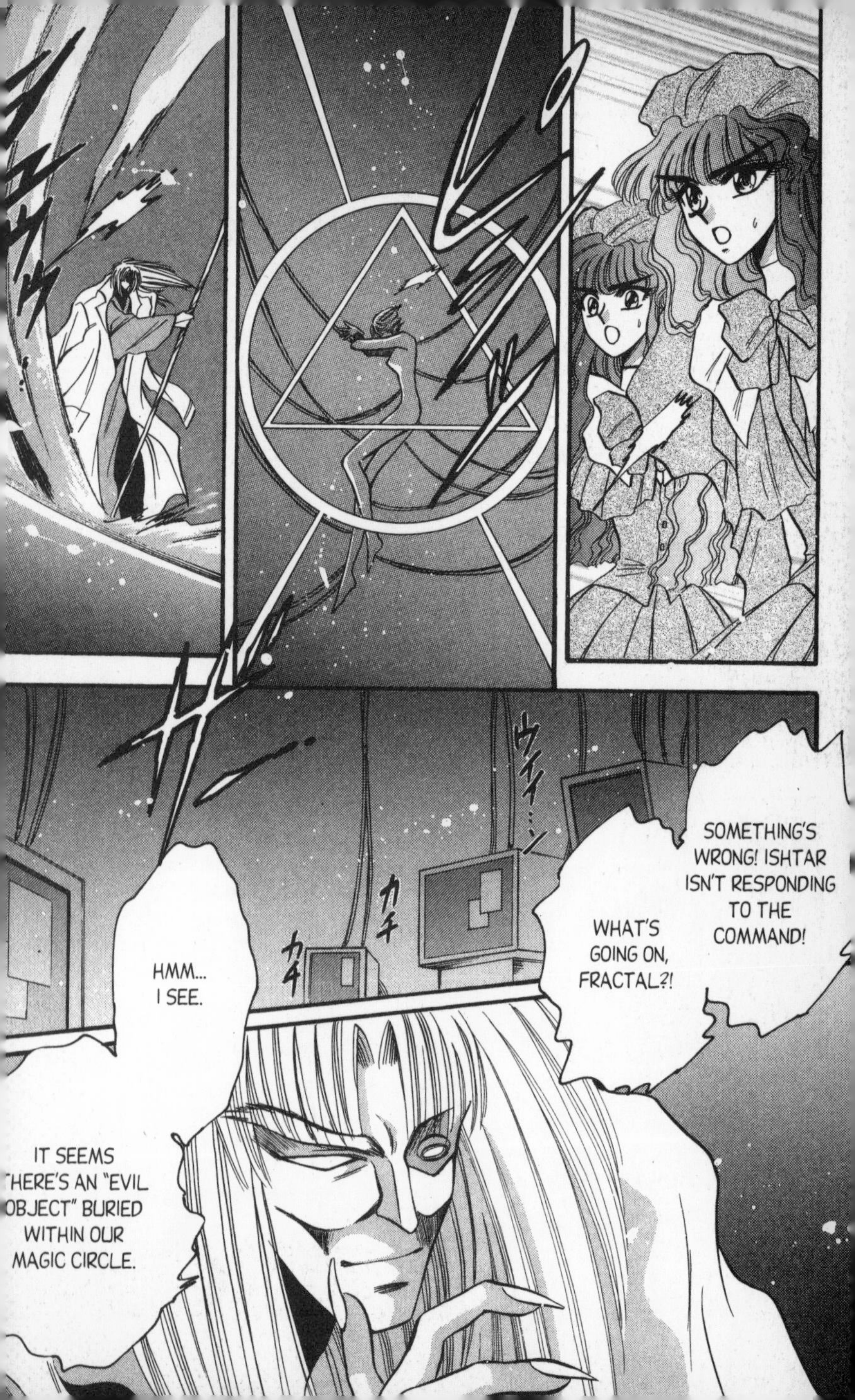
SOMETHING'S WRONG! ISHTAR ISN'T RESPONDING TO THE COMMAND!
WHAT'S GOING ON, FRACTAL?!
ウィィ…ン
カチ
カチ
HMM... I SEE.
IT SEEMS THERE'S AN "EVIL OBJECT" BURIED WITHIN OUR MAGIC CIRCLE.

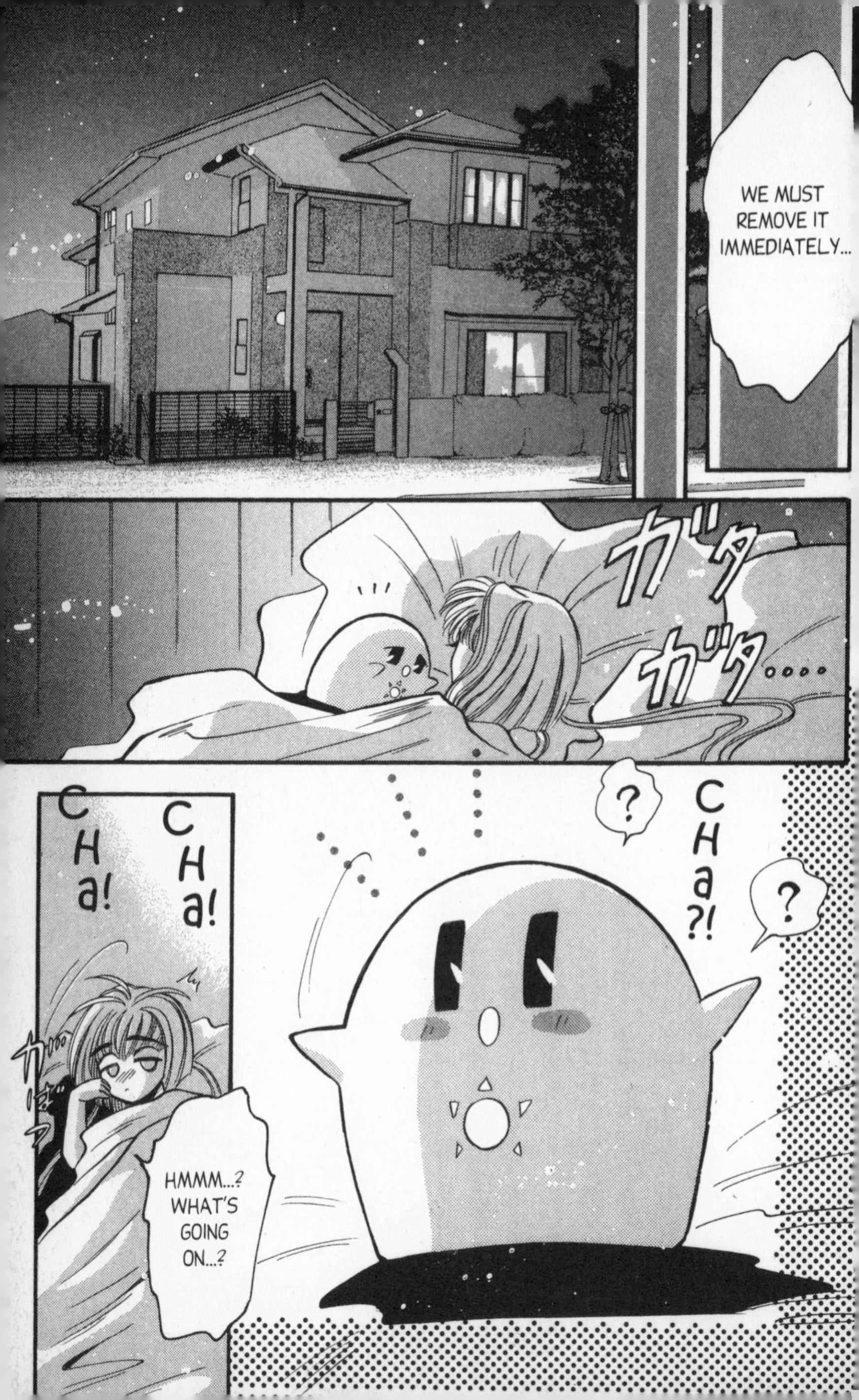
WE MUST REMOVE IT IMMEDIATELY...
ガタ
ガタ....
?
CHa?!
?
CHa!
CHa!
HMMM...? WHAT'S GOING ON...?

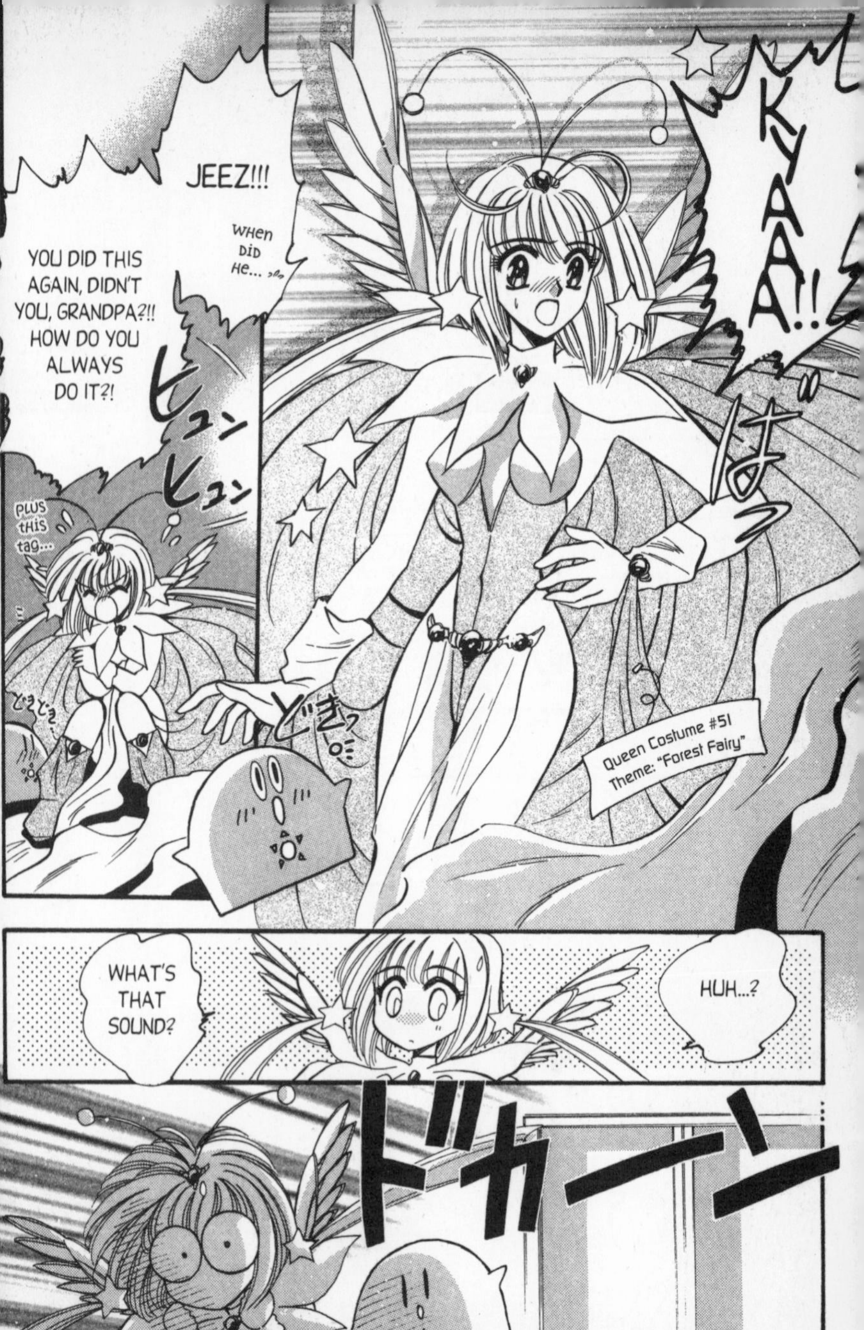
KYAAA!!
ばっ
どきっ
Queen Costume #51
Theme: "Forest Fairy"
JEEZ!!!
YOU DID THIS AGAIN, DIDN'T YOU, GRANDPA?!! HOW DO YOU ALWAYS DO IT?!
WHEN DID HE...
ヒュン
ヒュン
PLUS THIS TAG...
どきどき
HUH...?
WHAT'S THAT SOUND?
ドカーン

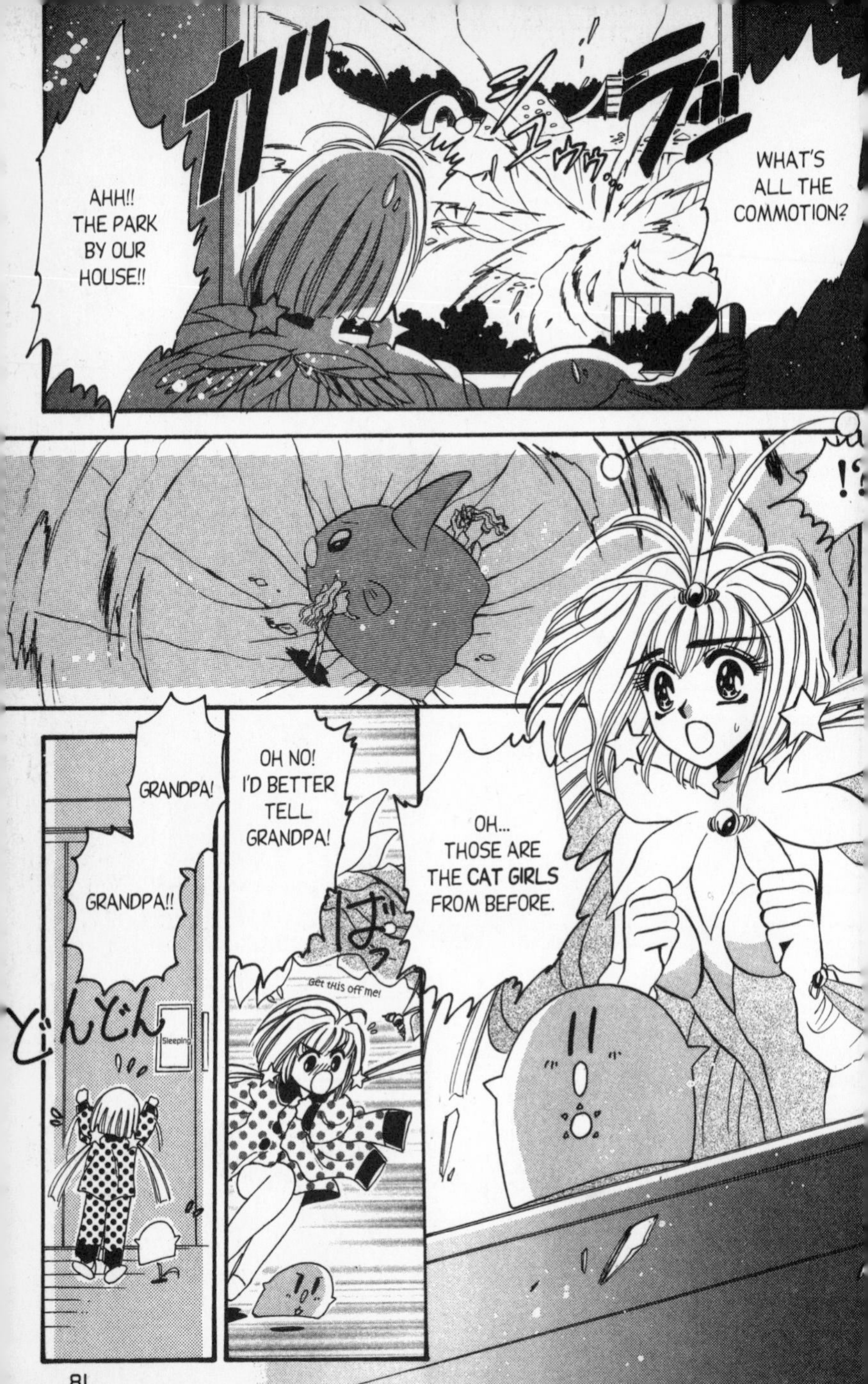
WHAT'S ALL THE COMMOTION?
AHH!! THE PARK BY OUR HOUSE!!
!?
OH... THOSE ARE THE CAT GIRLS FROM BEFORE.
OH NO! I'D BETTER TELL GRANDPA!
ぱっ
Get this off me!
GRANDPA!
GRANDPA!!
どんどん
Sleeping

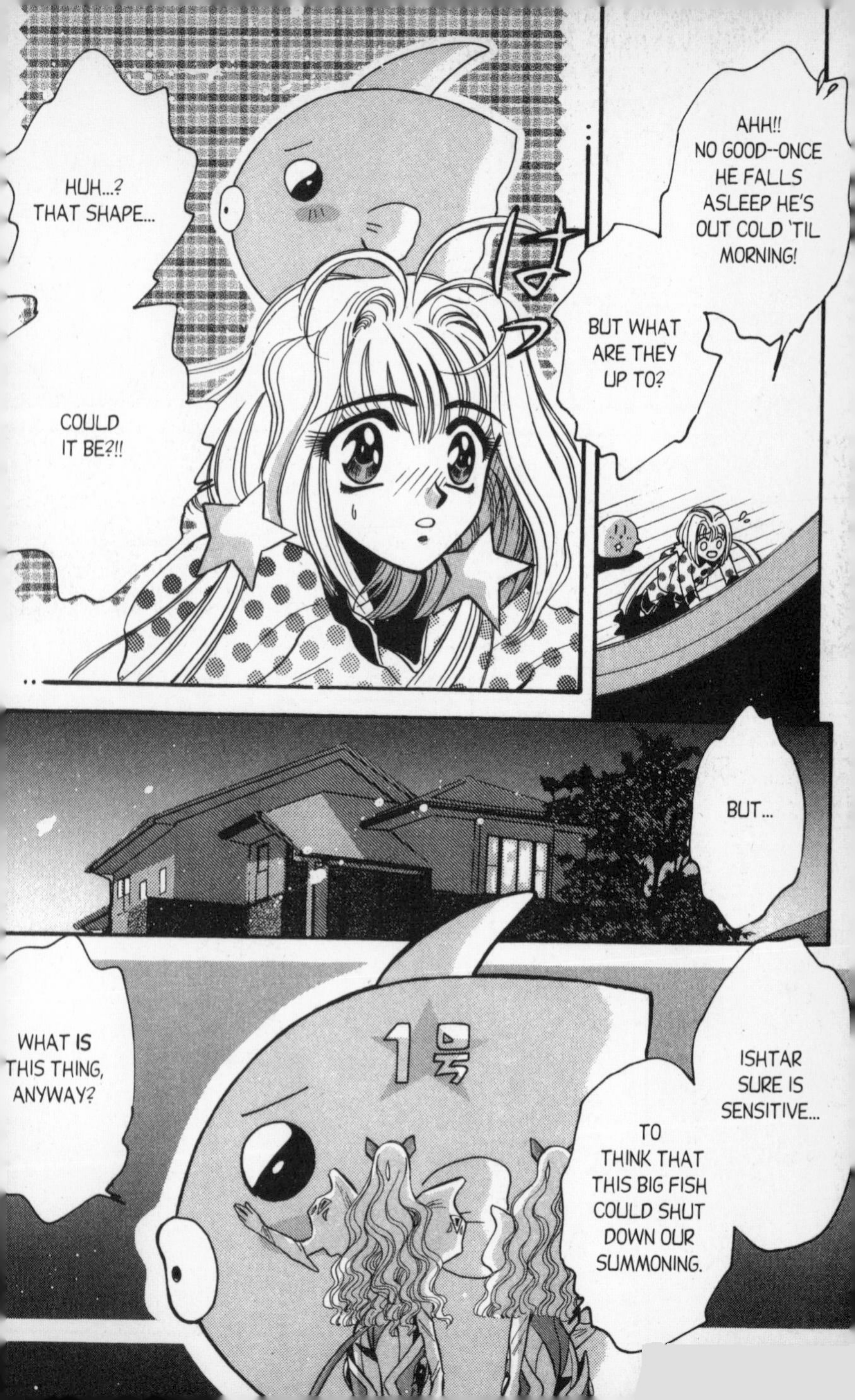
AHH!! NO GOOD--ONCE HE FALLS ASLEEP HE'S OUT COLD 'TIL MORNING!
BUT WHAT ARE THEY UP TO?
はっ
HUH...? THAT SHAPE...
COULD IT BE?!!
BUT...
1号
ISHTAR SURE IS SENSITIVE...
TO THINK THAT THIS BIG FISH COULD SHUT DOWN OUR SUMMONING.
WHAT IS THIS THING, ANYWAY?

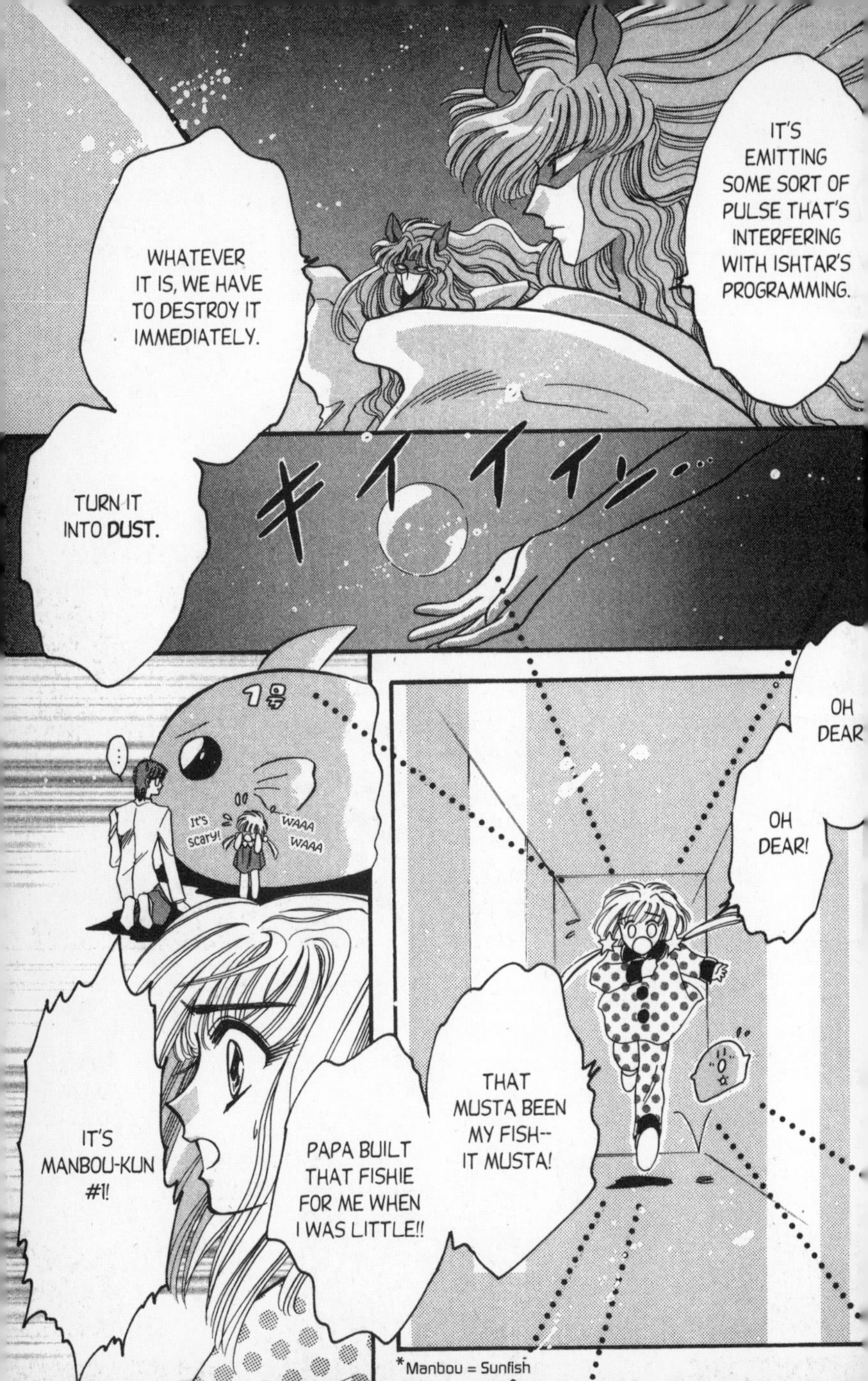
IT'S EMITTING SOME SORT OF PULSE THAT'S INTERFERING WITH ISHTAR'S PROGRAMMING.
WHATEVER IT IS, WE HAVE TO DESTROY IT IMMEDIATELY.
キイイイン...
TURN IT INTO DUST.
OH DEAR
OH DEAR!
THAT MUSTA BEEN MY FISH-- IT MUSTA!
1号
...
WAAA WAAA
It's scary!
PAPA BUILT THAT FISHIE FOR ME WHEN I WAS LITTLE!!
IT'S MANBOU-KUN #1!

*Manbou = Sunfish

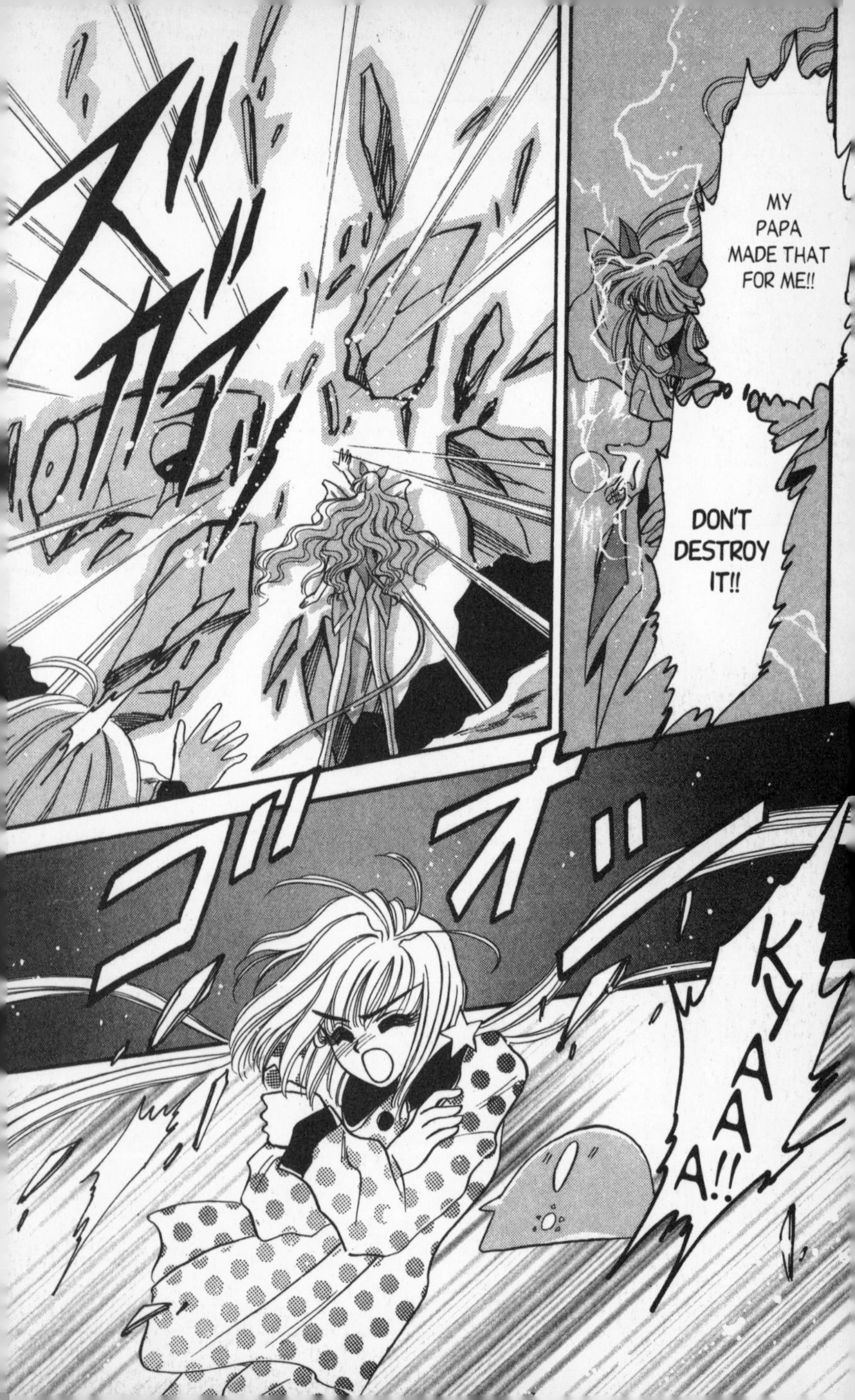
MY PAPA MADE THAT FOR ME!!
DON'T DESTROY IT!!
KYAAAA!!

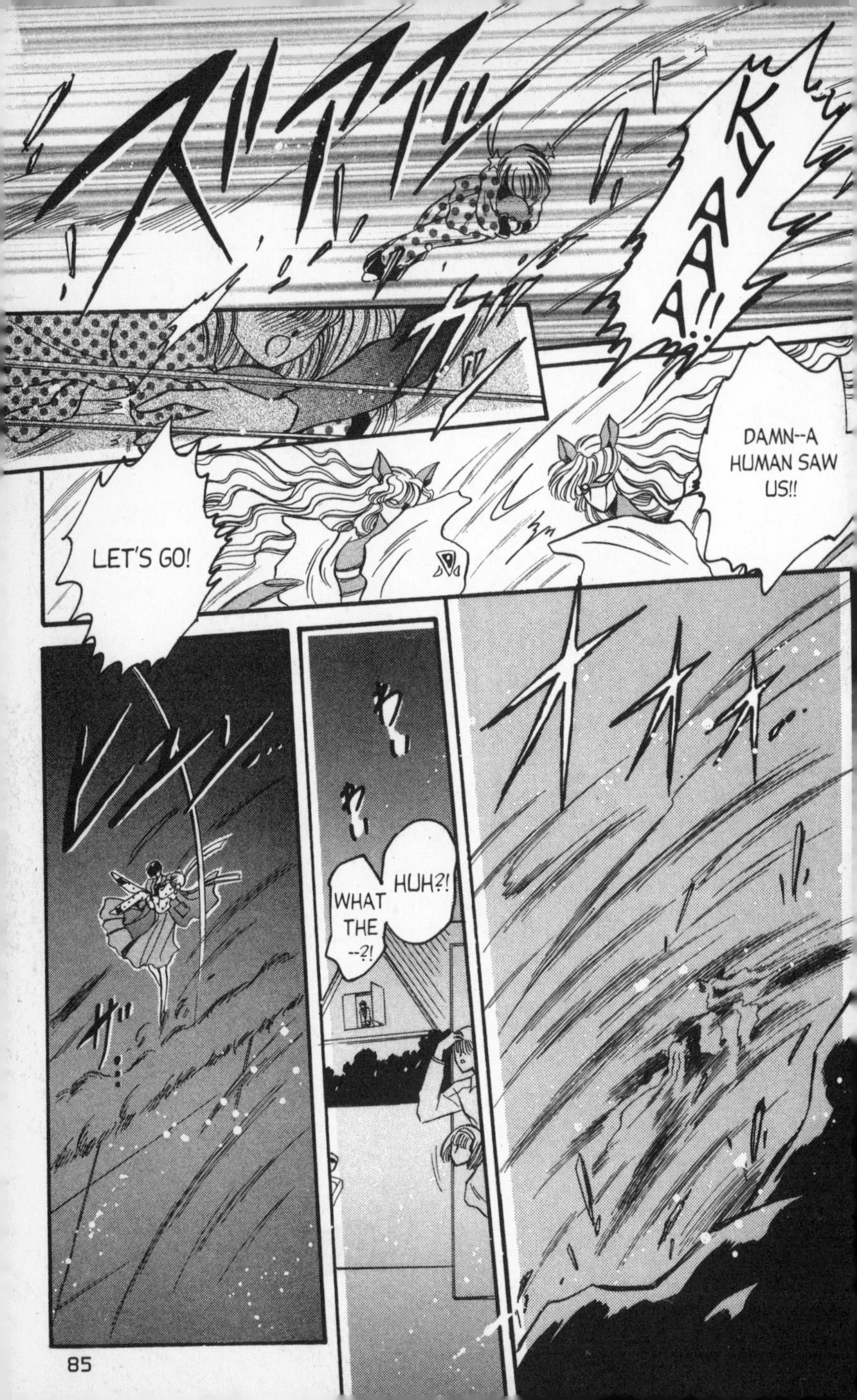
KYAAA!!
DAMN--A HUMAN SAW US!!
LET'S GO!
HUH?!
WHAT THE --?!

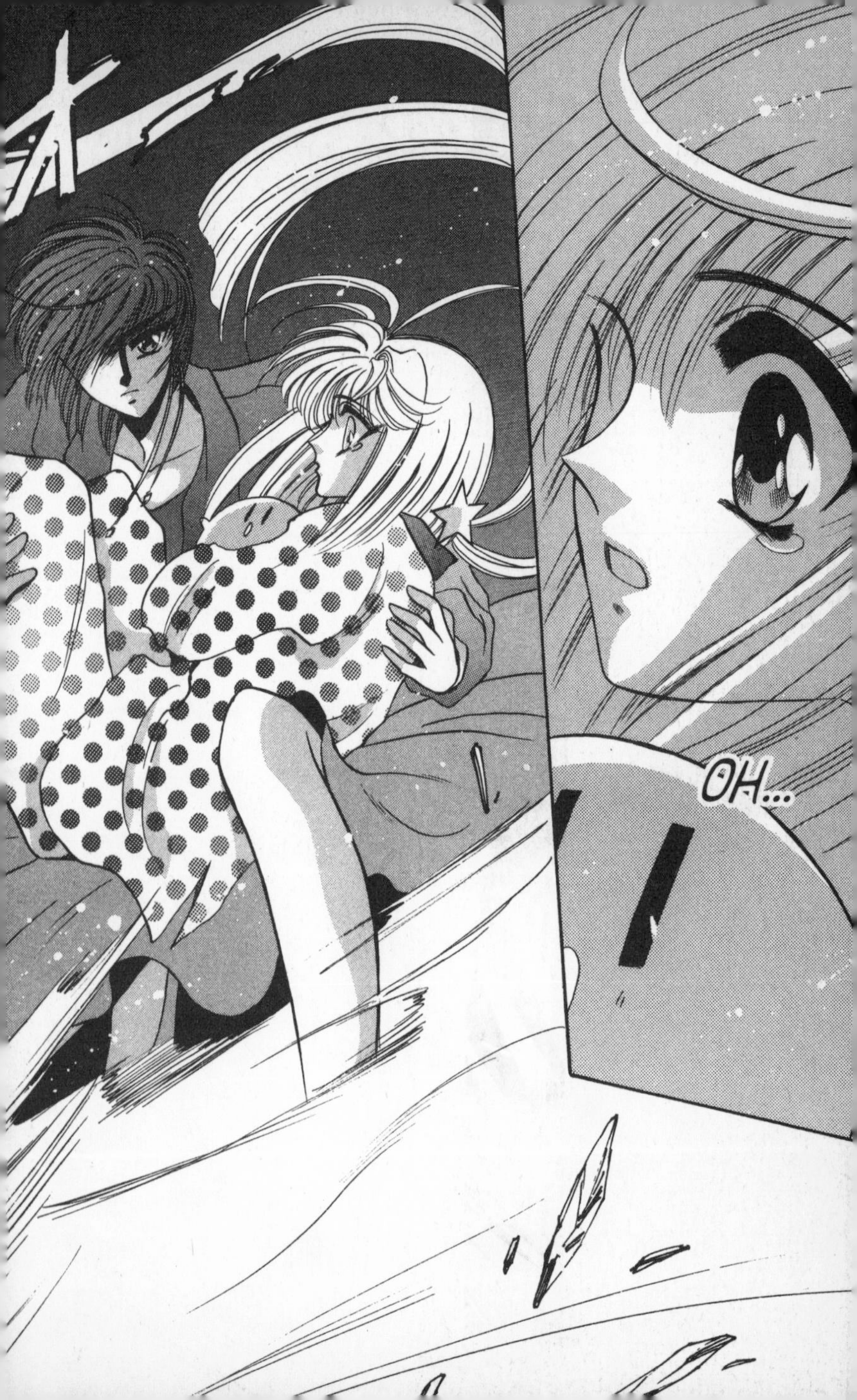
OH...

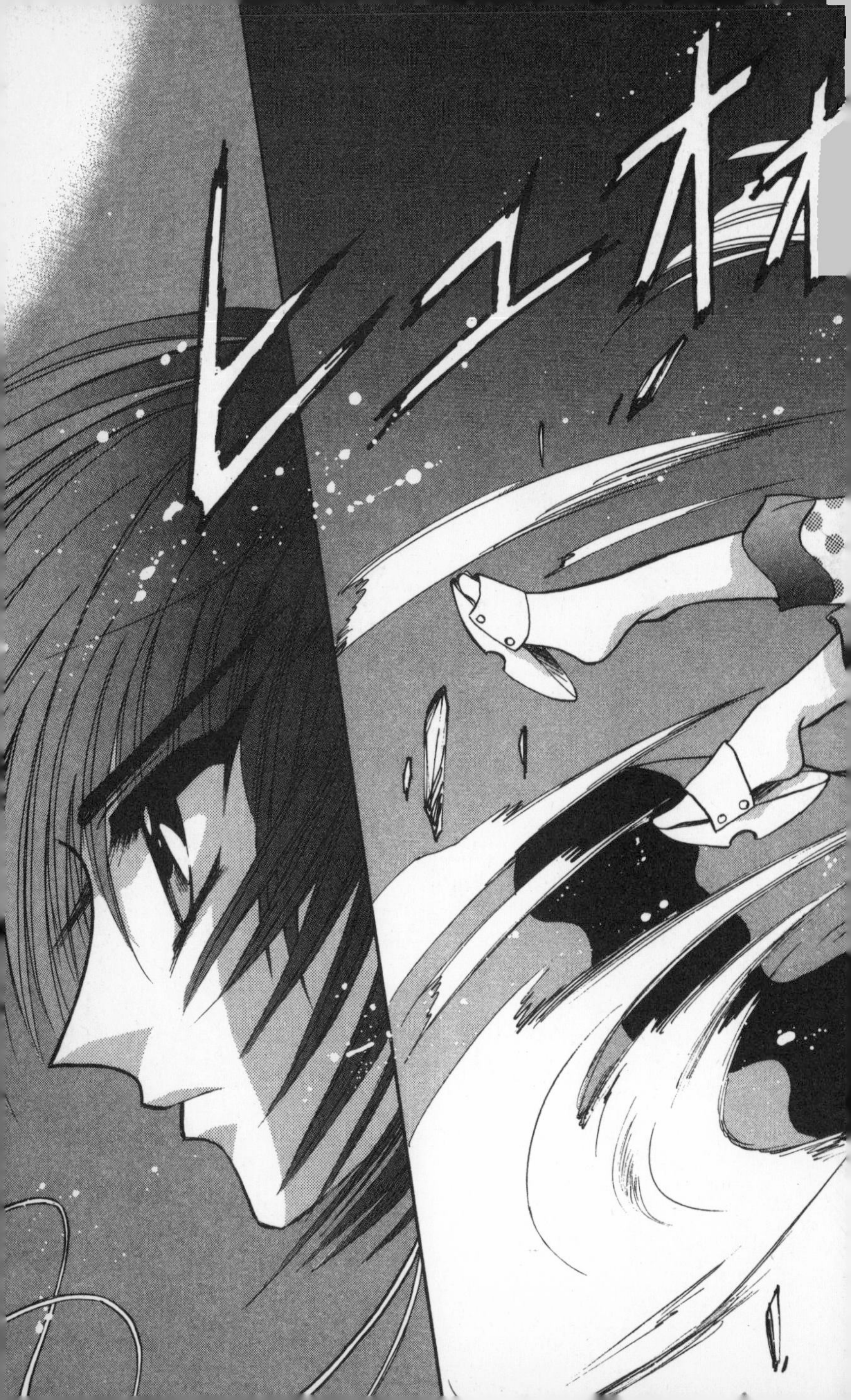
ヒュオオ

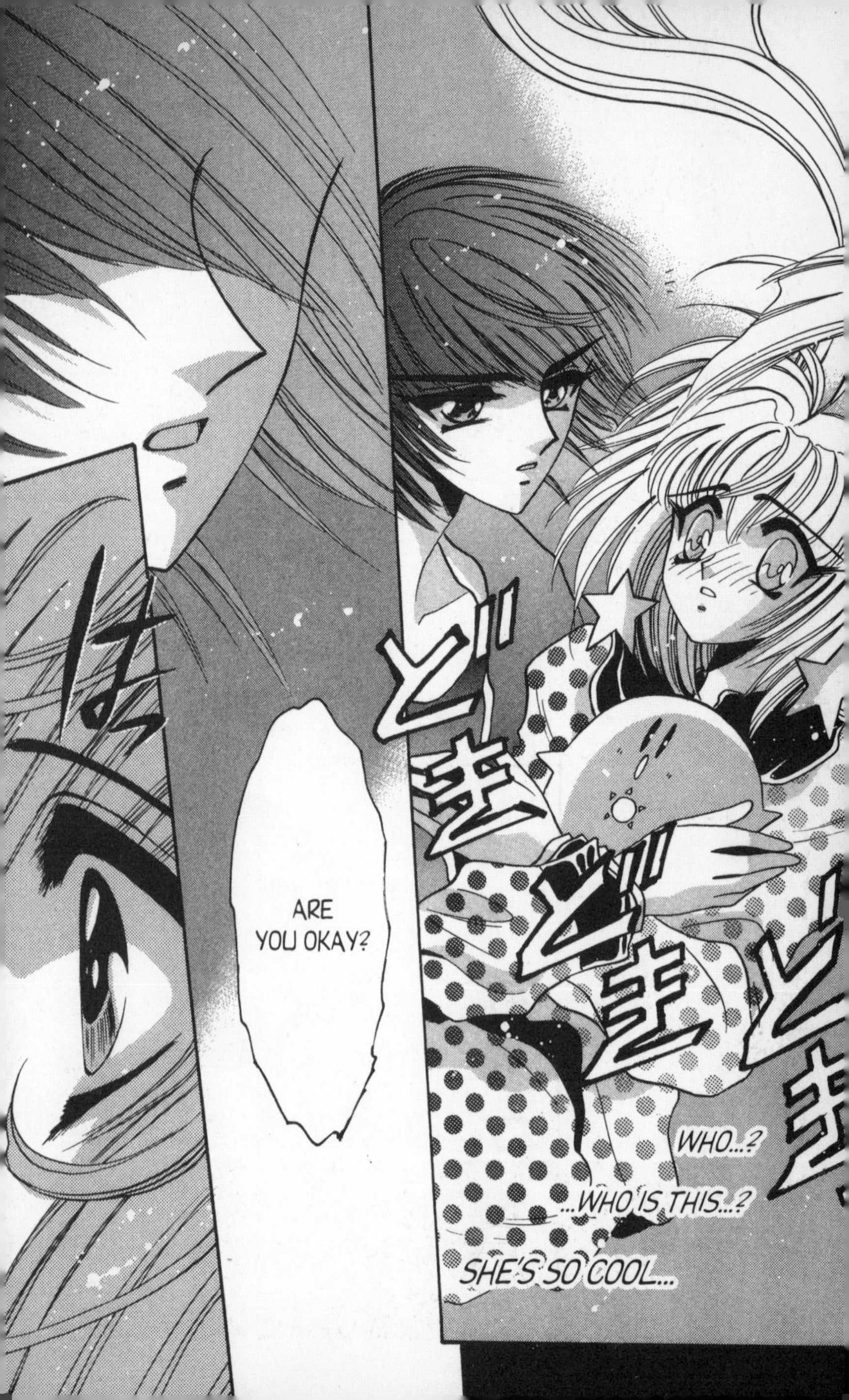

どき
どき
どき
WHO...?
...WHO IS THIS...?
SHE'S SO COOL...
ARE YOU OKAY?
はっ

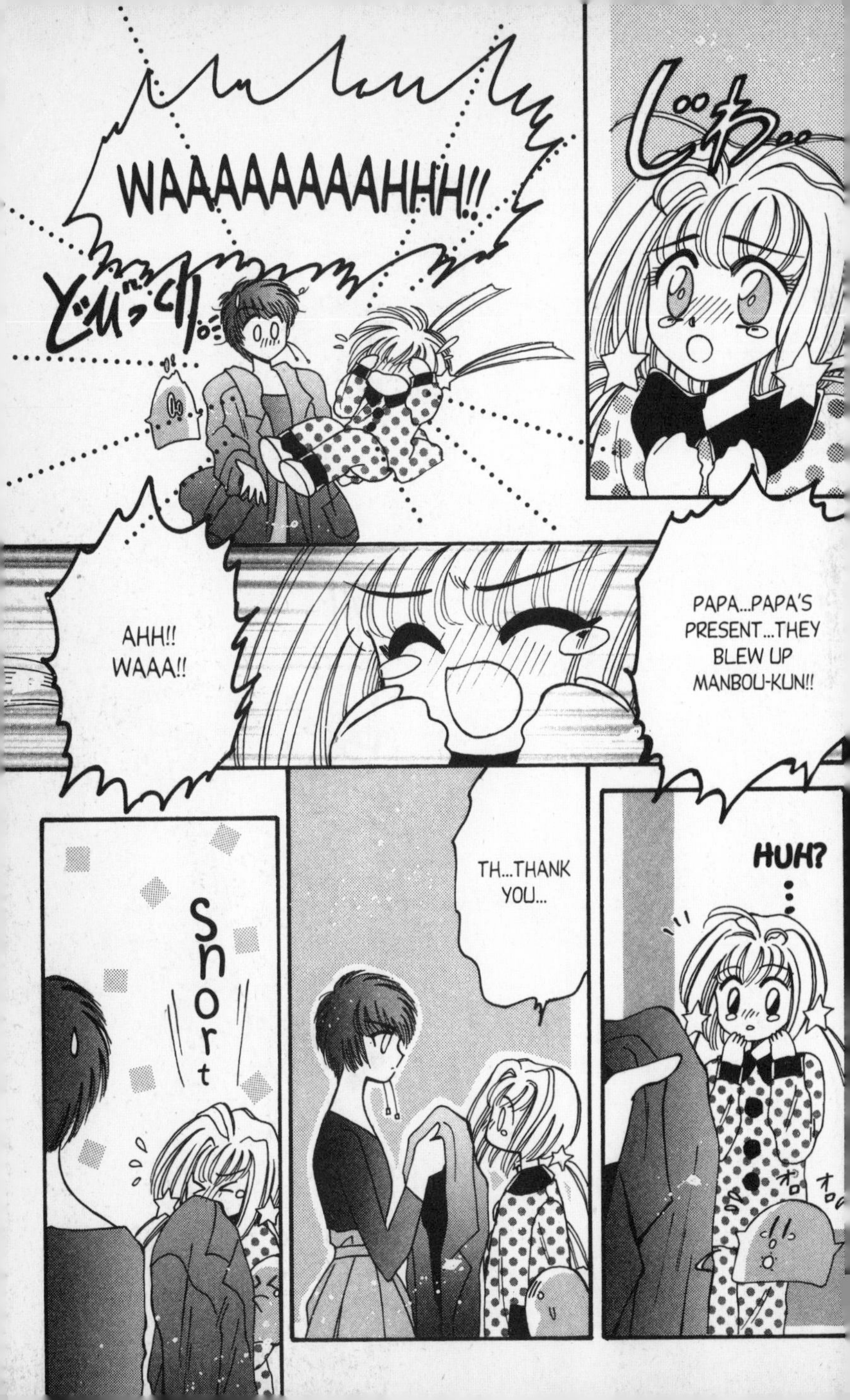
WAAAAAAAAHHH!!
PAPA...PAPA'S PRESENT...THEY BLEW UP MANBOU-KUN!!
AHH!! WAAA!!
HUH?
オロ オロ
TH...THANK YOU...
Snort

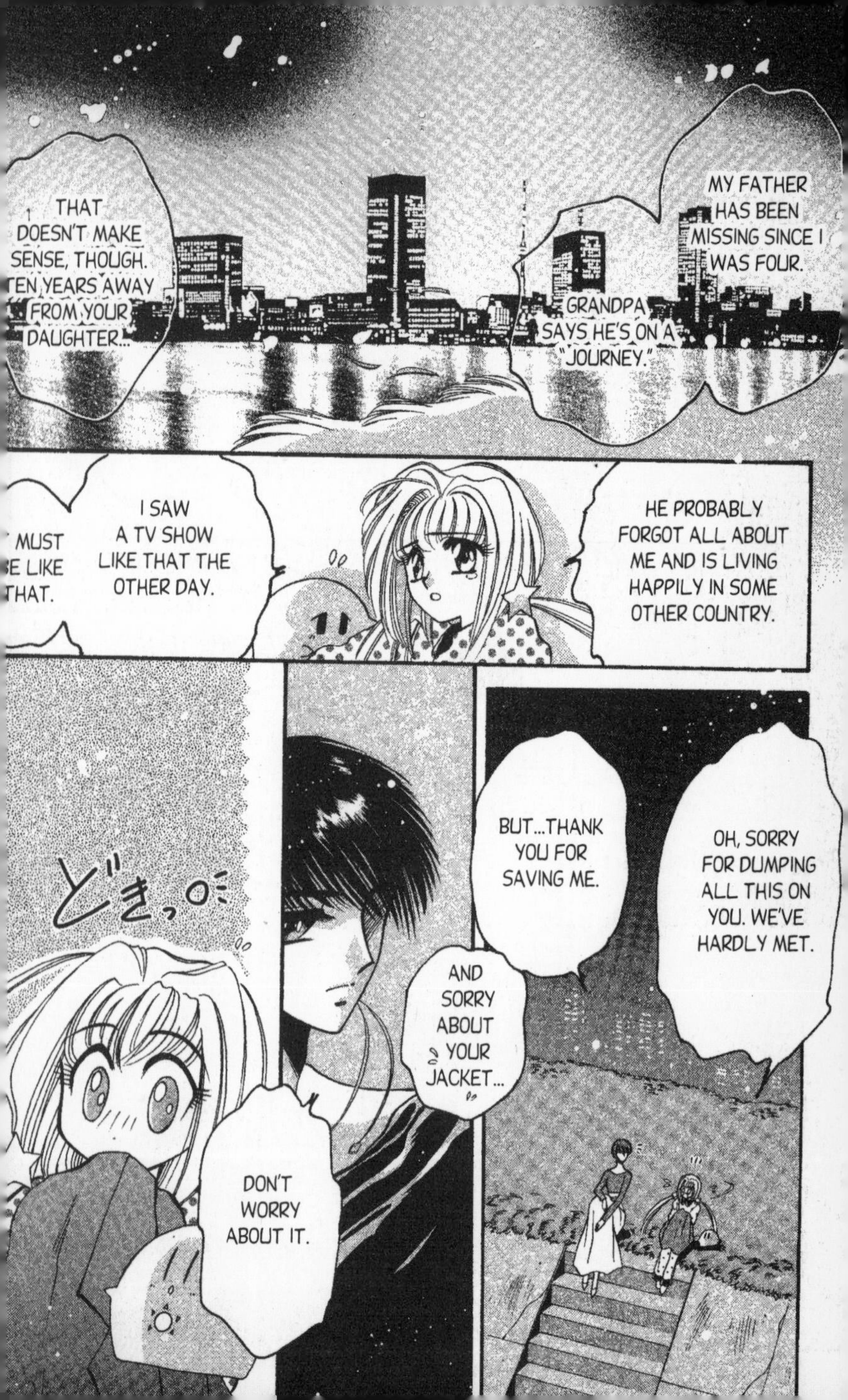
MY FATHER HAS BEEN MISSING SINCE I WAS FOUR.
GRANDPA SAYS HE'S ON A "JOURNEY."
THAT DOESN'T MAKE SENSE, THOUGH. TEN YEARS AWAY FROM YOUR DAUGHTER...
HE PROBABLY FORGOT ALL ABOUT ME AND IS LIVING HAPPILY IN SOME OTHER COUNTRY.
I SAW A TV SHOW LIKE THAT THE OTHER DAY.
MUST E LIKE THAT.
OH, SORRY FOR DUMPING ALL THIS ON YOU. WE'VE HARDLY MET.
BUT...THANK YOU FOR SAVING ME.
AND SORRY ABOUT YOUR JACKET...
どきっ
DON'T WORRY ABOUT IT.

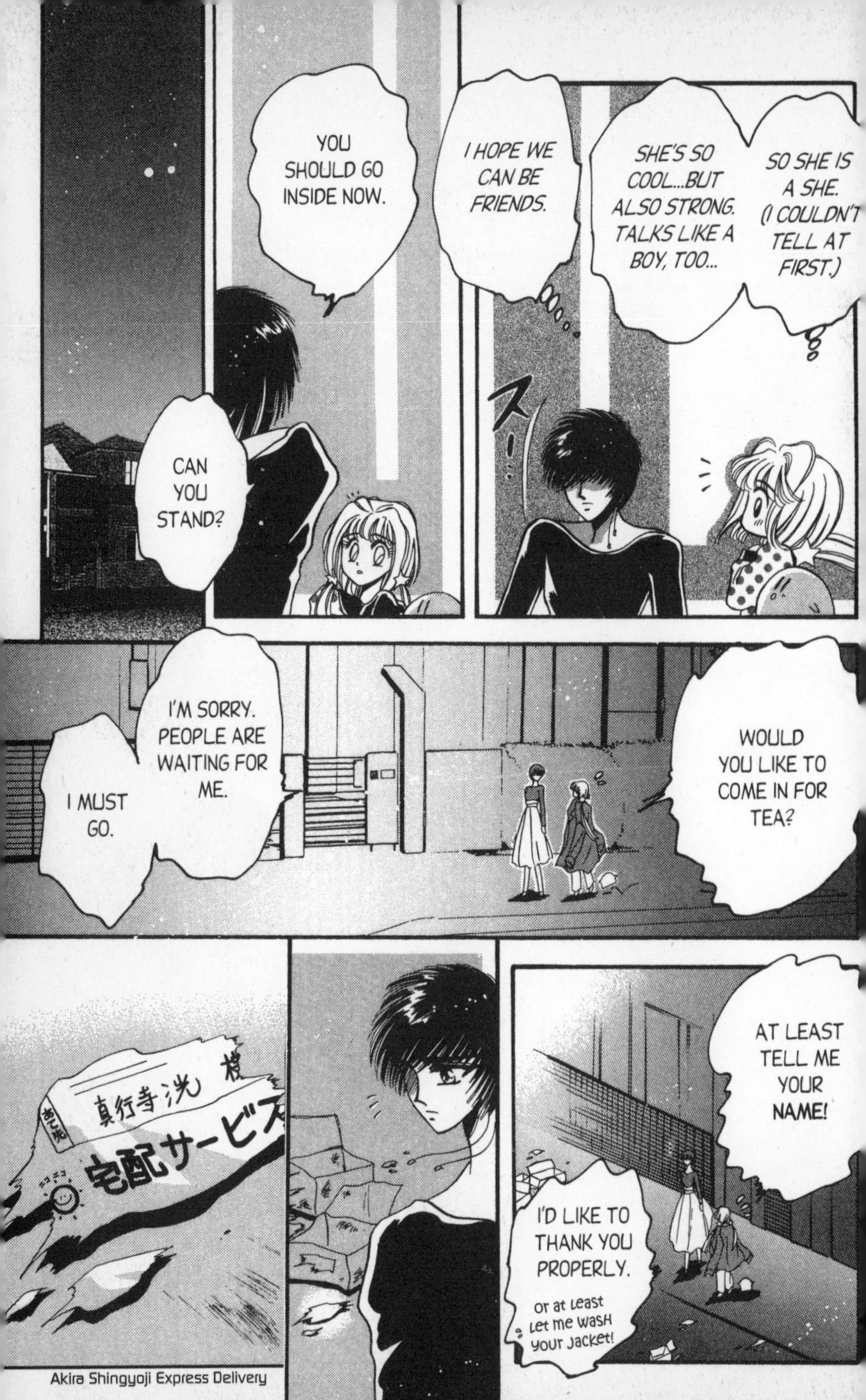
SO SHE IS A SHE. (I COULDN'T TELL AT FIRST.)
SHE'S SO COOL...BUT ALSO STRONG. TALKS LIKE A BOY, TOO...
I HOPE WE CAN BE FRIENDS.
ス…
YOU SHOULD GO INSIDE NOW.
CAN YOU STAND?
WOULD YOU LIKE TO COME IN FOR TEA?
I'M SORRY. PEOPLE ARE WAITING FOR ME.
I MUST GO.
AT LEAST TELL ME YOUR NAME!
I'D LIKE TO THANK YOU PROPERLY.
Or at least let me wash your jacket!
真行寺洸 様
宅配サービス

Akira Shingyoji Express Delivery

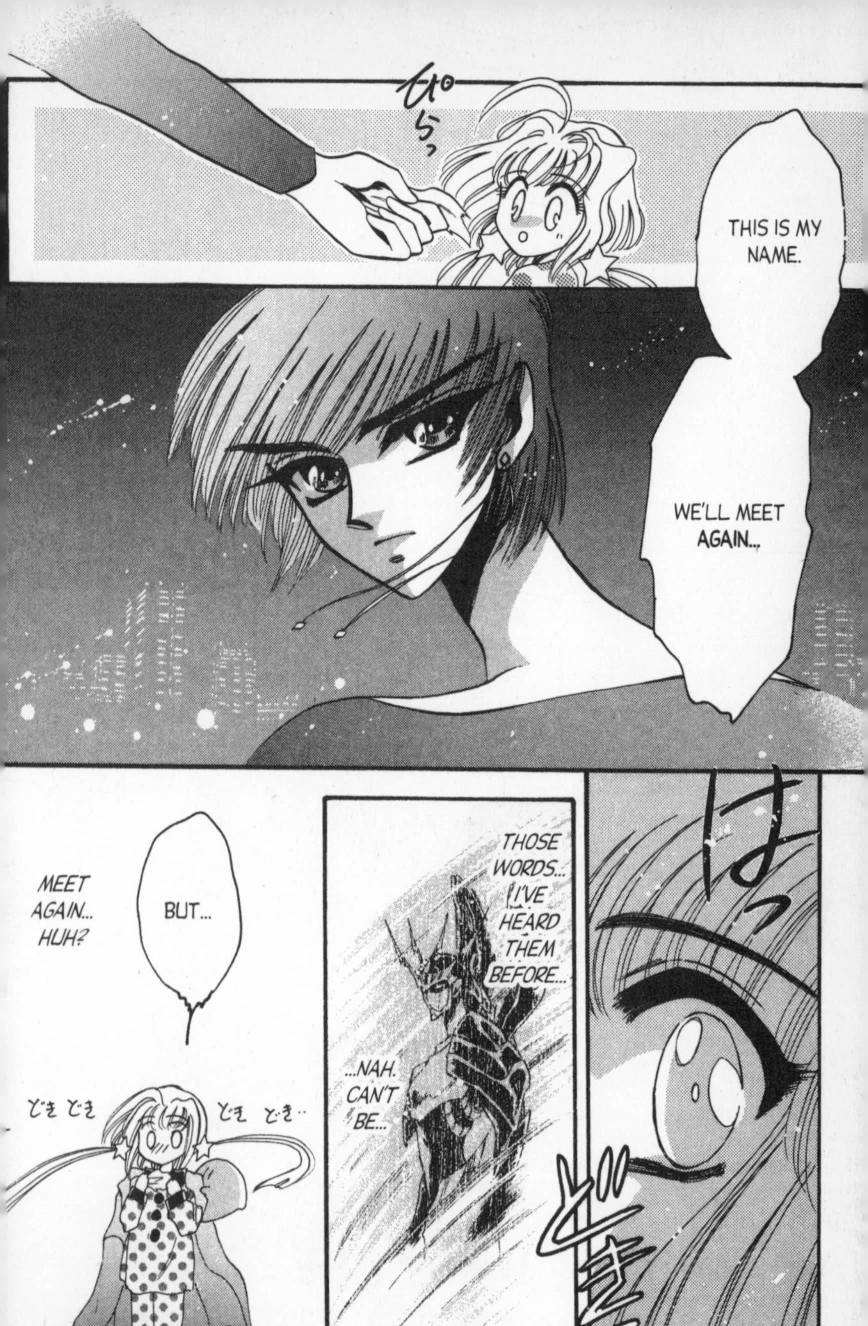
ぴらっ
THIS IS MY NAME.
WE'LL MEET AGAIN...
はっ
どきっ
THOSE WORDS... I'VE HEARD THEM BEFORE...
...NAH. CAN'T BE...
BUT...
MEET AGAIN... HUH?
どきどき どき どき‥

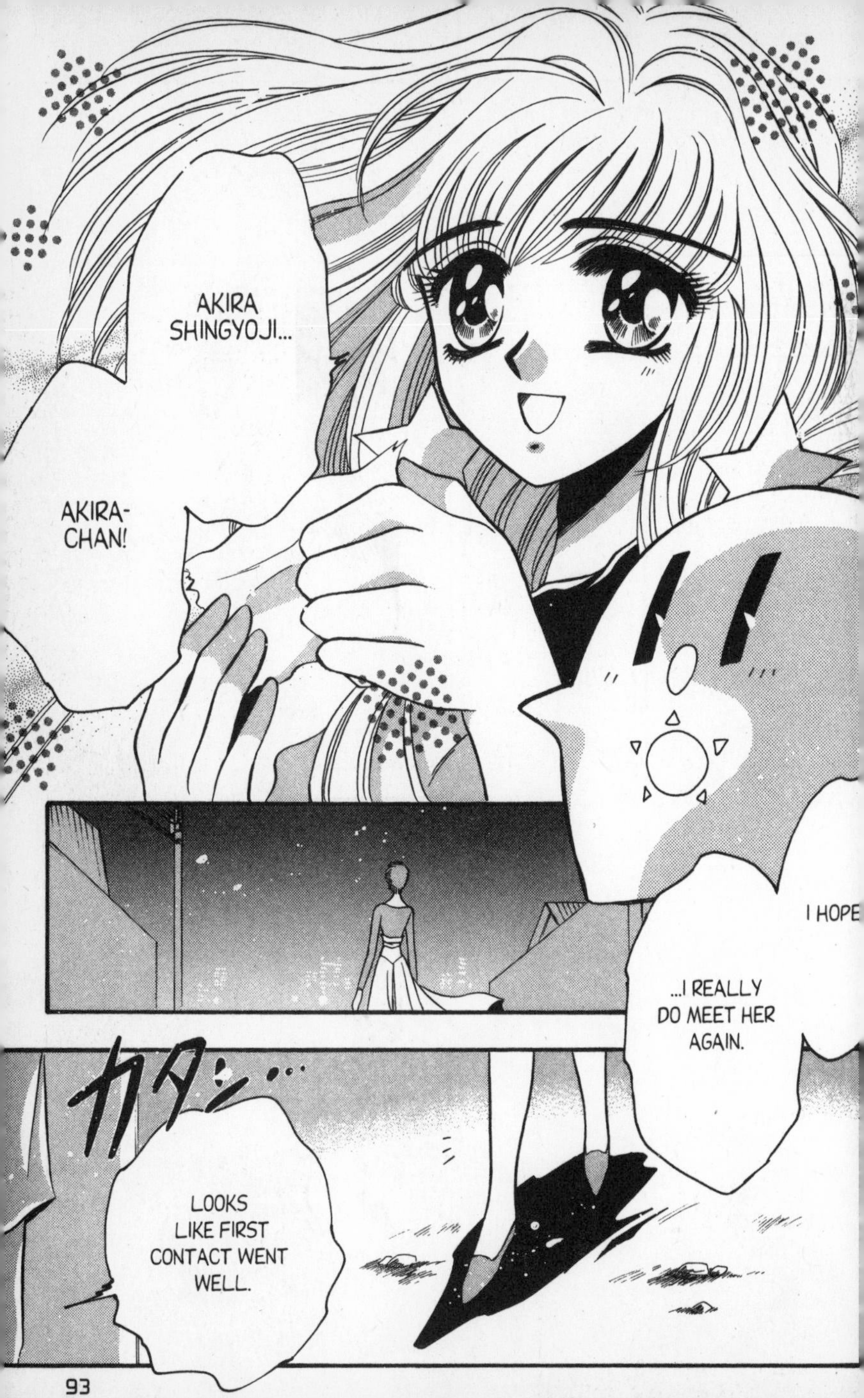
AKIRA SHINGYOJI...
AKIRA-CHAN!
I HOPE
...I REALLY DO MEET HER AGAIN.
カタン…
LOOKS LIKE FIRST CONTACT WENT WELL.

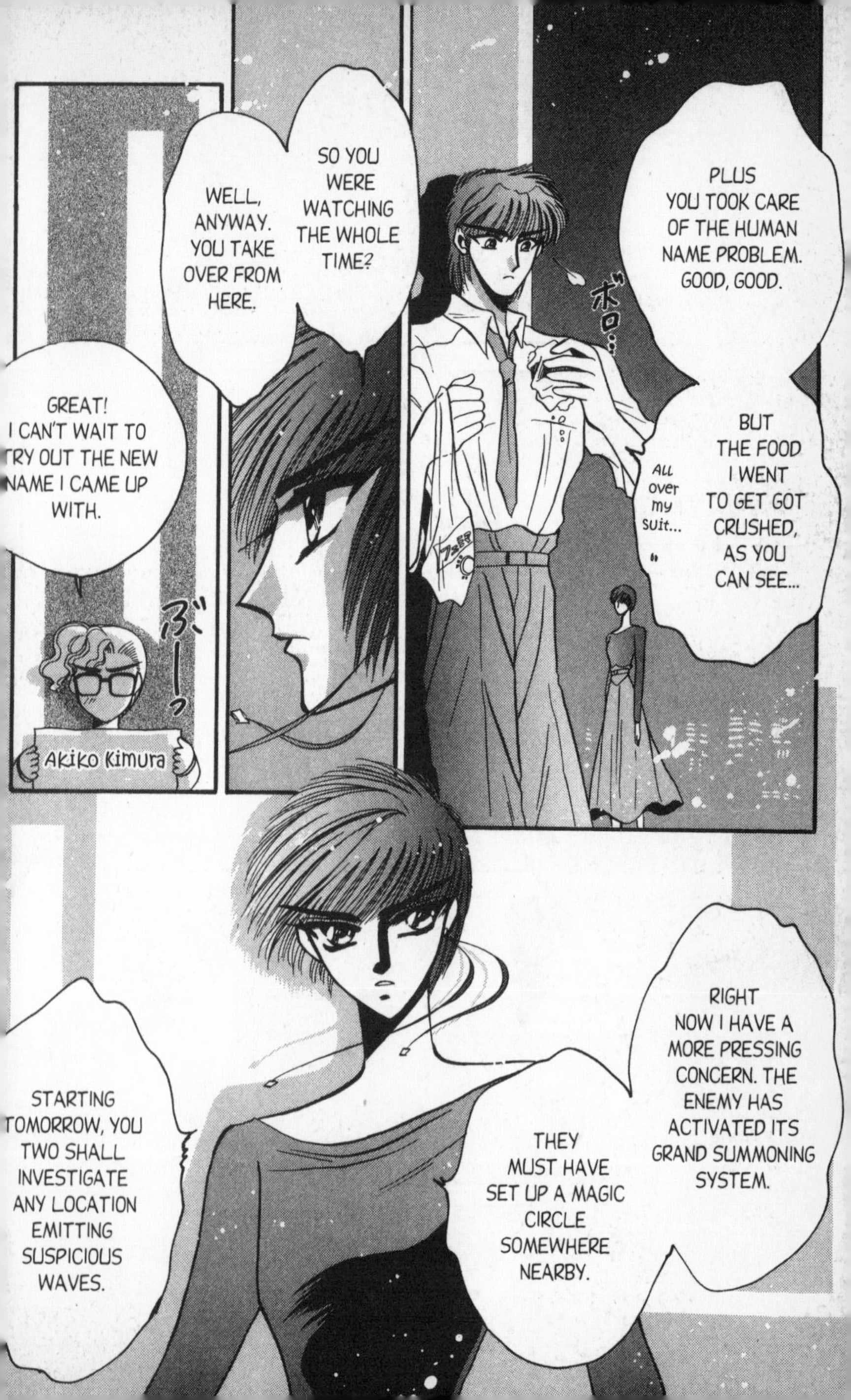
PLUS YOU TOOK CARE OF THE HUMAN NAME PROBLEM. GOOD, GOOD.
ボロ…
BUT THE FOOD I WENT TO GET GOT CRUSHED, AS YOU CAN SEE...
All over my suit...
SO YOU WERE WATCHING THE WHOLE TIME?
WELL, ANYWAY. YOU TAKE OVER FROM HERE.
GREAT! I CAN'T WAIT TO TRY OUT THE NEW NAME I CAME UP WITH.
ぶーっ
Akiko Kimura
RIGHT NOW I HAVE A MORE PRESSING CONCERN. THE ENEMY HAS ACTIVATED ITS GRAND SUMMONING SYSTEM.
THEY MUST HAVE SET UP A MAGIC CIRCLE SOMEWHERE NEARBY.
STARTING TOMORROW, YOU TWO SHALL INVESTIGATE ANY LOCATION EMITTING SUSPICIOUS WAVES.

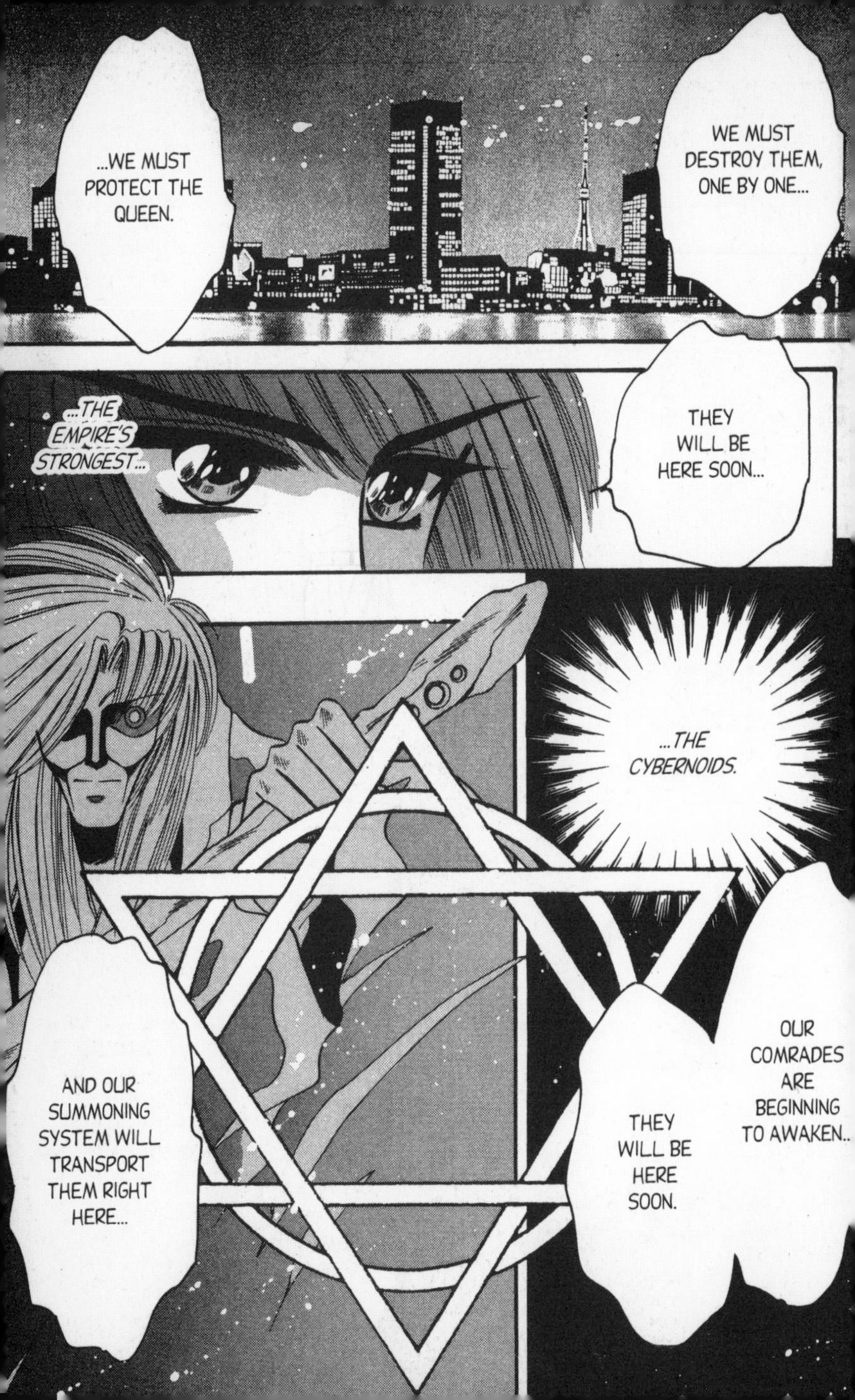
WE MUST DESTROY THEM, ONE BY ONE...
...WE MUST PROTECT THE QUEEN.
THEY WILL BE HERE SOON...
...THE EMPIRE'S STRONGEST...
...THE CYBERNOIDS.
OUR COMRADES ARE BEGINNING TO AWAKEN..
THEY WILL BE HERE SOON.
AND OUR SUMMONING SYSTEM WILL TRANSPORT THEM RIGHT HERE...

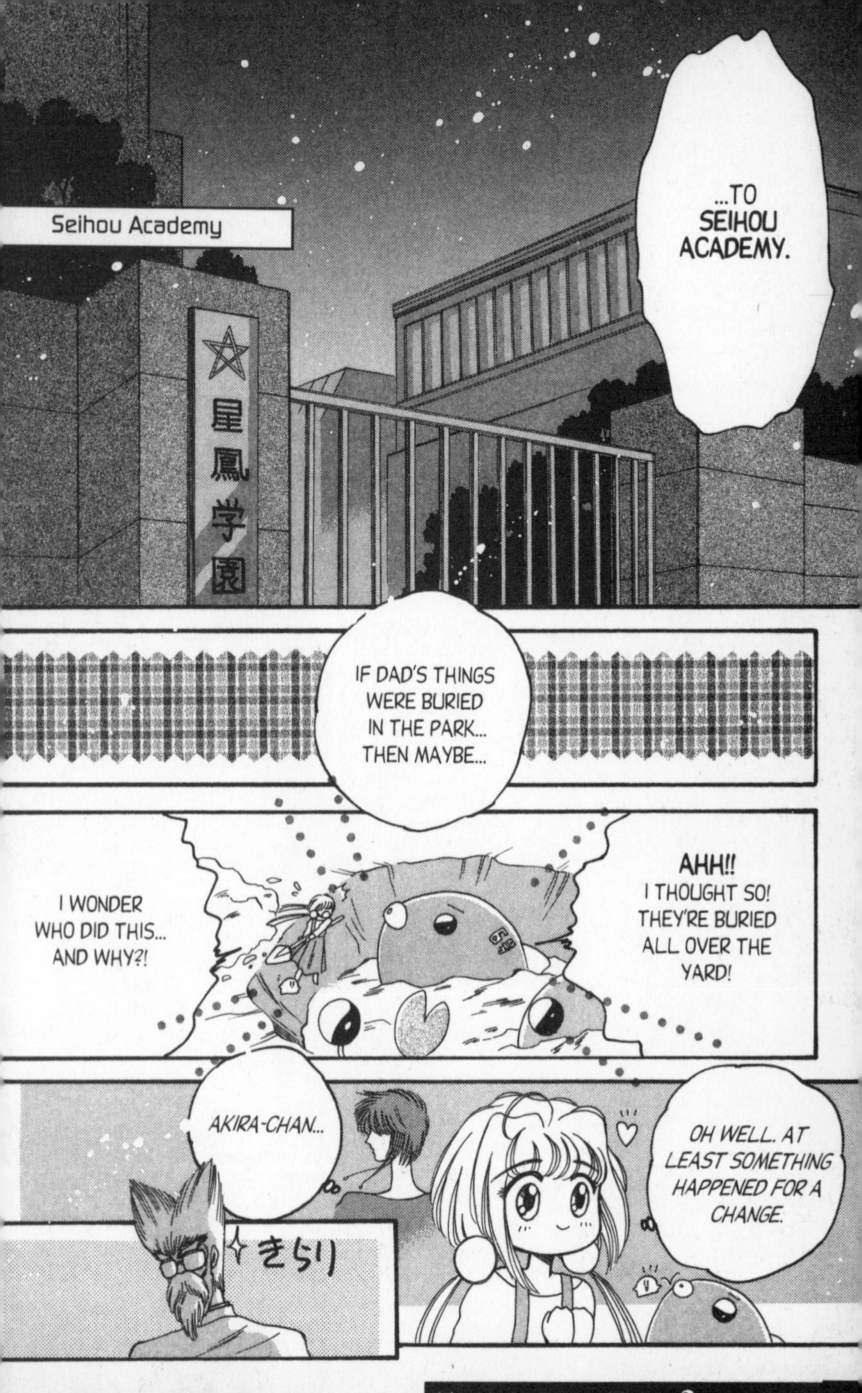
...TO SEIHOU ACADEMY.
Seihou Academy
星鳳学園
IF DAD'S THINGS WERE BURIED IN THE PARK... THEN MAYBE...
AHH!! I THOUGHT SO! THEY'RE BURIED ALL OVER THE YARD!
I WONDER WHO DID THIS... AND WHY?!
OH WELL. AT LEAST SOMETHING HAPPENED FOR A CHANGE.
AKIRA-CHAN...
きらり

TRANSFORMATION 2 —— END

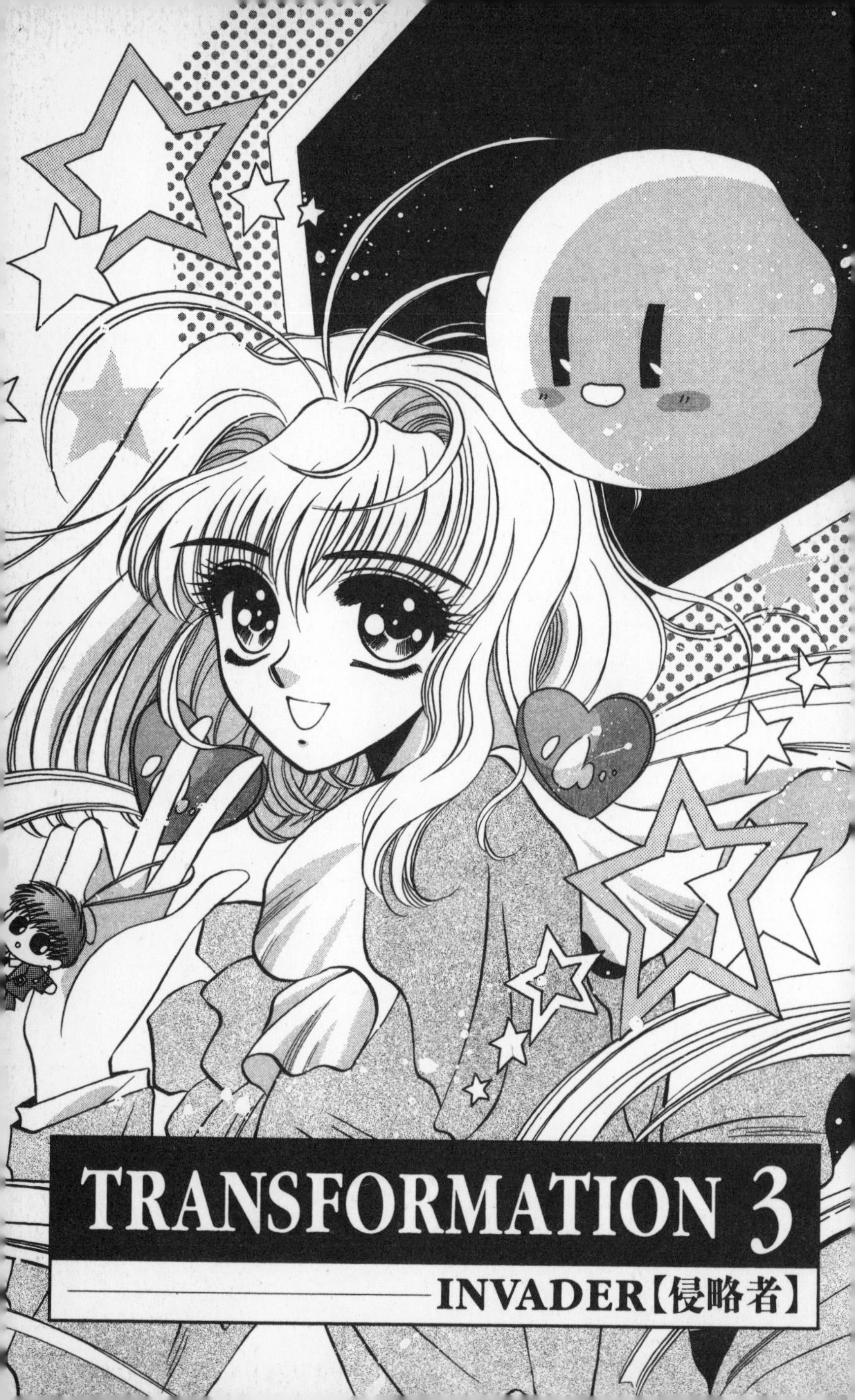

TRANSFORMATION 3

INVADER【侵略者】

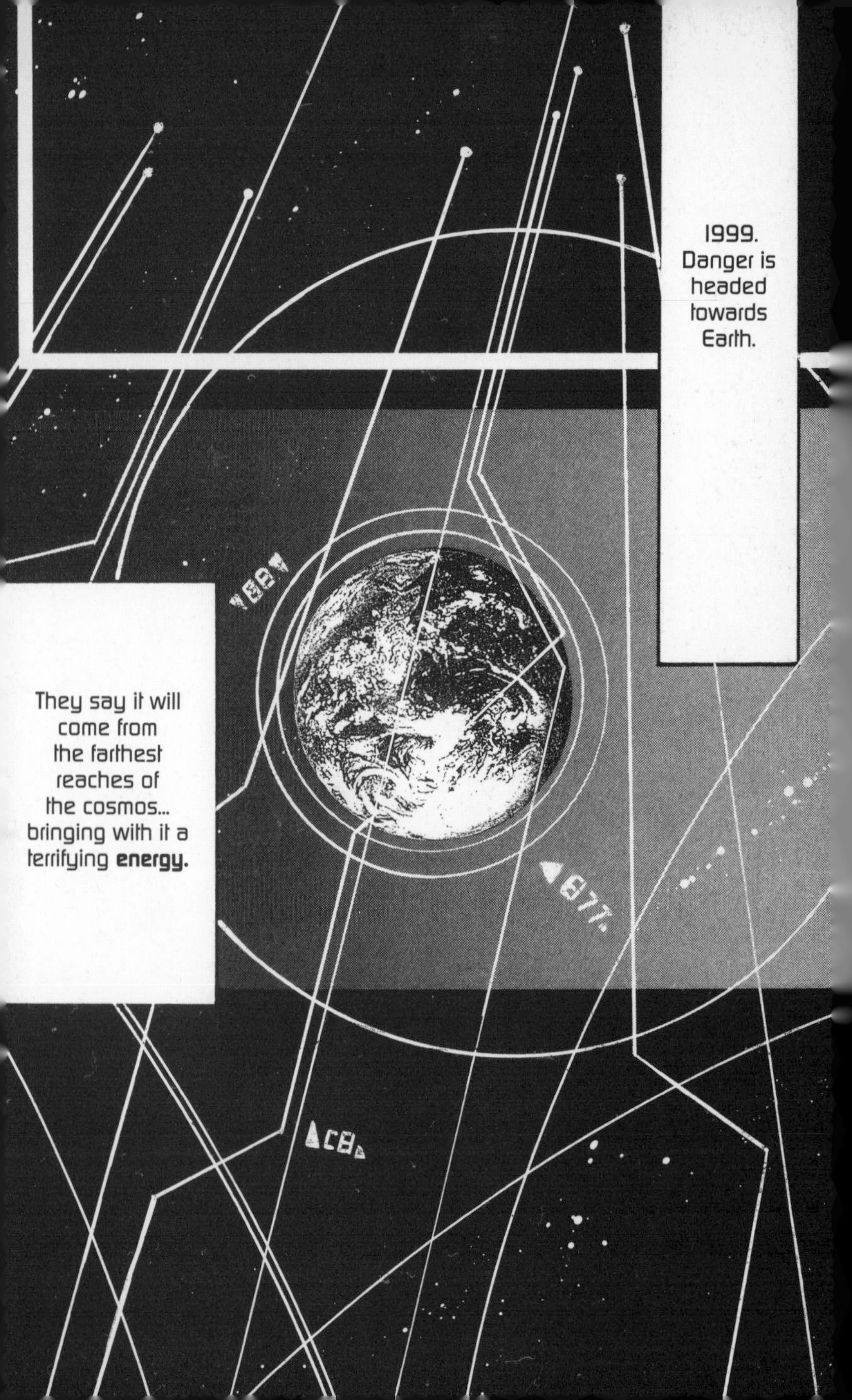
1999. Danger is headed towards Earth.
They say it will come from the farthest reaches of the cosmos... bringing with it a terrifying **energy.**

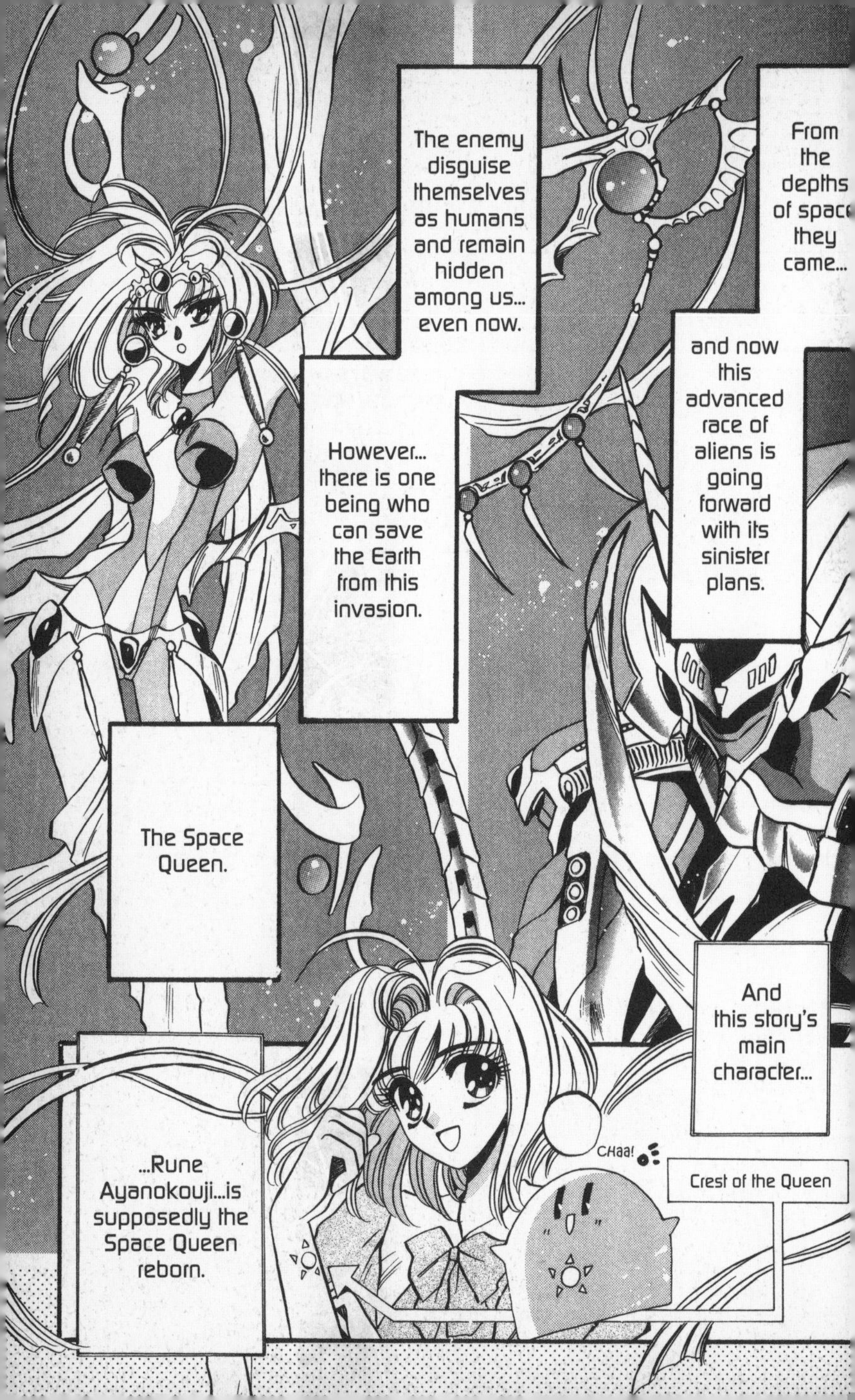
From the depths of space they came...
and now this advanced race of aliens is going forward with its sinister plans.
The enemy disguise themselves as humans and remain hidden among us... even now.
However... there is one being who can save the Earth from this invasion.
The Space Queen.
And this story's main character...
...Rune Ayanokouji...is supposedly the Space Queen reborn.
CHaa!
Crest of the Queen

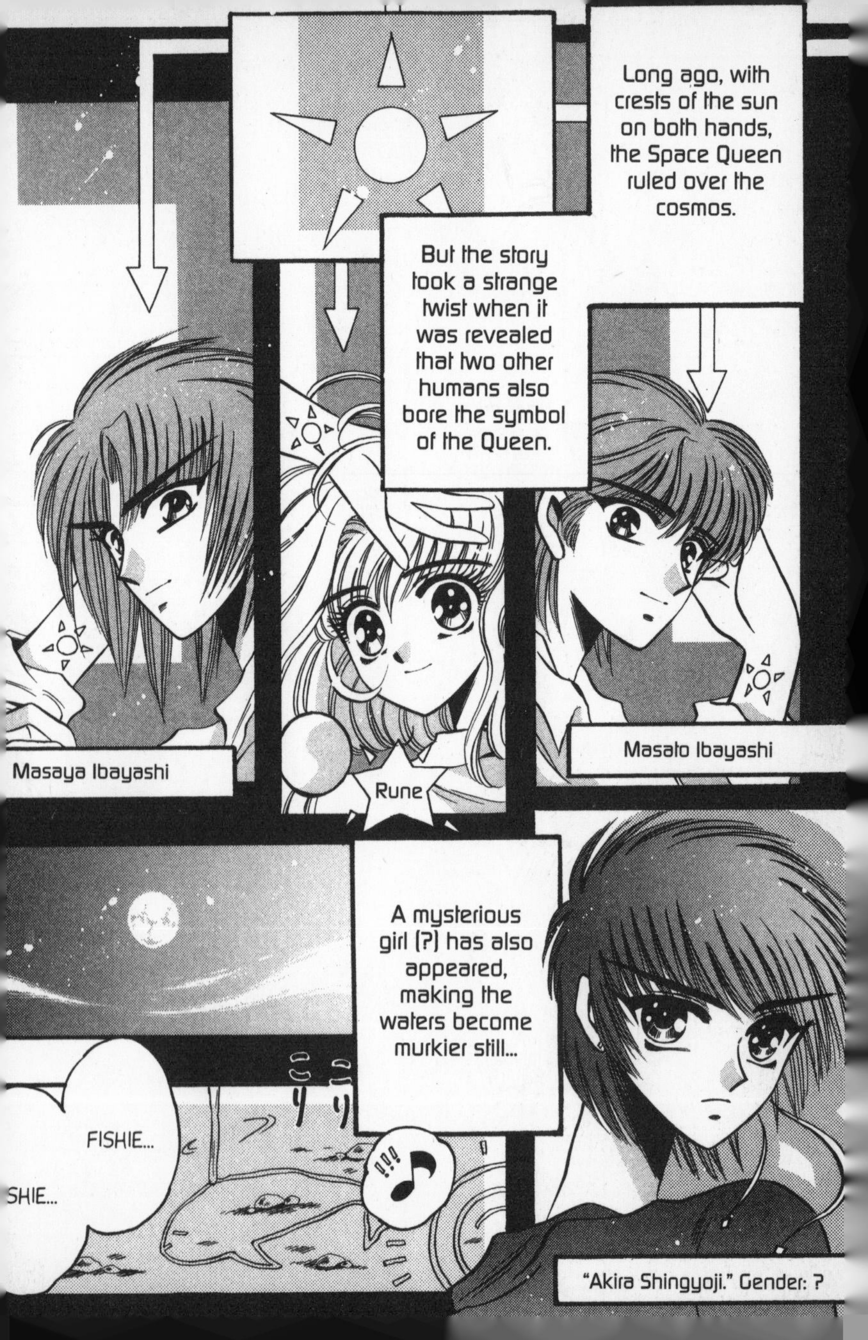
Long ago, with crests of the sun on both hands, the Space Queen ruled over the cosmos.
Masato Ibayashi
But the story took a strange twist when it was revealed that two other humans also bore the symbol of the Queen.
Rune
Masaya Ibayashi
A mysterious girl (?) has also appeared, making the waters become murkier still...
"Akira Shingyoji." Gender: ?
FISHIE...
SHIE...
!!!

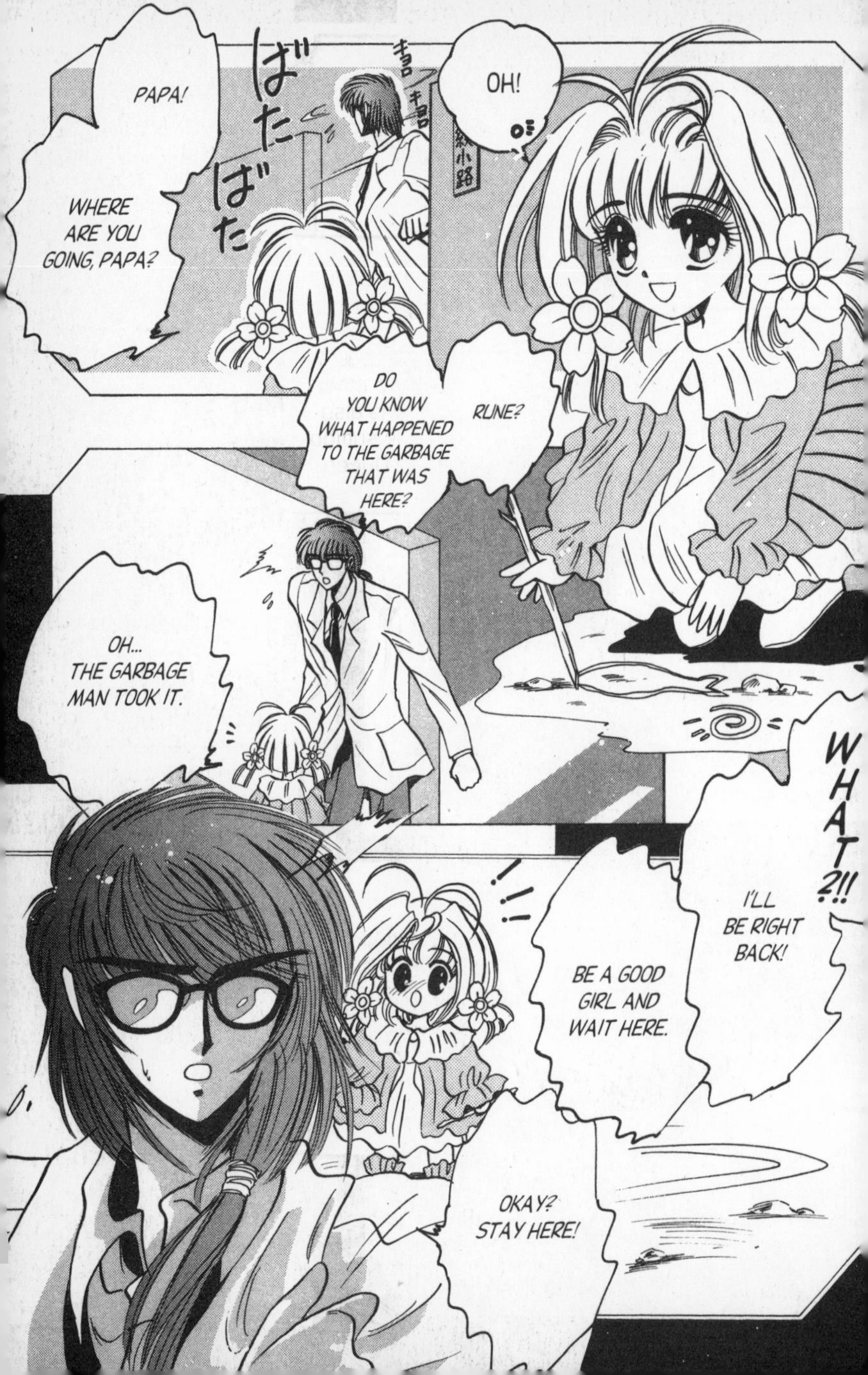

OH!
PAPA!
ばたばた
WHERE ARE YOU GOING, PAPA?
RUNE?
DO YOU KNOW WHAT HAPPENED TO THE GARBAGE THAT WAS HERE?
OH... THE GARBAGE MAN TOOK IT.
WHAT?!!
I'LL BE RIGHT BACK!
BE A GOOD GIRL AND WAIT HERE.
OKAY? STAY HERE!

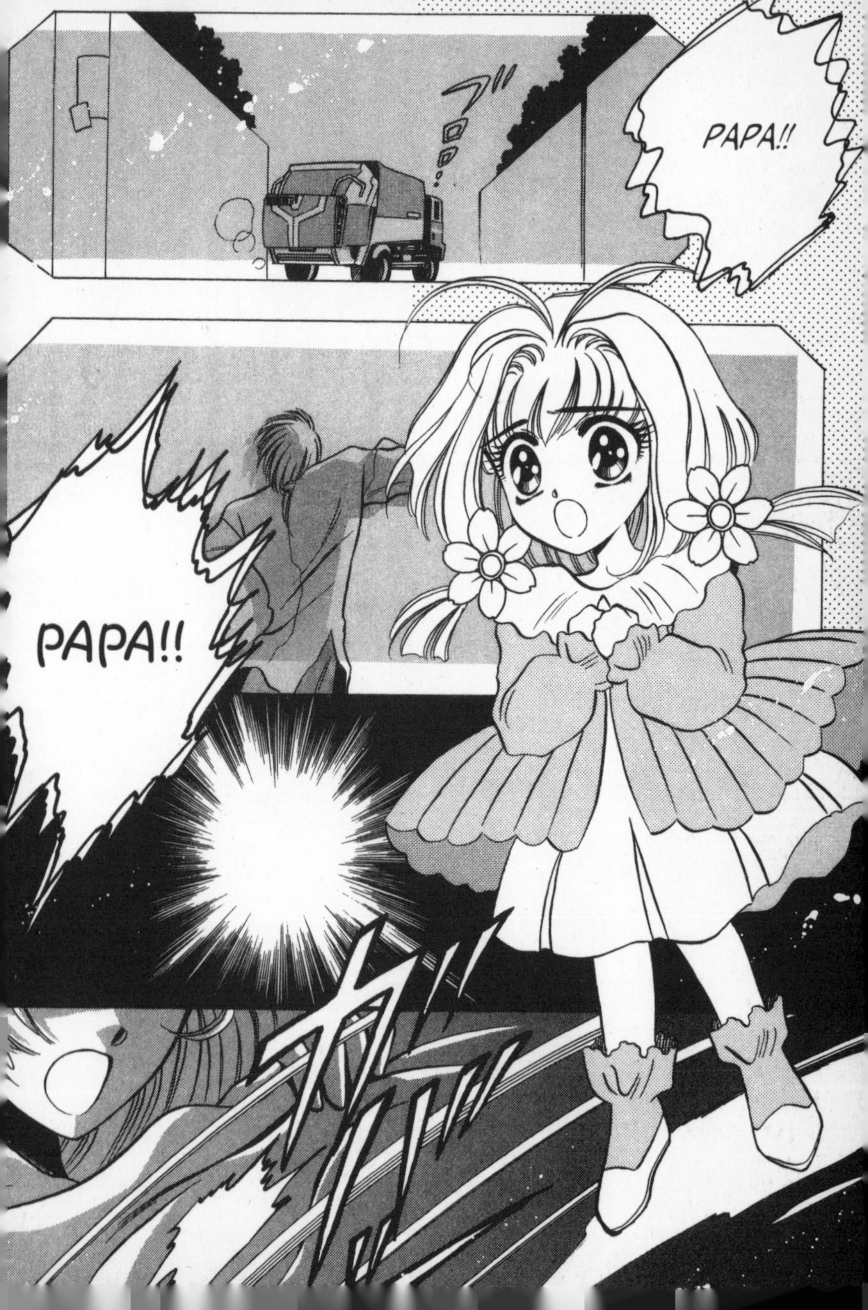
PAPA!!
PAPA!!

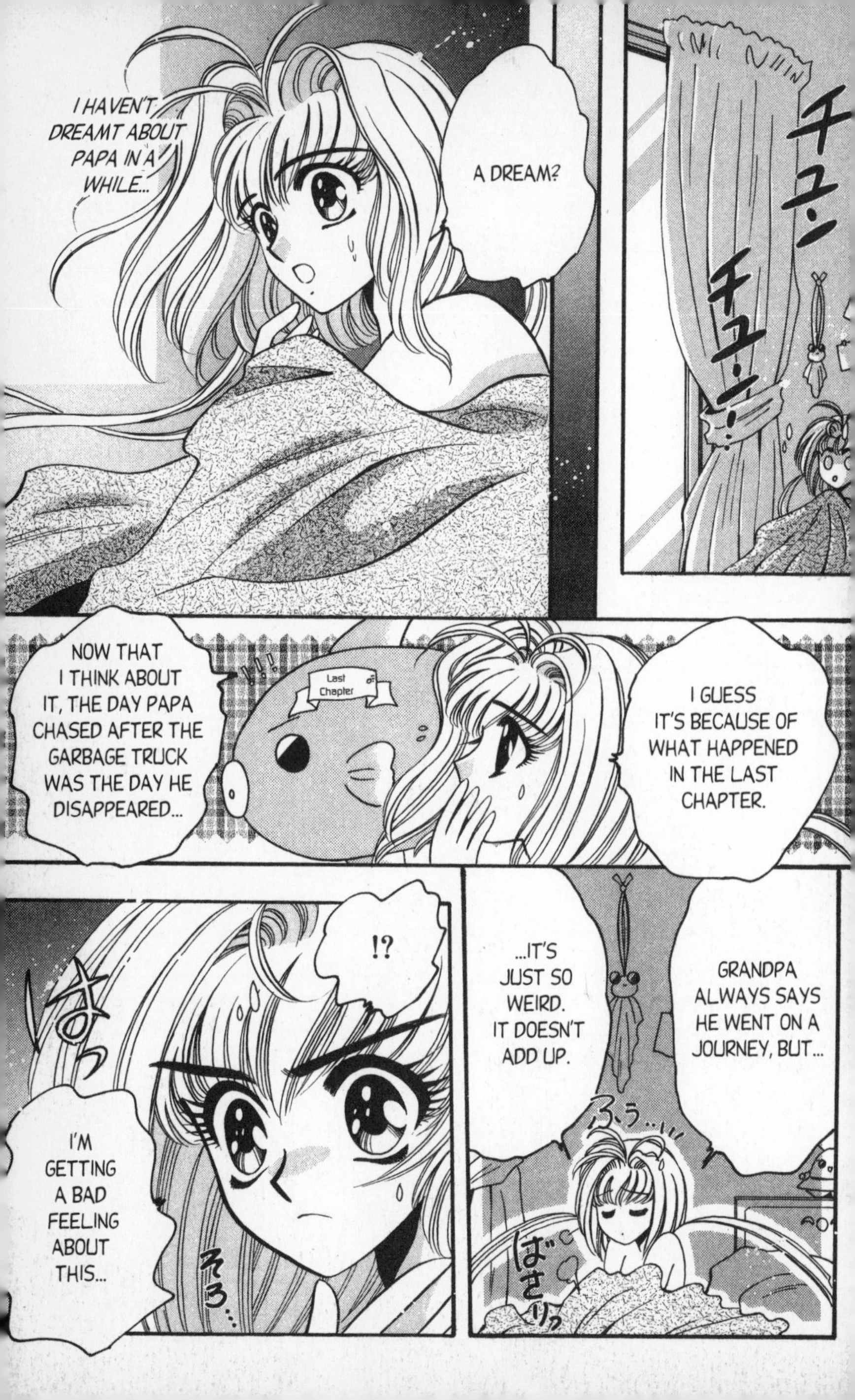
チュン
チュン!
A DREAM?
I HAVEN'T DREAMT ABOUT PAPA IN A WHILE...
I GUESS IT'S BECAUSE OF WHAT HAPPENED IN THE LAST CHAPTER.
Last Chapter
NOW THAT I THINK ABOUT IT, THE DAY PAPA CHASED AFTER THE GARBAGE TRUCK WAS THE DAY HE DISAPPEARED...
GRANDPA ALWAYS SAYS HE WENT ON A JOURNEY, BUT...
...IT'S JUST SO WEIRD. IT DOESN'T ADD UP.
ふう...
ばさりっ
!?
はっ
I'M GETTING A BAD FEELING ABOUT THIS...
そろ...

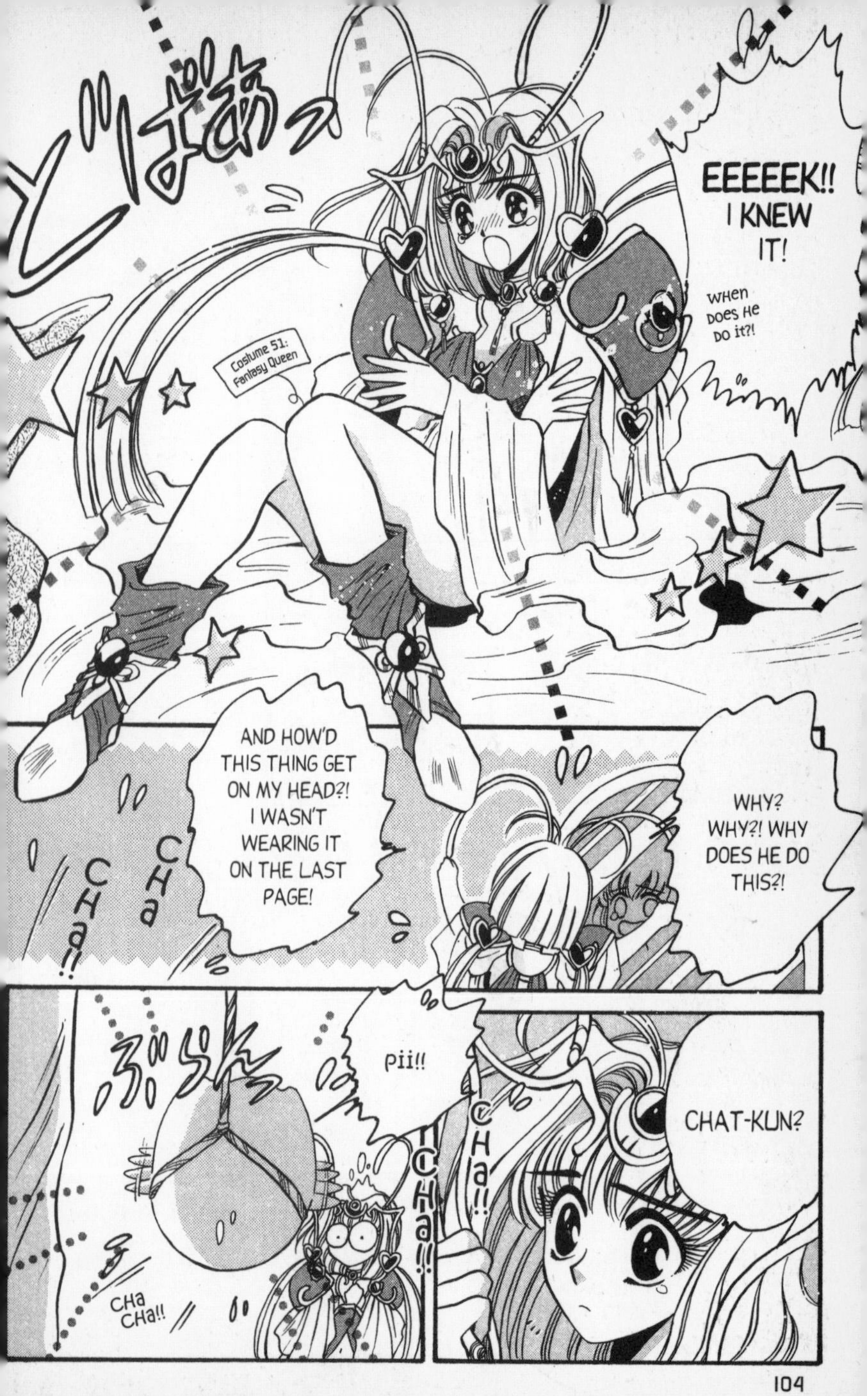
EEEEEK!! I KNEW IT!
When does he do it?!
どぱあっ
Costume 51: Fantasy Queen
WHY? WHY?! WHY DOES HE DO THIS?!
AND HOW'D THIS THING GET ON MY HEAD?! I WASN'T WEARING IT ON THE LAST PAGE!
CHa CHa!!
CHAT-KUN?
CHa CHa!!
pii!!
ぷらん
CHa CHa!!

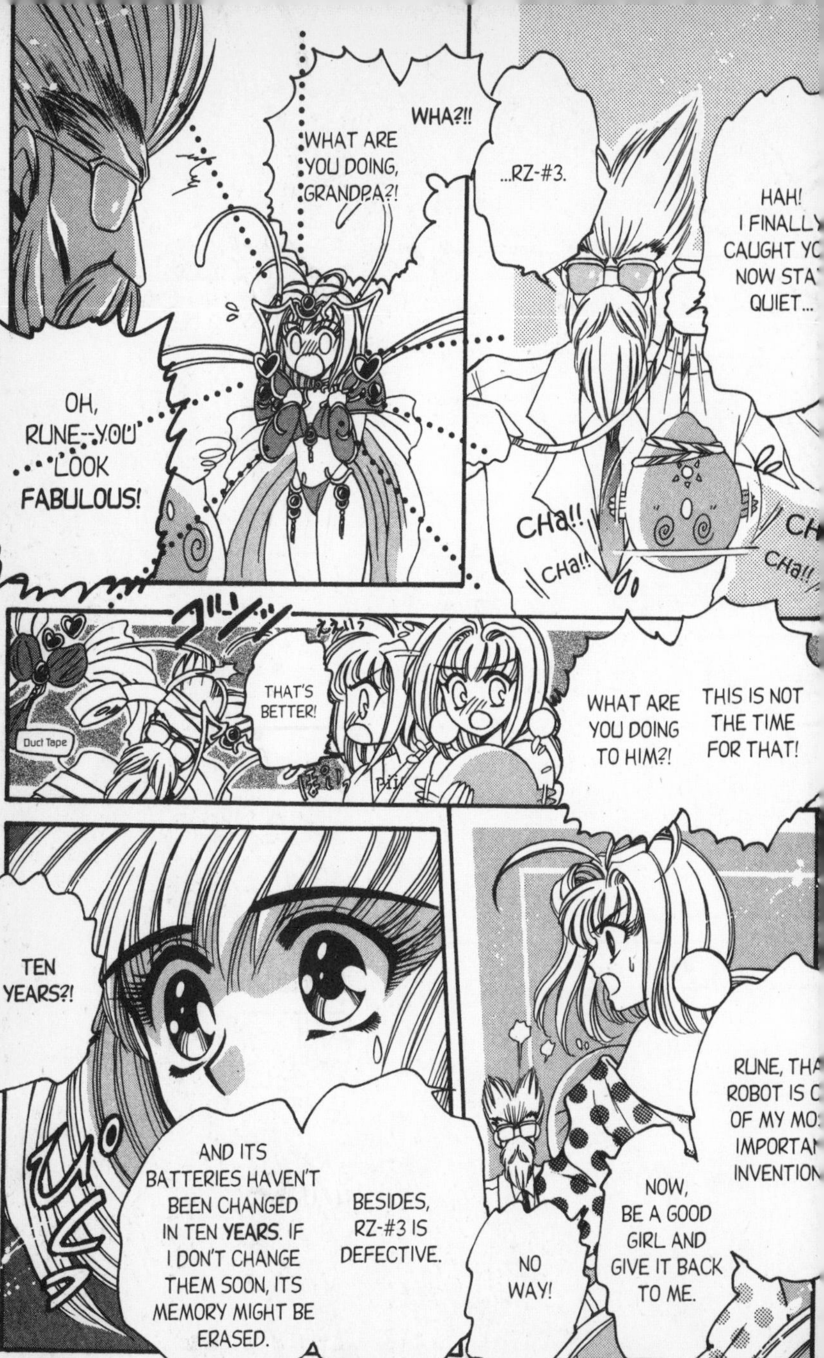
...RZ-#3.
HAH! I FINALLY CAUGHT YC NOW STA QUIET...
CHa!!
CHa!!
CH
CHa!!
WHA?!!
WHAT ARE YOU DOING, GRANDPA?!
OH, RUNE--YOU LOOK FABULOUS!
THIS IS NOT THE TIME FOR THAT!
WHAT ARE YOU DOING TO HIM?!
THAT'S BETTER!
Duct Tape
Pii!
RUNE, THA ROBOT IS O OF MY MOS IMPORTAN INVENTION
NOW, BE A GOOD GIRL AND GIVE IT BACK TO ME.
NO WAY!
BESIDES, RZ-#3 IS DEFECTIVE.
AND ITS BATTERIES HAVEN'T BEEN CHANGED IN TEN YEARS. IF I DON'T CHANGE THEM SOON, ITS MEMORY MIGHT BE ERASED.
TEN YEARS?!

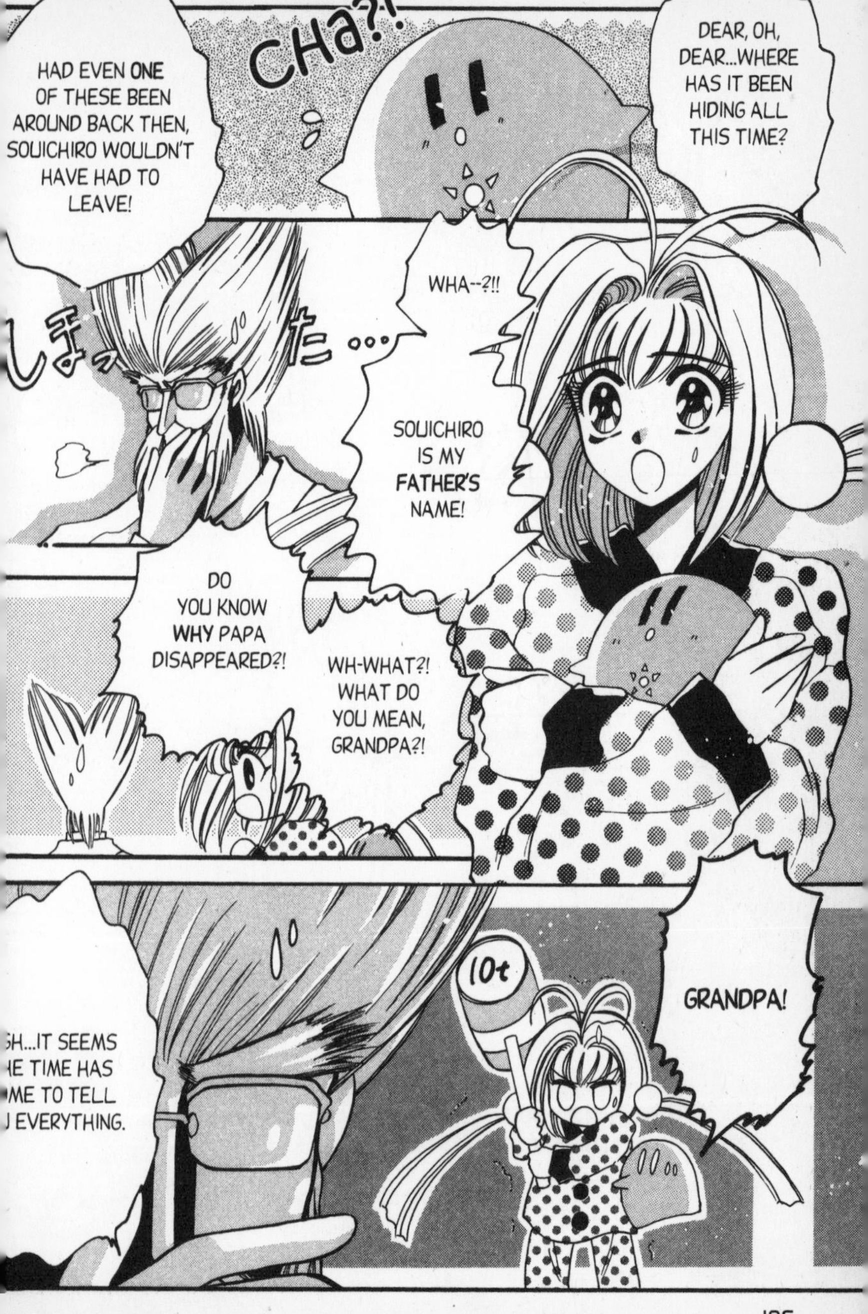
DEAR, OH, DEAR...WHERE HAS IT BEEN HIDING ALL THIS TIME?
CHa?!
HAD EVEN ONE OF THESE BEEN AROUND BACK THEN, SOUICHIRO WOULDN'T HAVE HAD TO LEAVE!
WHA--?!!
SOUICHIRO IS MY FATHER'S NAME!
しまった…
DO YOU KNOW WHY PAPA DISAPPEARED?!
WH-WHAT?! WHAT DO YOU MEAN, GRANDPA?!
GRANDPA!
10t
H...IT SEEMS E TIME HAS ME TO TELL U EVERYTHING.

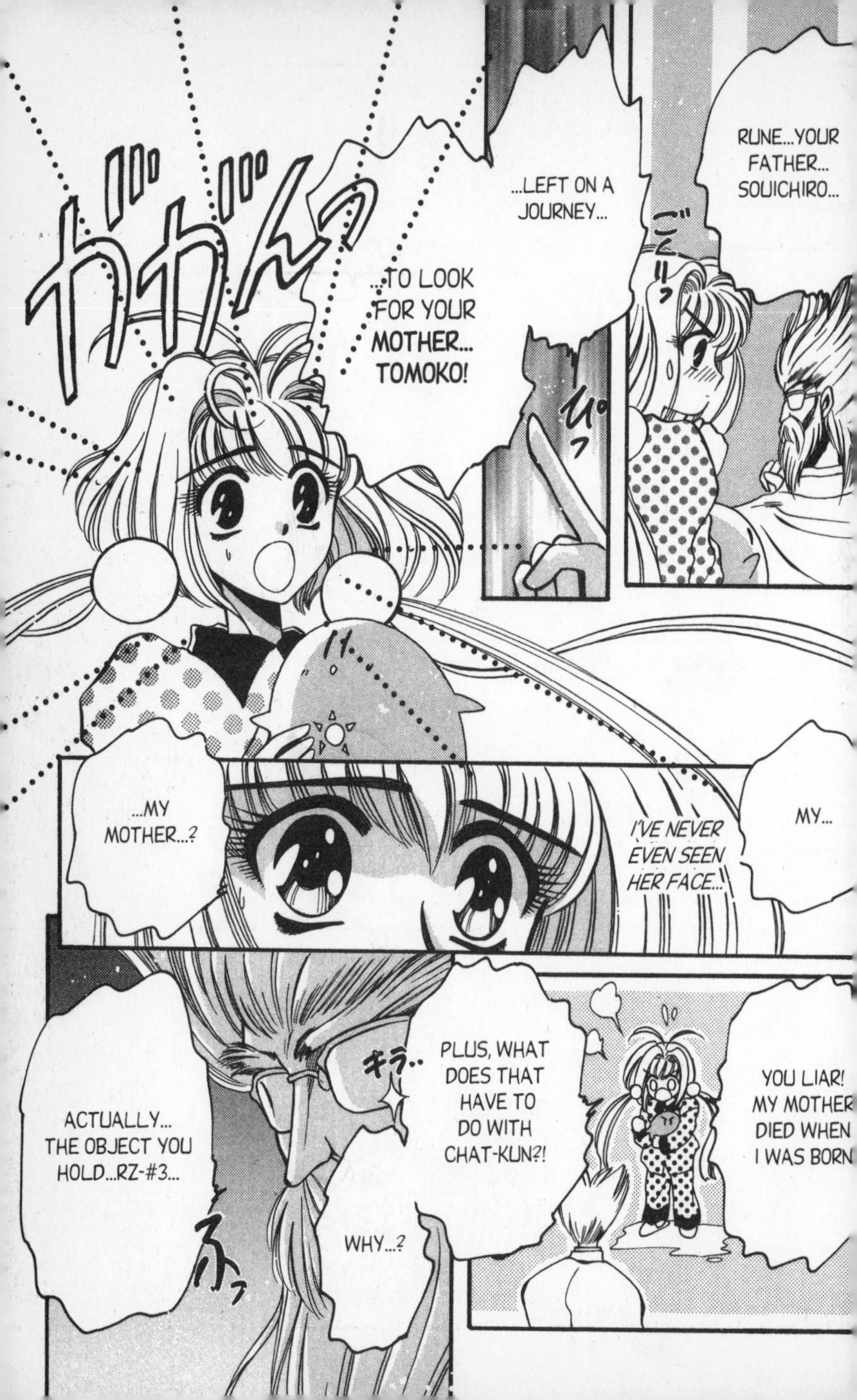
RUNE...YOUR FATHER... SOUICHIRO...
...LEFT ON A JOURNEY...
...TO LOOK FOR YOUR MOTHER... TOMOKO!
MY...
I'VE NEVER EVEN SEEN HER FACE...
...MY MOTHER...?
YOU LIAR! MY MOTHER DIED WHEN I WAS BORN
PLUS, WHAT DOES THAT HAVE TO DO WITH CHAT-KUN?!
WHY...?
ACTUALLY... THE OBJECT YOU HOLD...RZ-#3...

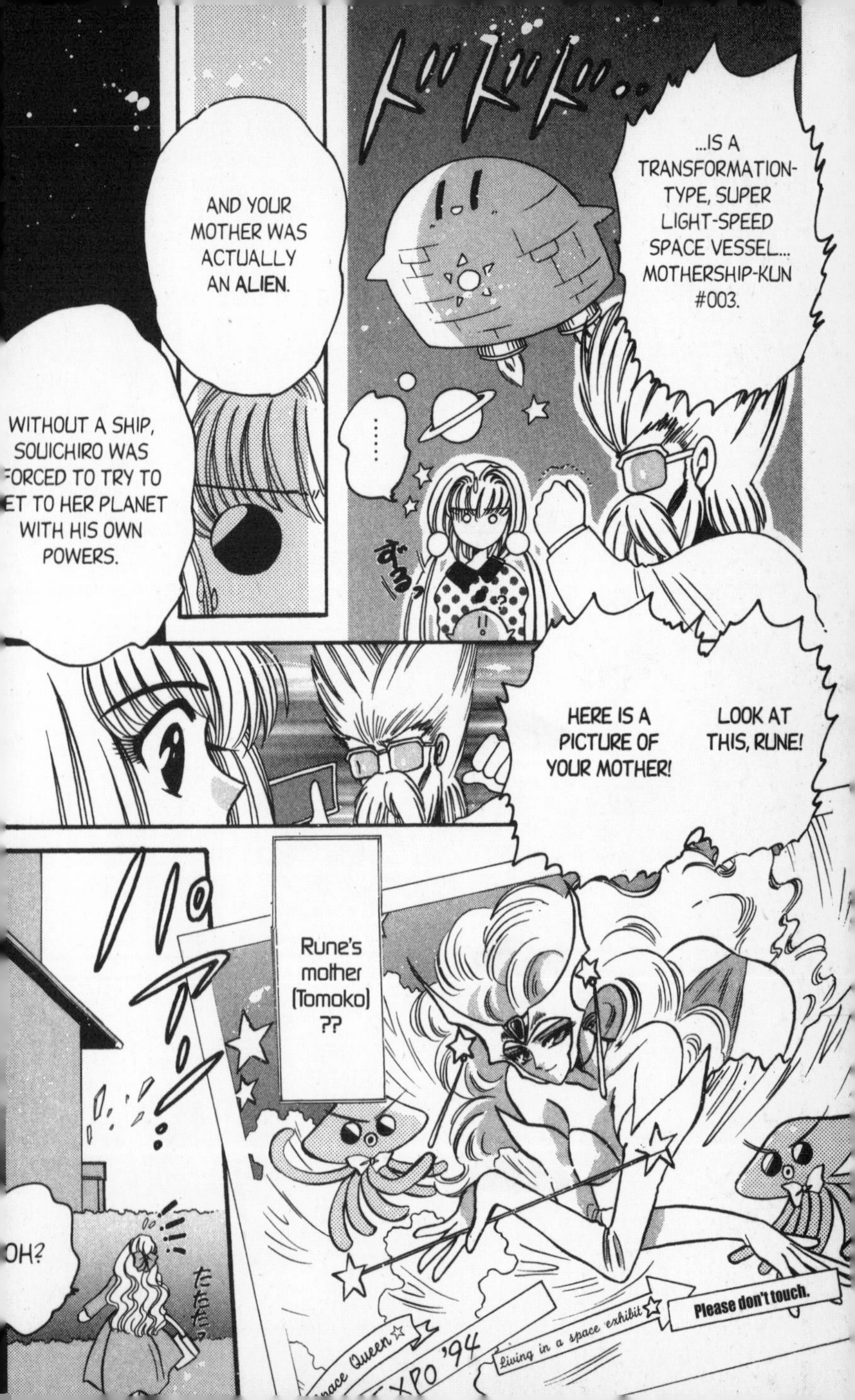
KOO KOO KOO...
...IS A TRANSFORMATION-TYPE, SUPER LIGHT-SPEED SPACE VESSEL... MOTHERSHIP-KUN #003.
......
AND YOUR MOTHER WAS ACTUALLY AN ALIEN.
WITHOUT A SHIP, SOUICHIRO WAS FORCED TO TRY TO ET TO HER PLANET WITH HIS OWN POWERS.
LOOK AT THIS, RUNE!
HERE IS A PICTURE OF YOUR MOTHER!
Rune's mother (Tomoko) ??
Please don't touch.
Living in a space exhibit
Space Queen
EXPO '94
OH?

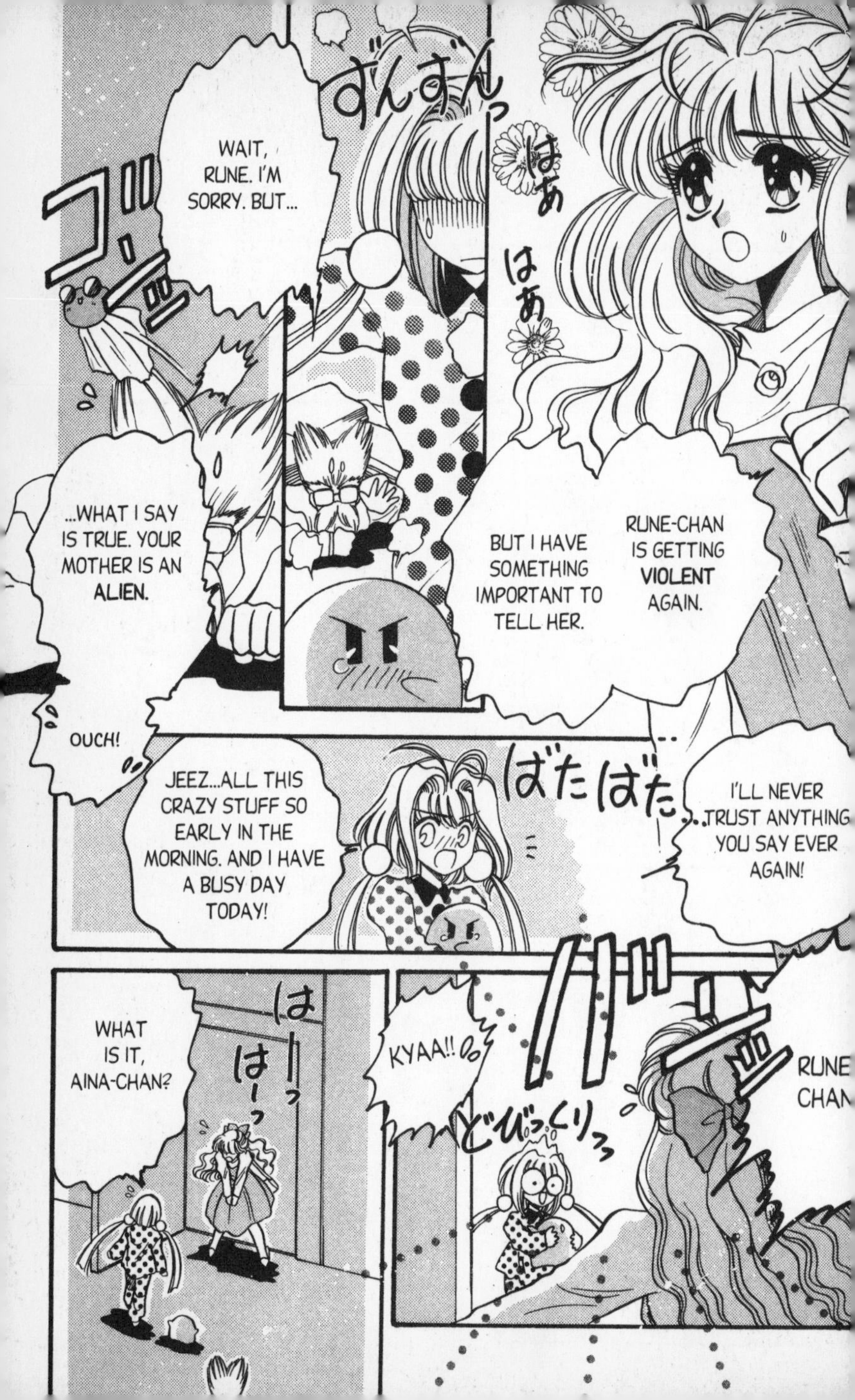

はぁ
はぁ
RUNE-CHAN IS GETTING VIOLENT AGAIN.
BUT I HAVE SOMETHING IMPORTANT TO TELL HER.
ずんずんっ
ゴッ
WAIT, RUNE. I'M SORRY. BUT...
...WHAT I SAY IS TRUE. YOUR MOTHER IS AN ALIEN.
OUCH!
I'LL NEVER TRUST ANYTHING YOU SAY EVER AGAIN!
ばたばた
JEEZ...ALL THIS CRAZY STUFF SO EARLY IN THE MORNING. AND I HAVE A BUSY DAY TODAY!
バン
RUNE CHAN
KYAA!!
どびっくりっ
はーっ
はーっ
WHAT IS IT, AINA-CHAN?

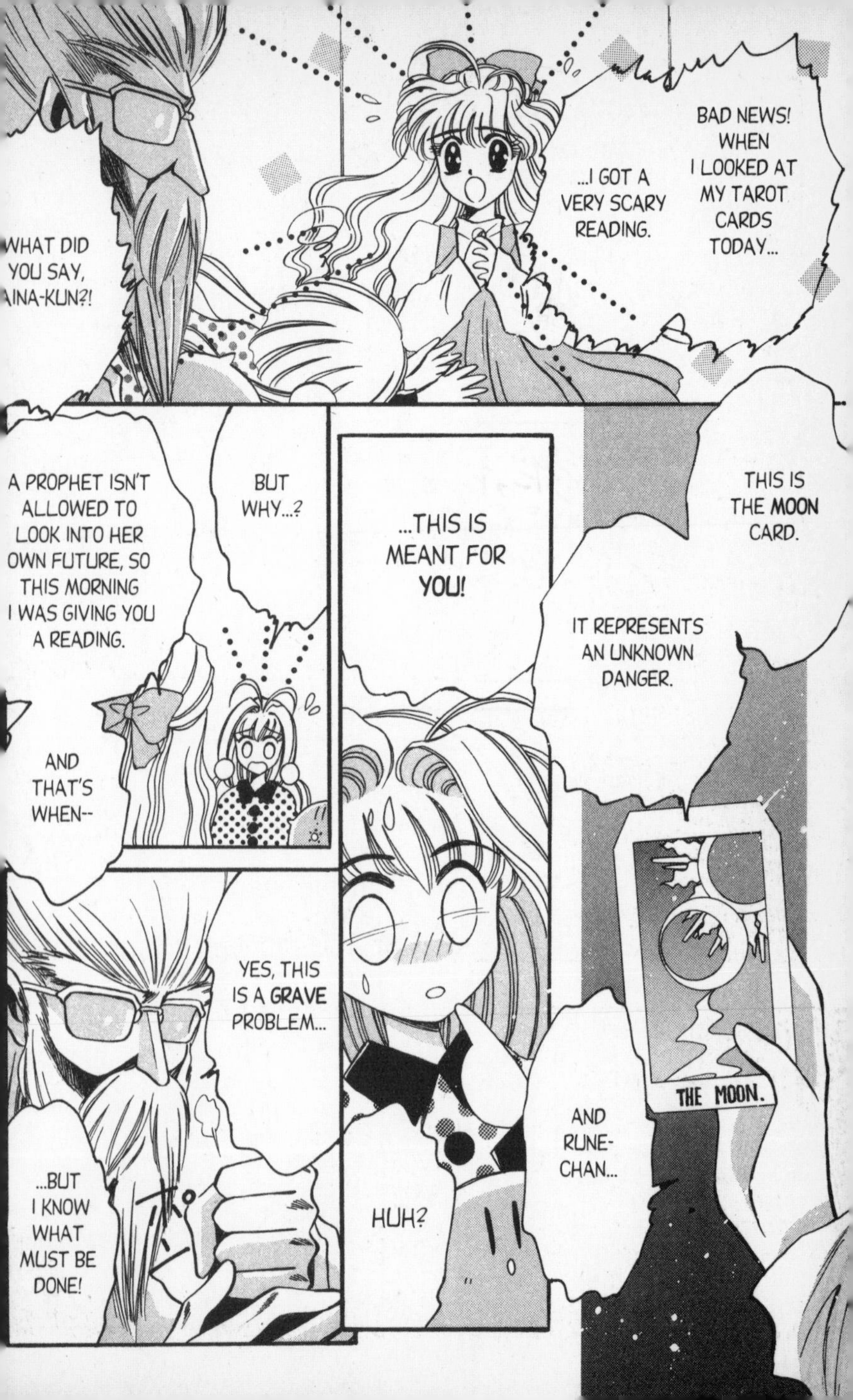
BAD NEWS! WHEN I LOOKED AT MY TAROT CARDS TODAY...
...I GOT A VERY SCARY READING.
WHAT DID YOU SAY, INA-KUN?!
THIS IS THE MOON CARD.
IT REPRESENTS AN UNKNOWN DANGER.
THE MOON.
AND RUNE-CHAN...
...THIS IS MEANT FOR YOU!
HUH?
BUT WHY...?
A PROPHET ISN'T ALLOWED TO LOOK INTO HER OWN FUTURE, SO THIS MORNING I WAS GIVING YOU A READING.
AND THAT'S WHEN--
YES, THIS IS A GRAVE PROBLEM...
...BUT I KNOW WHAT MUST BE DONE!

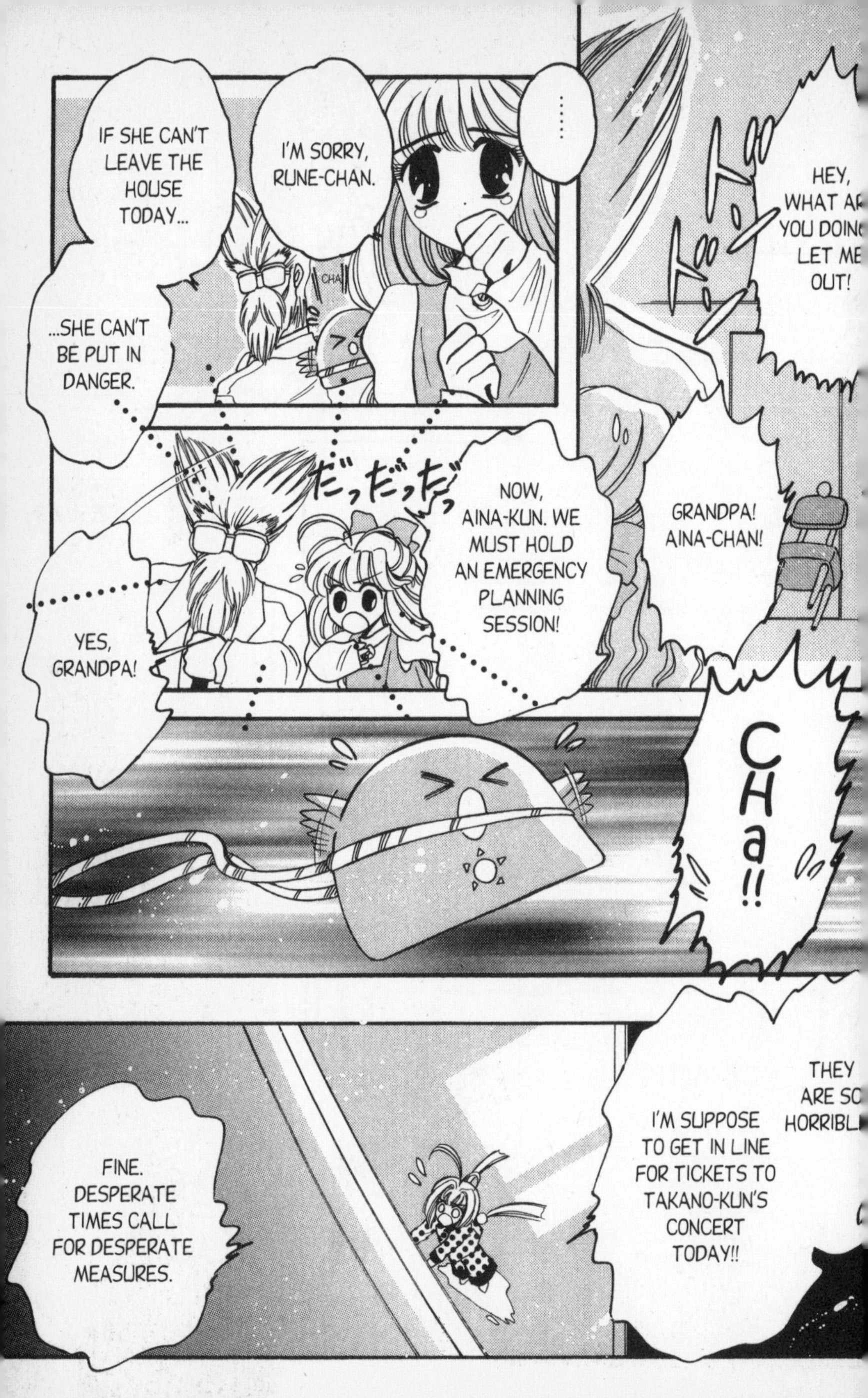

HEY, WHAT AR YOU DOIN LET ME OUT!
GRANDPA! AINA-CHAN!
……
I'M SORRY, RUNE-CHAN.
CHA
IF SHE CAN'T LEAVE THE HOUSE TODAY...
...SHE CAN'T BE PUT IN DANGER.
だっだっだっ
NOW, AINA-KUN. WE MUST HOLD AN EMERGENCY PLANNING SESSION!
YES, GRANDPA!
CHa!!
THEY ARE SO HORRIBL
I'M SUPPOSE TO GET IN LINE FOR TICKETS TO TAKANO-KUN'S CONCERT TODAY!!
FINE. DESPERATE TIMES CALL FOR DESPERATE MEASURES.

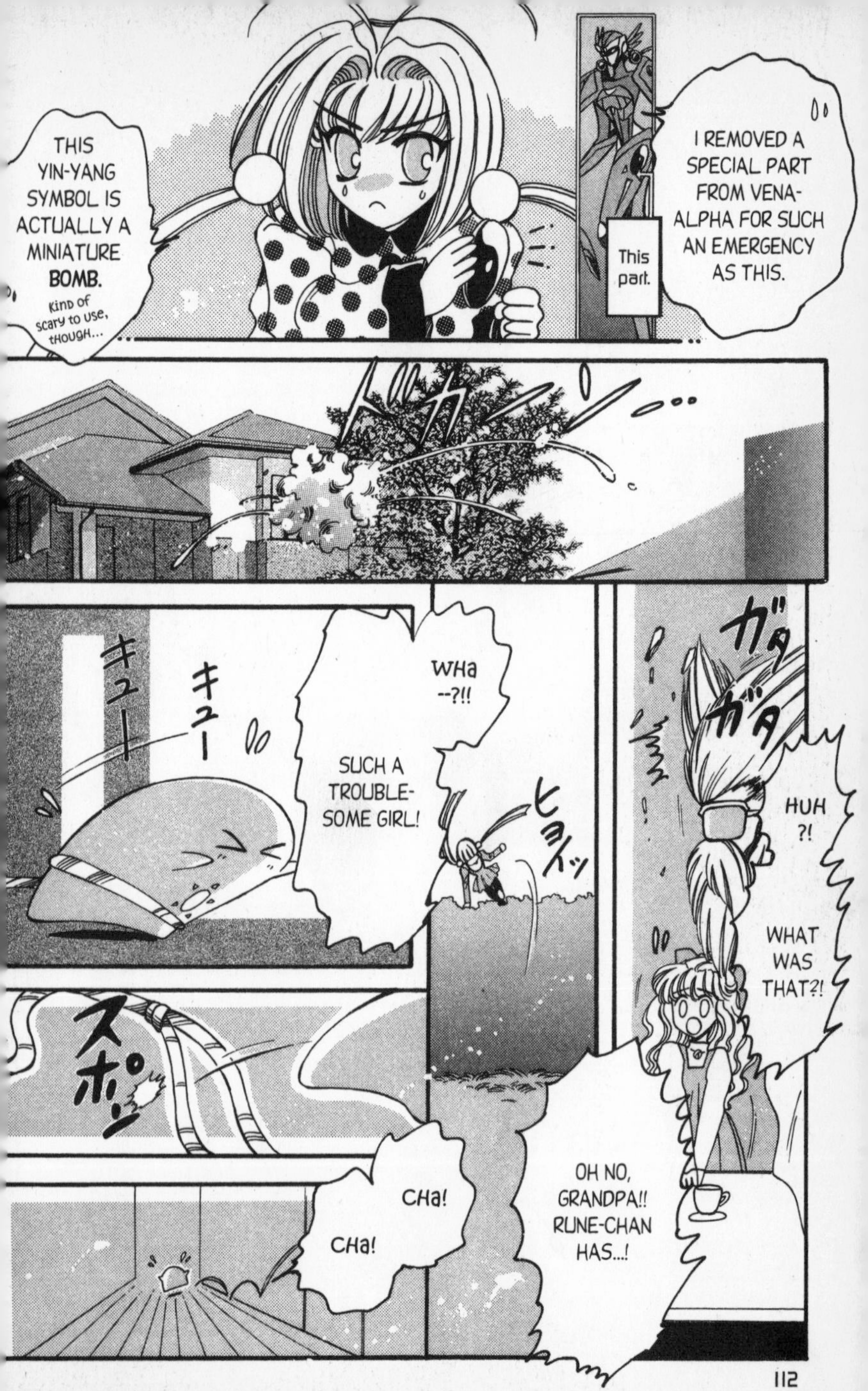
I REMOVED A SPECIAL PART FROM VENA-ALPHA FOR SUCH AN EMERGENCY AS THIS.
This part.
THIS YIN-YANG SYMBOL IS ACTUALLY A MINIATURE **BOMB.**
Kind of scary to use, though...
ガタ
ガタ
HUH?!
WHAT WAS THAT?!
OH NO, GRANDPA!! RUNE-CHAN HAS...!
WHA--?!!
SUCH A TROUBLE-SOME GIRL!
ヒョイッ
キュー
キュー
スポン
CHA!
CHA!

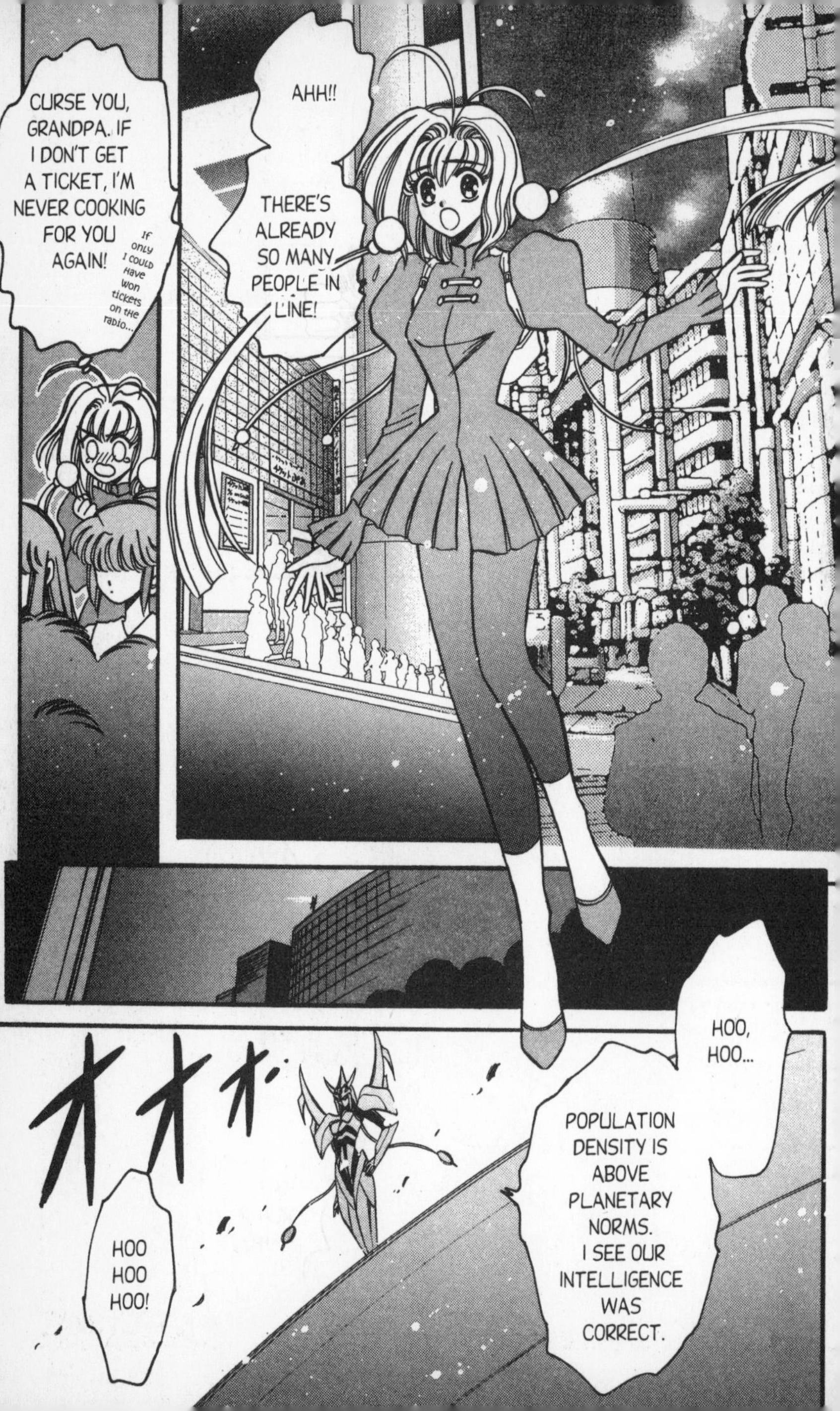
AHH!!
THERE'S ALREADY SO MANY PEOPLE IN LINE!
CURSE YOU, GRANDPA. IF I DON'T GET A TICKET, I'M NEVER COOKING FOR YOU AGAIN!
If only I could have won tickets on the radio...
HOO, HOO...
POPULATION DENSITY IS ABOVE PLANETARY NORMS. I SEE OUR INTELLIGENCE WAS CORRECT.
HOO HOO HOO!
オオオ

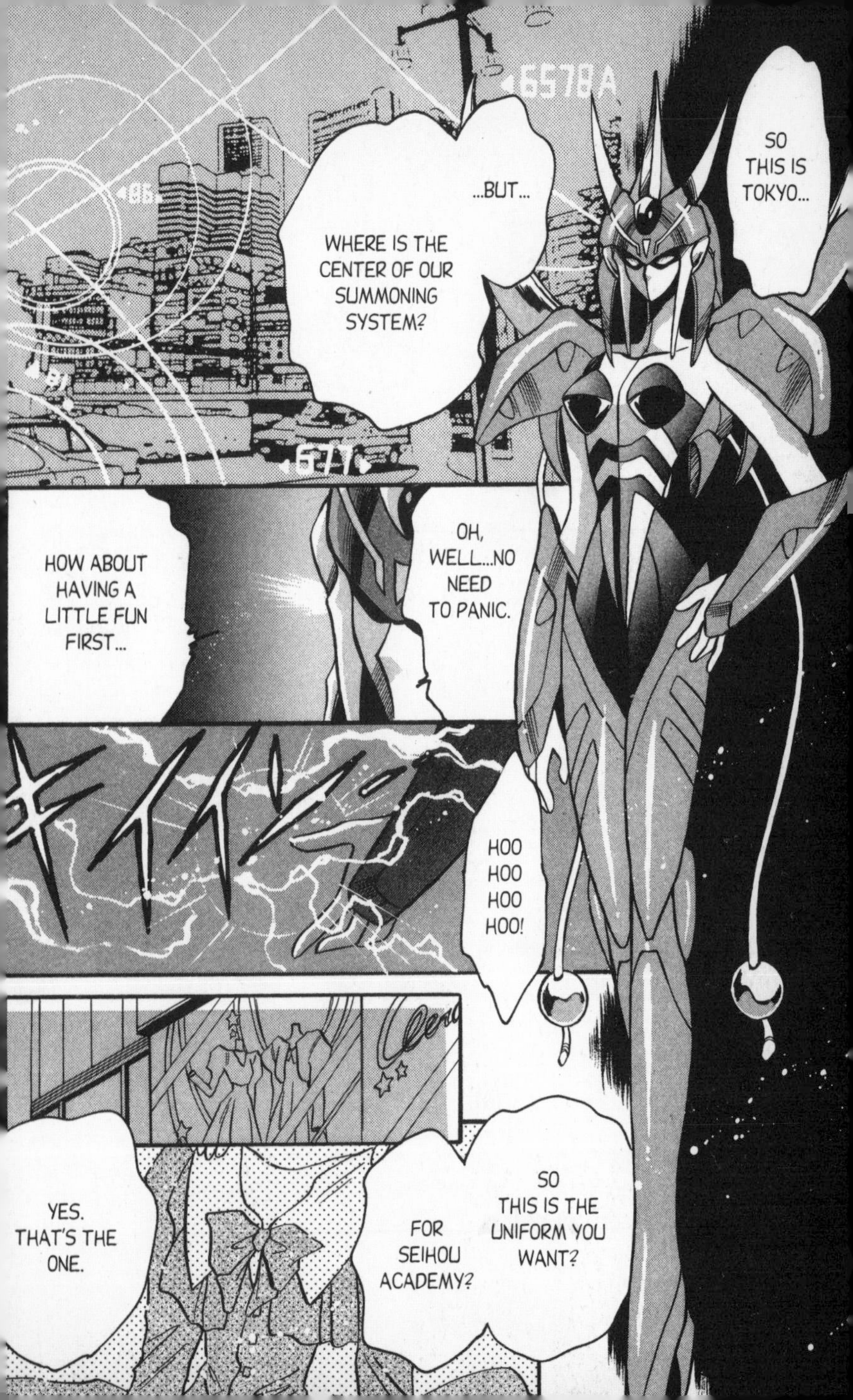
SO THIS IS TOKYO...
...BUT...
WHERE IS THE CENTER OF OUR SUMMONING SYSTEM?
OH, WELL...NO NEED TO PANIC.
HOW ABOUT HAVING A LITTLE FUN FIRST...
HOO HOO HOO HOO!
SO THIS IS THE UNIFORM YOU WANT?
FOR SEIHOU ACADEMY?
YES. THAT'S THE ONE.

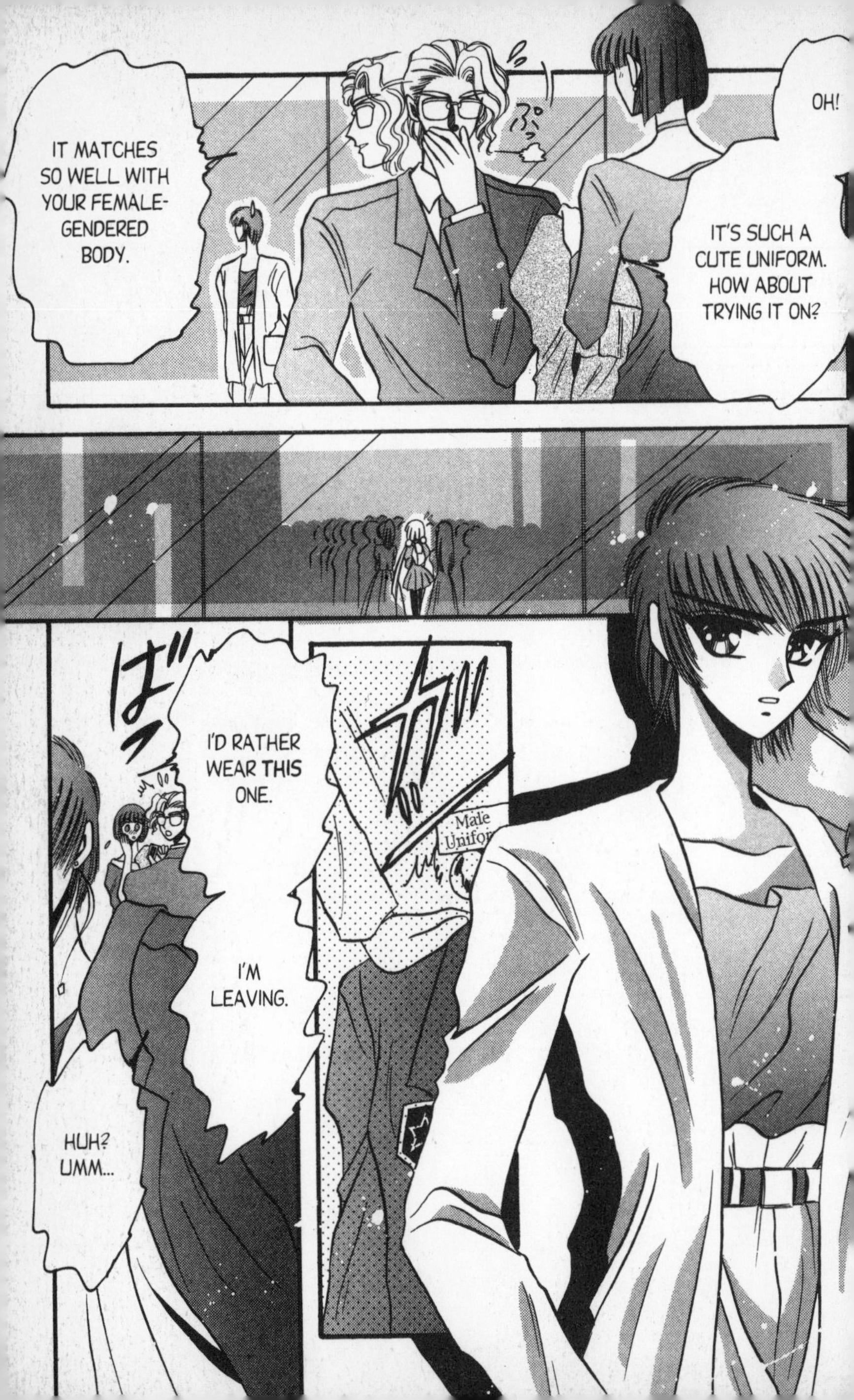
OH!
IT'S SUCH A CUTE UNIFORM. HOW ABOUT TRYING IT ON?
IT MATCHES SO WELL WITH YOUR FEMALE-GENDERED BODY.
ばっ
I'D RATHER WEAR THIS ONE.
I'M LEAVING.
HUH? UMM...

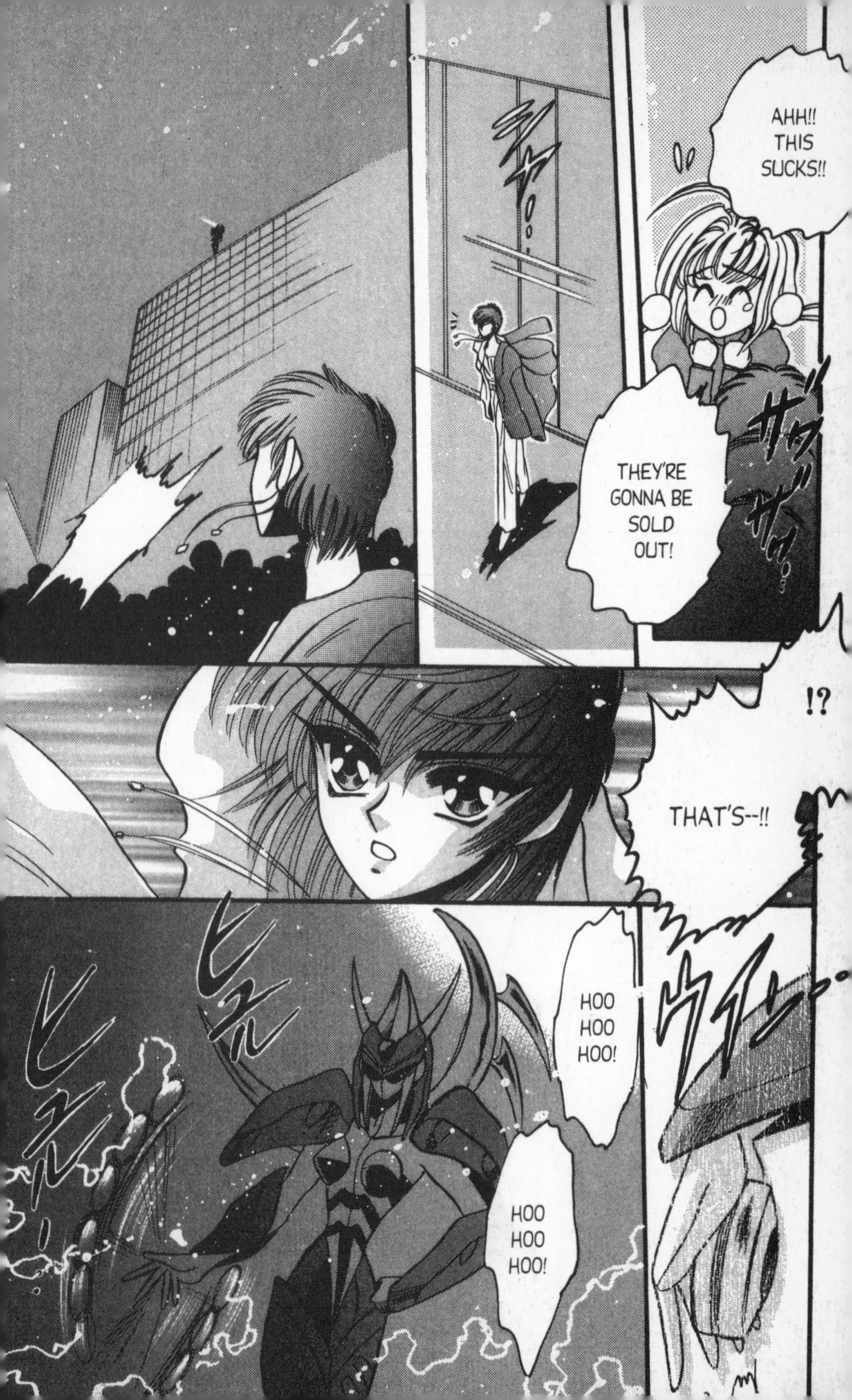
AHH!! THIS SUCKS!!
THEY'RE GONNA BE SOLD OUT!
!?
THAT'S--!!
HOO HOO HOO!
HOO HOO HOO!

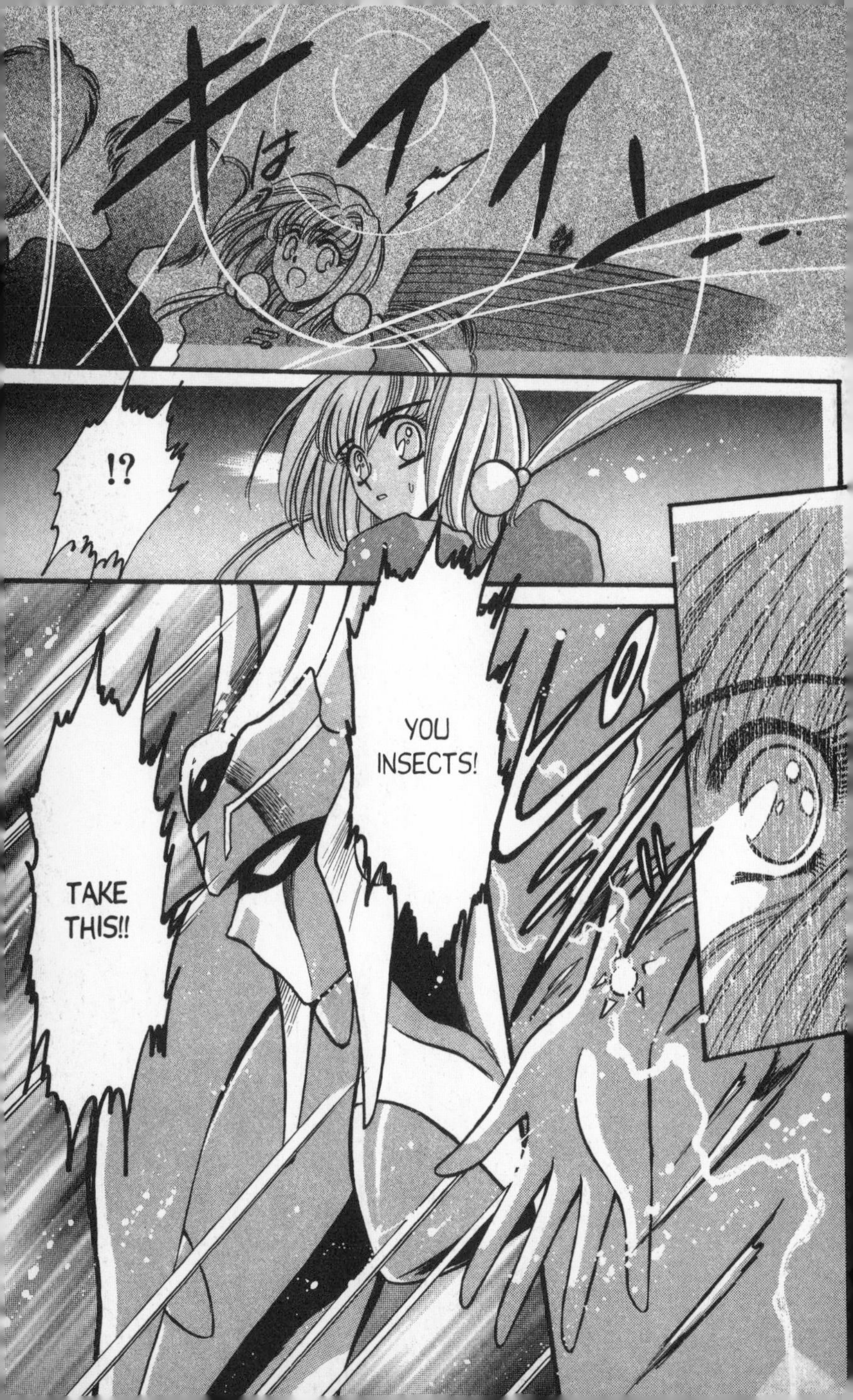

!?
YOU INSECTS!
TAKE THIS!!

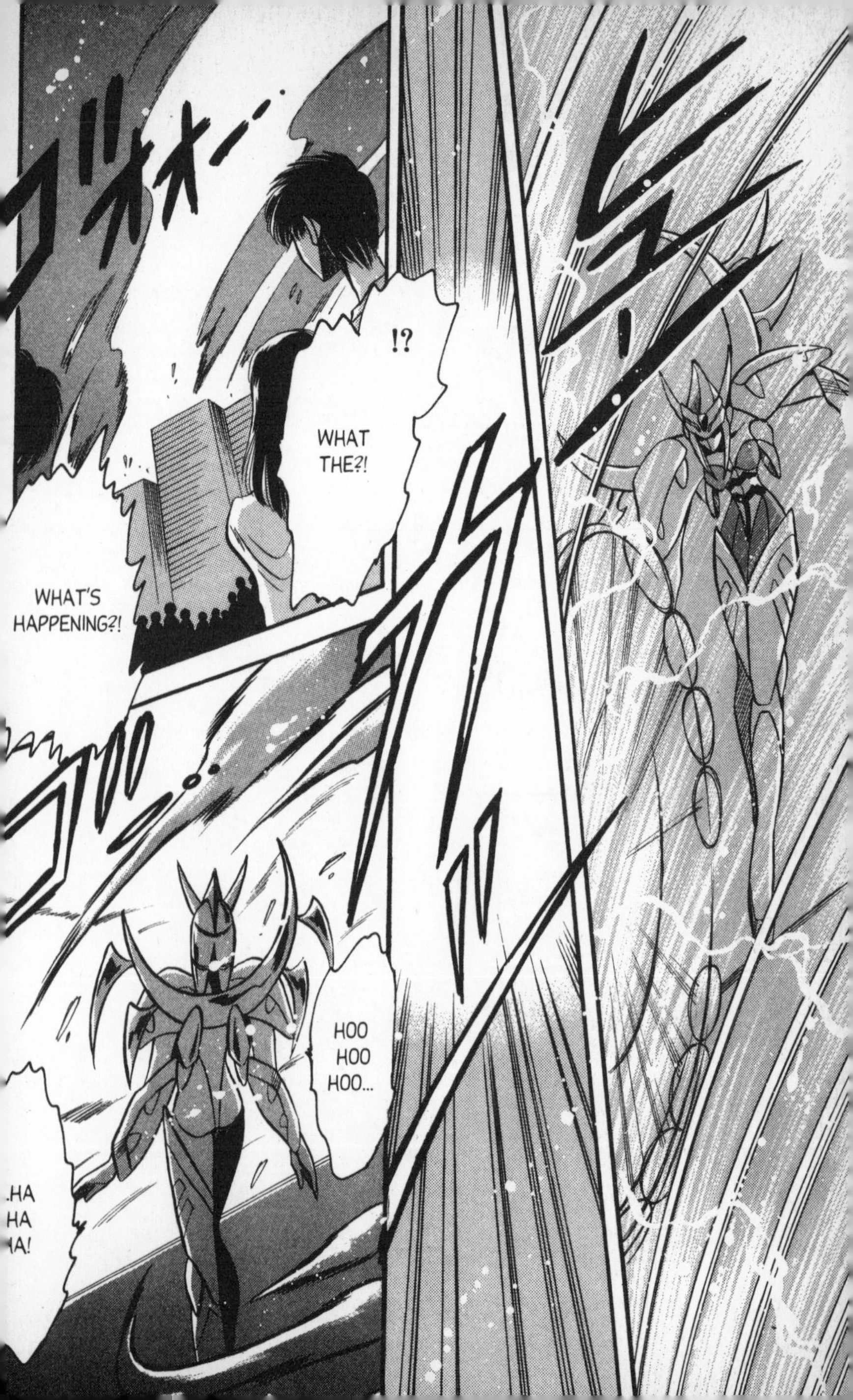
!?
WHAT THE?!
WHAT'S HAPPENING?!
HOO HOO HOO...
HA HA HA!

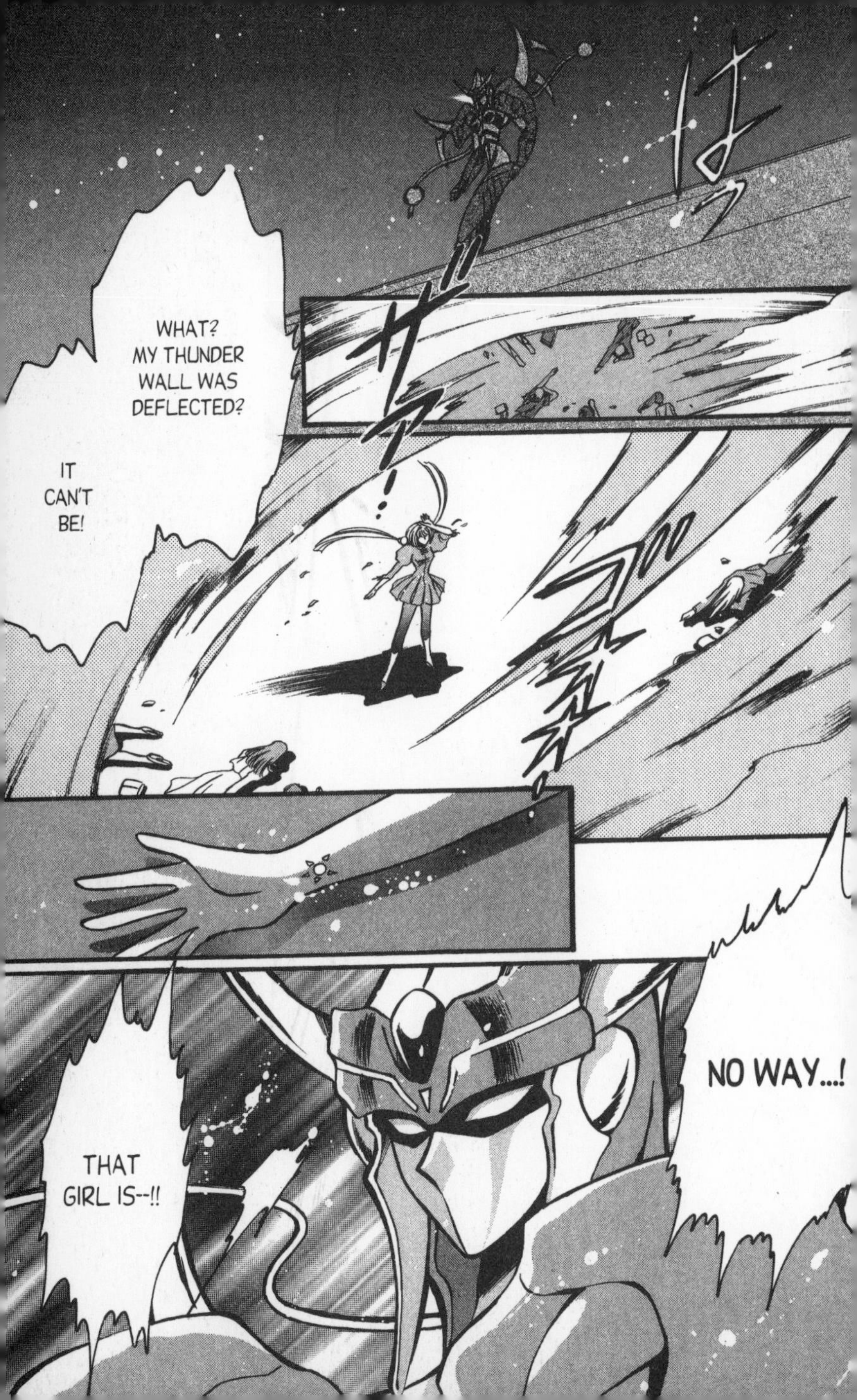
はっ
WHAT? MY THUNDER WALL WAS DEFLECTED?
IT CAN'T BE!
NO WAY...!
THAT GIRL IS--!!

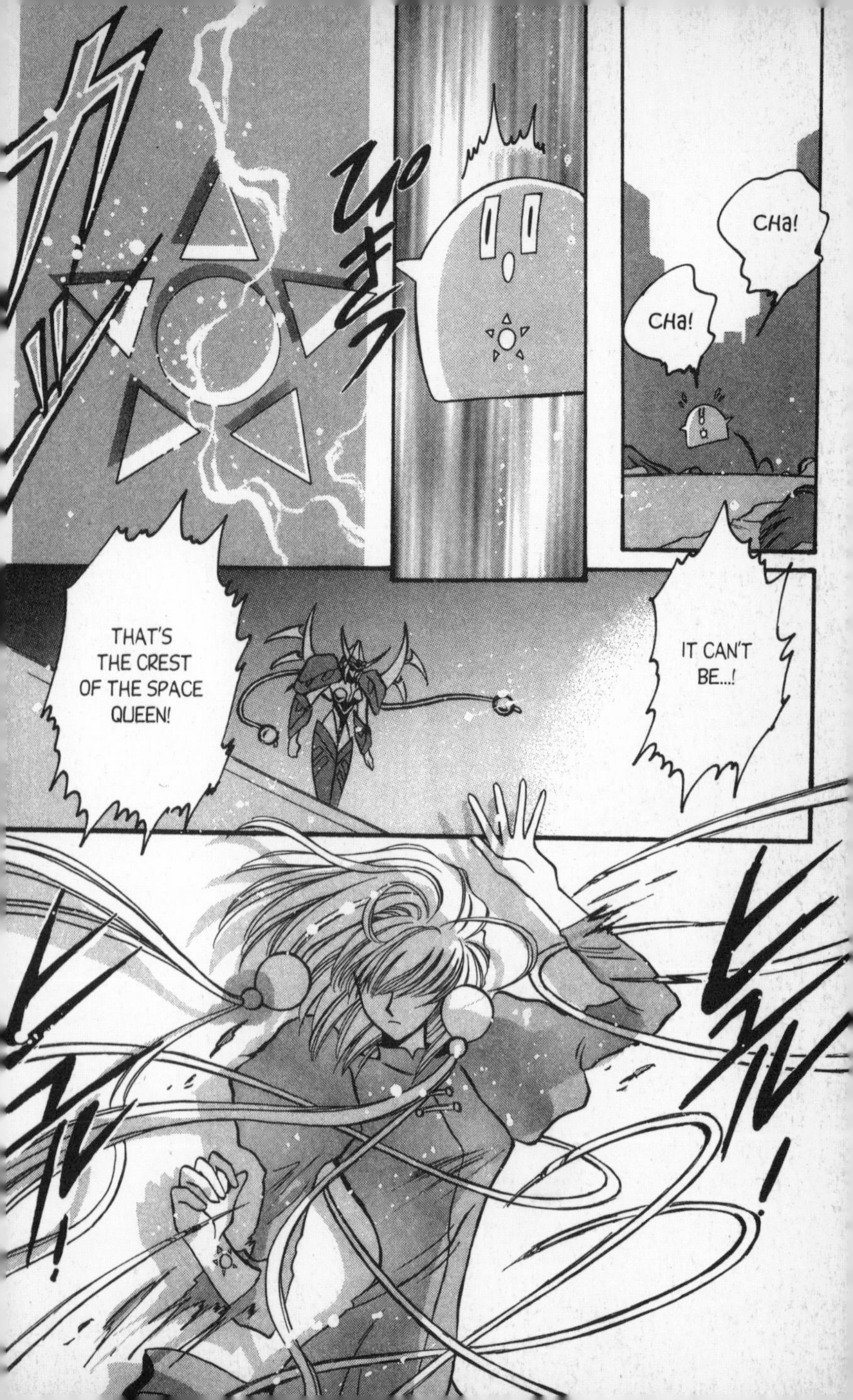
CHa!
CHa!
IT CAN'T BE...!
THAT'S THE CREST OF THE SPACE QUEEN!

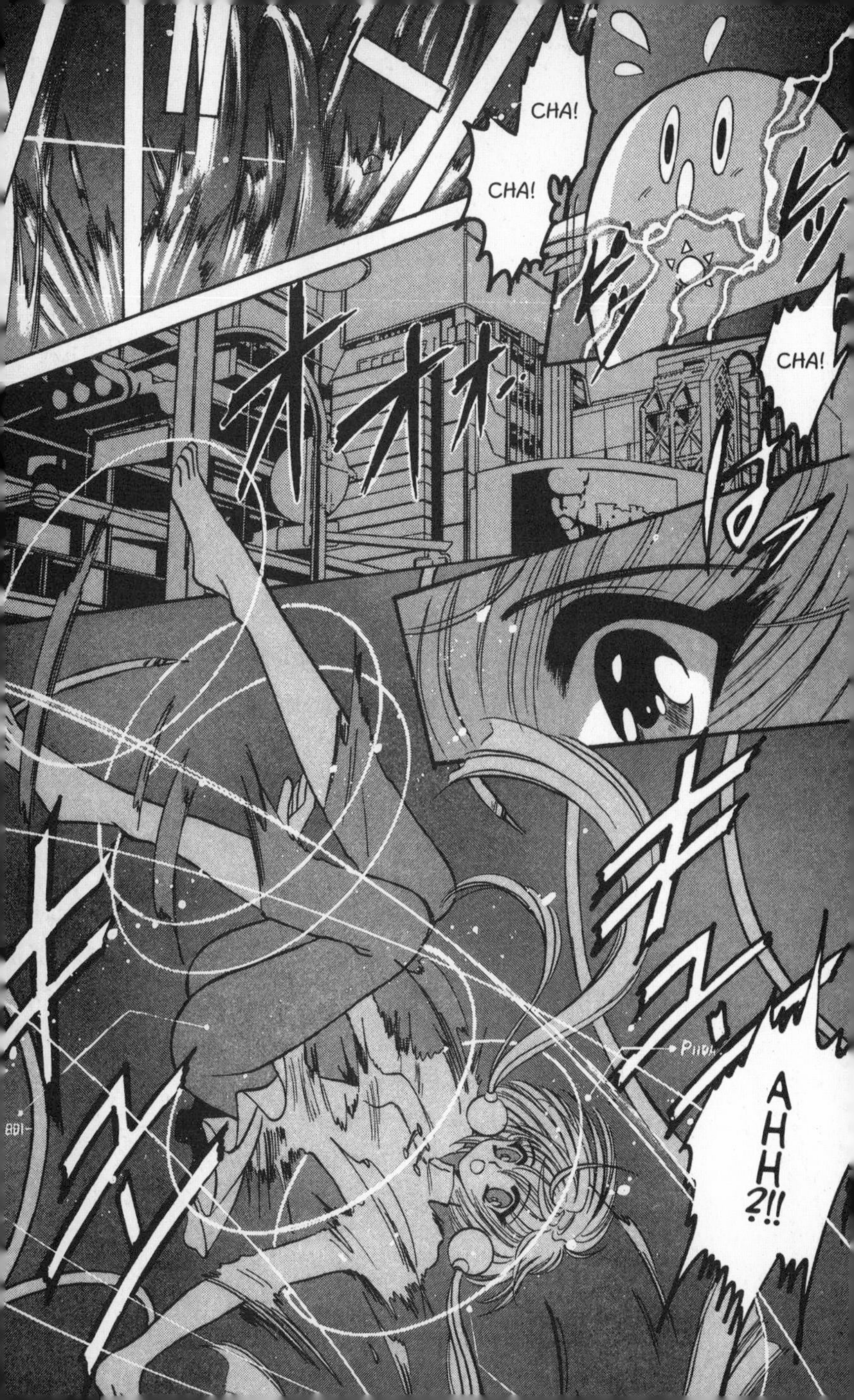
CHA!
CHA!
CHA!
AHH?!!

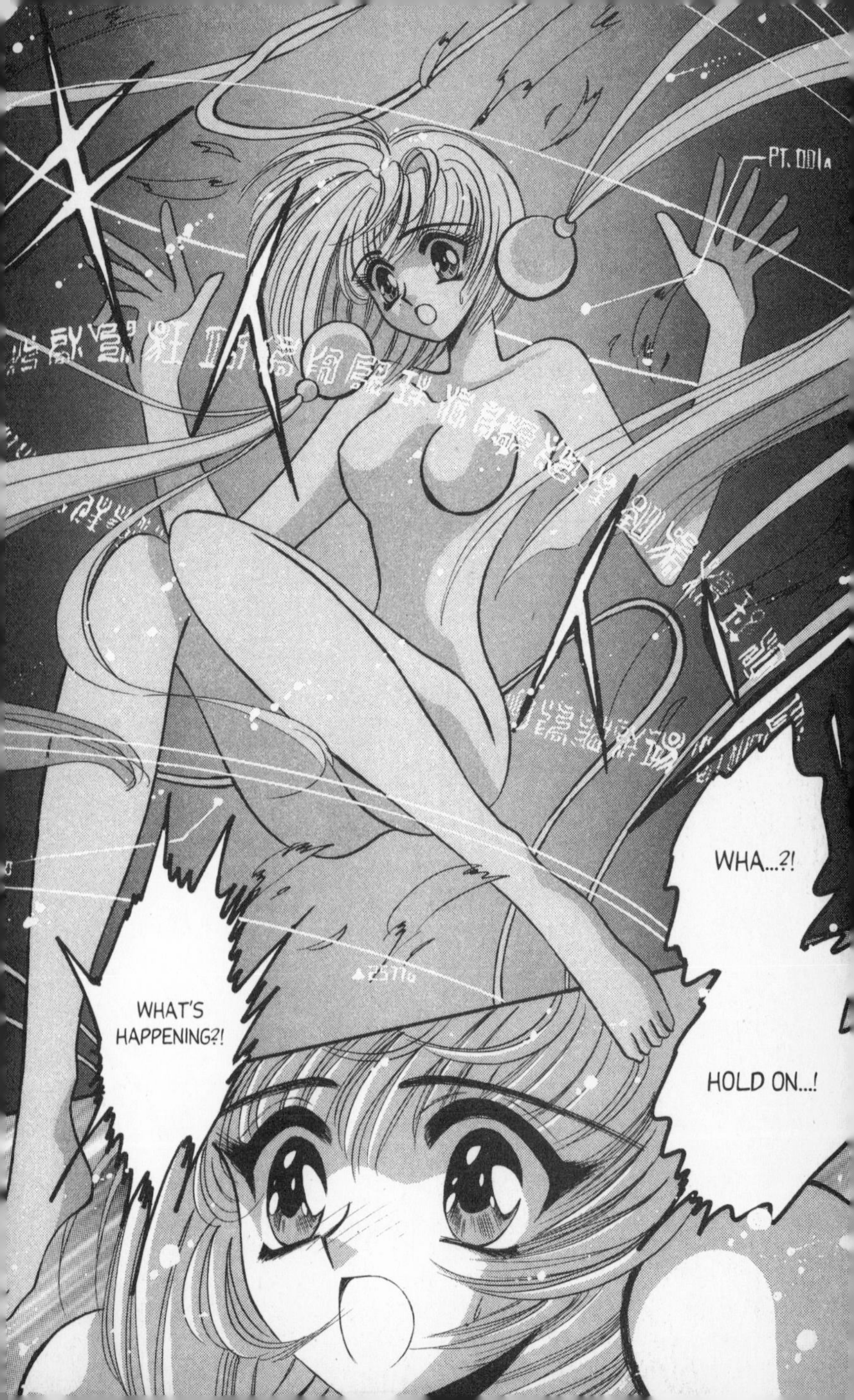
PT. 001A
WHA...?!
HOLD ON...!
WHAT'S HAPPENING?!
▲25716

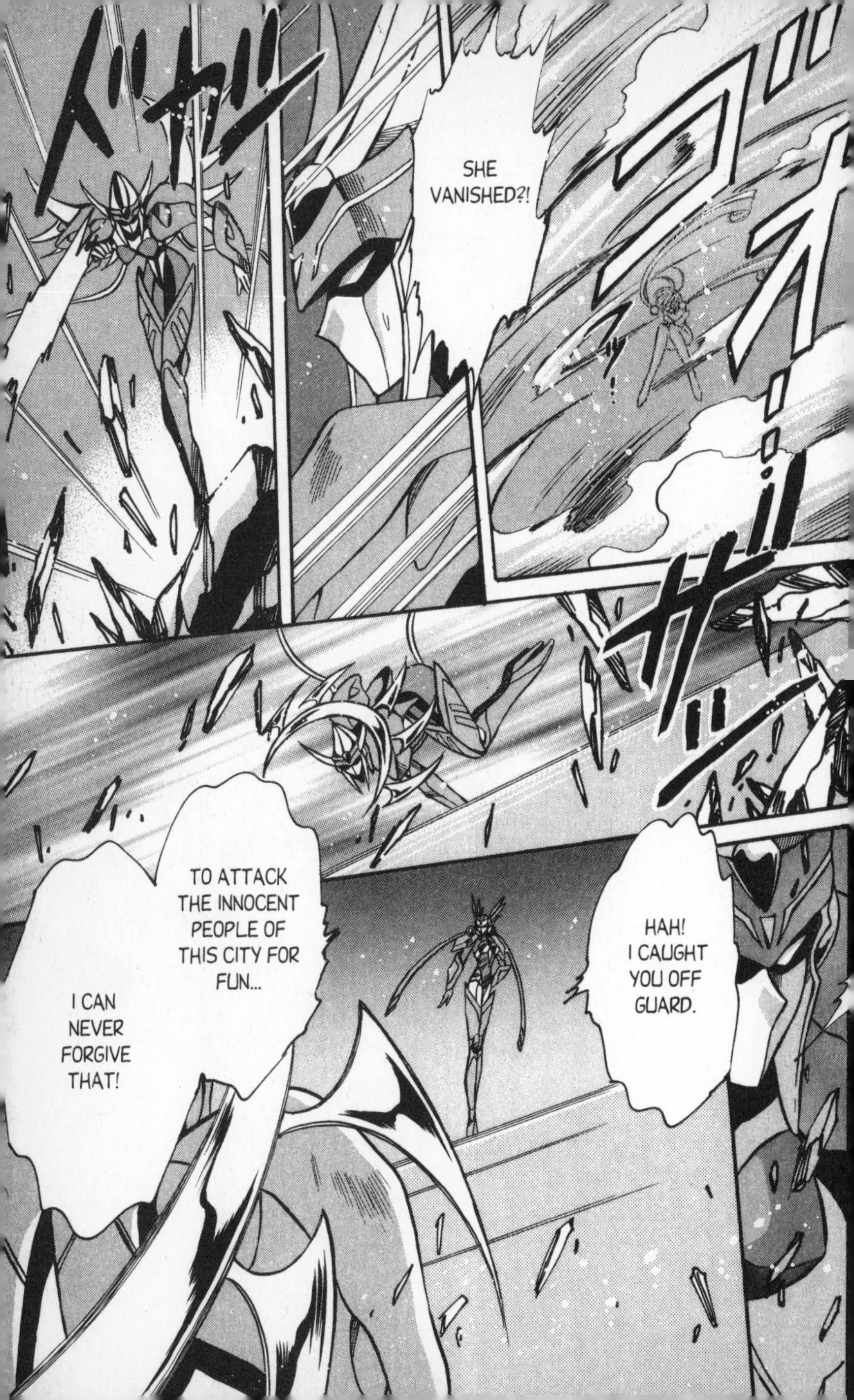
SHE VANISHED?!
HAH! I CAUGHT YOU OFF GUARD.
TO ATTACK THE INNOCENT PEOPLE OF THIS CITY FOR FUN...
I CAN NEVER FORGIVE THAT!

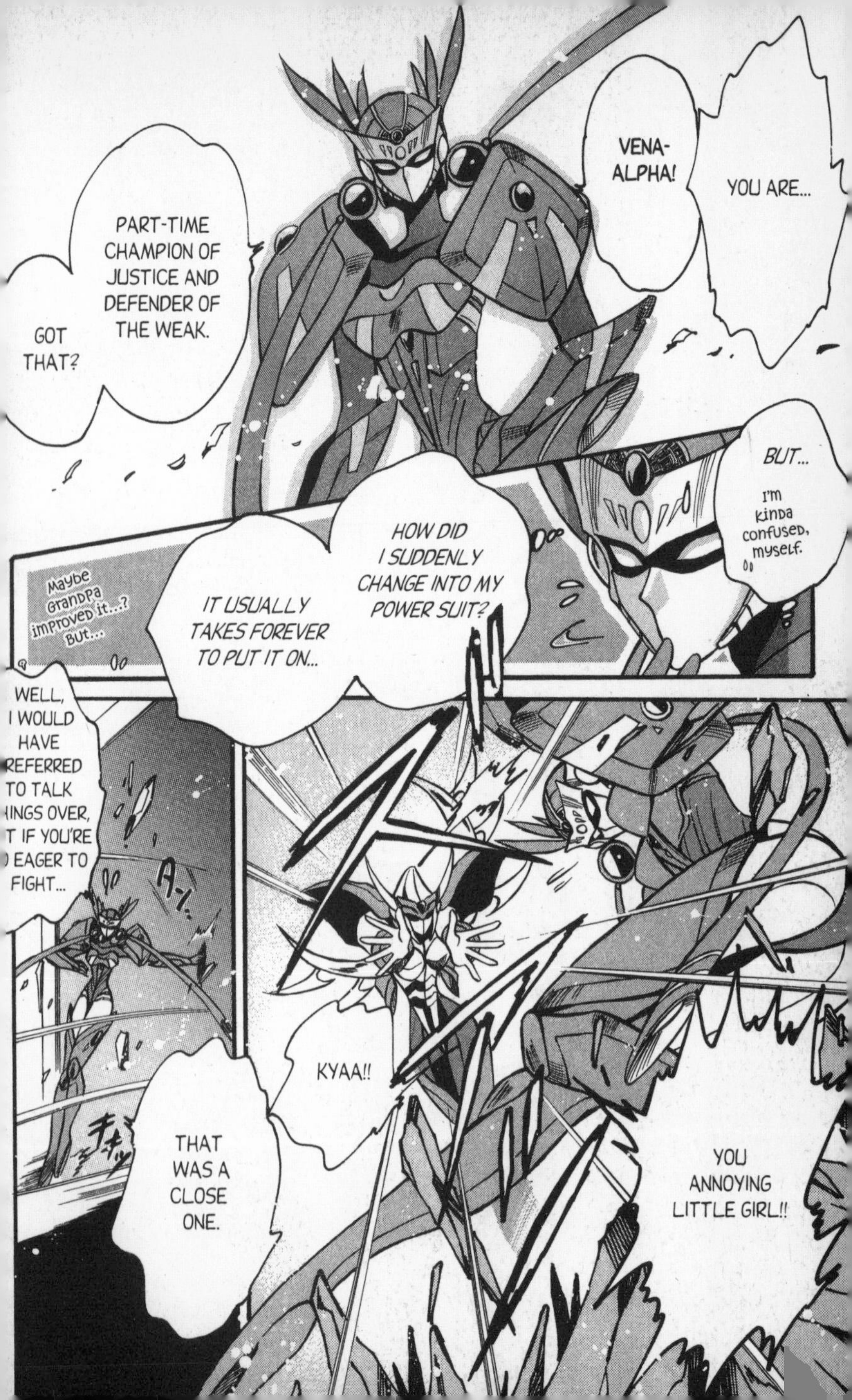
YOU ARE...
VENA-ALPHA!
PART-TIME CHAMPION OF JUSTICE AND DEFENDER OF THE WEAK.
GOT THAT?
BUT...
I'm kinda confused, myself.
HOW DID I SUDDENLY CHANGE INTO MY POWER SUIT?
IT USUALLY TAKES FOREVER TO PUT IT ON...
Maybe Grandpa improved it...? But...
YOU ANNOYING LITTLE GIRL!!
KYAA!!
THAT WAS A CLOSE ONE.
WELL, I WOULD HAVE REFERRED TO TALK HINGS OVER, T IF YOU'RE EAGER TO FIGHT...
A-!

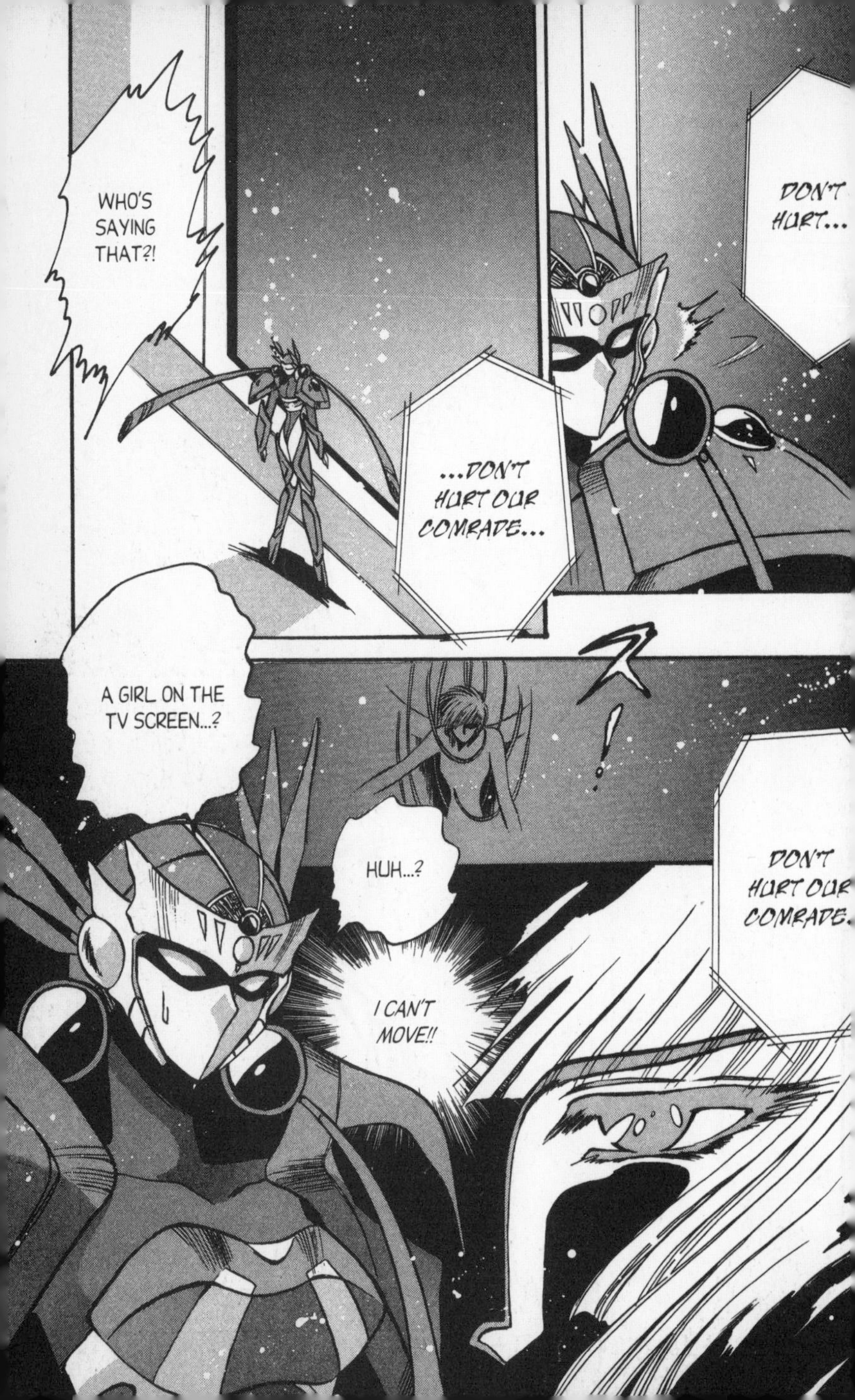
DON'T HURT...
...DON'T HURT OUR COMRADE...
WHO'S SAYING THAT?!
ス
!
A GIRL ON THE TV SCREEN...?
DON'T HURT OUR COMRADE...
HUH...?
I CAN'T MOVE!!

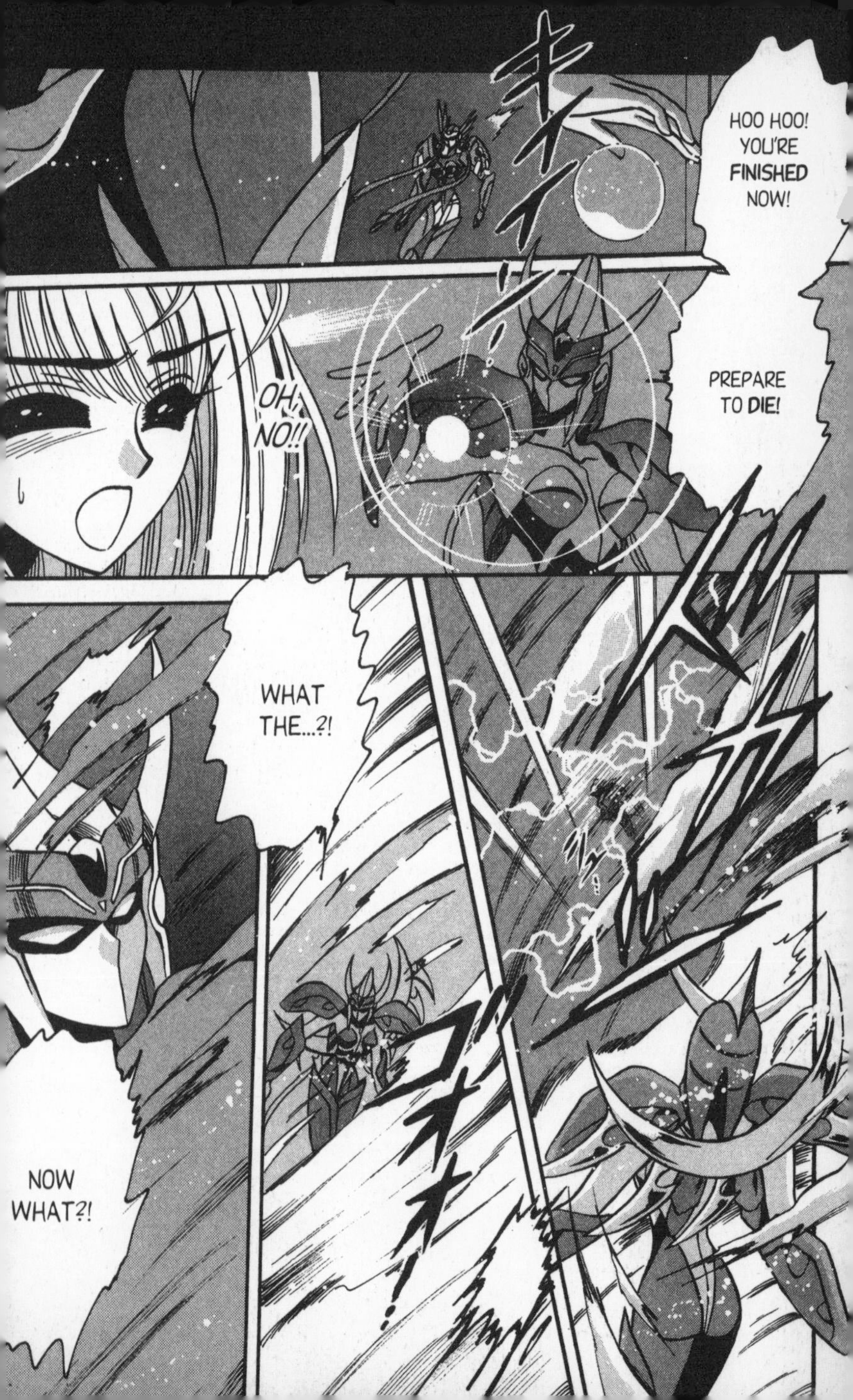
HOO HOO! YOU'RE FINISHED NOW!
PREPARE TO DIE!
OH, NO!!
WHAT THE...?!
NOW WHAT?!

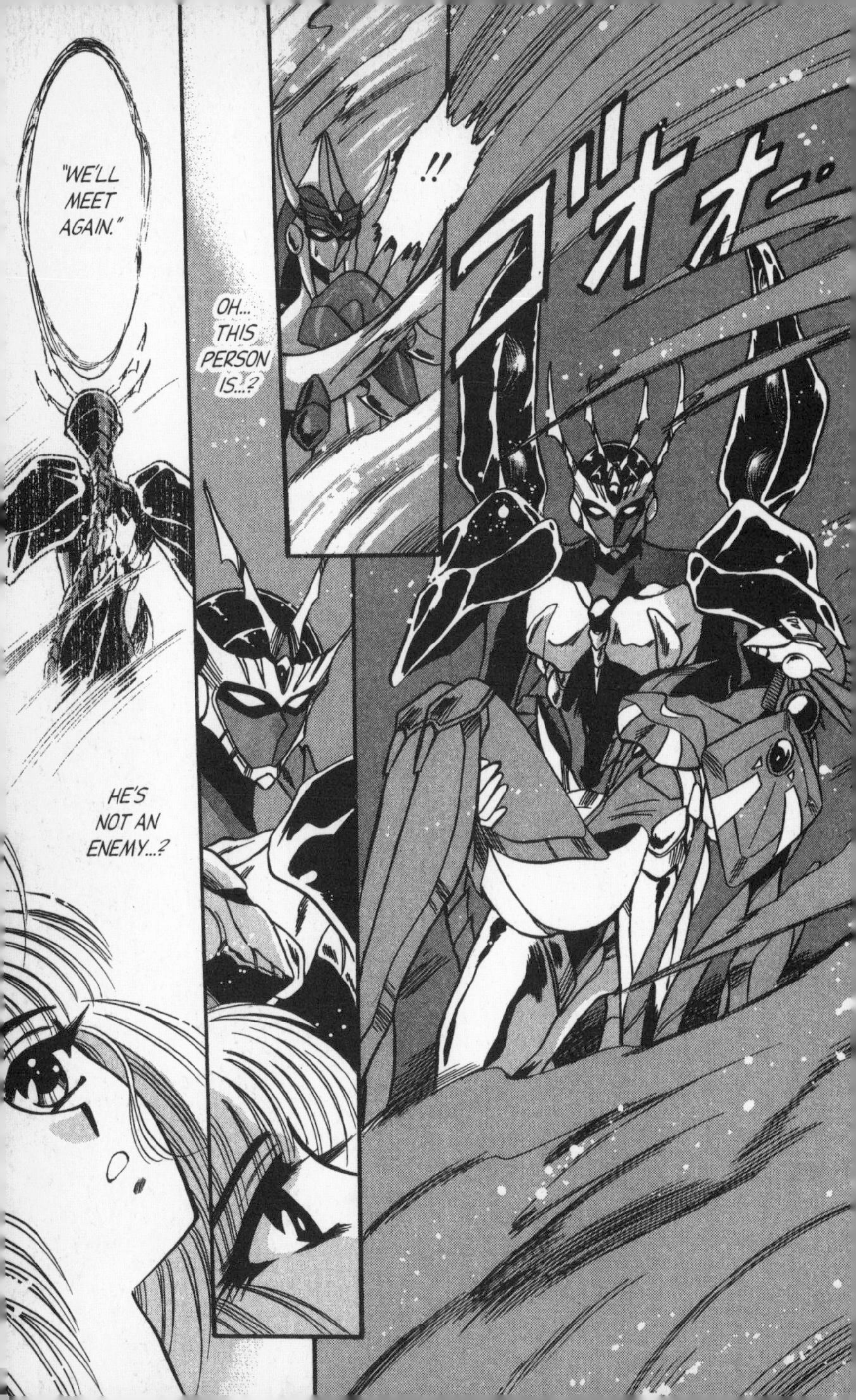
ゴオオー
!!
OH... THIS PERSON IS...?
"WE'LL MEET AGAIN."
HE'S NOT AN ENEMY...?

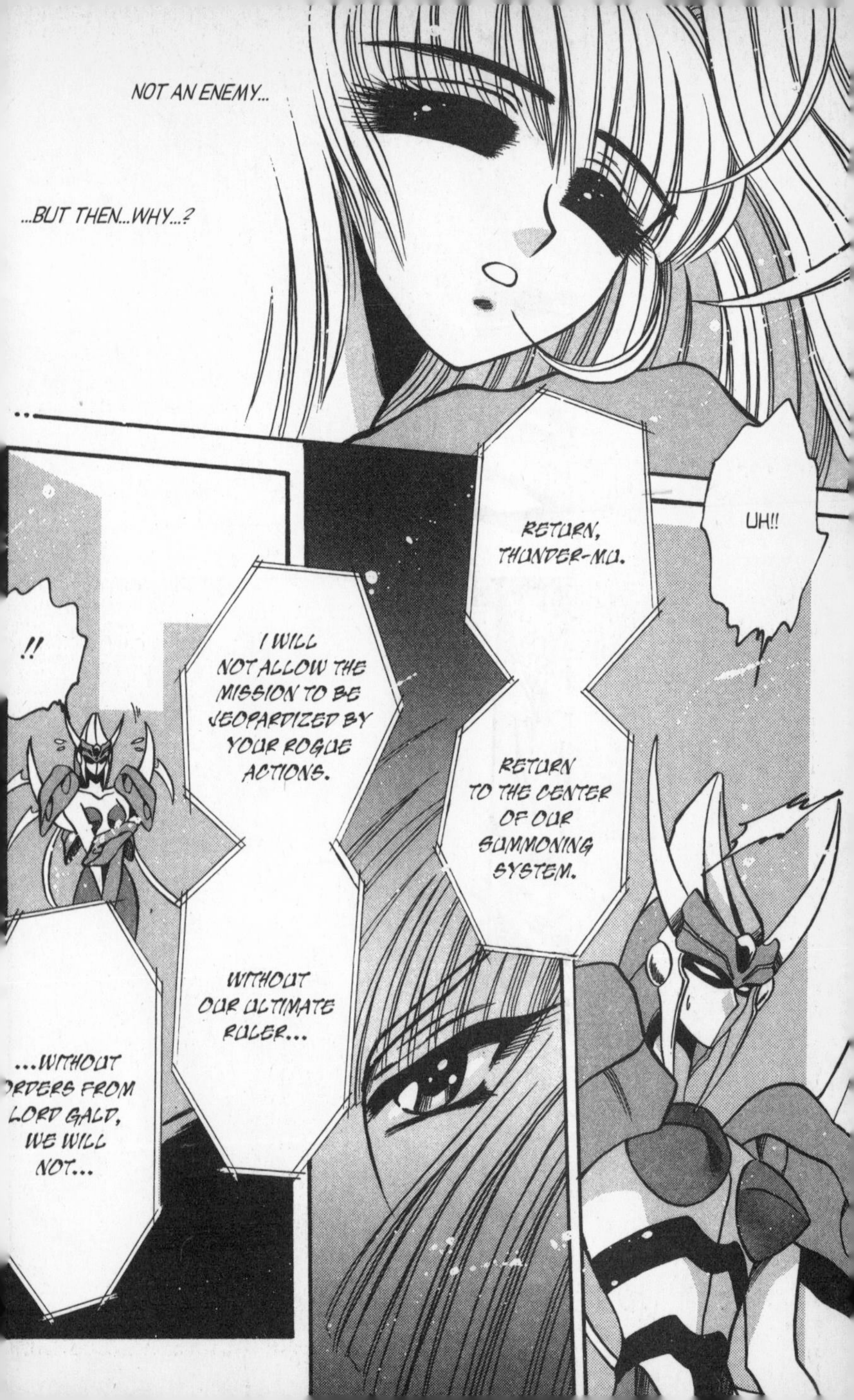
NOT AN ENEMY...
...BUT THEN...WHY...?
...
UH!!
RETURN, THUNDER-MU.
RETURN TO THE CENTER OF OUR SUMMONING SYSTEM.
I WILL NOT ALLOW THE MISSION TO BE JEOPARDIZED BY YOUR ROGUE ACTIONS.
WITHOUT OUR ULTIMATE RULER...
!!
...WITHOUT ORDERS FROM LORD GALD, WE WILL NOT...

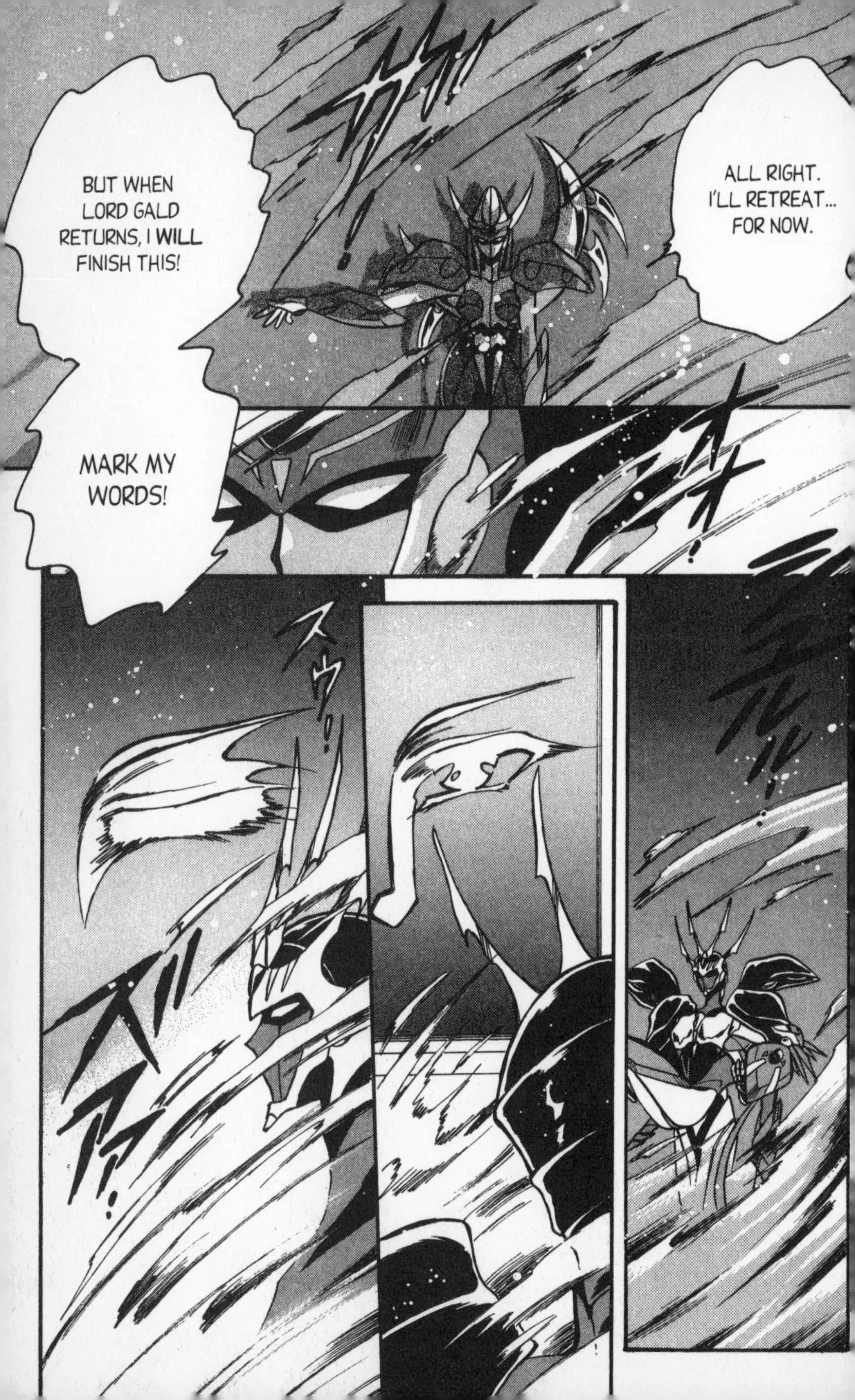
ALL RIGHT. I'LL RETREAT... FOR NOW.
BUT WHEN LORD GALD RETURNS, I WILL FINISH THIS!
MARK MY WORDS!

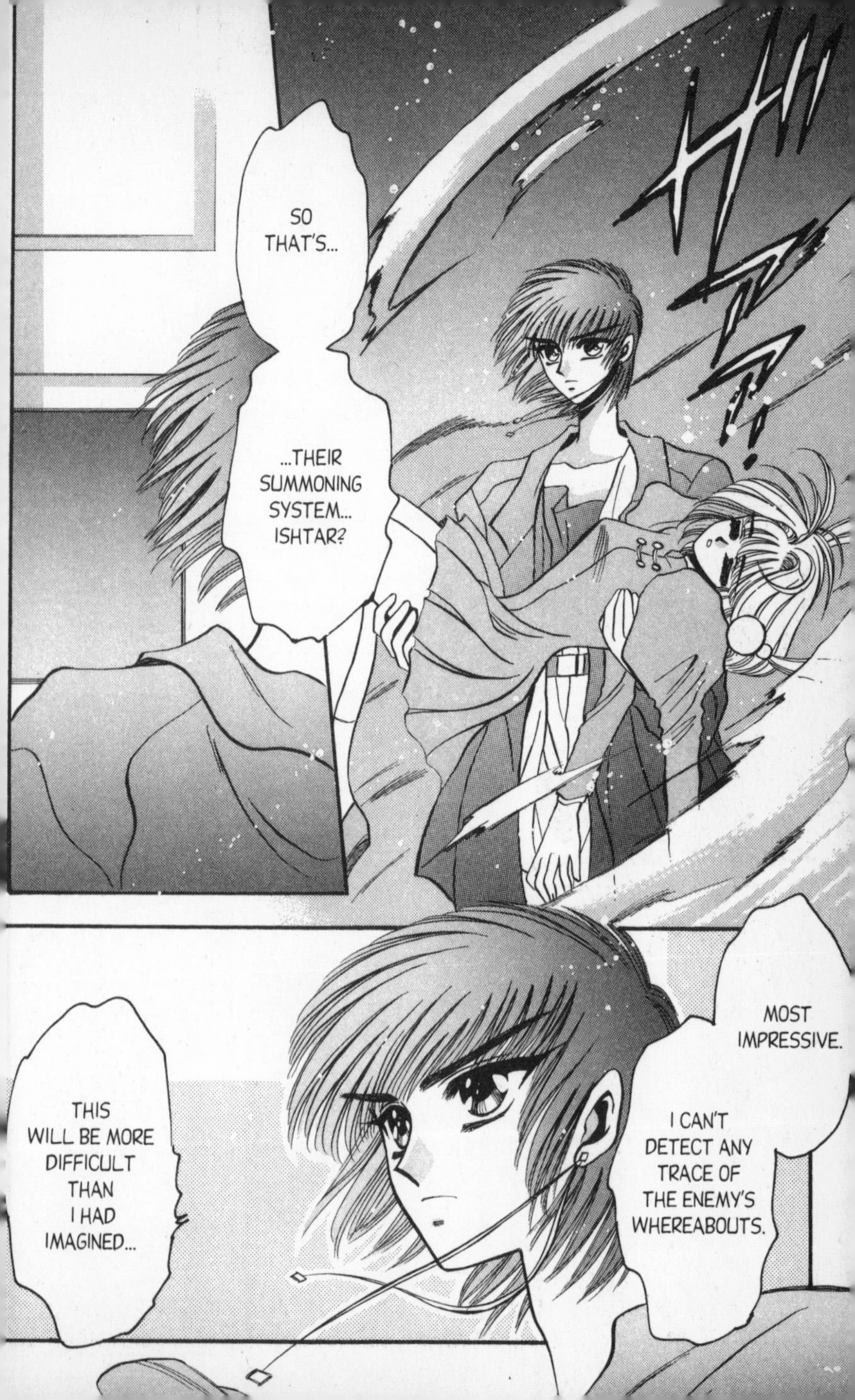
SO THAT'S...
...THEIR SUMMONING SYSTEM... ISHTAR?
MOST IMPRESSIVE.
I CAN'T DETECT ANY TRACE OF THE ENEMY'S WHEREABOUTS.
THIS WILL BE MORE DIFFICULT THAN I HAD IMAGINED...

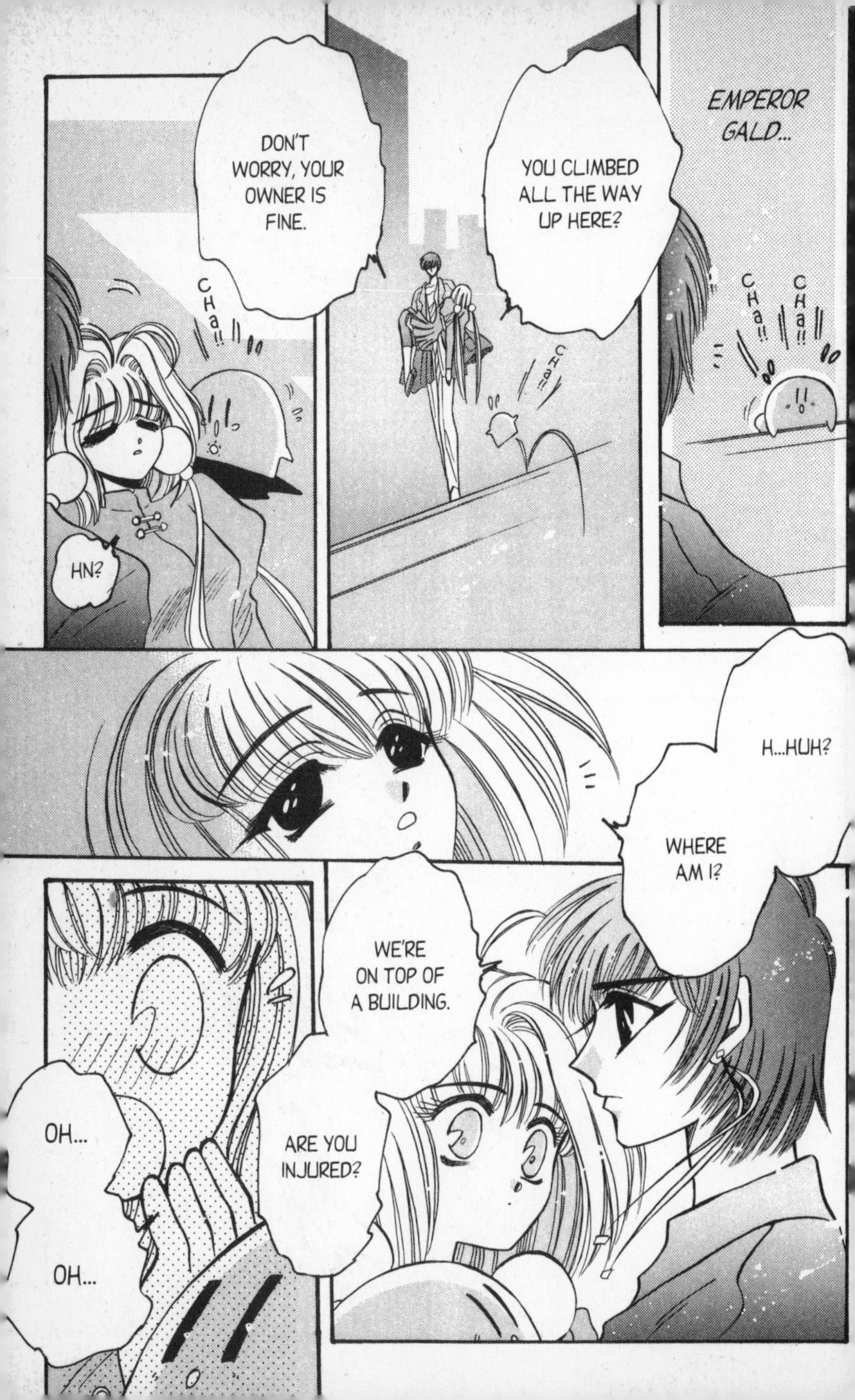
EMPEROR GALD...
CHa!! CHa!!
YOU CLIMBED ALL THE WAY UP HERE?
CHa!!
DON'T WORRY, YOUR OWNER IS FINE.
CHa!!
HN?
H...HUH?
WHERE AM I?
WE'RE ON TOP OF A BUILDING.
ARE YOU INJURED?
OH...
OH...

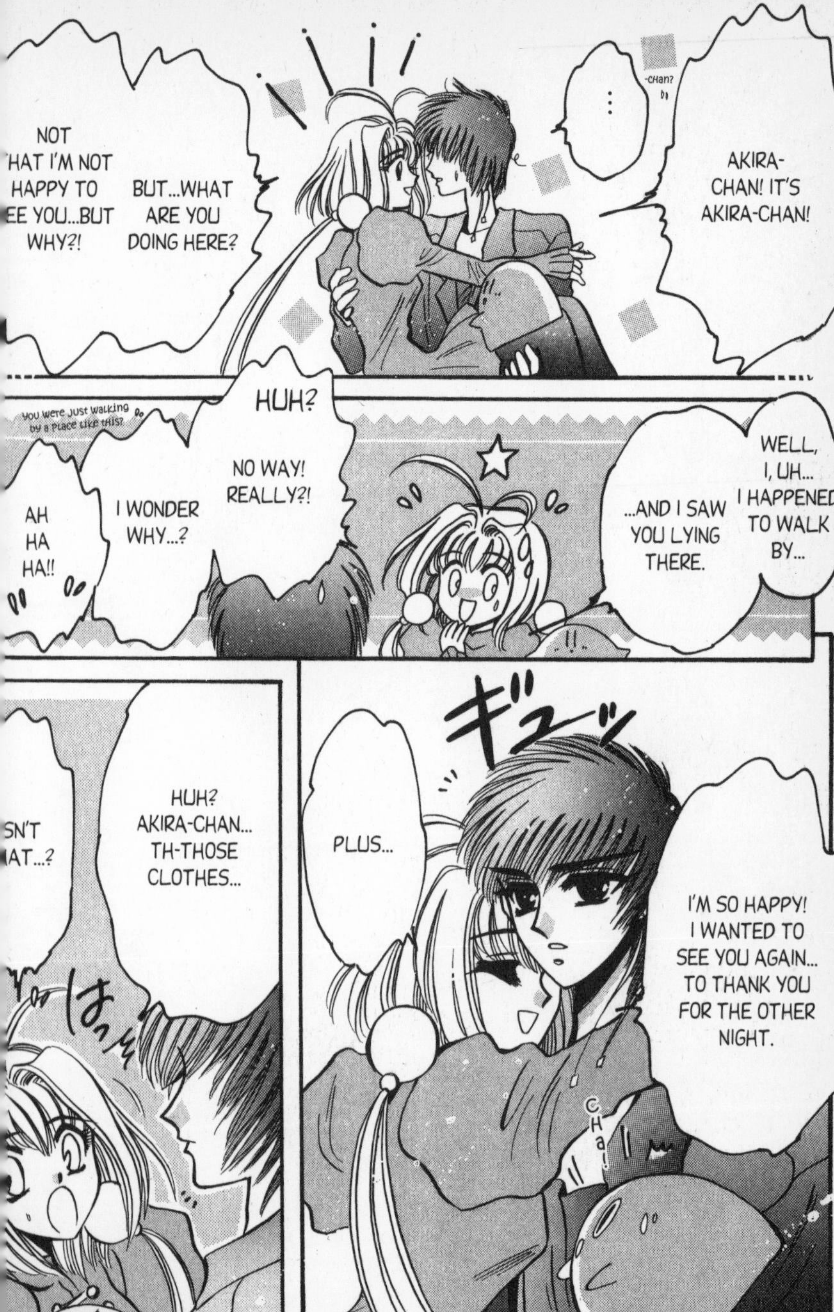
AKIRA-CHAN! IT'S AKIRA-CHAN!
-chan?
...
BUT...WHAT ARE YOU DOING HERE?
NOT HAT I'M NOT HAPPY TO EE YOU...BUT WHY?!
WELL, I, UH... I HAPPENED TO WALK BY...
...AND I SAW YOU LYING THERE.
HUH?
NO WAY! REALLY?!
I WONDER WHY...?
AH HA HA!!
You were just walking by a place like this?
ギューッ
I'M SO HAPPY! I WANTED TO SEE YOU AGAIN... TO THANK YOU FOR THE OTHER NIGHT.
PLUS...
Cha!
HUH? AKIRA-CHAN... TH-THOSE CLOTHES...
SN'T AT...?
はっ

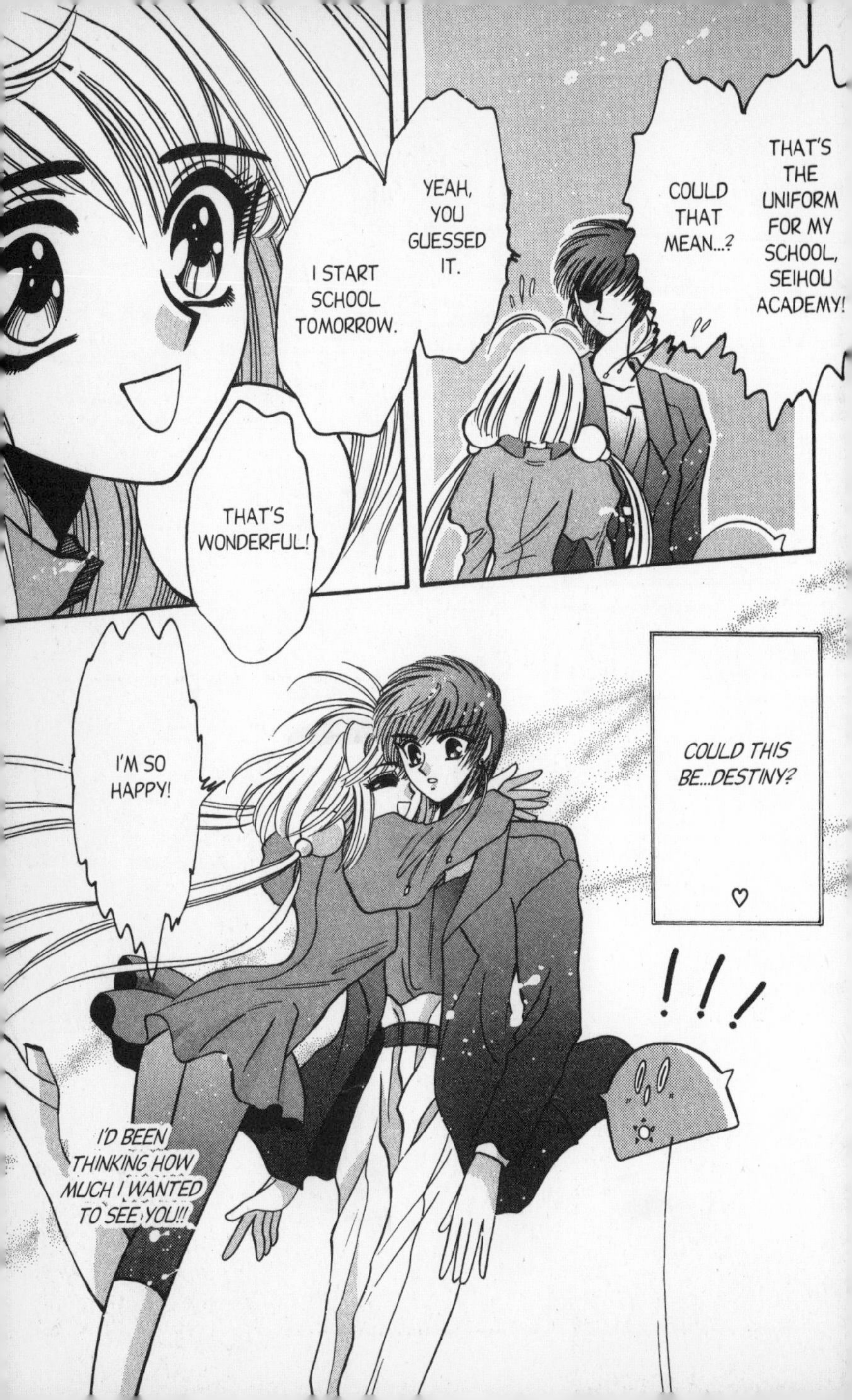
THAT'S THE UNIFORM FOR MY SCHOOL, SEIHOU ACADEMY!
COULD THAT MEAN...?
YEAH, YOU GUESSED IT.
I START SCHOOL TOMORROW.
THAT'S WONDERFUL!
COULD THIS BE...DESTINY? ♡
!!!
I'M SO HAPPY!
I'D BEEN THINKING HOW MUCH I WANTED TO SEE YOU!!

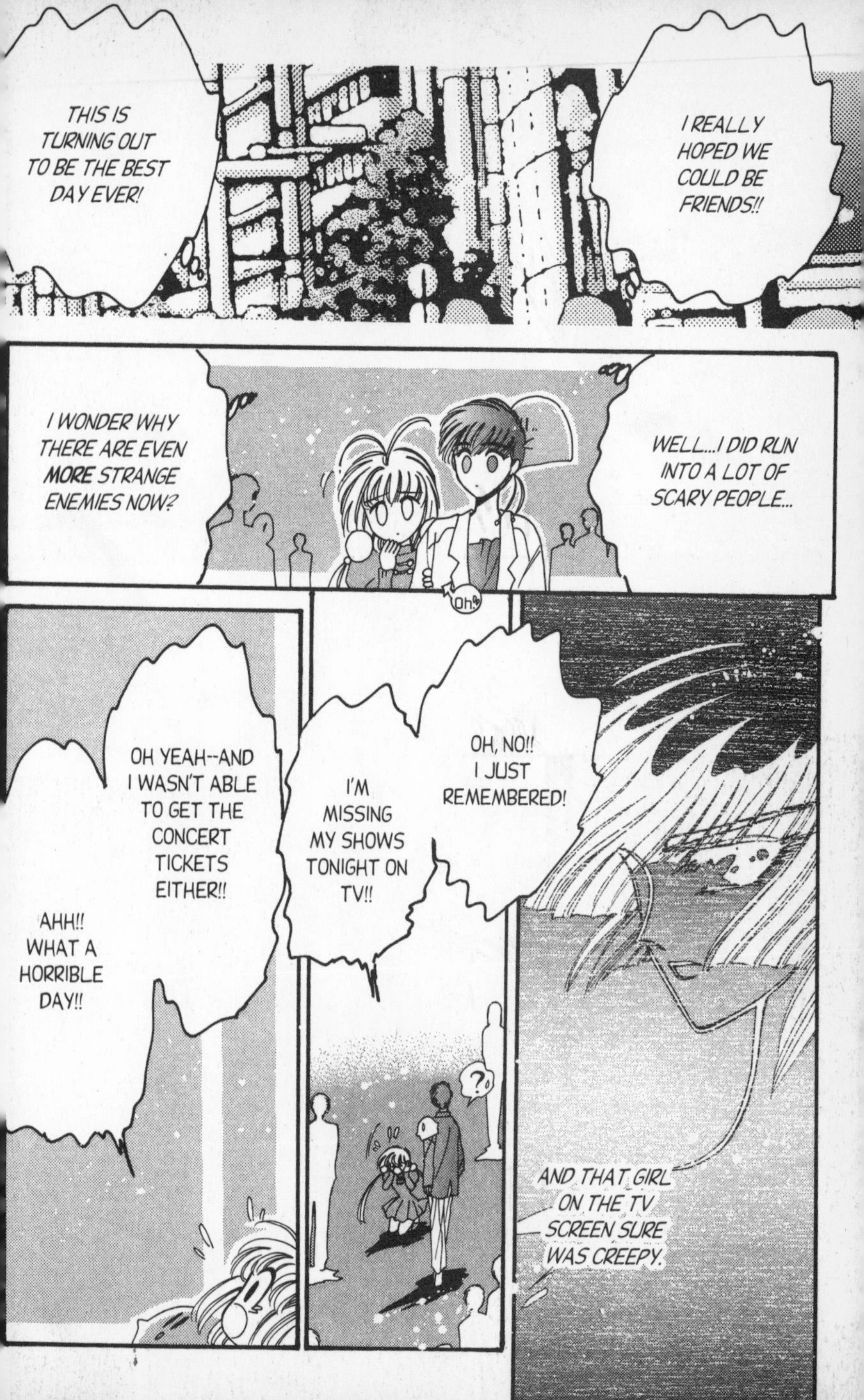
I REALLY HOPED WE COULD BE FRIENDS!!
THIS IS TURNING OUT TO BE THE BEST DAY EVER!
WELL...I DID RUN INTO A LOT OF SCARY PEOPLE...
I WONDER WHY THERE ARE EVEN MORE STRANGE ENEMIES NOW?
Oh
AND THAT GIRL ON THE TV SCREEN SURE WAS CREEPY.
OH, NO!! I JUST REMEMBERED!
I'M MISSING MY SHOWS TONIGHT ON TV!!
?
OH YEAH--AND I WASN'T ABLE TO GET THE CONCERT TICKETS EITHER!!
AHH!! WHAT A HORRIBLE DAY!!

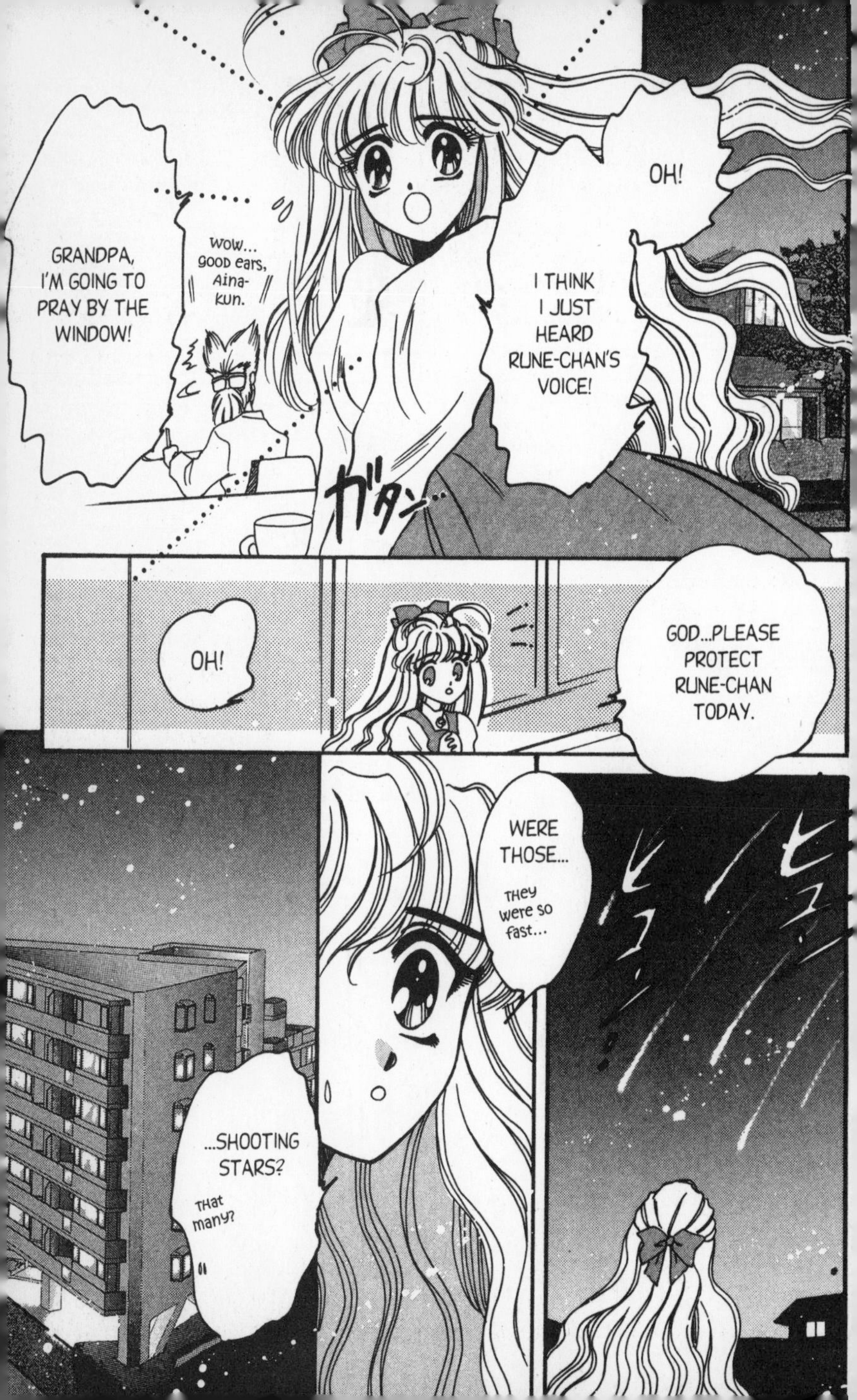
OH!
I THINK I JUST HEARD RUNE-CHAN'S VOICE!
WOW... GOOD ears, Aina-kun.
GRANDPA, I'M GOING TO PRAY BY THE WINDOW!
ガタン
GOD...PLEASE PROTECT RUNE-CHAN TODAY.
OH!
WERE THOSE...
THey were so fast...
...SHOOTING STARS?
THat many?

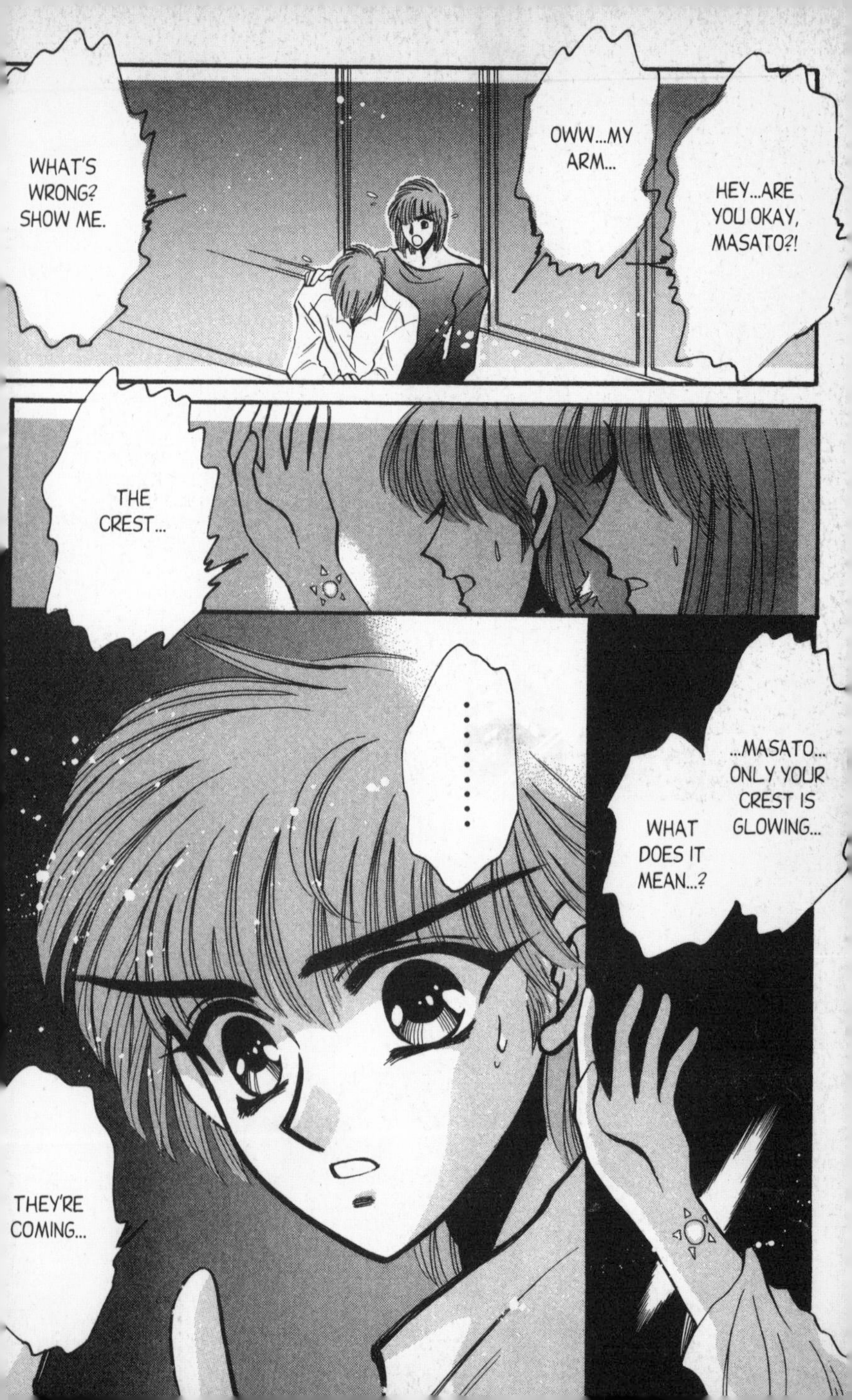
HEY...ARE YOU OKAY, MASATO?!
OWW...MY ARM...
WHAT'S WRONG? SHOW ME.
THE CREST...
...MASATO... ONLY YOUR CREST IS GLOWING...
WHAT DOES IT MEAN...?
....
THEY'RE COMING...

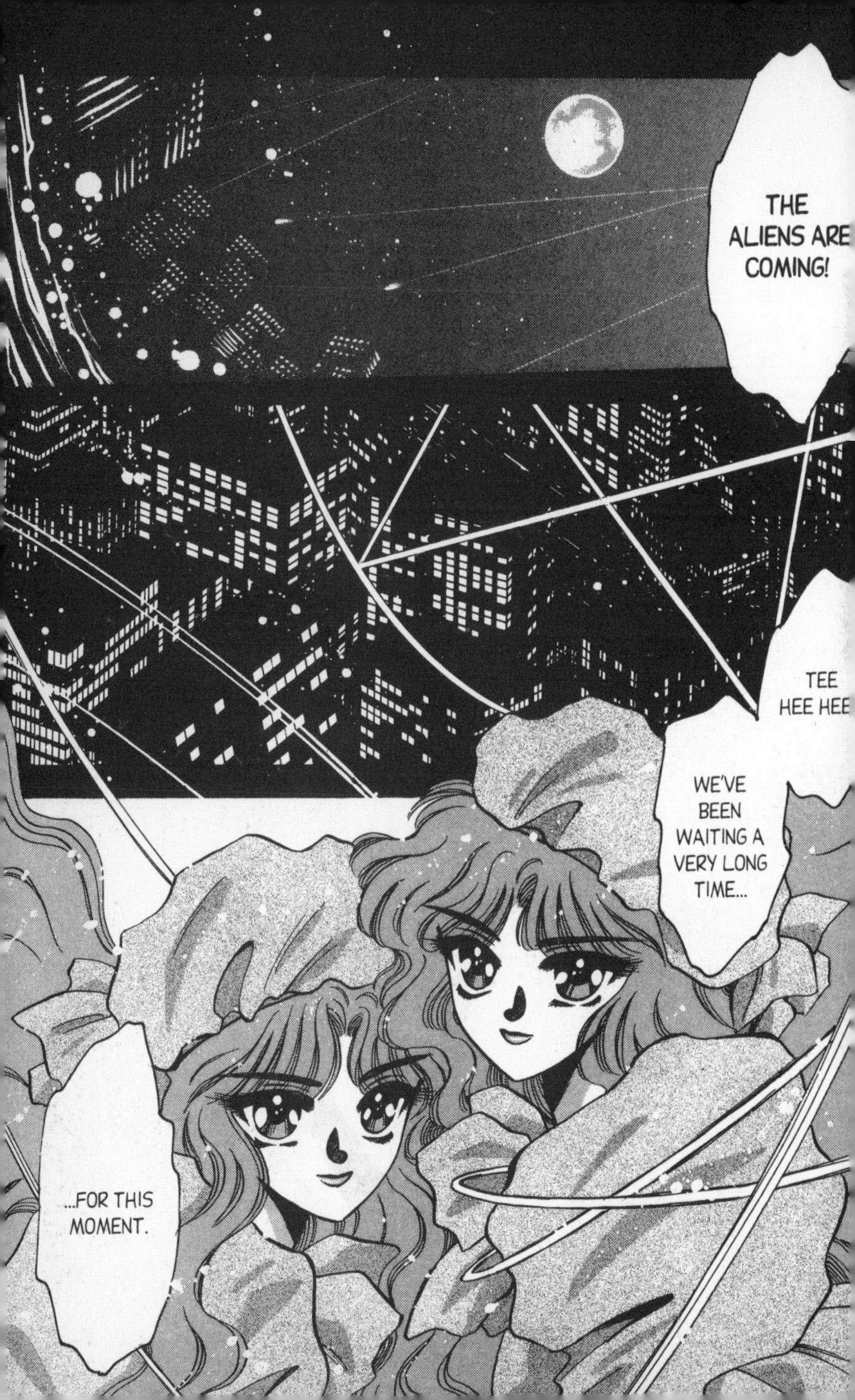
THE ALIENS ARE COMING!
TEE HEE HEE
WE'VE BEEN WAITING A VERY LONG TIME...
...FOR THIS MOMENT.

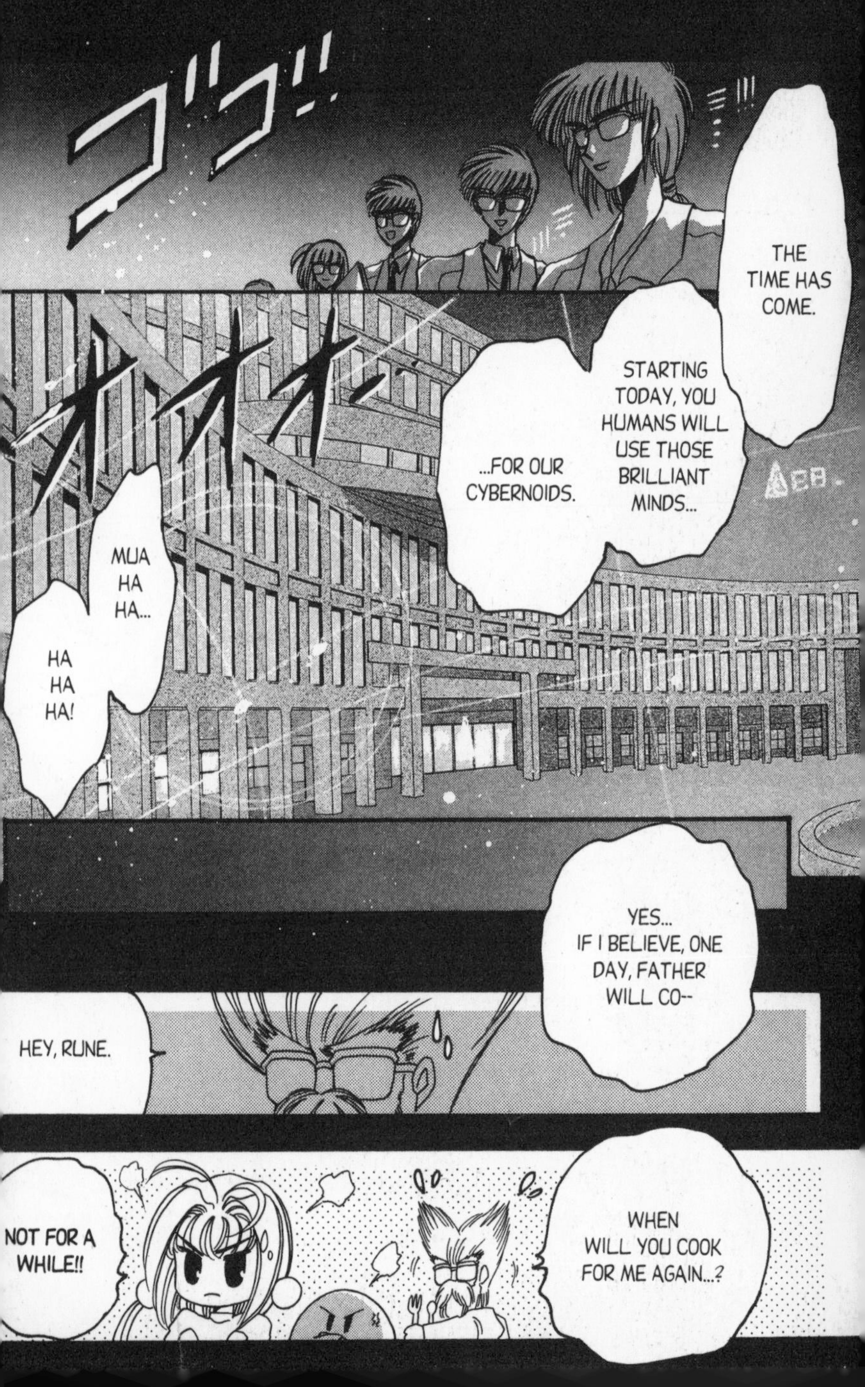
ゴゴ!!
THE TIME HAS COME.
STARTING TODAY, YOU HUMANS WILL USE THOSE BRILLIANT MINDS...
...FOR OUR CYBERNOIDS.
オオオ
MUA HA HA...
HA HA HA!
YES... IF I BELIEVE, ONE DAY, FATHER WILL CO--
HEY, RUNE.
WHEN WILL YOU COOK FOR ME AGAIN...?
NOT FOR A WHILE!!

TRANSFORMATION 4

EXPLOSION【急展開】

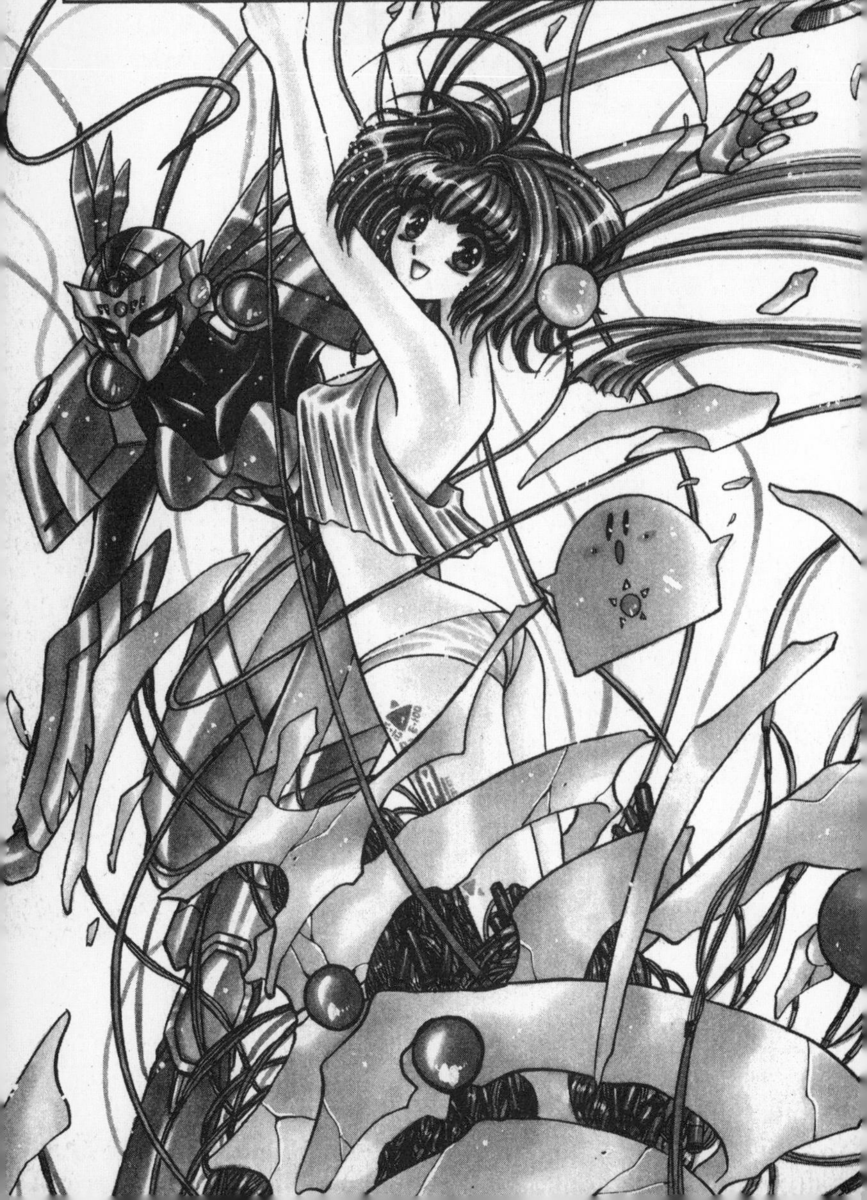

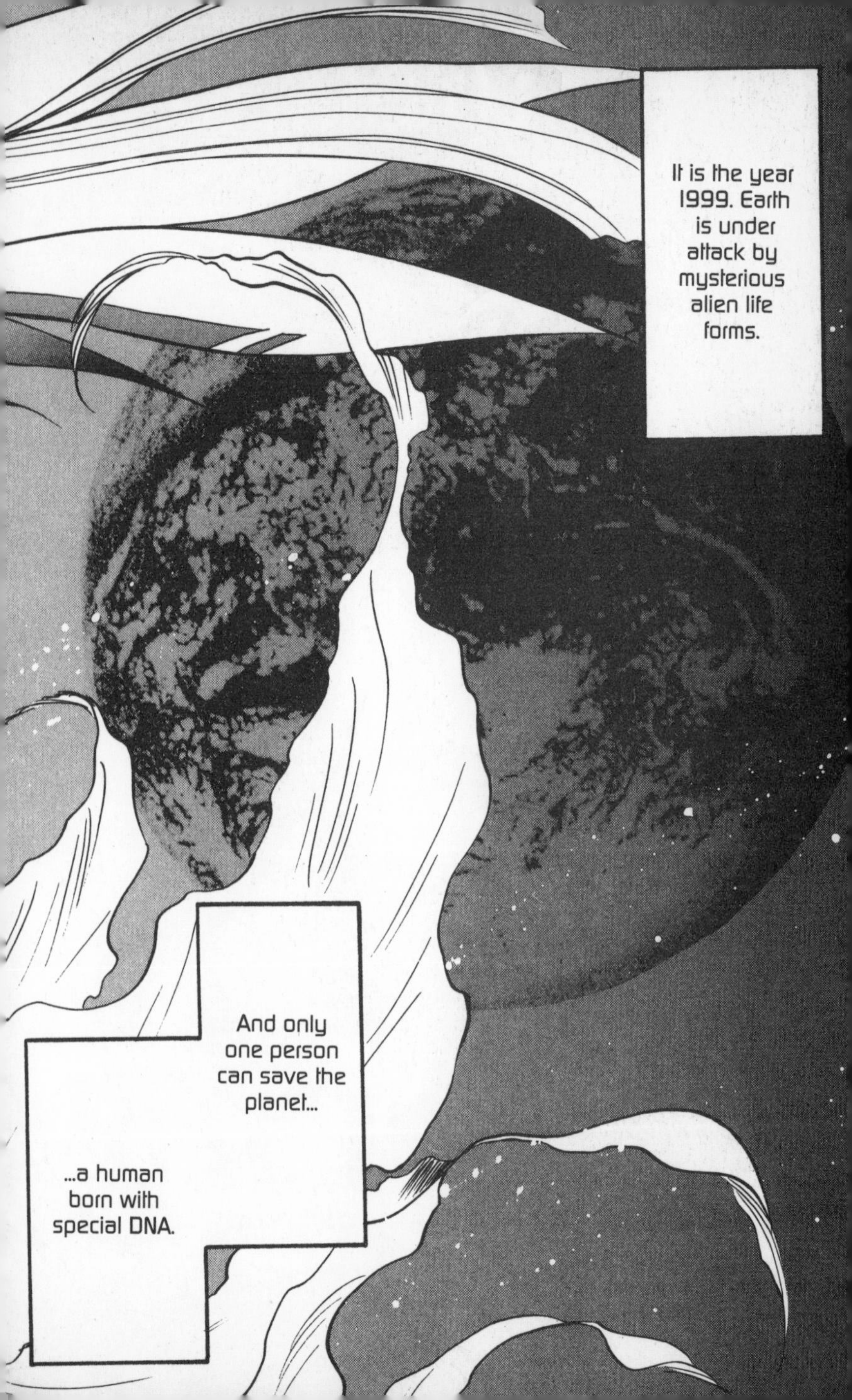
It is the year 1999. Earth is under attack by mysterious alien life forms.
And only one person can save the planet...
...a human born with special DNA.

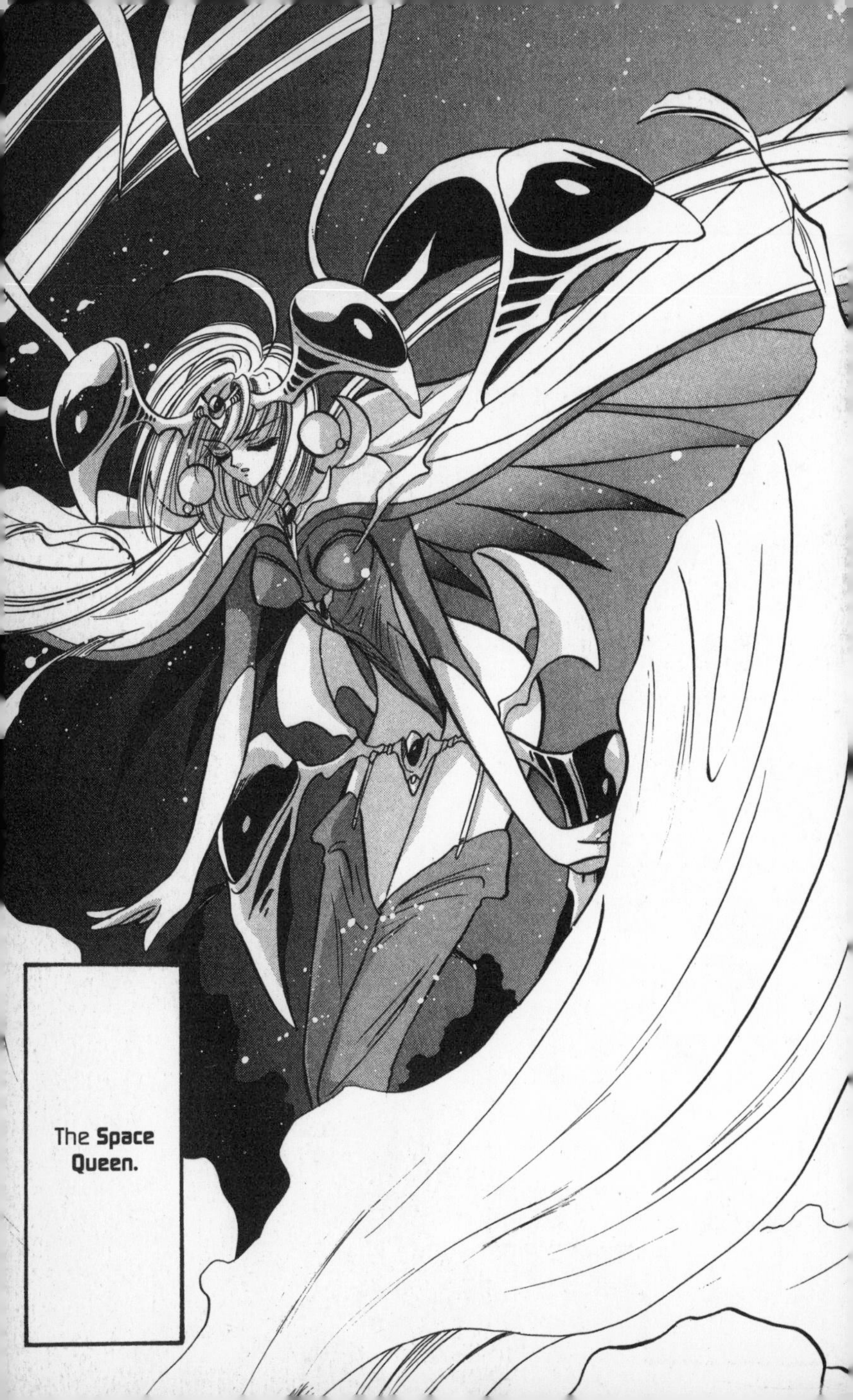
The Space Queen.

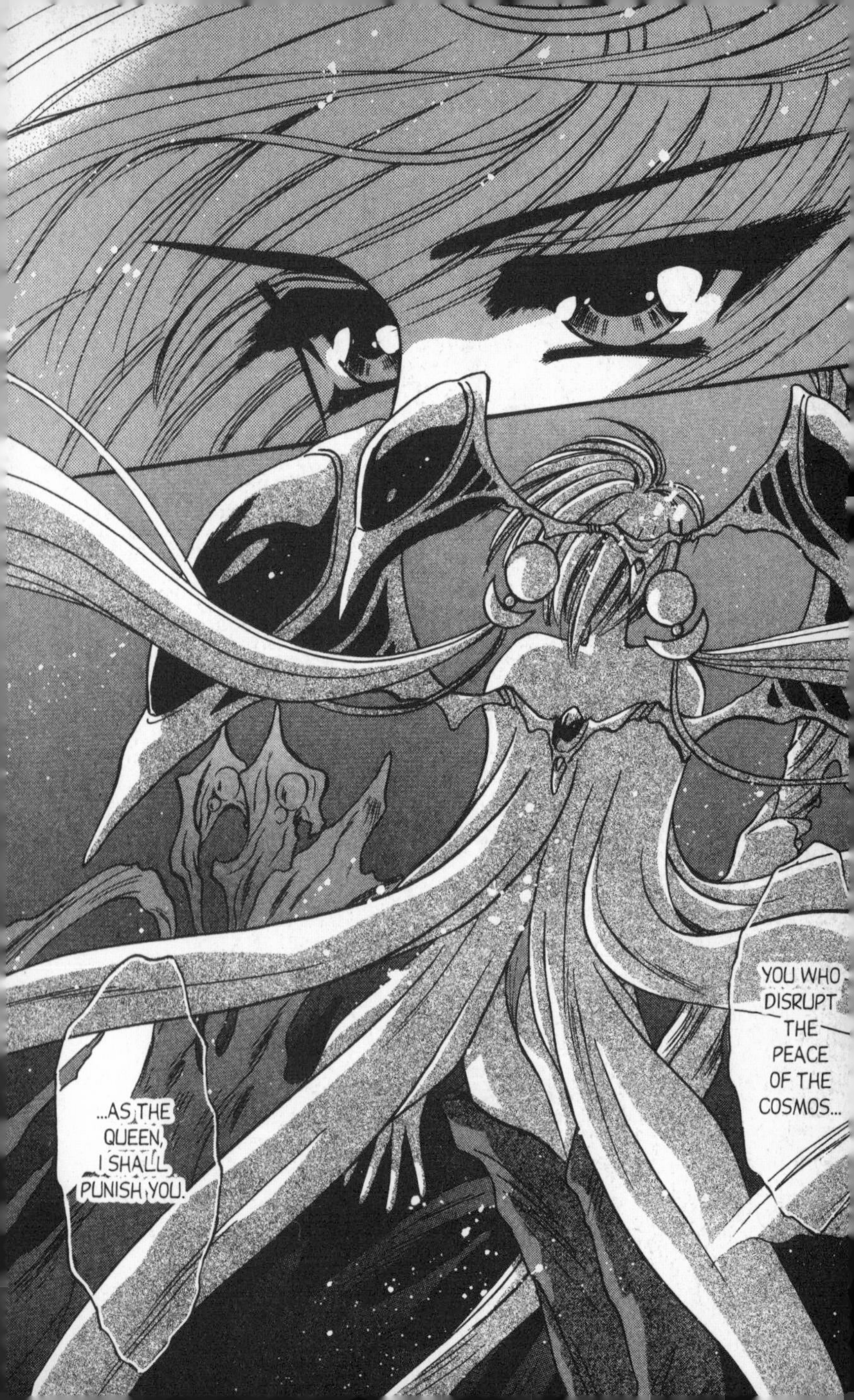
YOU WHO DISRUPT THE PEACE OF THE COSMOS...
...AS THE QUEEN, I SHALL PUNISH YOU.

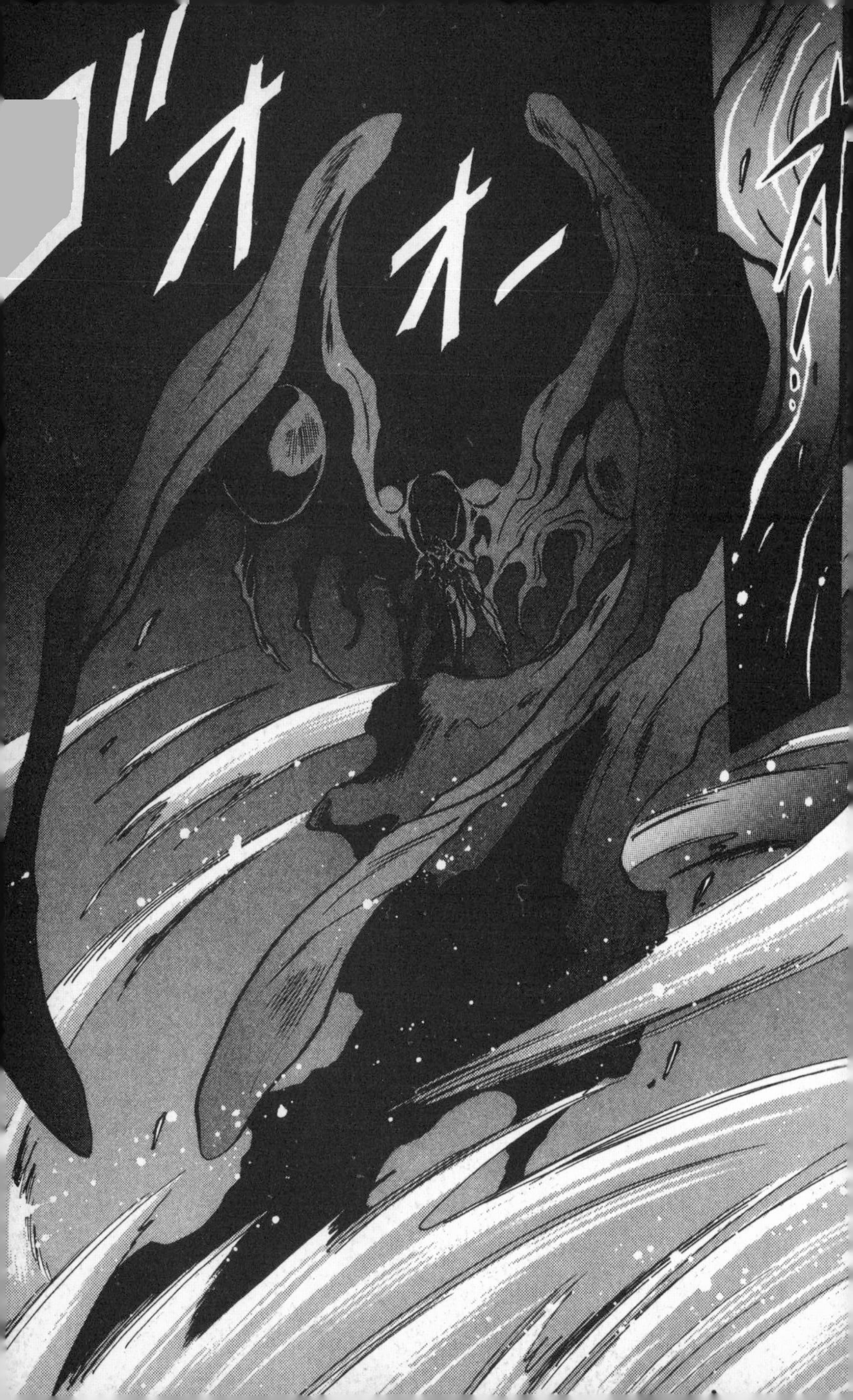
ゴオオー

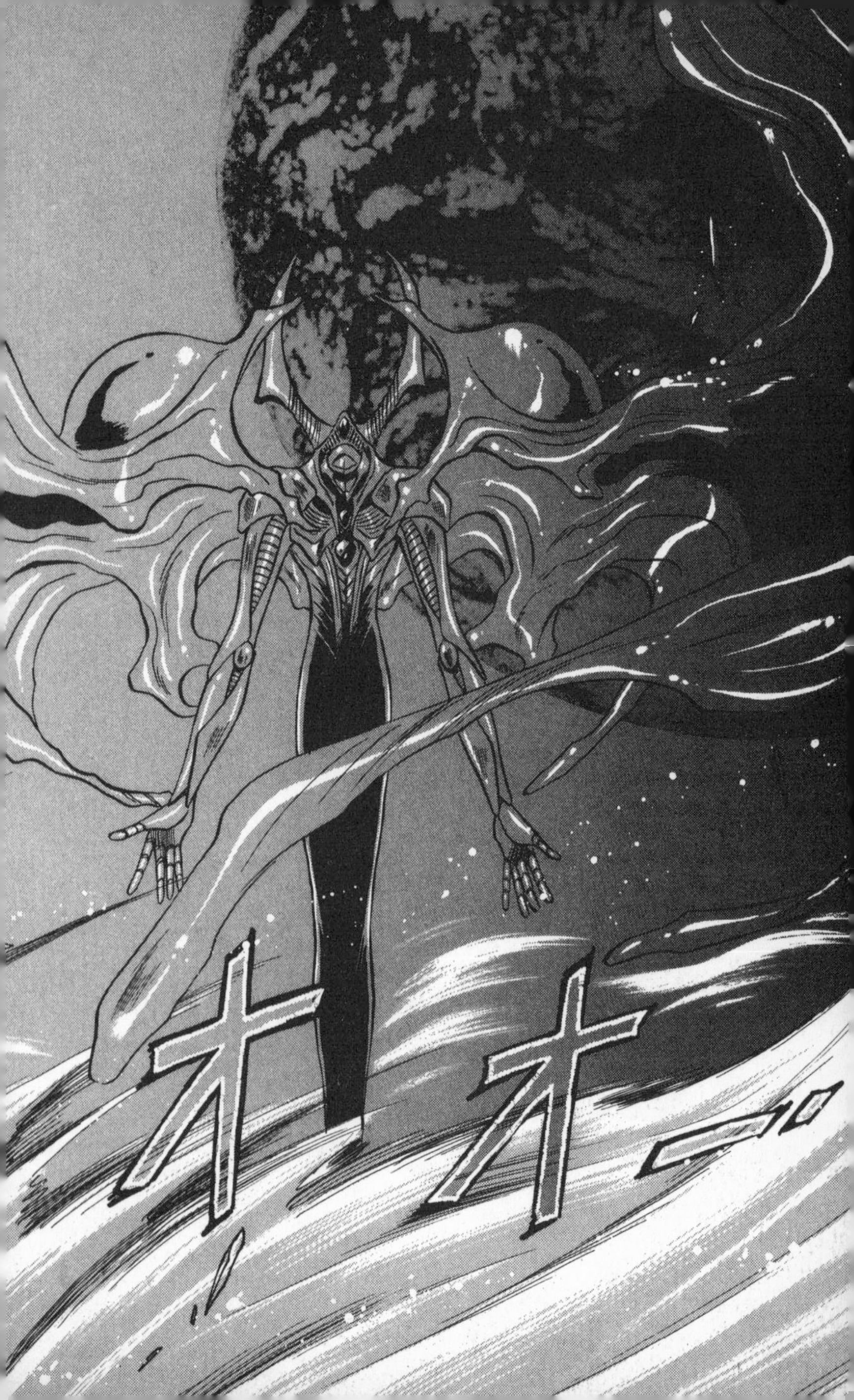
オオ—ン

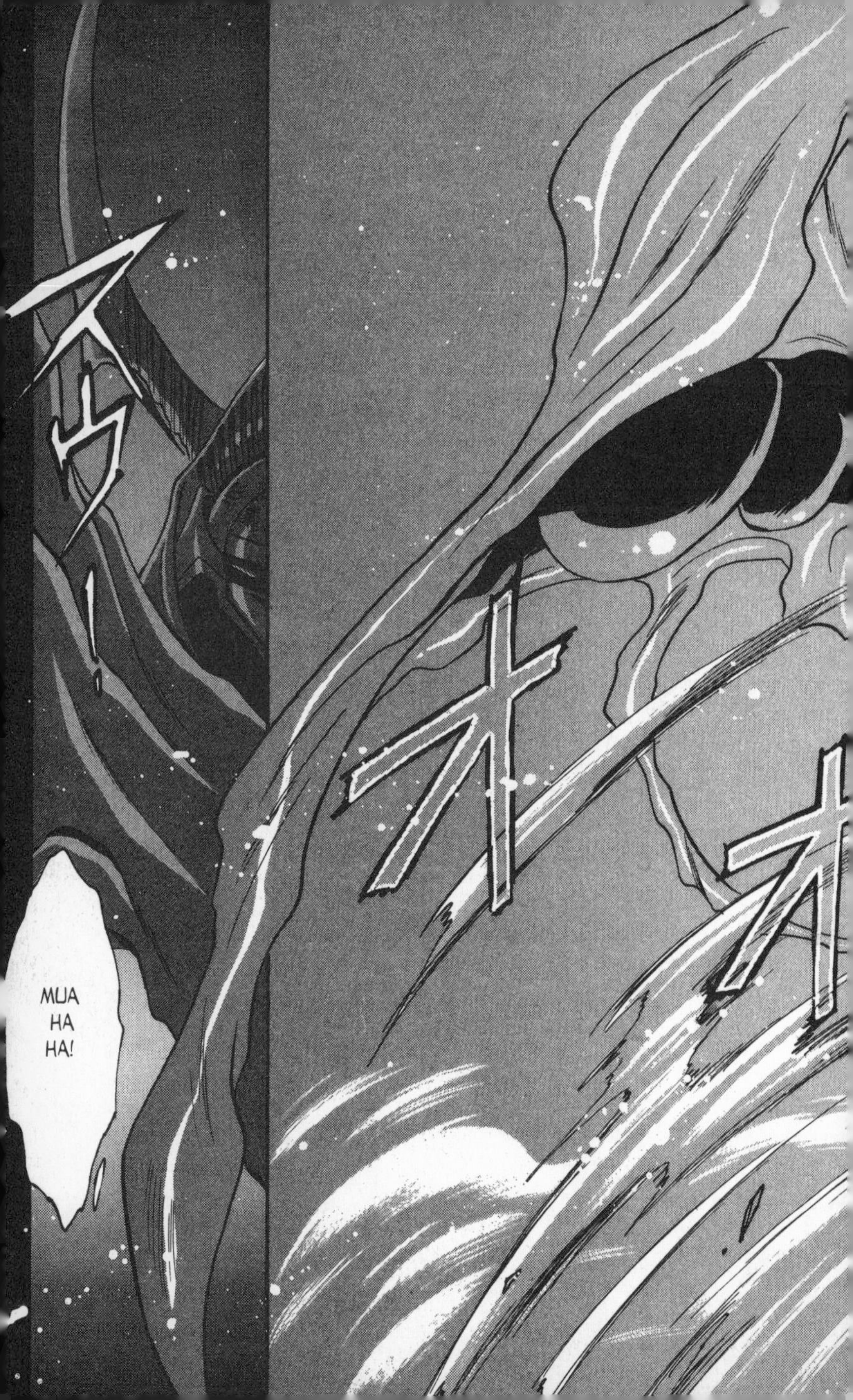
オオ
スッ!
MUA
HA
HA!

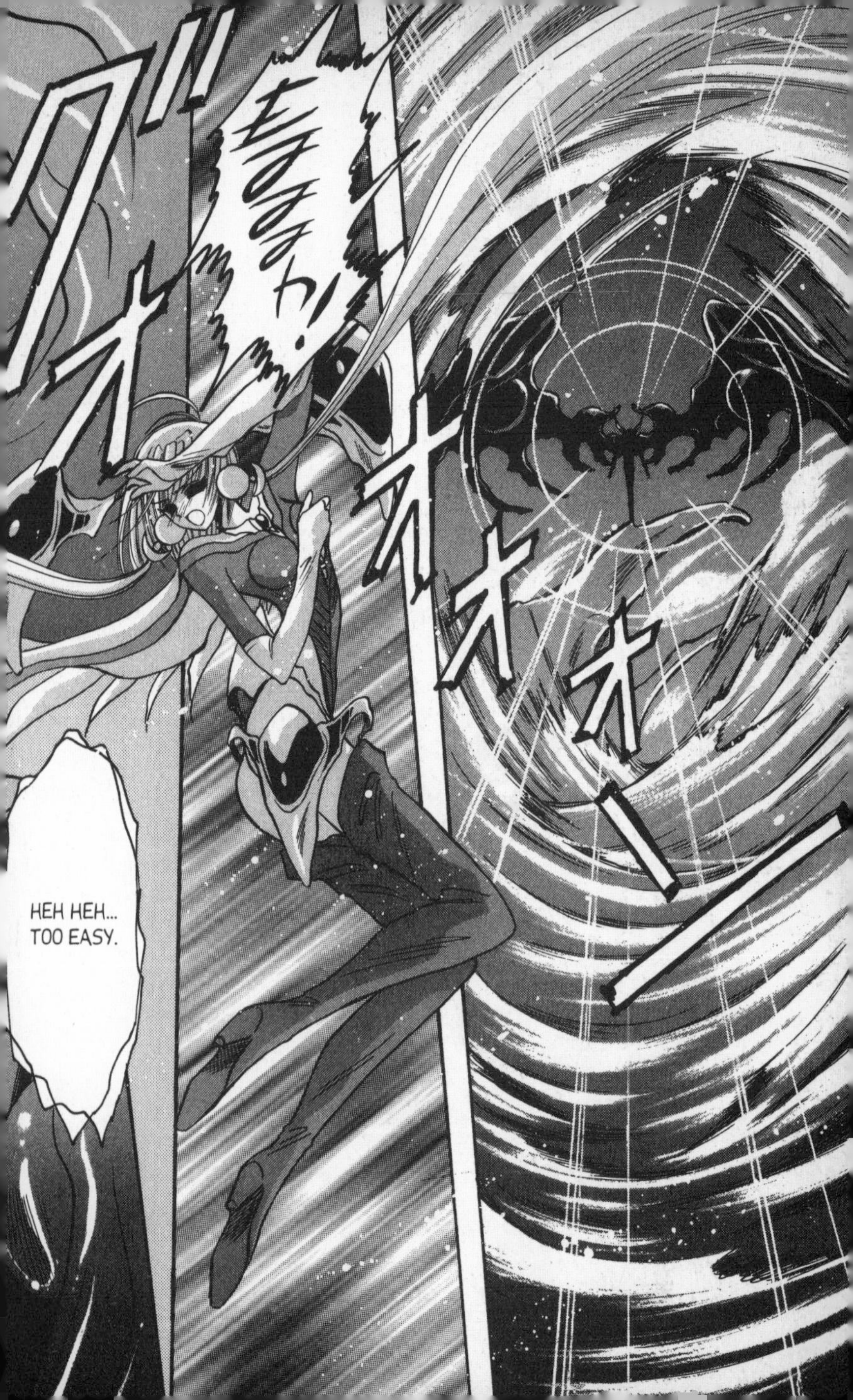
HEH HEH...
TOO EASY.

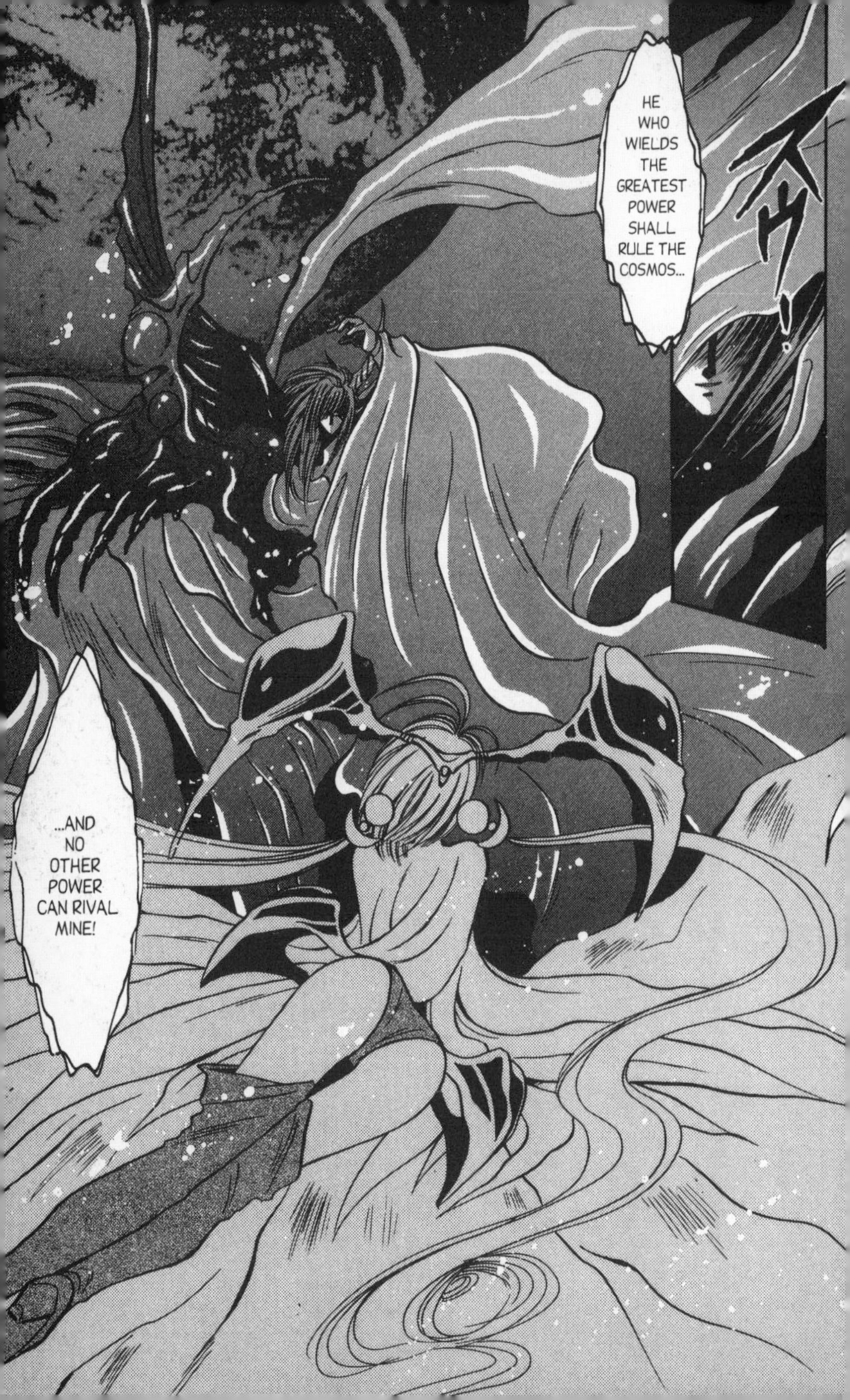
HE WHO WIELDS THE GREATEST POWER SHALL RULE THE COSMOS...
...AND NO OTHER POWER CAN RIVAL MINE!

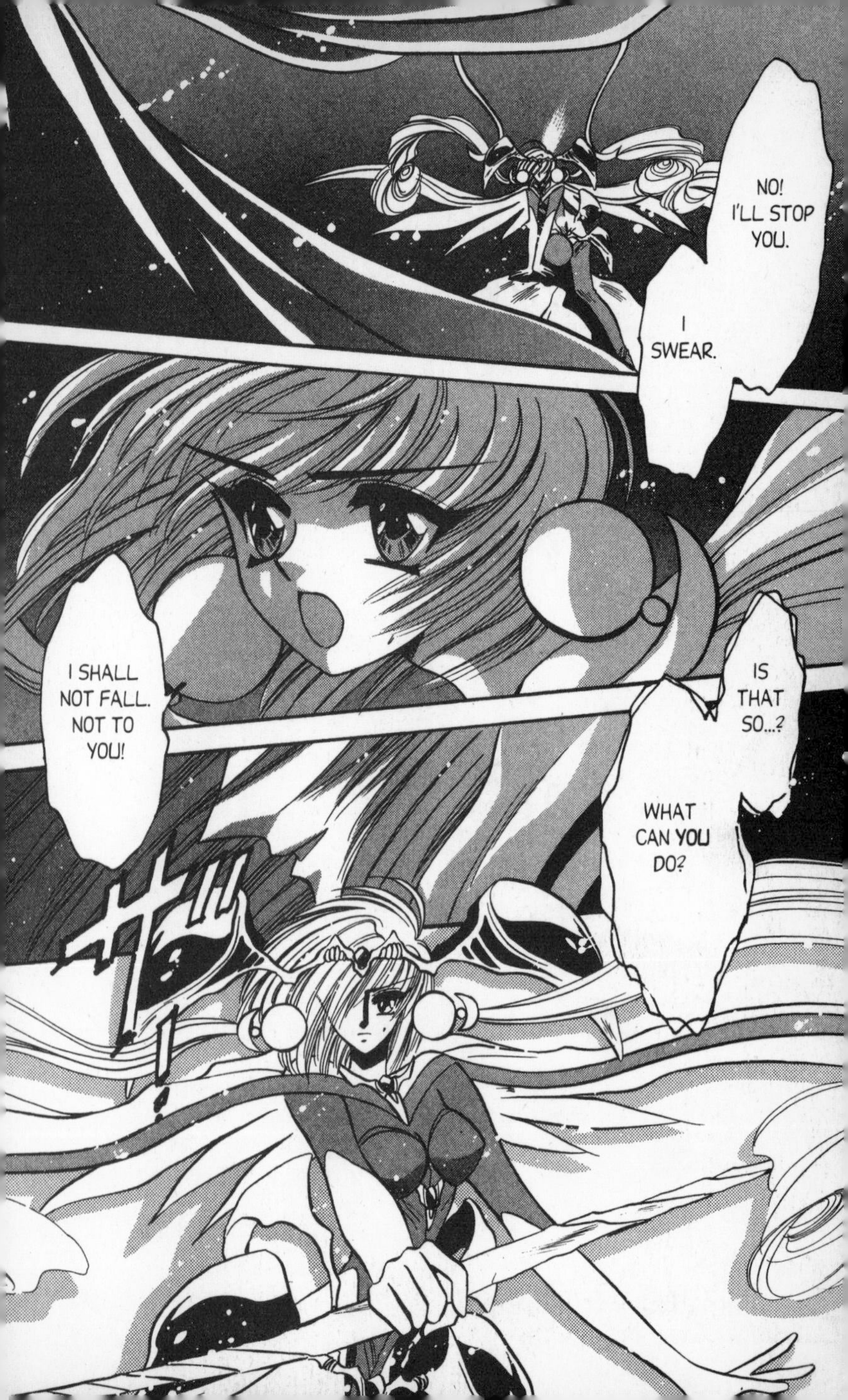
NO! I'LL STOP YOU.
I SWEAR.
I SHALL NOT FALL. NOT TO YOU!
IS THAT SO...?
WHAT CAN YOU DO?

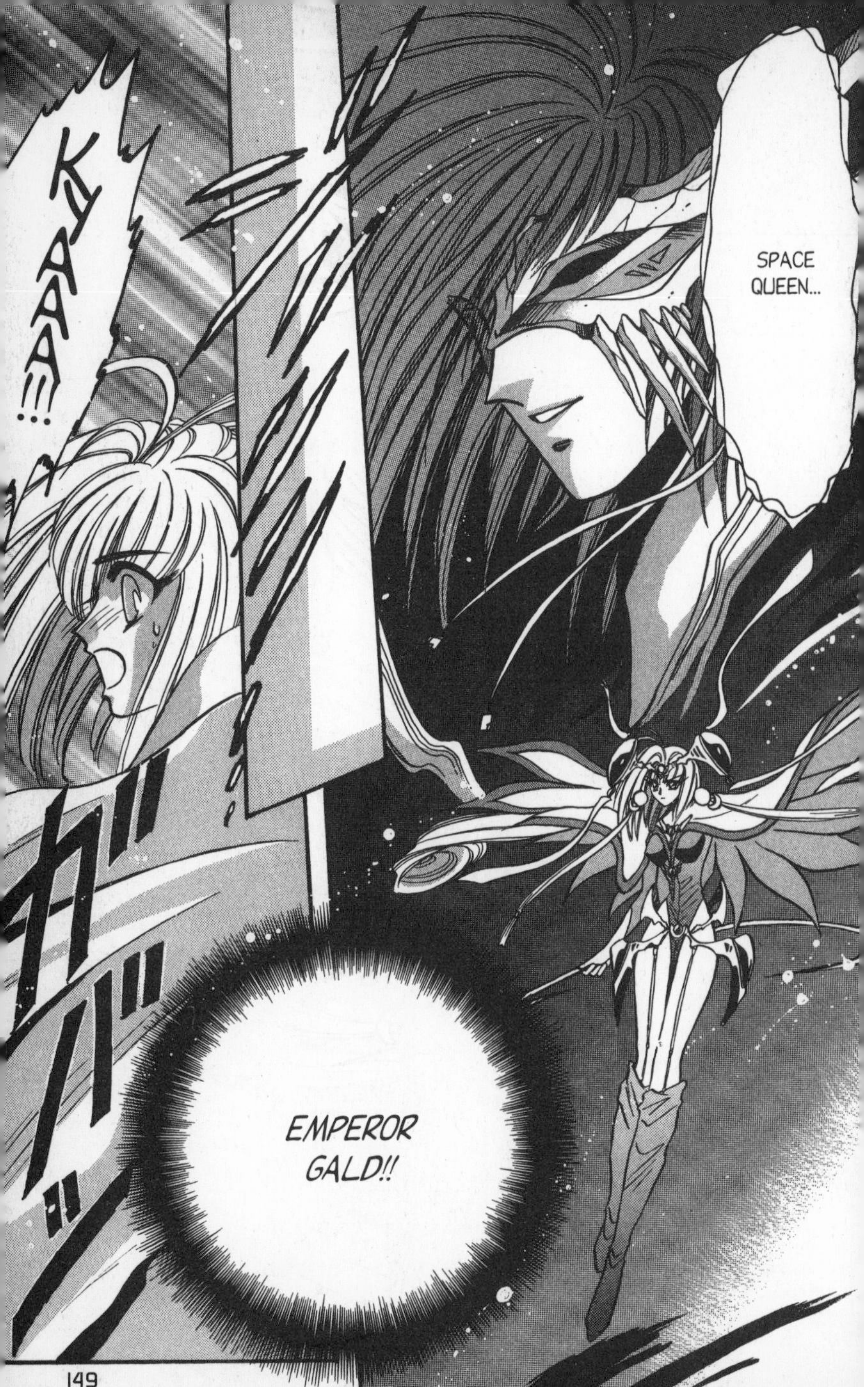
SPACE QUEEN...
EMPEROR GALD!!
KYAAA!!!

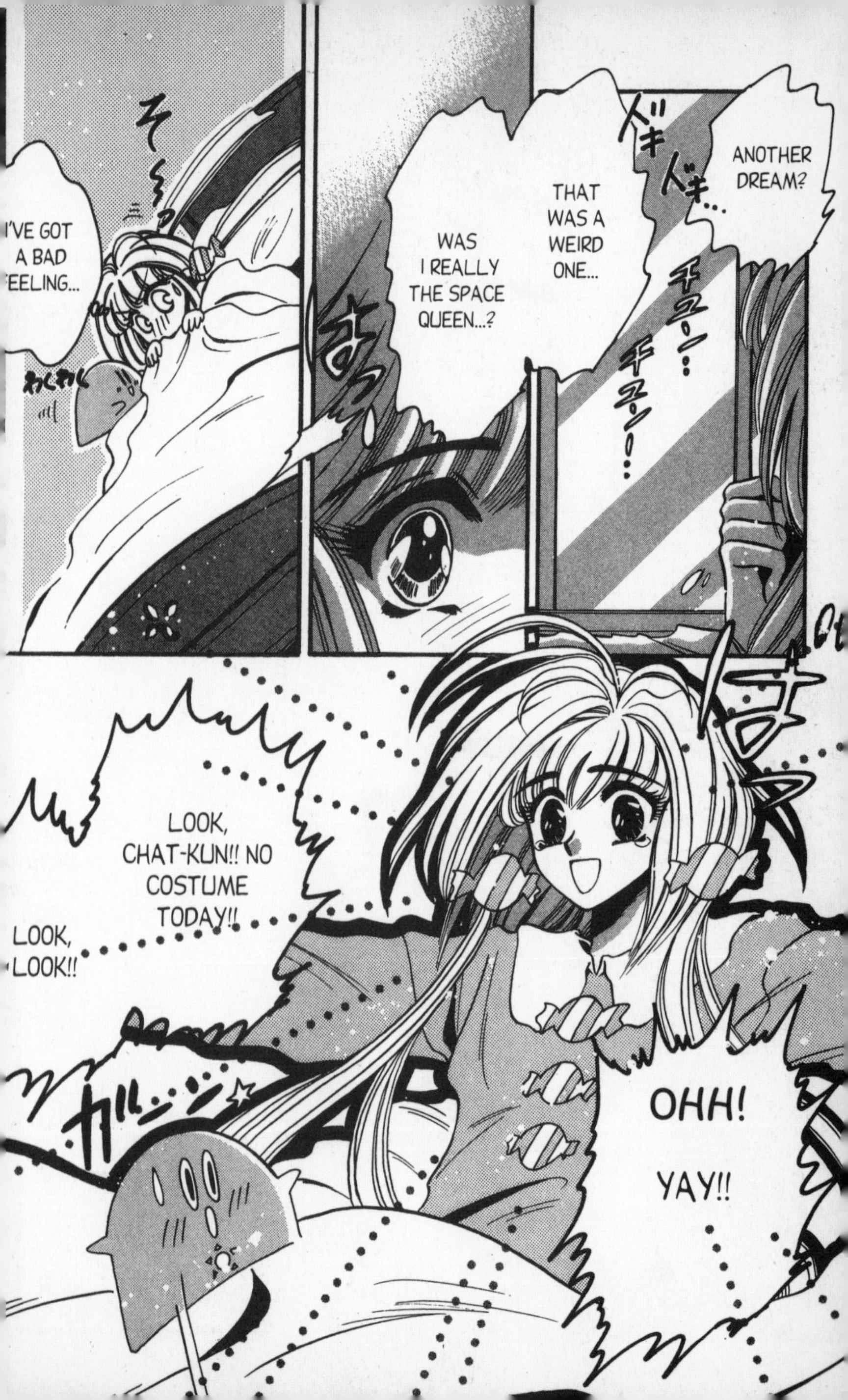
ANOTHER DREAM?
THAT WAS A WEIRD ONE...
WAS I REALLY THE SPACE QUEEN...?
I'VE GOT A BAD FEELING...
LOOK, CHAT-KUN!! NO COSTUME TODAY!!
LOOK, LOOK!!
OHH!
YAY!!

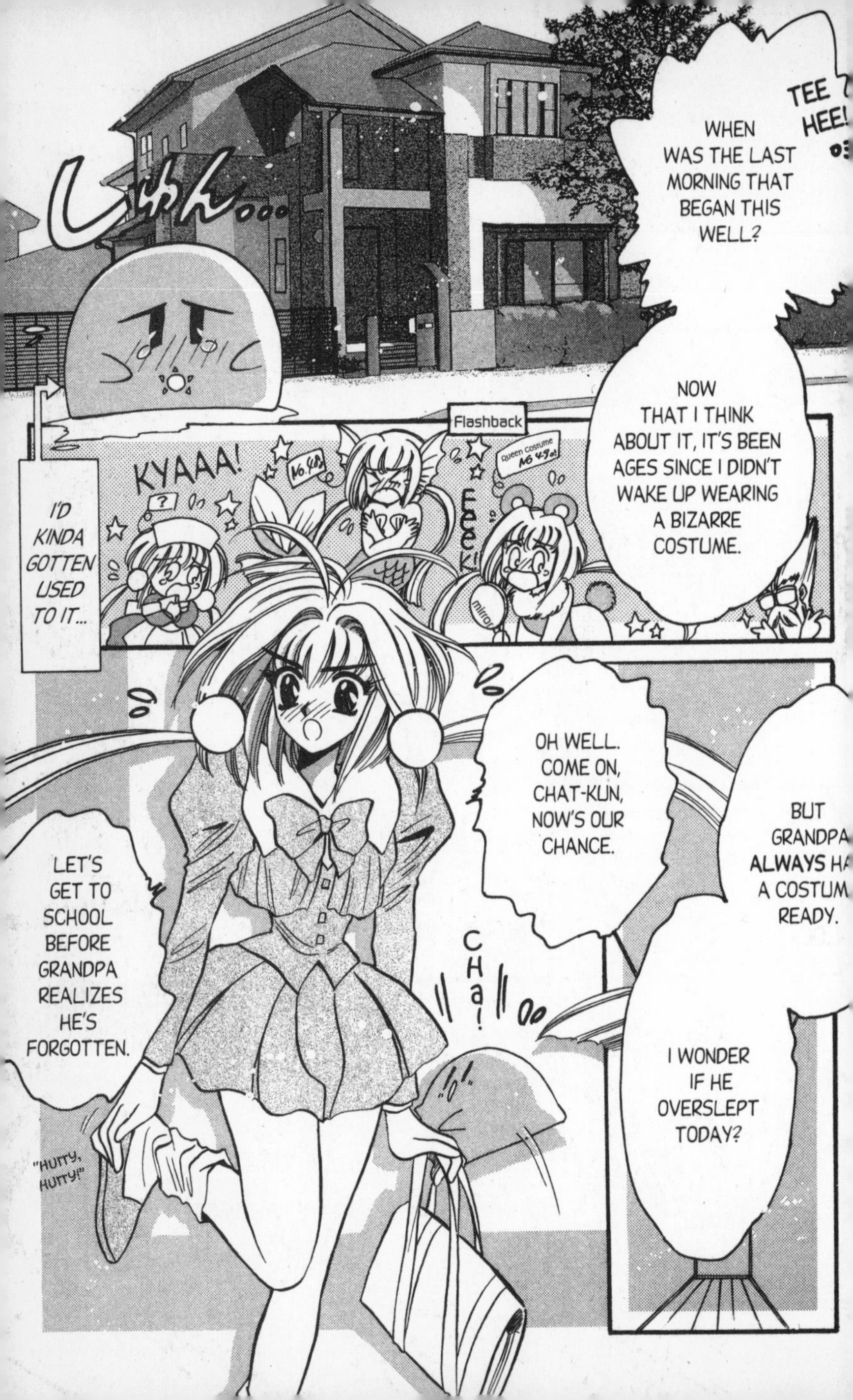
TEE HEE!
WHEN WAS THE LAST MORNING THAT BEGAN THIS WELL?
しゅん...
NOW THAT I THINK ABOUT IT, IT'S BEEN AGES SINCE I DIDN'T WAKE UP WEARING A BIZARRE COSTUME.
Flashback
Queen Costume
Eeek!
No.48
KYAAA!
I'D KINDA GOTTEN USED TO IT...
BUT GRANDPA ALWAYS HA A COSTUM READY.
I WONDER IF HE OVERSLEPT TODAY?
OH WELL. COME ON, CHAT-KUN, NOW'S OUR CHANCE.
CHa!
LET'S GET TO SCHOOL BEFORE GRANDPA REALIZES HE'S FORGOTTEN.
"HUTTY, HUTTY!"

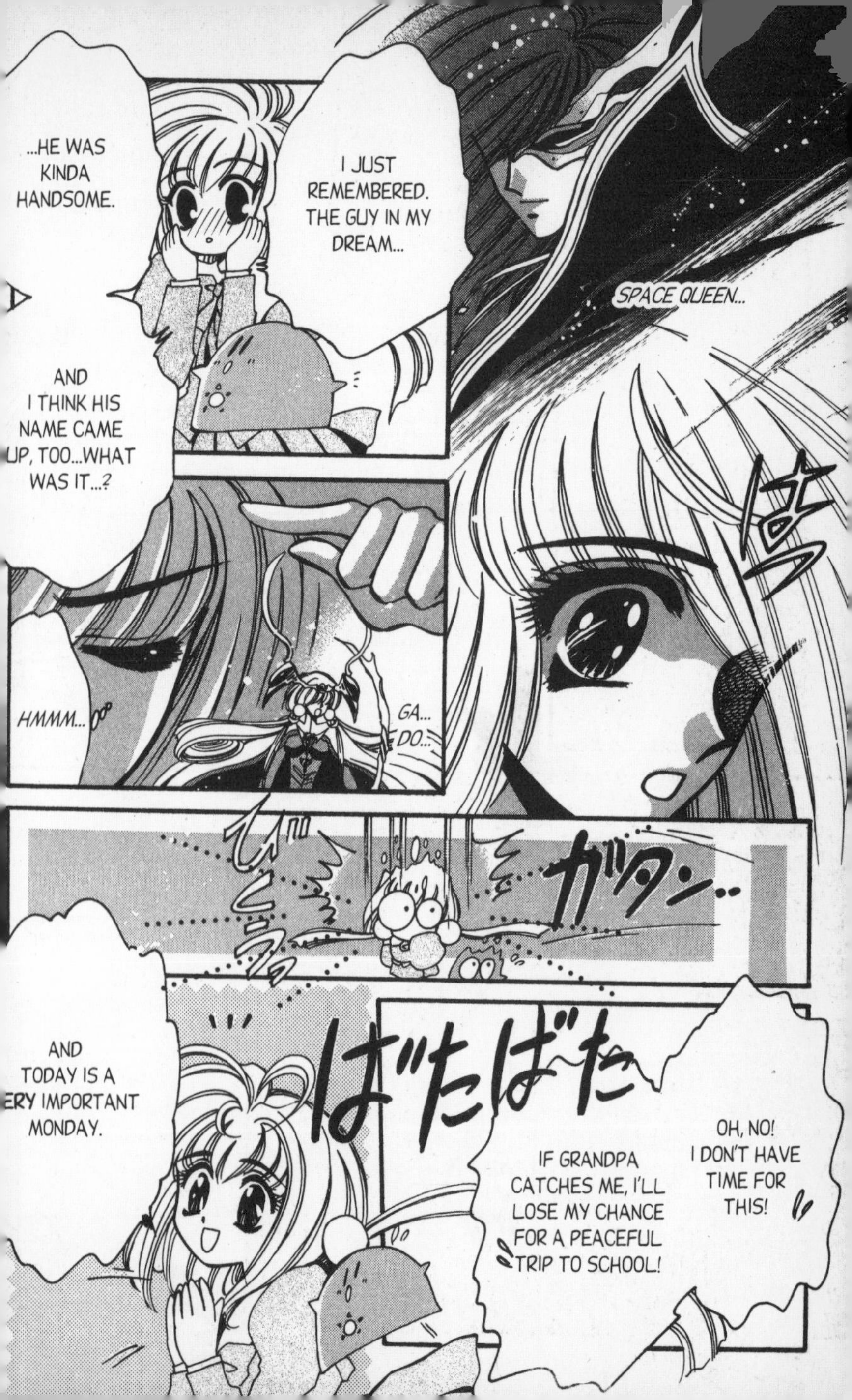
SPACE QUEEN...
は
I JUST REMEMBERED. THE GUY IN MY DREAM...
...HE WAS KINDA HANDSOME.
AND I THINK HIS NAME CAME UP, TOO...WHAT WAS IT...?
GA... DO...
HMMM...
ガタン…
OH, NO! I DON'T HAVE TIME FOR THIS!
IF GRANDPA CATCHES ME, I'LL LOSE MY CHANCE FOR A PEACEFUL TRIP TO SCHOOL!
ばたばた
AND TODAY IS A ERY IMPORTANT MONDAY.

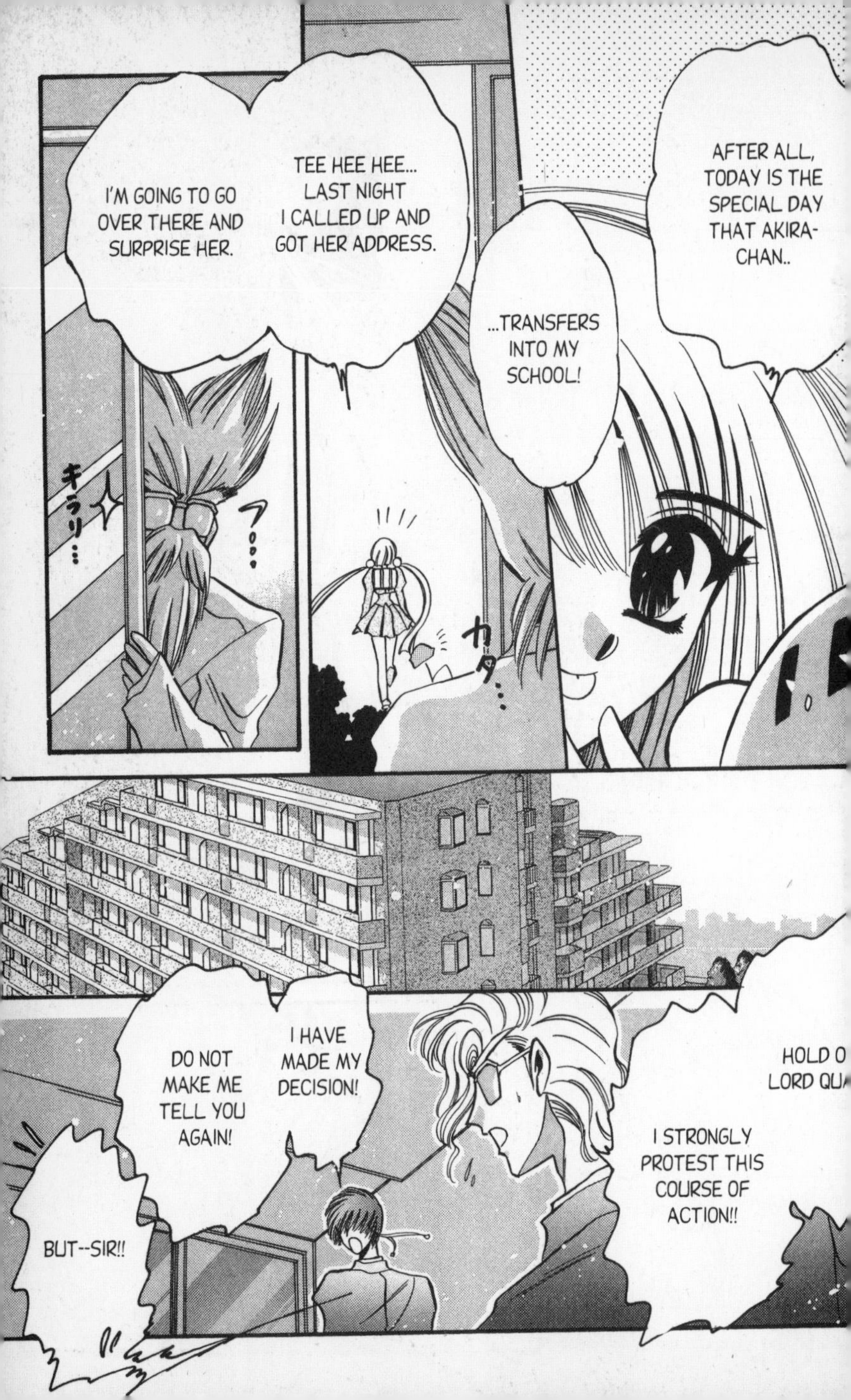
AFTER ALL, TODAY IS THE SPECIAL DAY THAT AKIRA-CHAN..
...TRANSFERS INTO MY SCHOOL!
カタ…
TEE HEE HEE... LAST NIGHT I CALLED UP AND GOT HER ADDRESS.
I'M GOING TO GO OVER THERE AND SURPRISE HER.
フ…
キラリ…
HOLD O
LORD QUA
I STRONGLY PROTEST THIS COURSE OF ACTION!!
I HAVE MADE MY DECISION!
DO NOT MAKE ME TELL YOU AGAIN!
BUT--SIR!!

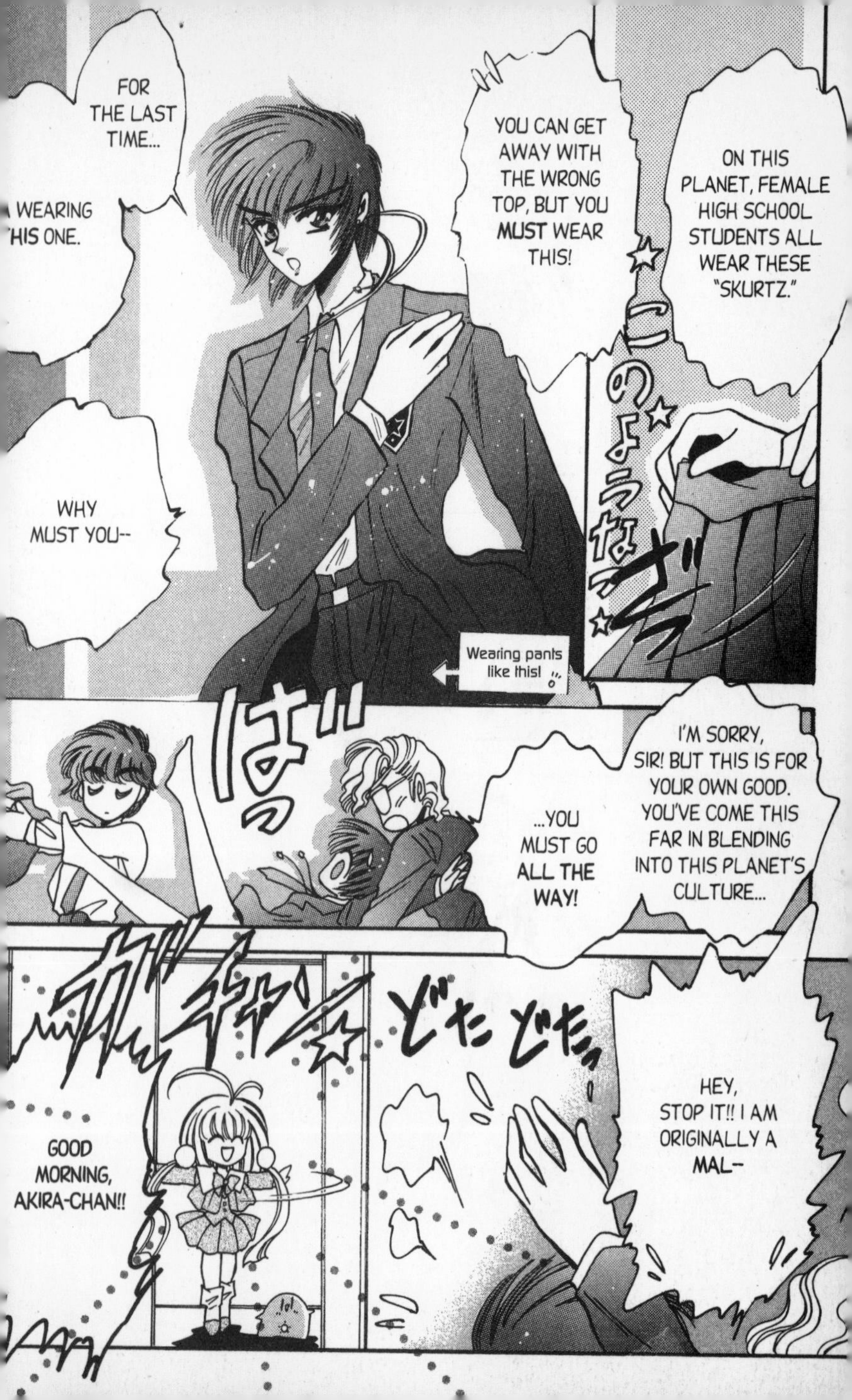

ON THIS PLANET, FEMALE HIGH SCHOOL STUDENTS ALL WEAR THESE "SKURTZ."
このようなっ☆
ざっ
YOU CAN GET AWAY WITH THE WRONG TOP, BUT YOU **MUST** WEAR THIS!
FOR THE LAST TIME...
WEARING **THIS** ONE.
WHY MUST YOU--
Wearing pants like this!
I'M SORRY, SIR! BUT THIS IS FOR YOUR OWN GOOD. YOU'VE COME THIS FAR IN BLENDING INTO THIS PLANET'S CULTURE...
...YOU MUST GO **ALL THE WAY!**
ばっ
HEY, STOP IT!! I AM ORIGINALLY A **MAL-**
どたどたっ
ガチャ☆
GOOD MORNING, AKIRA-CHAN!!

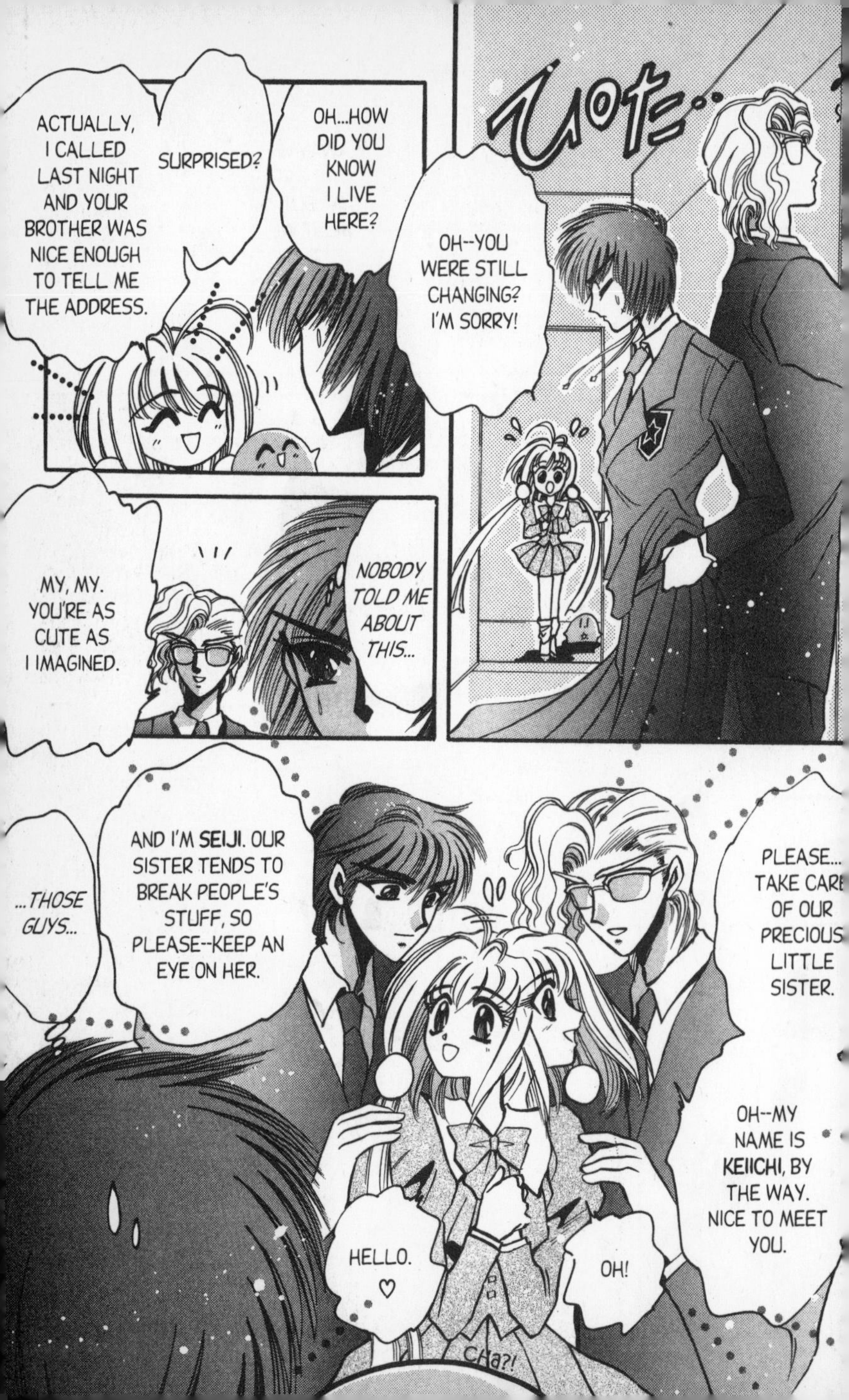
ひやっ
OH--YOU WERE STILL CHANGING? I'M SORRY!
OH...HOW DID YOU KNOW I LIVE HERE?
SURPRISED?
ACTUALLY, I CALLED LAST NIGHT AND YOUR BROTHER WAS NICE ENOUGH TO TELL ME THE ADDRESS.
NOBODY TOLD ME ABOUT THIS...
MY, MY. YOU'RE AS CUTE AS I IMAGINED.
PLEASE... TAKE CARE OF OUR PRECIOUS LITTLE SISTER.
OH--MY NAME IS KEIICHI, BY THE WAY. NICE TO MEET YOU.
OH!
AND I'M SEIJI. OUR SISTER TENDS TO BREAK PEOPLE'S STUFF, SO PLEASE--KEEP AN EYE ON HER.
HELLO. ♡
CHA?!
...THOSE GUYS...

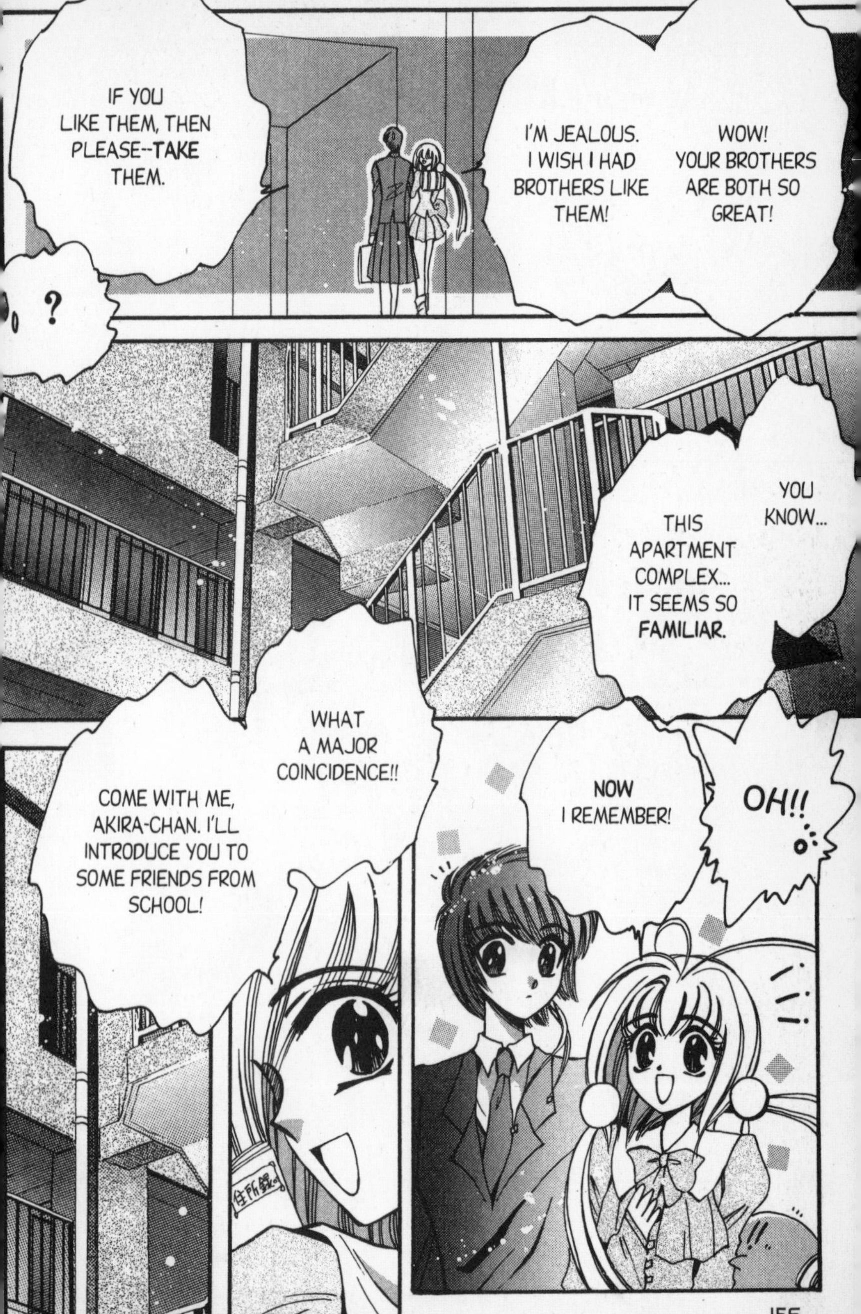
WOW! YOUR BROTHERS ARE BOTH SO GREAT!
I'M JEALOUS. I WISH I HAD BROTHERS LIKE THEM!
IF YOU LIKE THEM, THEN PLEASE--**TAKE** THEM.
?
YOU KNOW...
THIS APARTMENT COMPLEX... IT SEEMS SO **FAMILIAR.**
OH!!
NOW I REMEMBER!
住所録
WHAT A MAJOR COINCIDENCE!!
COME WITH ME, AKIRA-CHAN. I'LL INTRODUCE YOU TO SOME FRIENDS FROM SCHOOL!

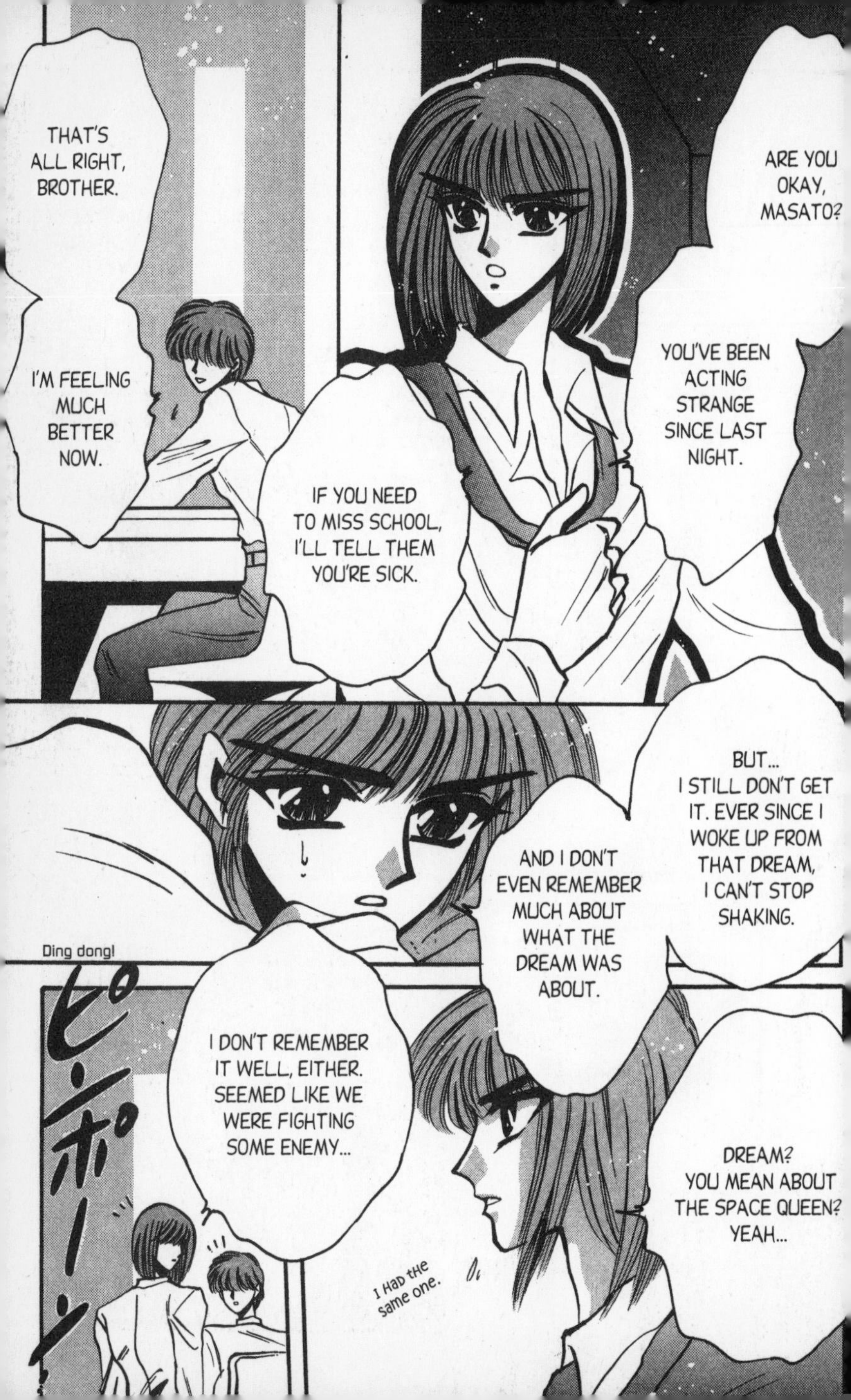
ARE YOU OKAY, MASATO?
YOU'VE BEEN ACTING STRANGE SINCE LAST NIGHT.
IF YOU NEED TO MISS SCHOOL, I'LL TELL THEM YOU'RE SICK.
THAT'S ALL RIGHT, BROTHER.
I'M FEELING MUCH BETTER NOW.
BUT... I STILL DON'T GET IT. EVER SINCE I WOKE UP FROM THAT DREAM, I CAN'T STOP SHAKING.
AND I DON'T EVEN REMEMBER MUCH ABOUT WHAT THE DREAM WAS ABOUT.
DREAM? YOU MEAN ABOUT THE SPACE QUEEN? YEAH...
I HAD THE SAME ONE.
I DON'T REMEMBER IT WELL, EITHER. SEEMED LIKE WE WERE FIGHTING SOME ENEMY...
Ding dong!
ピンポーン

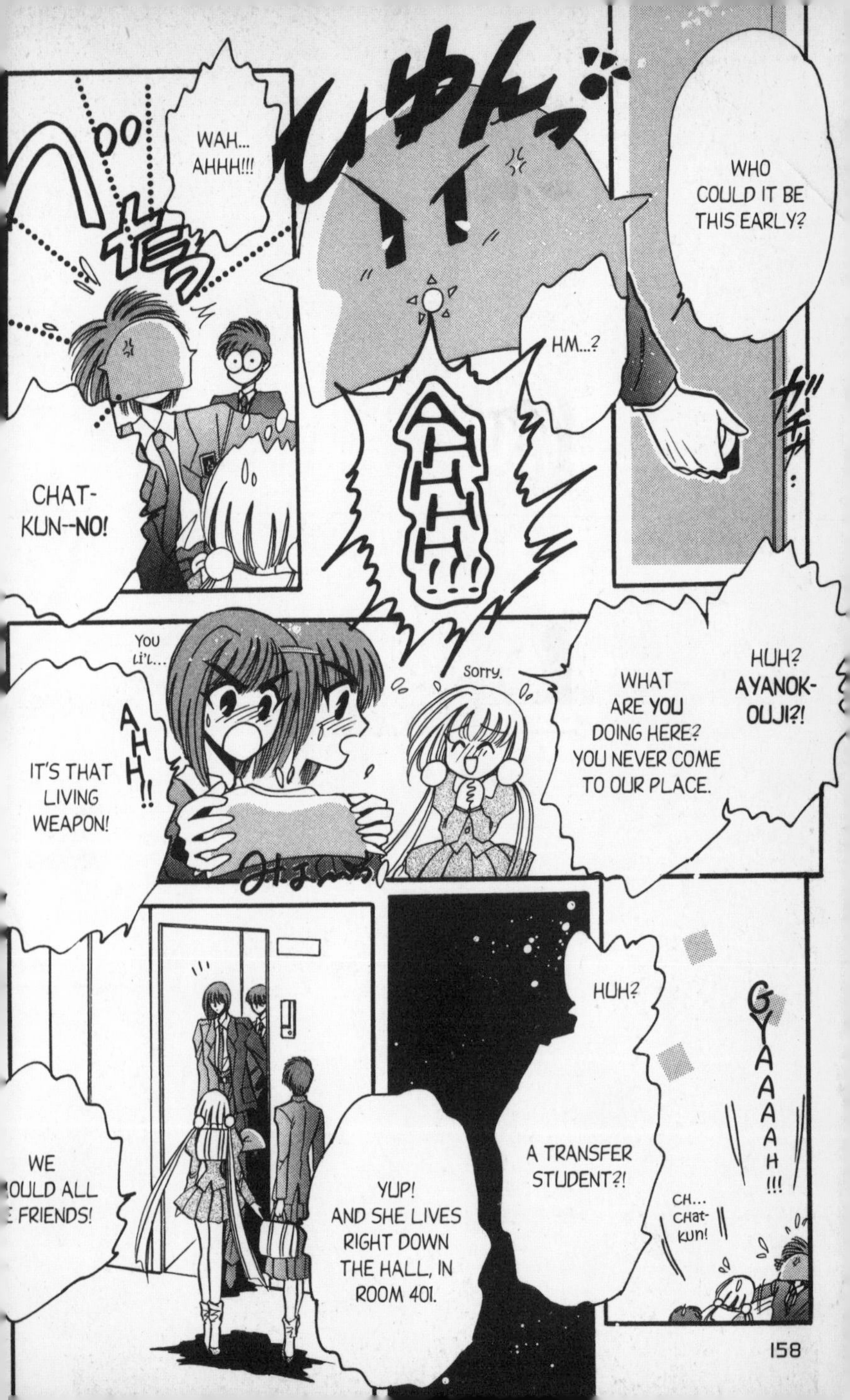
WHO COULD IT BE THIS EARLY?
HM...?
WAH... AHHH!!!
DO
CHAT-KUN--NO!
AHHH!!!
HUH? AYANOK-OUJI?!
WHAT ARE YOU DOING HERE? YOU NEVER COME TO OUR PLACE.
Sorry.
YOU LI'L...
AHHH!!
IT'S THAT LIVING WEAPON!
GYAAAAAH!!!
CH... CHAT-KUN!
HUH?
A TRANSFER STUDENT?!
YUP! AND SHE LIVES RIGHT DOWN THE HALL, IN ROOM 401.
WE
OULD ALL
E FRIENDS!

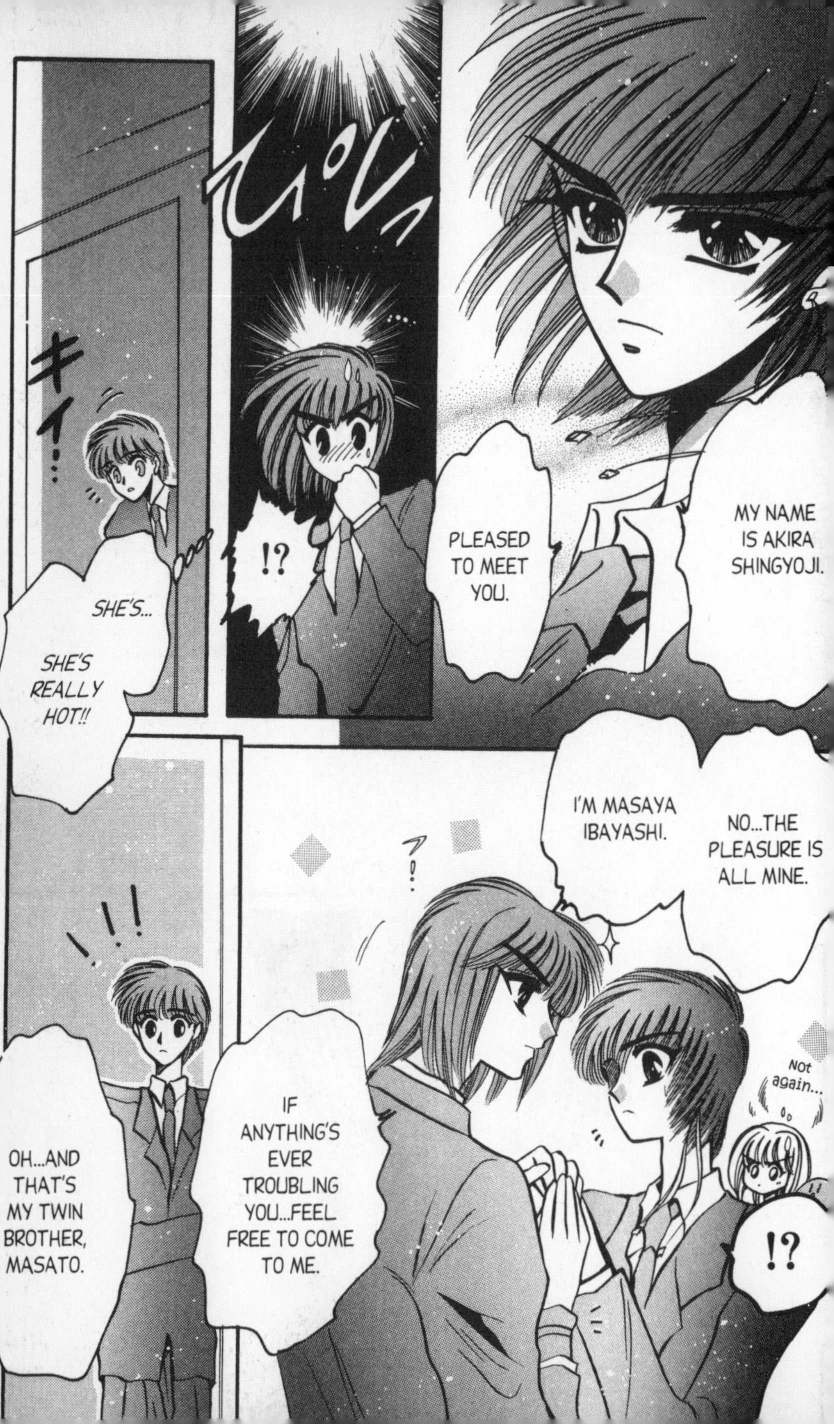
MY NAME IS AKIRA SHINGYOJI.
PLEASED TO MEET YOU.
!?
キイ…
SHE'S...
SHE'S REALLY HOT!!
NO...THE PLEASURE IS ALL MINE.
I'M MASAYA IBAYASHI.
Not again...
!?
IF ANYTHING'S EVER TROUBLING YOU...FEEL FREE TO COME TO ME.
OH...AND THAT'S MY TWIN BROTHER, MASATO.

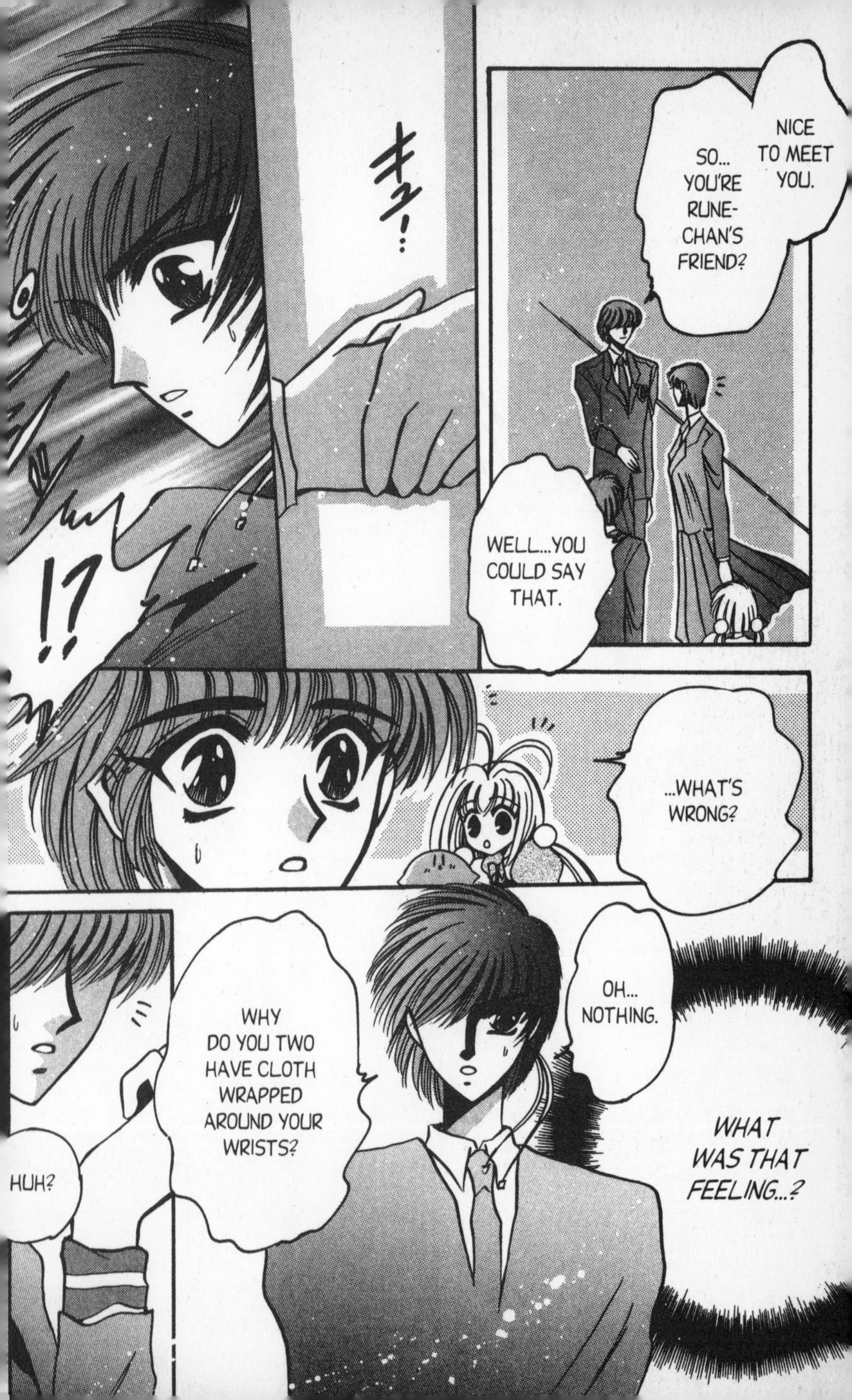

NICE TO MEET YOU.
SO... YOU'RE RUNE-CHAN'S FRIEND?
WELL...YOU COULD SAY THAT.
キュ!
!?
...WHAT'S WRONG?
OH... NOTHING.
WHAT WAS THAT FEELING...?
WHY DO YOU TWO HAVE CLOTH WRAPPED AROUND YOUR WRISTS?
HUH?

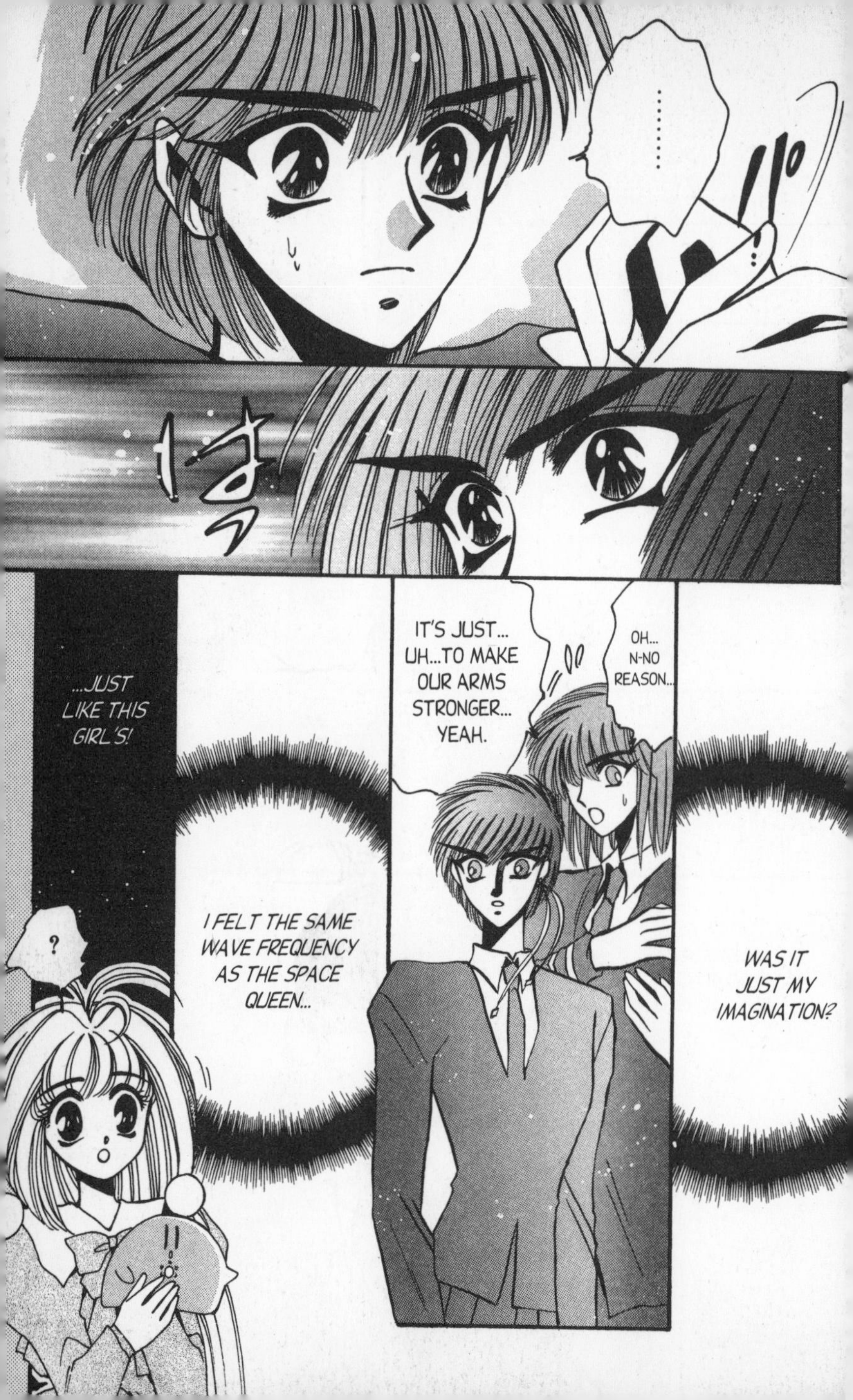
......
パ
はっ
OH... N-NO REASON...
IT'S JUST... UH...TO MAKE OUR ARMS STRONGER... YEAH.
WAS IT JUST MY IMAGINATION?
I FELT THE SAME WAVE FREQUENCY AS THE SPACE QUEEN...
...JUST LIKE THIS GIRL'S!
?

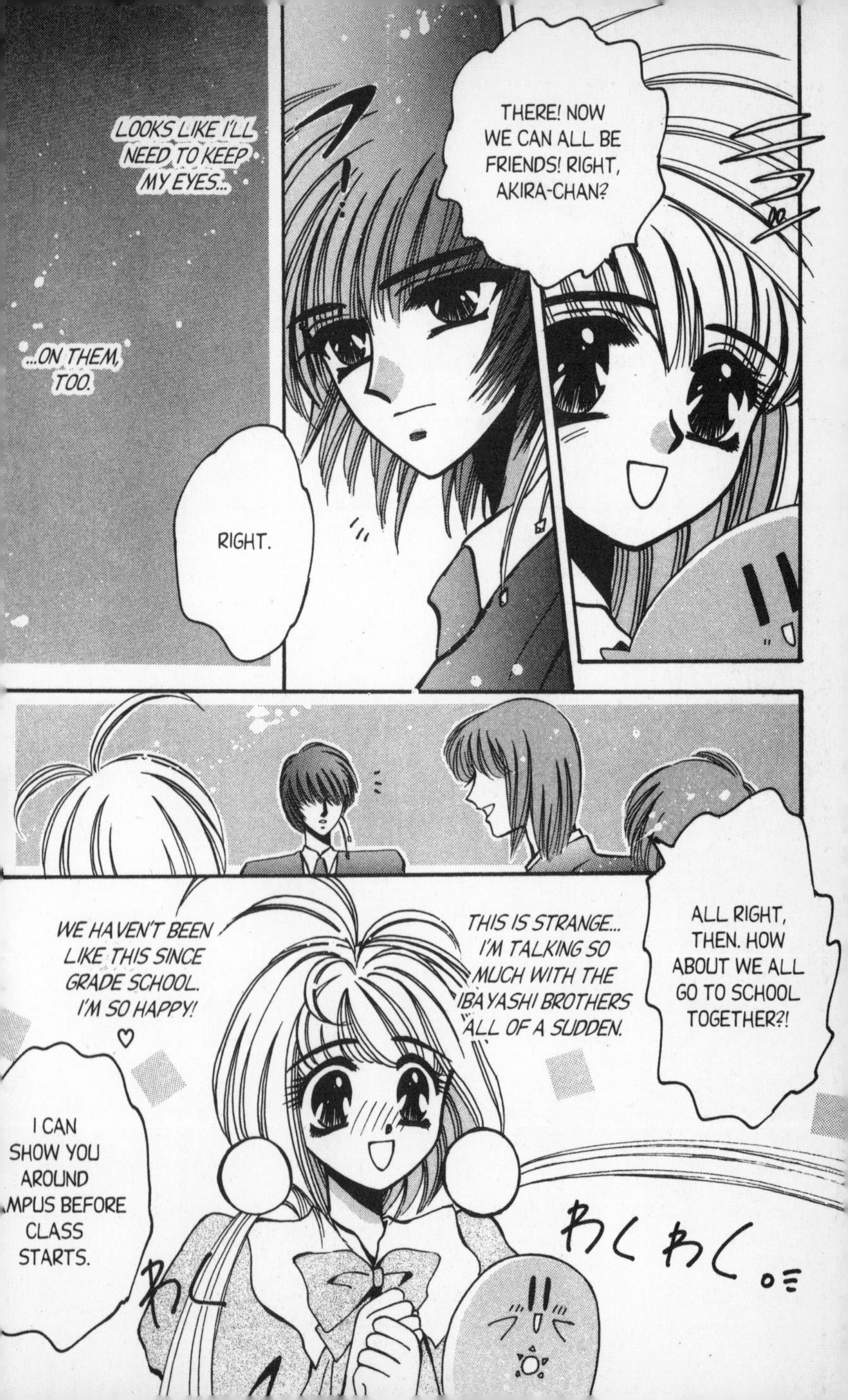
THERE! NOW WE CAN ALL BE FRIENDS! RIGHT, AKIRA-CHAN?
RIGHT.
LOOKS LIKE I'LL NEED TO KEEP MY EYES...
...ON THEM, TOO.
ALL RIGHT, THEN. HOW ABOUT WE ALL GO TO SCHOOL TOGETHER?!
THIS IS STRANGE... I'M TALKING SO MUCH WITH THE IBAYASHI BROTHERS ALL OF A SUDDEN.
WE HAVEN'T BEEN LIKE THIS SINCE GRADE SCHOOL. I'M SO HAPPY! ♡
I CAN SHOW YOU AROUND MPUS BEFORE CLASS STARTS.
わくわく。
わく

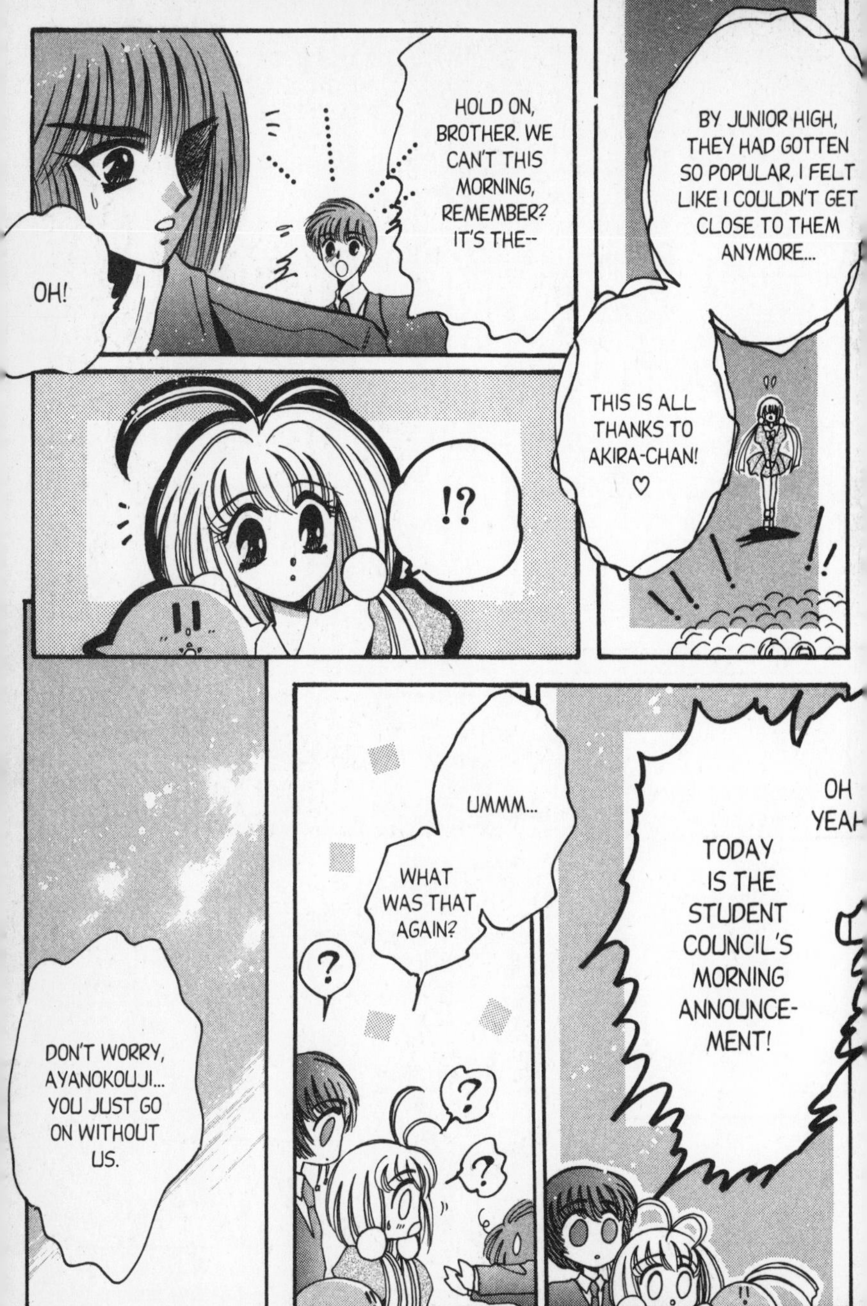
BY JUNIOR HIGH, THEY HAD GOTTEN SO POPULAR, I FELT LIKE I COULDN'T GET CLOSE TO THEM ANYMORE...
THIS IS ALL THANKS TO AKIRA-CHAN! ♡
HOLD ON, BROTHER. WE CAN'T THIS MORNING, REMEMBER? IT'S THE--
OH!
!?
OH YEAH
TODAY IS THE STUDENT COUNCIL'S MORNING ANNOUNCE-MENT!
UMMM...
WHAT WAS THAT AGAIN?
?
?
?
DON'T WORRY, AYANOKOUJI... YOU JUST GO ON WITHOUT US.

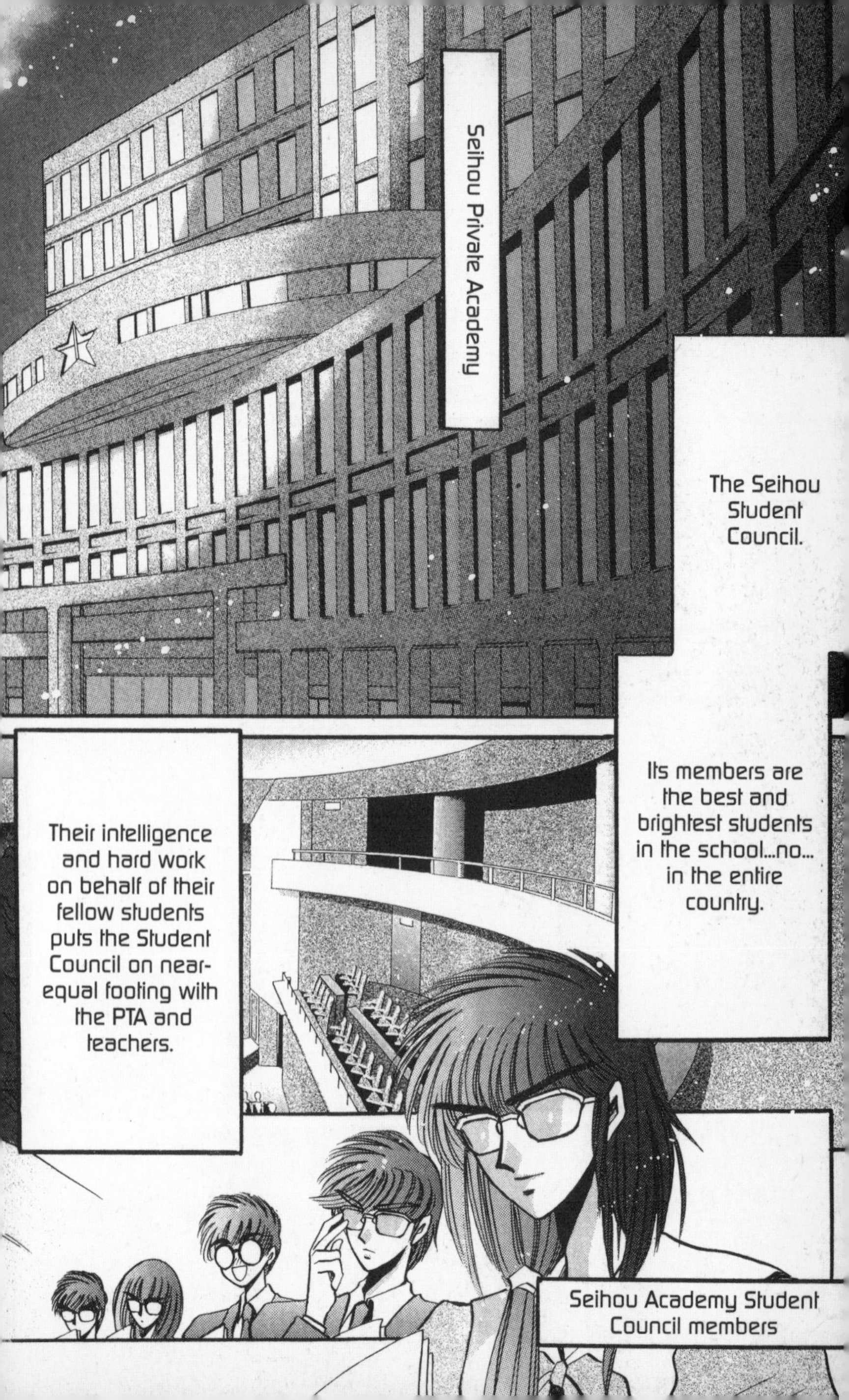
Seihou Private Academy
The Seihou Student Council.
Its members are the best and brightest students in the school...no... in the entire country.
Their intelligence and hard work on behalf of their fellow students puts the Student Council on near-equal footing with the PTA and teachers.
Seihou Academy Student Council members

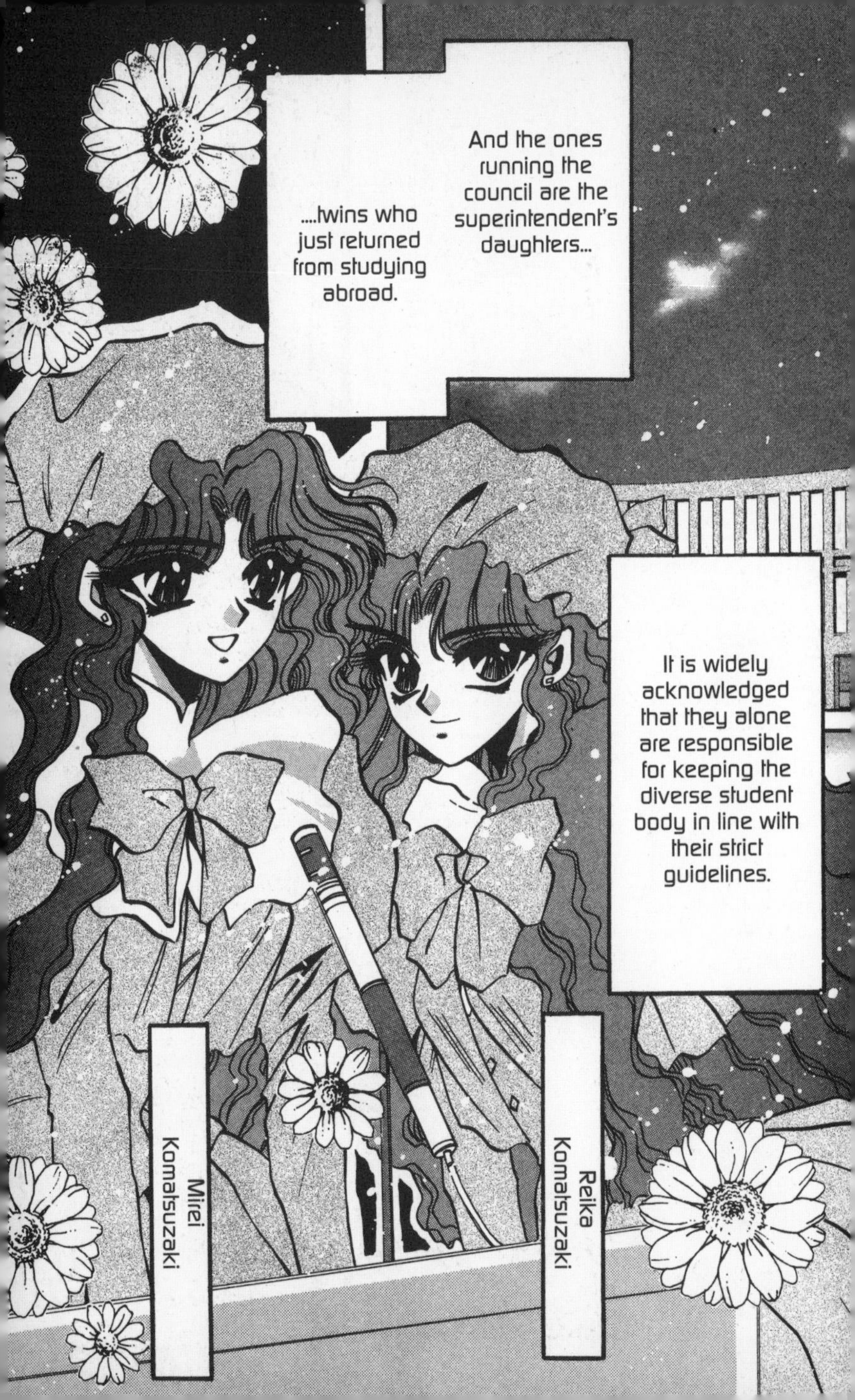
And the ones running the council are the superintendent's daughters...
....twins who just returned from studying abroad.
It is widely acknowledged that they alone are responsible for keeping the diverse student body in line with their strict guidelines.
Reika Komatsuzaki
Mirei Komatsuzaki

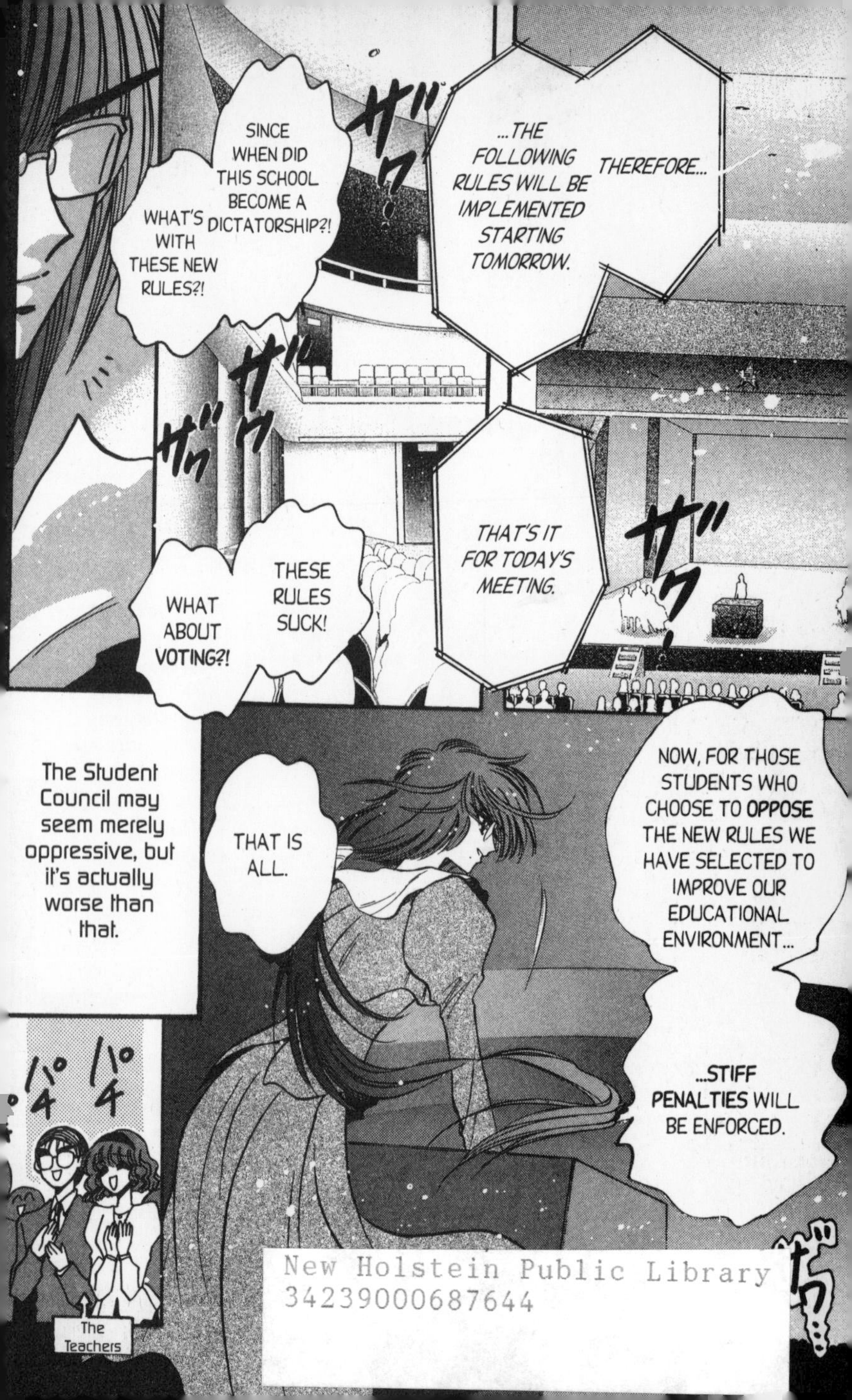
THEREFORE...
...THE FOLLOWING RULES WILL BE IMPLEMENTED STARTING TOMORROW.
ザワ
THAT'S IT FOR TODAY'S MEETING.
ザワ
SINCE WHEN DID THIS SCHOOL BECOME A DICTATORSHIP?!
WHAT'S WITH THESE NEW RULES?!
ザワ
ザワ
THESE RULES SUCK!
WHAT ABOUT VOTING?!
NOW, FOR THOSE STUDENTS WHO CHOOSE TO **OPPOSE** THE NEW RULES WE HAVE SELECTED TO IMPROVE OUR EDUCATIONAL ENVIRONMENT...
...**STIFF PENALTIES** WILL BE ENFORCED.
THAT IS ALL.
The Student Council may seem merely oppressive, but it's actually worse than that.
パチ
パチ
The Teachers

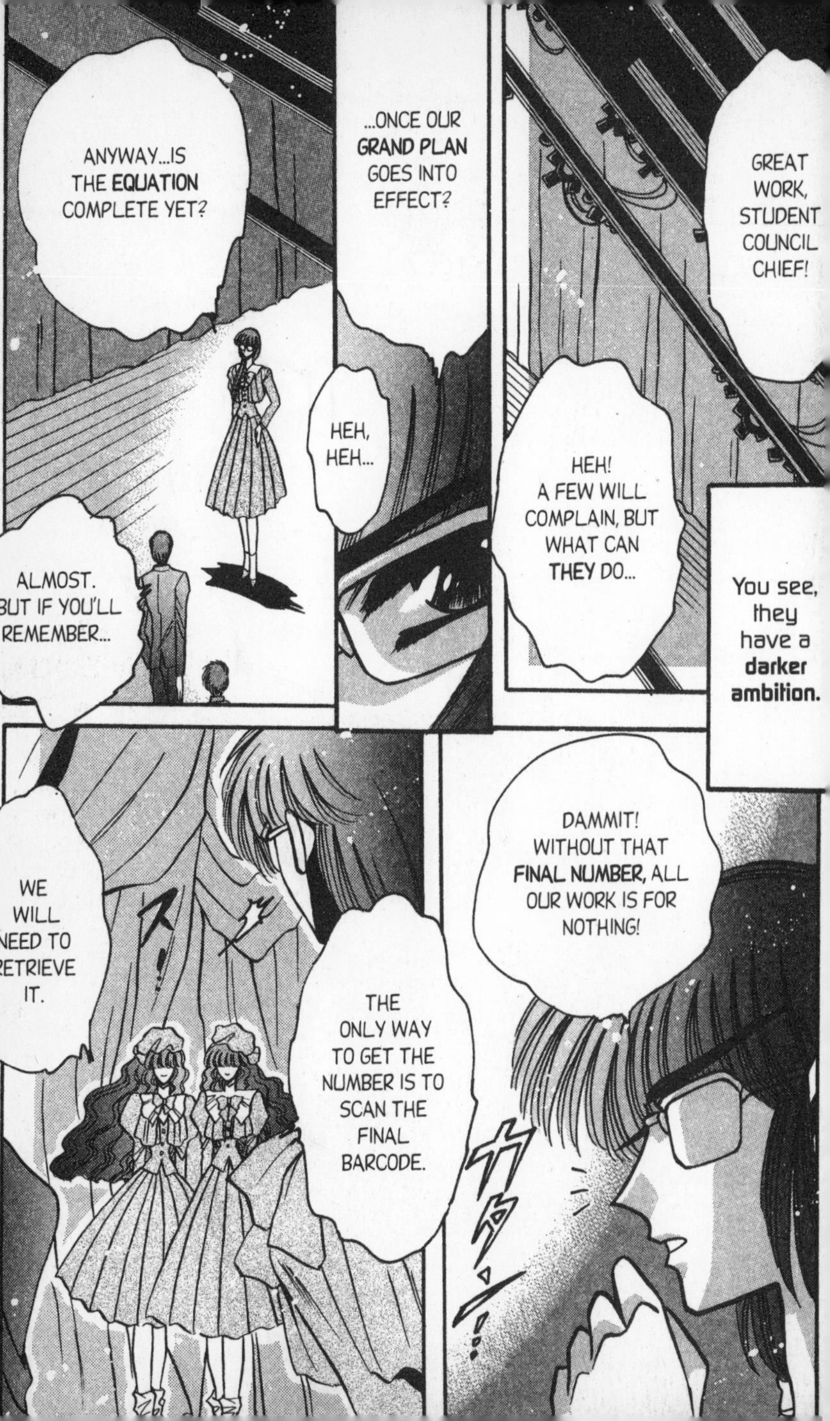
GREAT WORK, STUDENT COUNCIL CHIEF!
HEH! A FEW WILL COMPLAIN, BUT WHAT CAN THEY DO...
You see, they have a darker ambition.
...ONCE OUR GRAND PLAN GOES INTO EFFECT?
HEH, HEH...
ANYWAY...IS THE EQUATION COMPLETE YET?
ALMOST. BUT IF YOU'LL REMEMBER...
DAMMIT! WITHOUT THAT FINAL NUMBER, ALL OUR WORK IS FOR NOTHING!
THE ONLY WAY TO GET THE NUMBER IS TO SCAN THE FINAL BARCODE.
WE WILL NEED TO RETRIEVE IT.

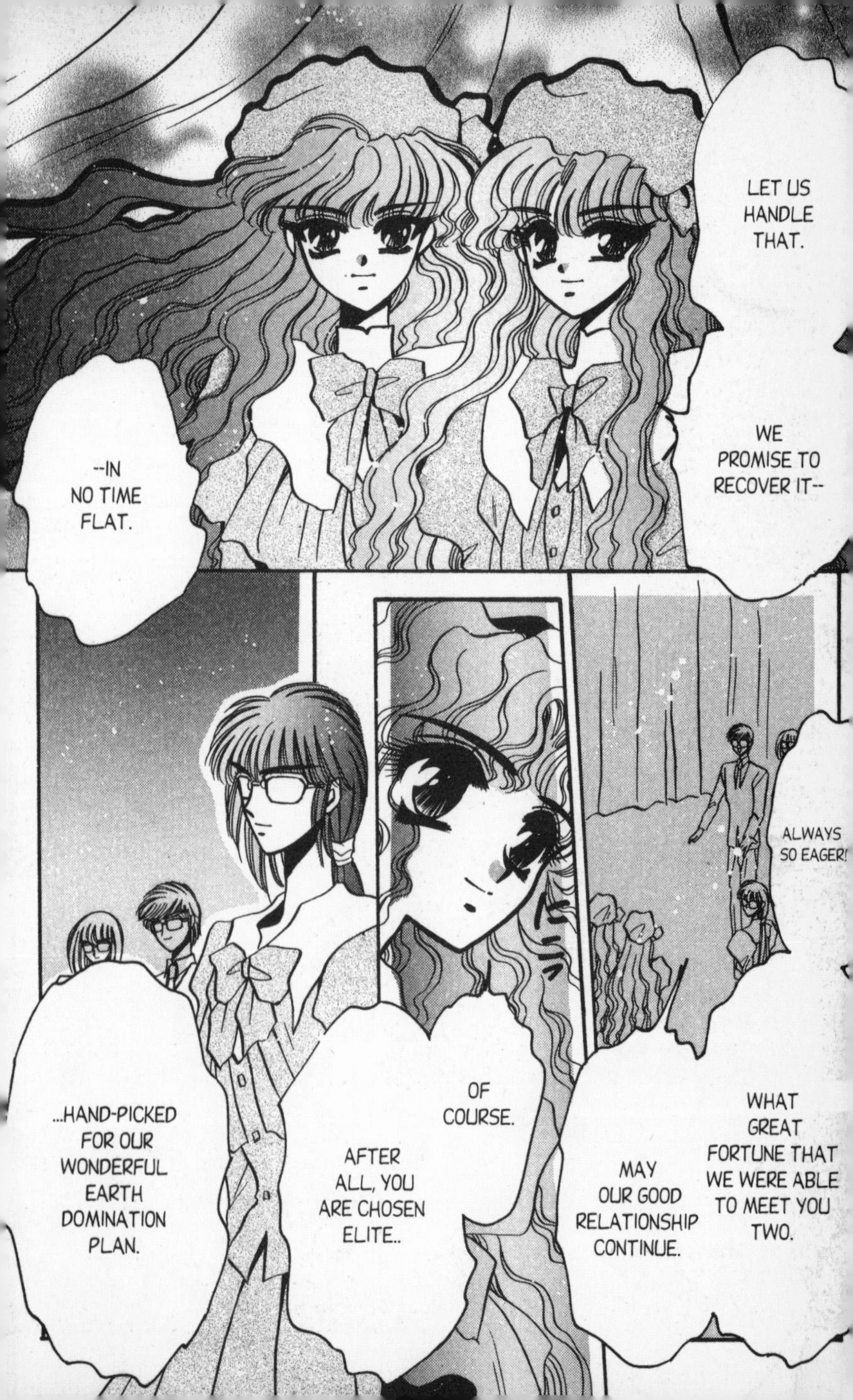
LET US HANDLE THAT.
WE PROMISE TO RECOVER IT--
--IN NO TIME FLAT.
ALWAYS SO EAGER!
WHAT GREAT FORTUNE THAT WE WERE ABLE TO MEET YOU TWO.
MAY OUR GOOD RELATIONSHIP CONTINUE.
OF COURSE.
AFTER ALL, YOU ARE CHOSEN ELITE..
...HAND-PICKED FOR OUR WONDERFUL EARTH DOMINATION PLAN.

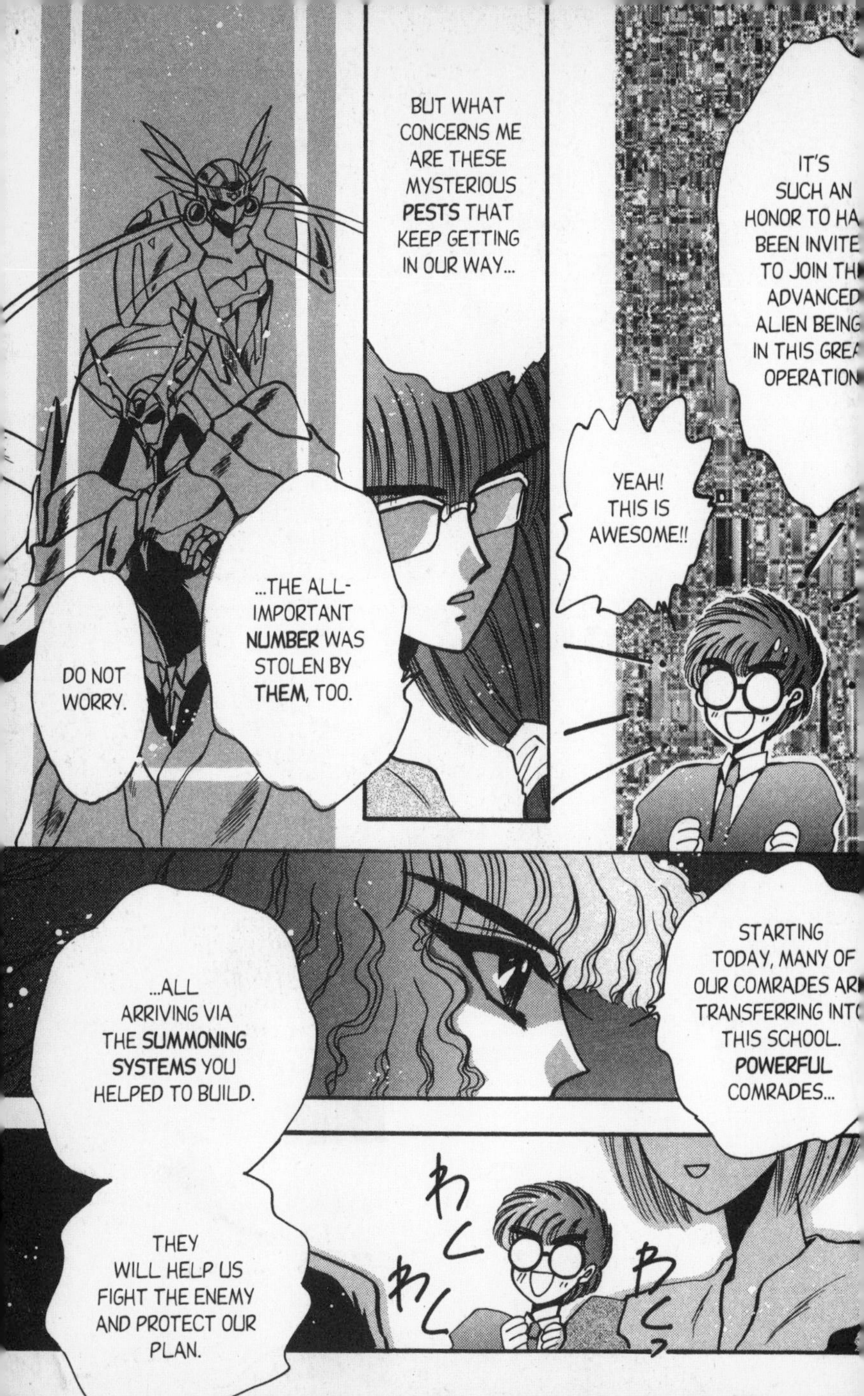
IT'S SUCH AN HONOR TO HA BEEN INVITE TO JOIN TH ADVANCED ALIEN BEING IN THIS GREA OPERATION
YEAH! THIS IS AWESOME!!
BUT WHAT CONCERNS ME ARE THESE MYSTERIOUS **PESTS** THAT KEEP GETTING IN OUR WAY...
...THE ALL-IMPORTANT **NUMBER** WAS STOLEN BY **THEM**, TOO.
DO NOT WORRY.
STARTING TODAY, MANY OF OUR COMRADES AR TRANSFERRING INT THIS SCHOOL. **POWERFUL** COMRADES...
...ALL ARRIVING VIA THE **SUMMONING SYSTEMS** YOU HELPED TO BUILD.
THEY WILL HELP US FIGHT THE ENEMY AND PROTECT OUR PLAN.
わく
わく
わく

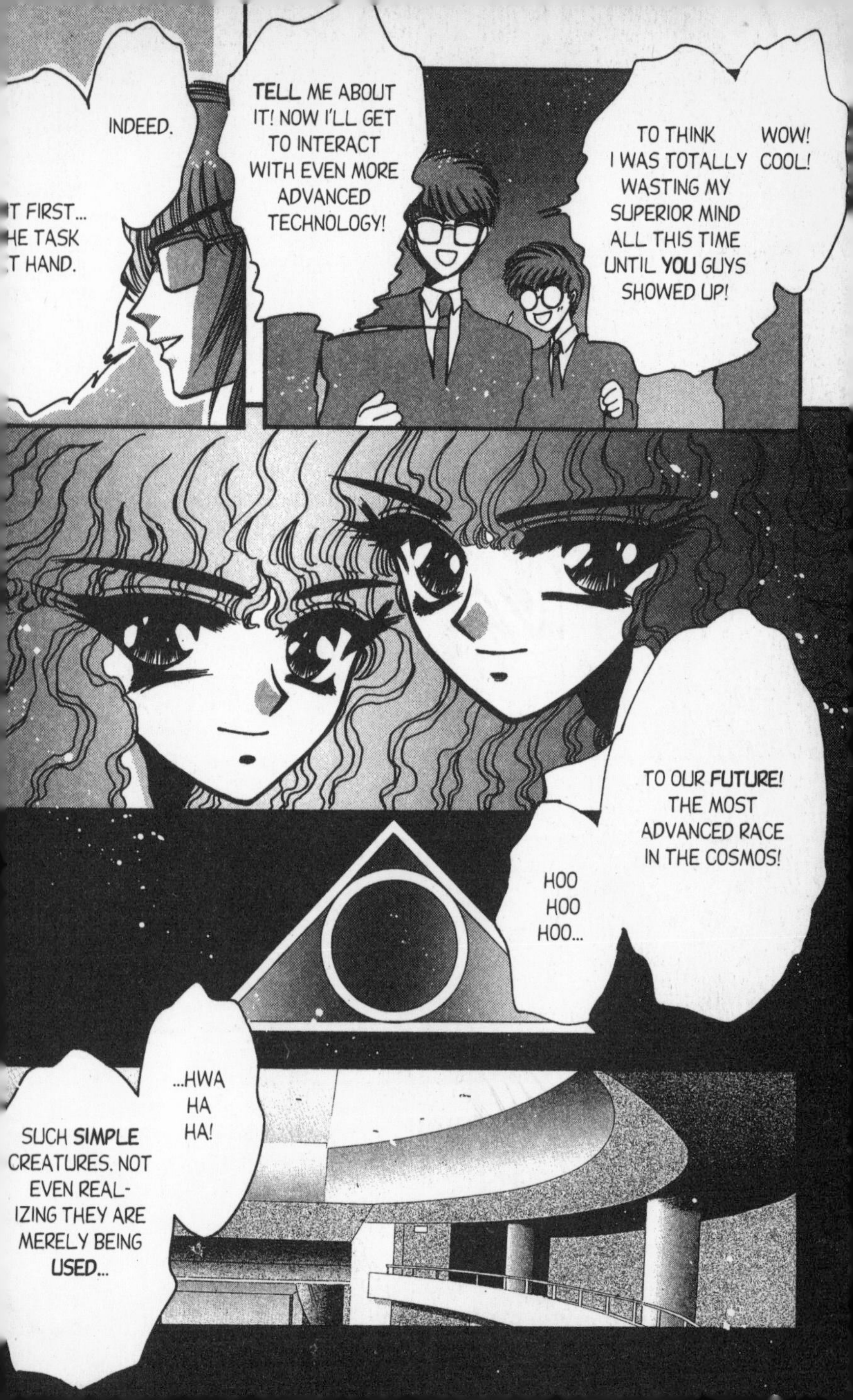
WOW! COOL!
TO THINK I WAS TOTALLY WASTING MY SUPERIOR MIND ALL THIS TIME UNTIL YOU GUYS SHOWED UP!
TELL ME ABOUT IT! NOW I'LL GET TO INTERACT WITH EVEN MORE ADVANCED TECHNOLOGY!
INDEED.
T FIRST... HE TASK T HAND.
TO OUR FUTURE! THE MOST ADVANCED RACE IN THE COSMOS!
HOO HOO HOO...
...HWA HA HA!
SUCH SIMPLE CREATURES. NOT EVEN REAL-IZING THEY ARE MERELY BEING USED...

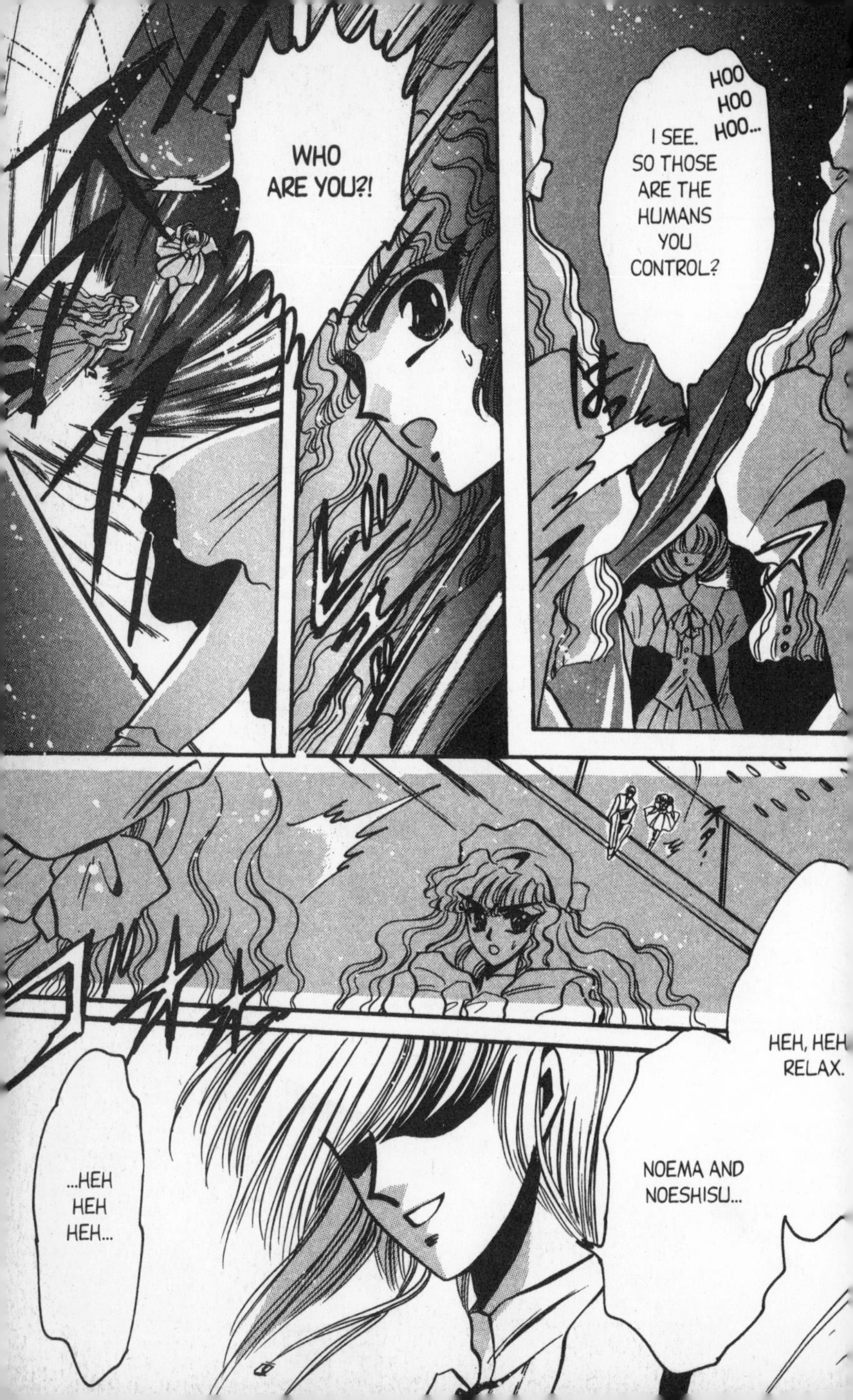
HOO HOO HOO...
I SEE. SO THOSE ARE THE HUMANS YOU CONTROL?
WHO ARE YOU?!
HEH, HEH RELAX.
NOEMA AND NOESHISU...
...HEH HEH HEH...

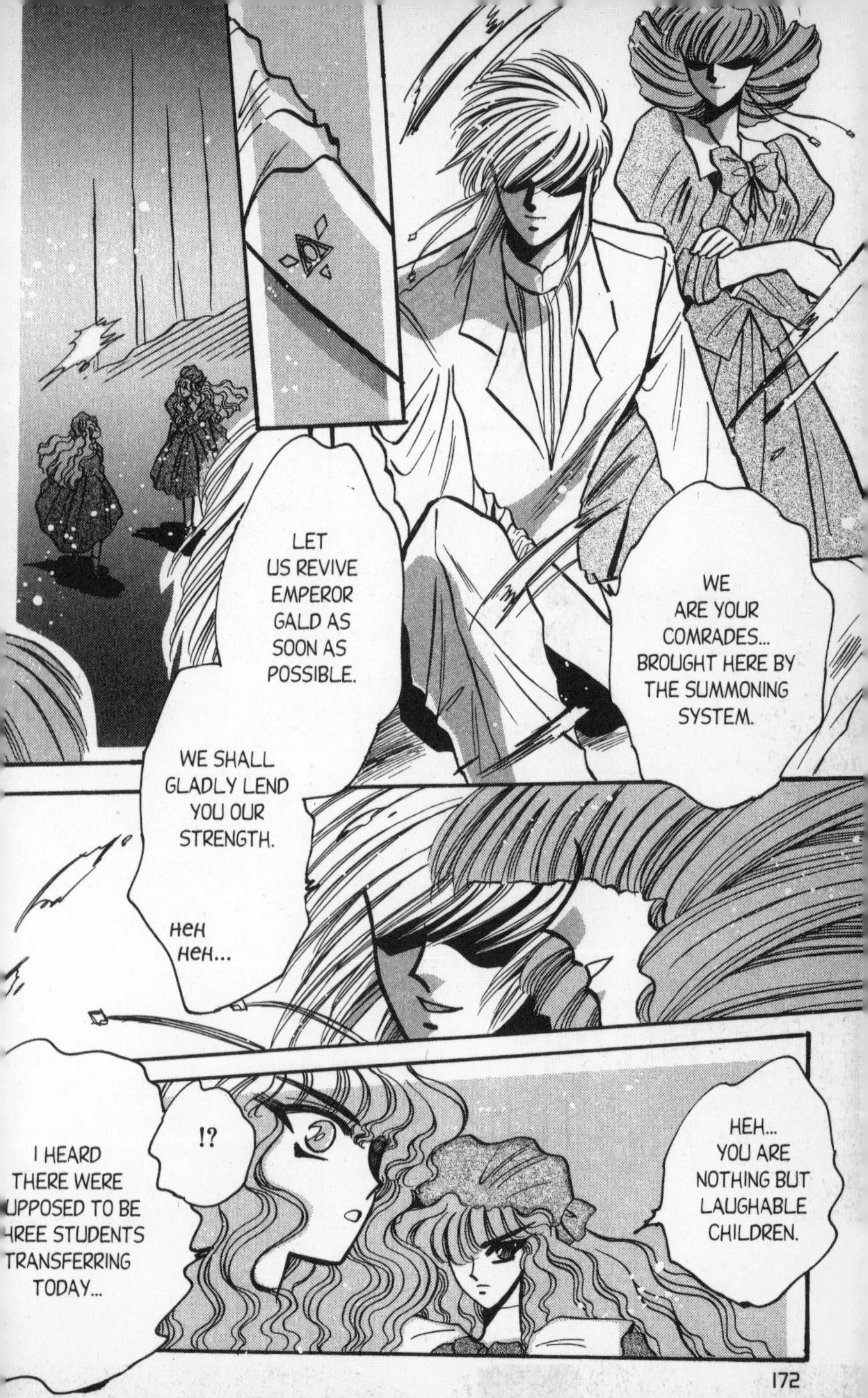
WE ARE YOUR COMRADES... BROUGHT HERE BY THE SUMMONING SYSTEM.
LET US REVIVE EMPEROR GALD AS SOON AS POSSIBLE.
WE SHALL GLADLY LEND YOU OUR STRENGTH.
HEH HEH...
HEH... YOU ARE NOTHING BUT LAUGHABLE CHILDREN.
!?
I HEARD THERE WERE UPPOSED TO BE HREE STUDENTS TRANSFERRING TODAY...

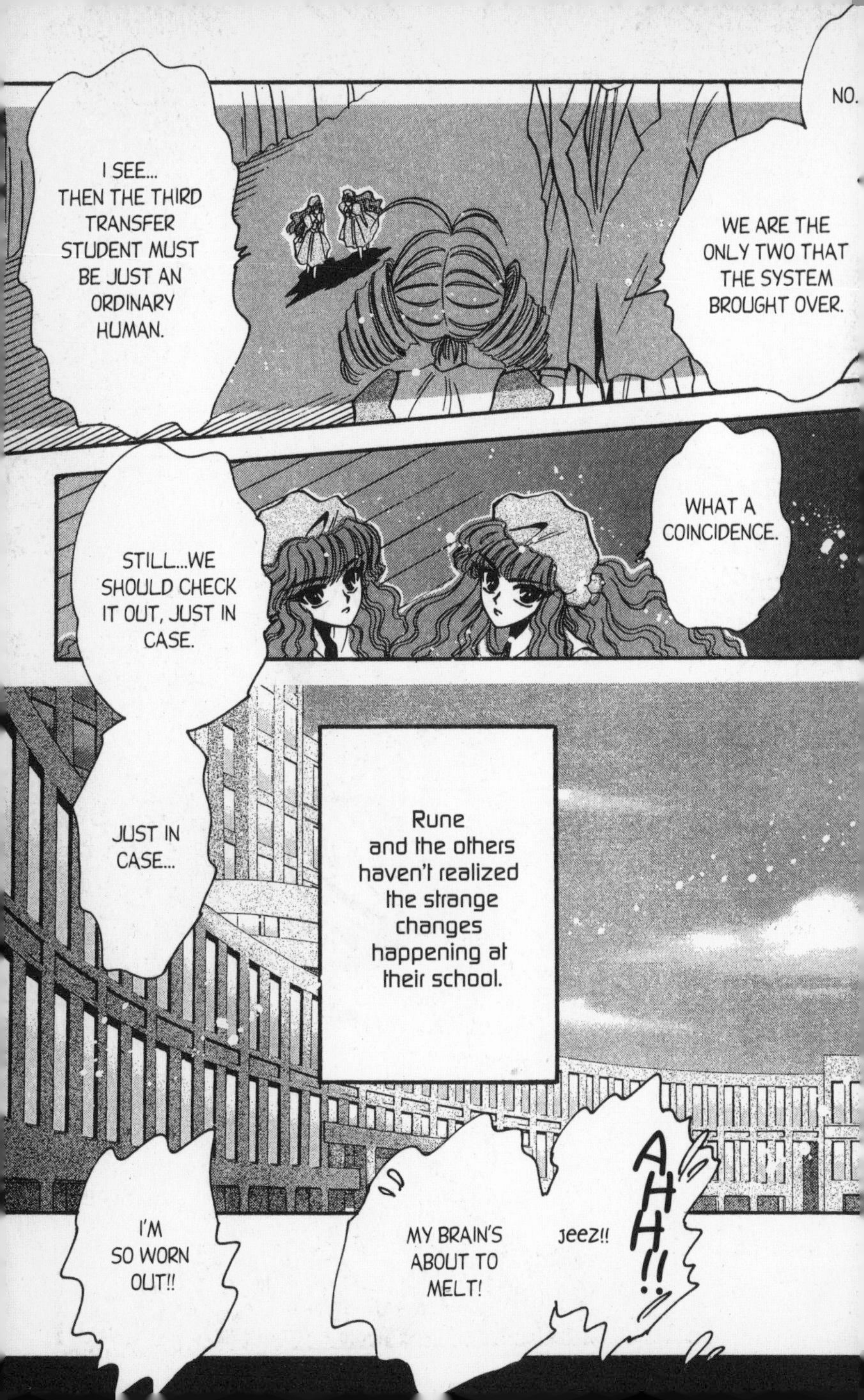
NO.
WE ARE THE ONLY TWO THAT THE SYSTEM BROUGHT OVER.
I SEE... THEN THE THIRD TRANSFER STUDENT MUST BE JUST AN ORDINARY HUMAN.
WHAT A COINCIDENCE.
STILL...WE SHOULD CHECK IT OUT, JUST IN CASE.
JUST IN CASE...
Rune and the others haven't realized the strange changes happening at their school.
AHH!!
Jeez!!
MY BRAIN'S ABOUT TO MELT!
I'M SO WORN OUT!!

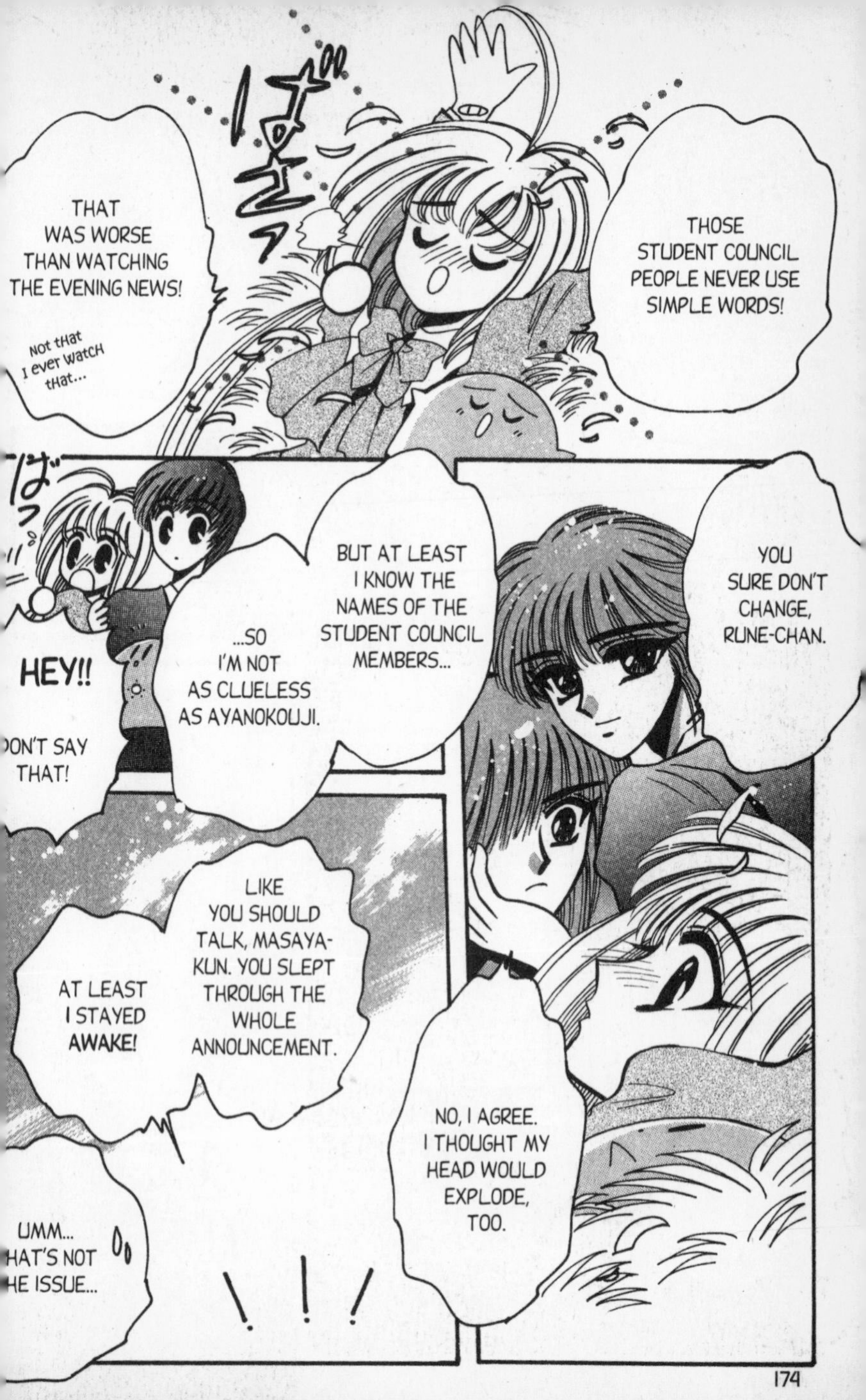
THOSE STUDENT COUNCIL PEOPLE NEVER USE SIMPLE WORDS!
THAT WAS WORSE THAN WATCHING THE EVENING NEWS!
Not that I ever watch that...
YOU SURE DON'T CHANGE, RUNE-CHAN.
NO, I AGREE. I THOUGHT MY HEAD WOULD EXPLODE, TOO.
BUT AT LEAST I KNOW THE NAMES OF THE STUDENT COUNCIL MEMBERS...
...SO I'M NOT AS CLUELESS AS AYANOKOUJI.
ばっ
HEY!!
DON'T SAY THAT!
LIKE YOU SHOULD TALK, MASAYA-KUN. YOU SLEPT THROUGH THE WHOLE ANNOUNCEMENT.
AT LEAST I STAYED AWAKE!
UMM... HAT'S NOT HE ISSUE...
!!!

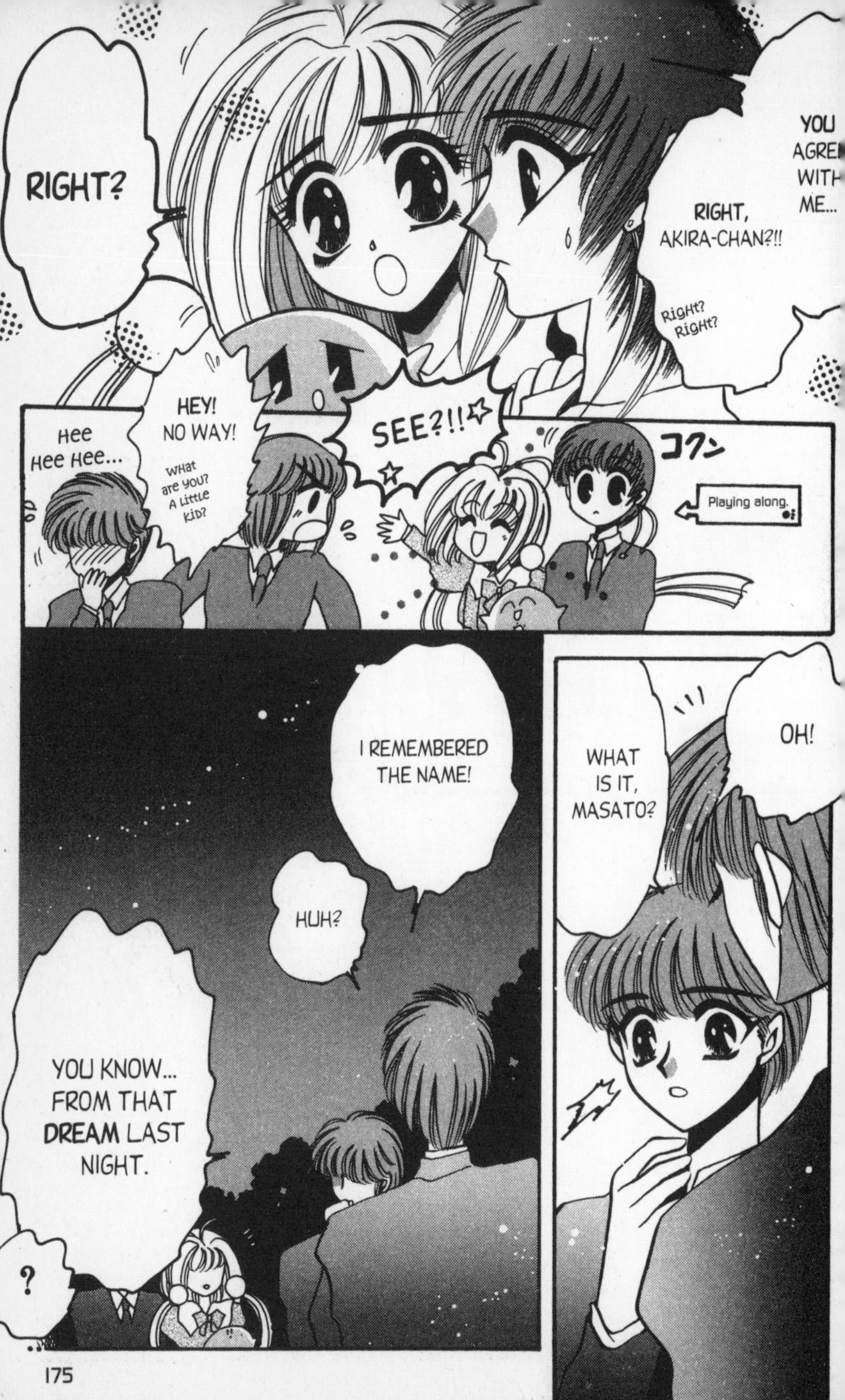

YOU AGRE WITH ME...
RIGHT, AKIRA-CHAN?!!
Right? Right?
RIGHT?
コクン
Playing along.
SEE?!!
HEY! NO WAY!
What are you? A little kid?
Hee hee hee...
OH!
WHAT IS IT, MASATO?
I REMEMBERED THE NAME!
HUH?
YOU KNOW... FROM THAT **DREAM** LAST NIGHT.
?

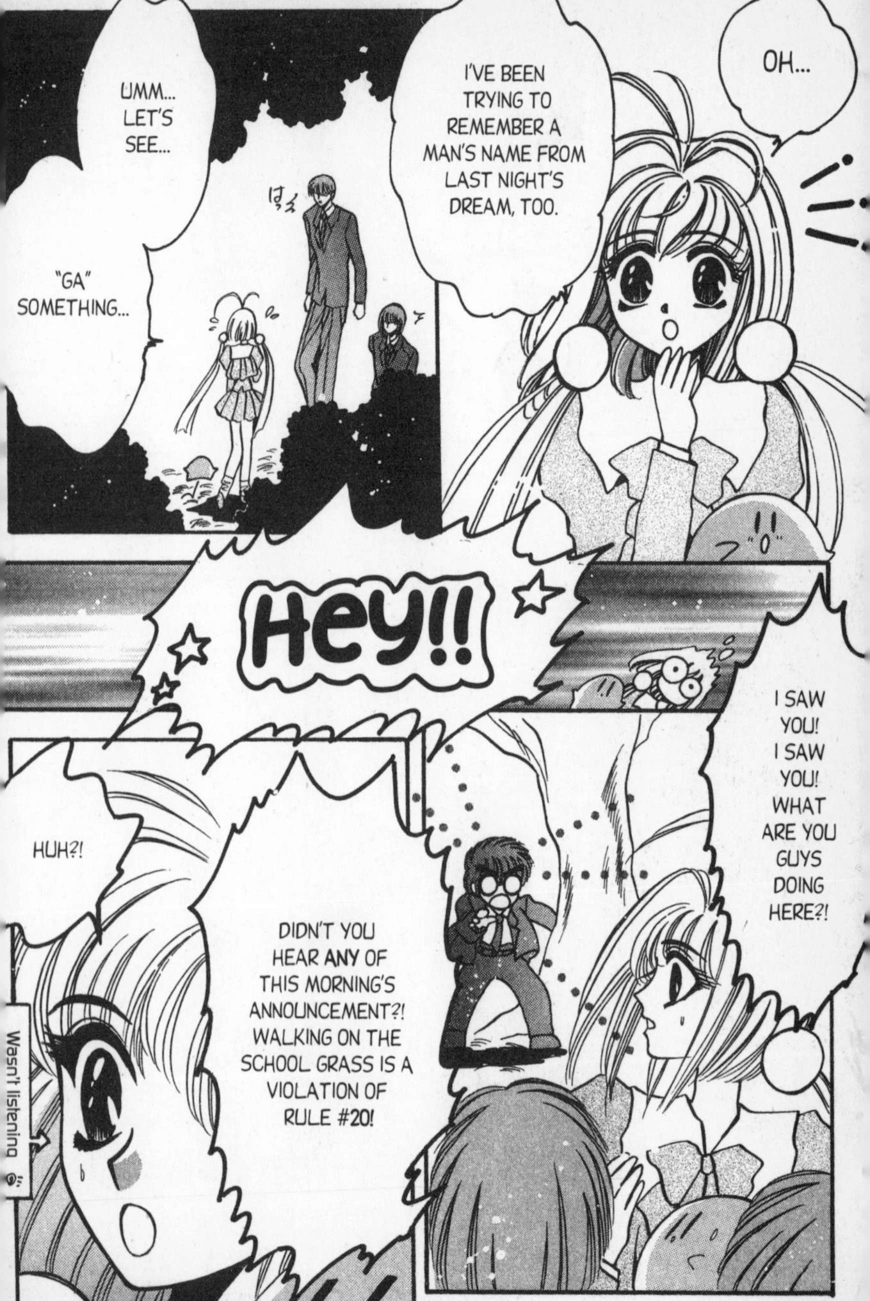
OH...
I'VE BEEN TRYING TO REMEMBER A MAN'S NAME FROM LAST NIGHT'S DREAM, TOO.
UMM... LET'S SEE...
"GA" SOMETHING...
Hey!!
I SAW YOU! I SAW YOU! WHAT ARE YOU GUYS DOING HERE?!
DIDN'T YOU HEAR **ANY** OF THIS MORNING'S ANNOUNCEMENT?! WALKING ON THE SCHOOL GRASS IS A VIOLATION OF RULE #20!
HUH?!
Wasn't listening

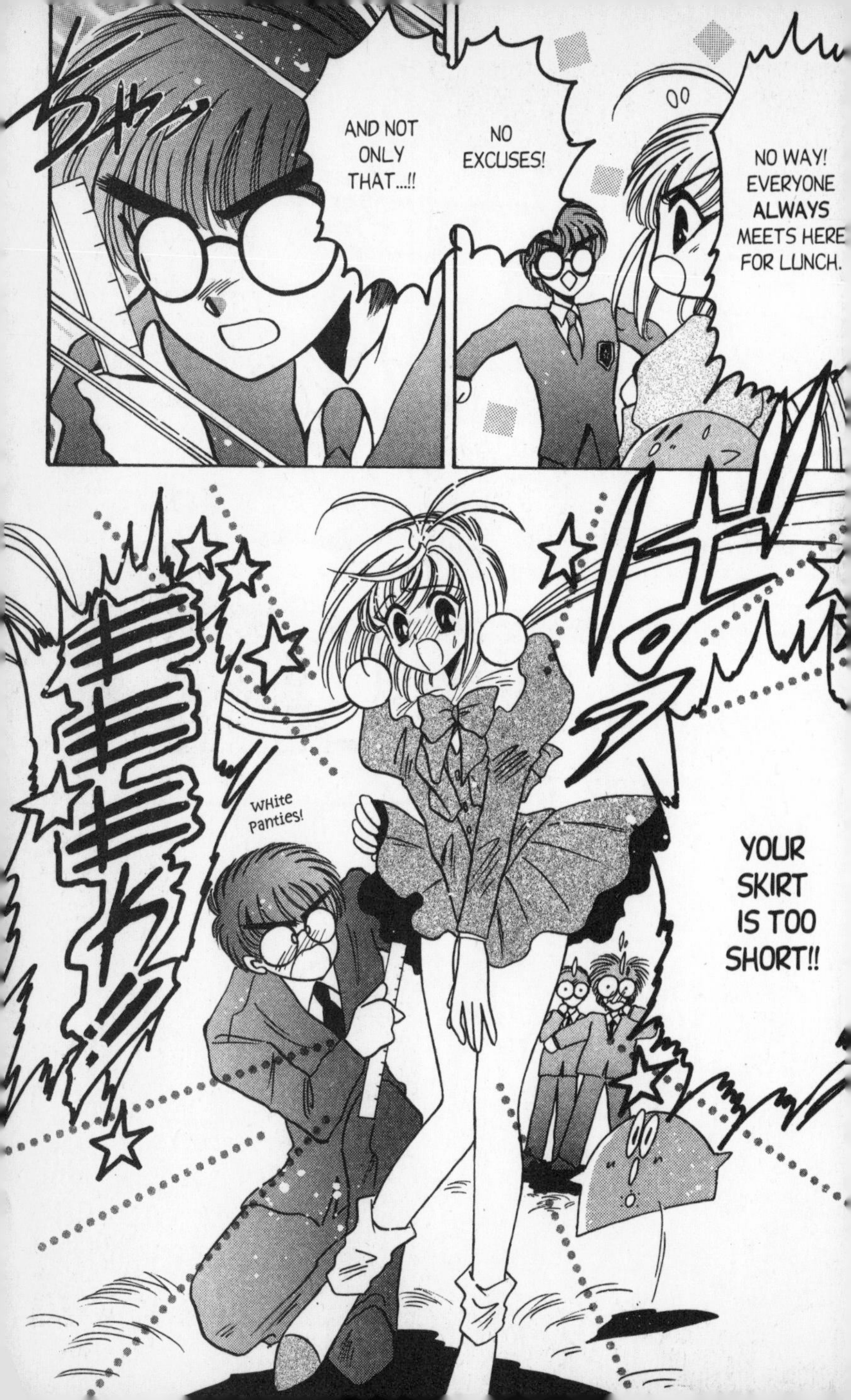
NO WAY! EVERYONE ALWAYS MEETS HERE FOR LUNCH.
NO EXCUSES!
AND NOT ONLY THAT...!!
YOUR SKIRT IS TOO SHORT!!
WHite Panties!

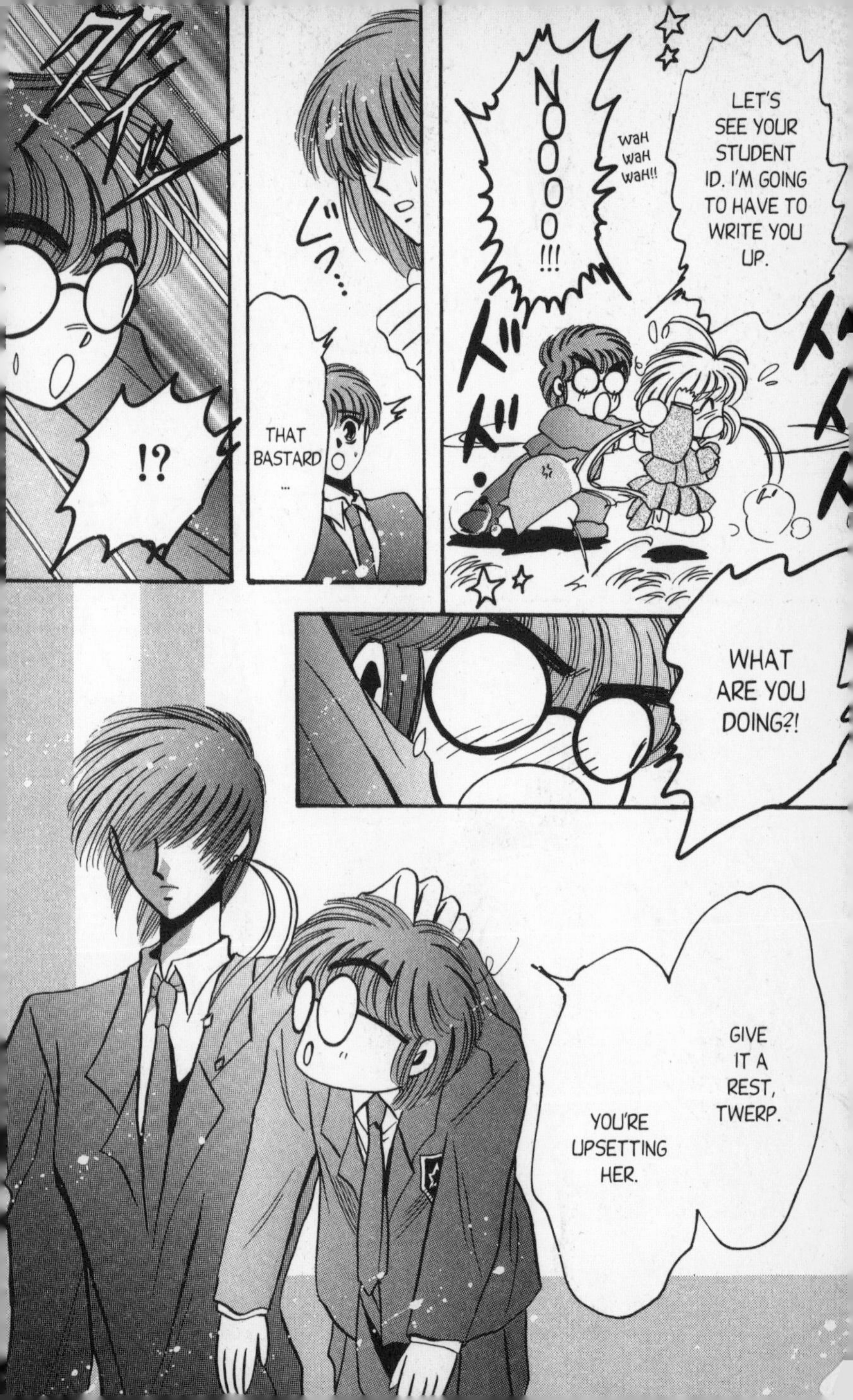
LET'S SEE YOUR STUDENT ID. I'M GOING TO HAVE TO WRITE YOU UP.
NOOOOO!!!
WAH WAH WAH!!
THAT BASTARD ...
!?
WHAT ARE YOU DOING?!
GIVE IT A REST, TWERP.
YOU'RE UPSETTING HER.

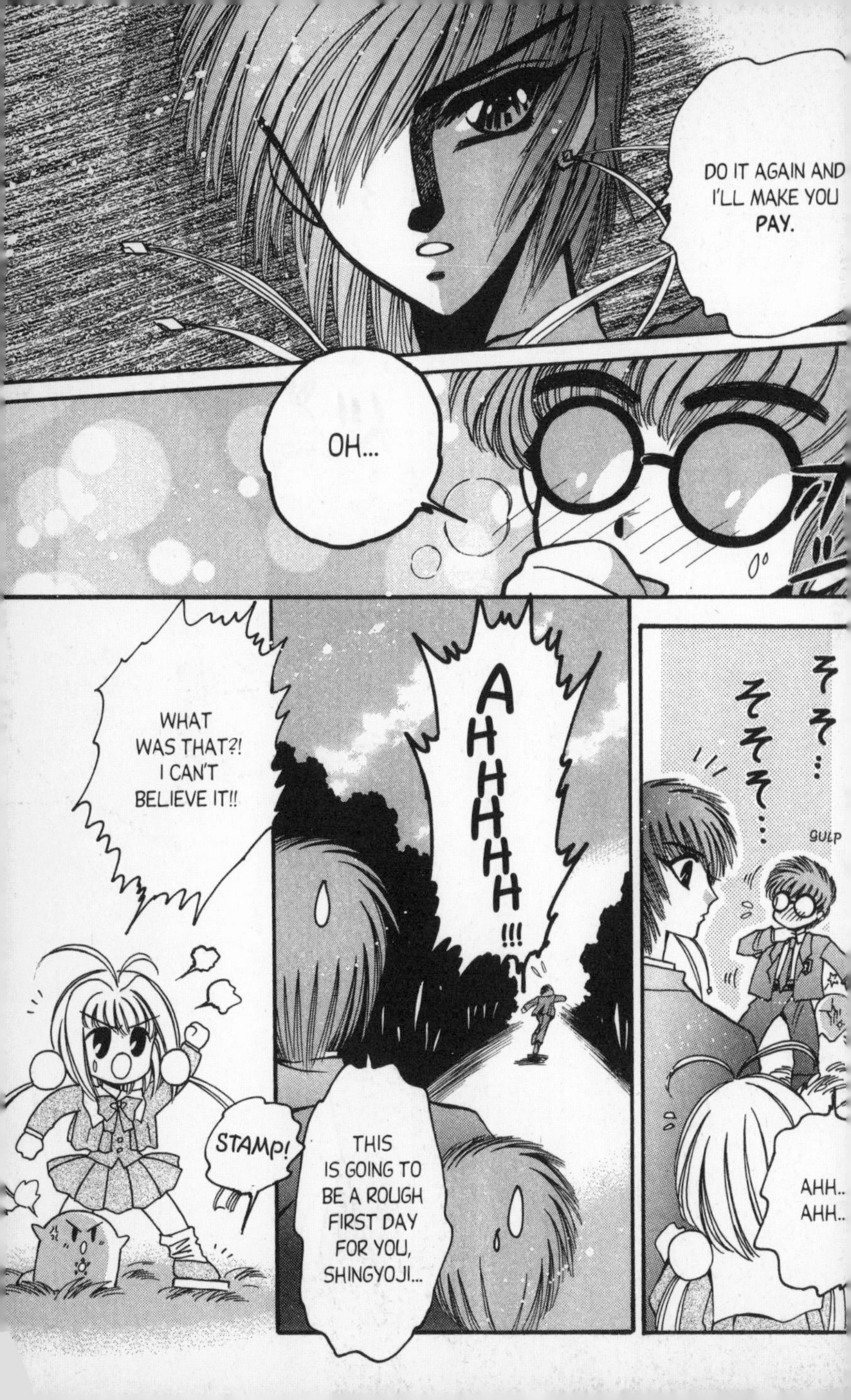
DO IT AGAIN AND I'LL MAKE YOU PAY.
OH...
そそ…
そそそ…
GULP
AHH.. AHH..
AHHHHH!!!
THIS IS GOING TO BE A ROUGH FIRST DAY FOR YOU, SHINGYOJI...
WHAT WAS THAT?! I CAN'T BELIEVE IT!!
STAMP!

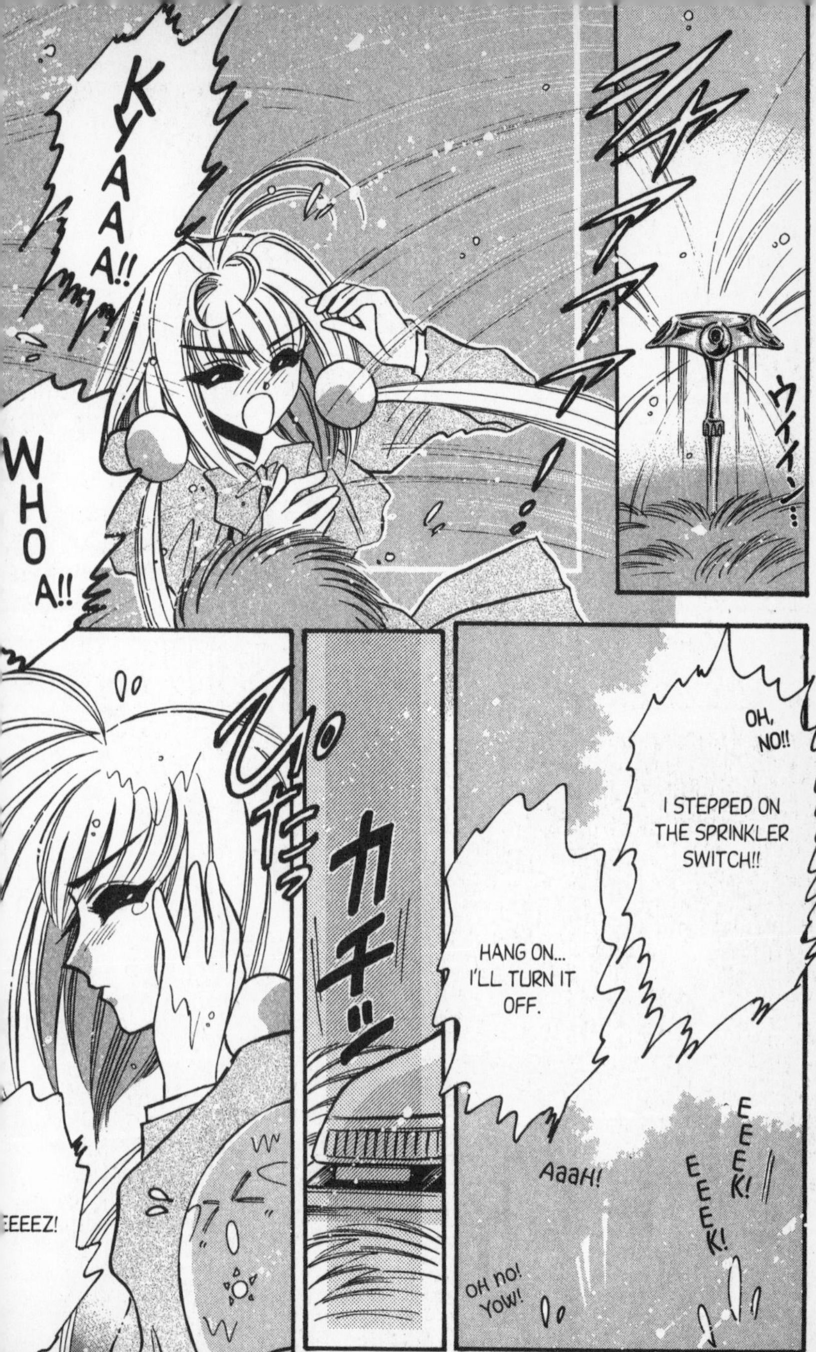
ウィイイン…
KYAAAA!!
WHOA!!
OH, NO!!
I STEPPED ON THE SPRINKLER SWITCH!!
HANG ON... I'LL TURN IT OFF.
AaaH!
EEEEK!
EEEK!
OH no! YOW!
カチッ
EEEEZ!

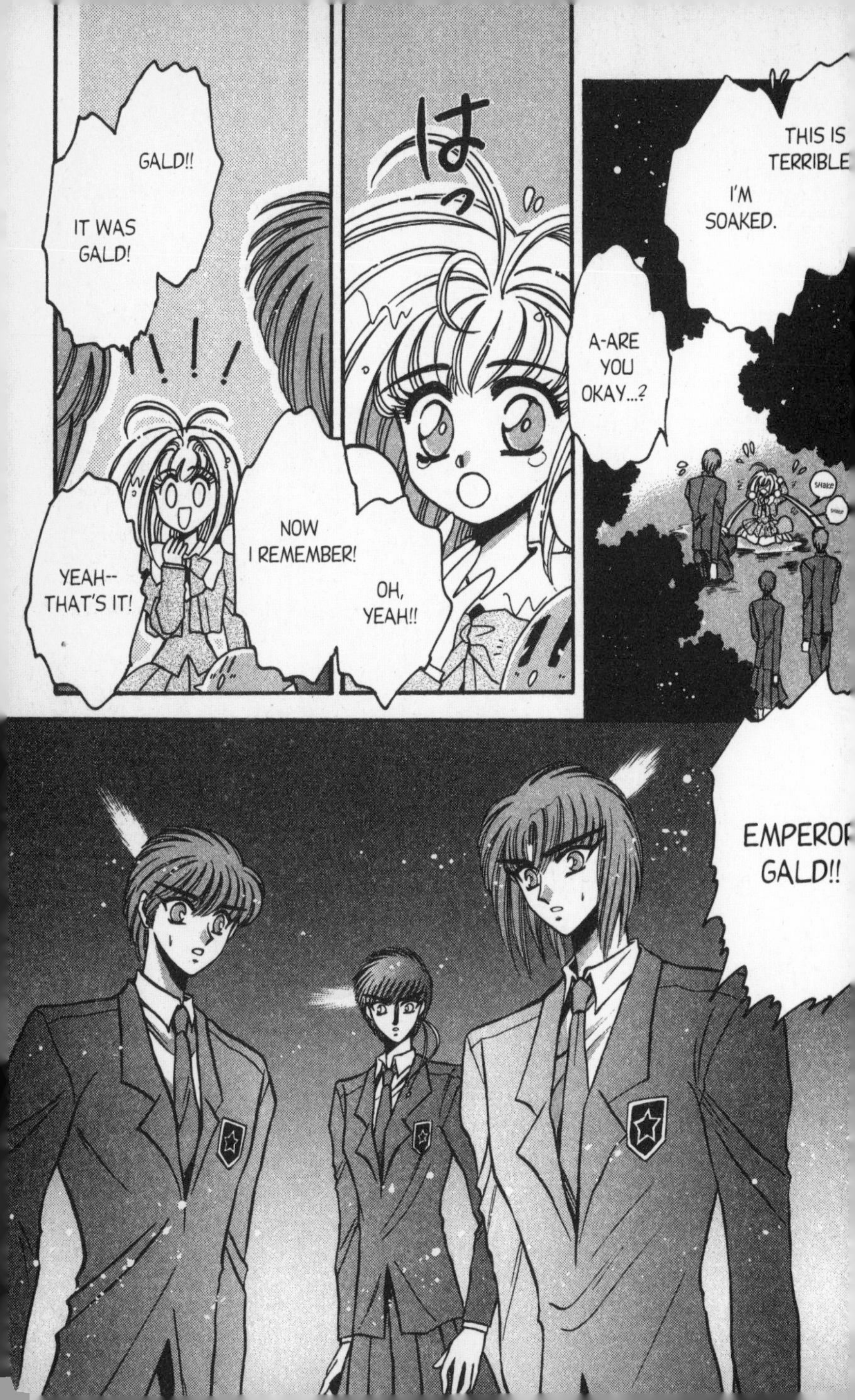
THIS IS TERRIBLE
I'M SOAKED.
A-ARE YOU OKAY...?
SHAKE
SHAKE
はっ
OH, YEAH!!
NOW I REMEMBER!
GALD!!
IT WAS GALD!
!!!
YEAH-- THAT'S IT!
EMPEROR GALD!!

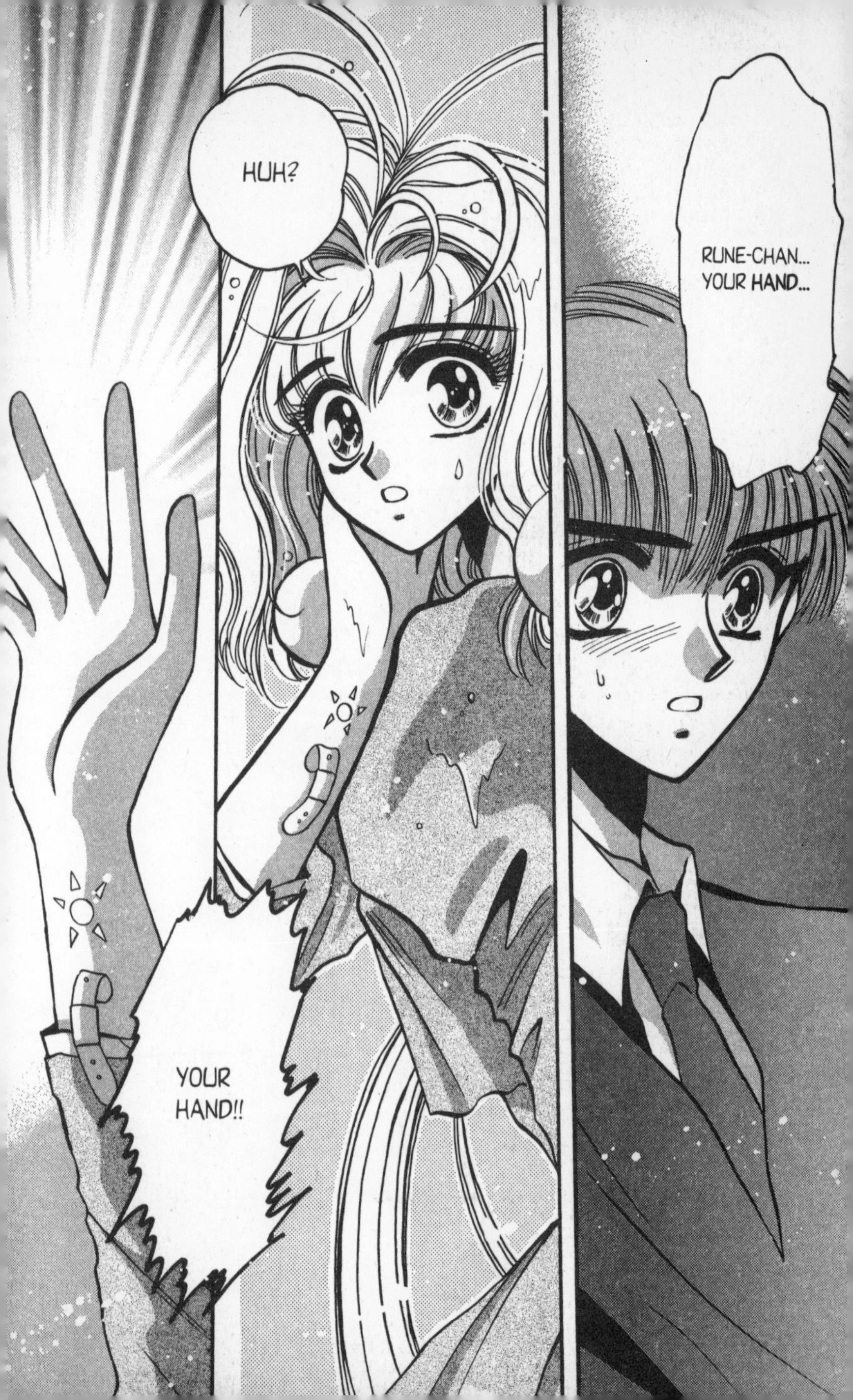
RUNE-CHAN... YOUR HAND...
HUH?
YOUR HAND!!

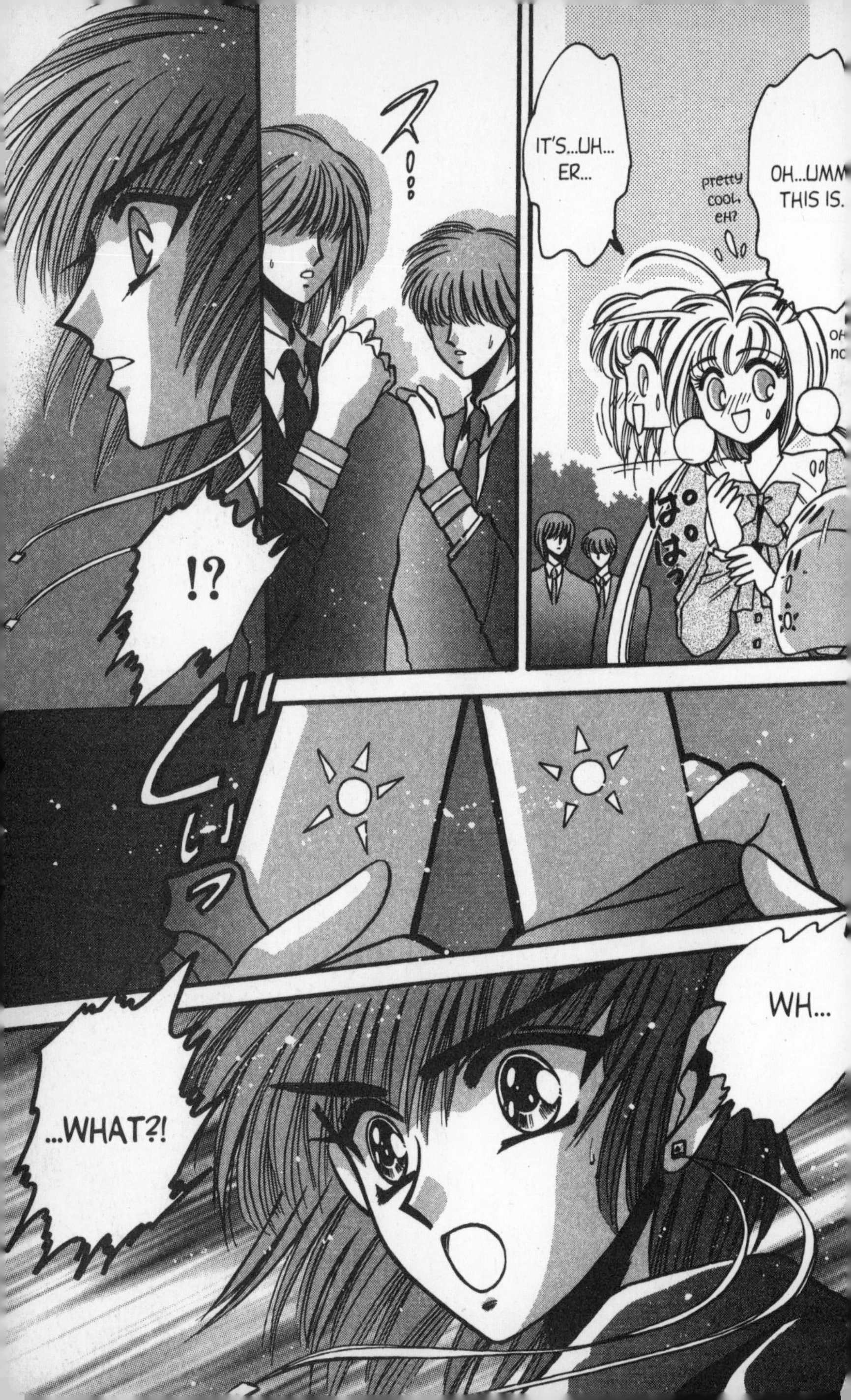
OH...UMM THIS IS.
pretty cool, eH?
IT'S...UH... ER...
ス
!?
WH...
...WHAT?!

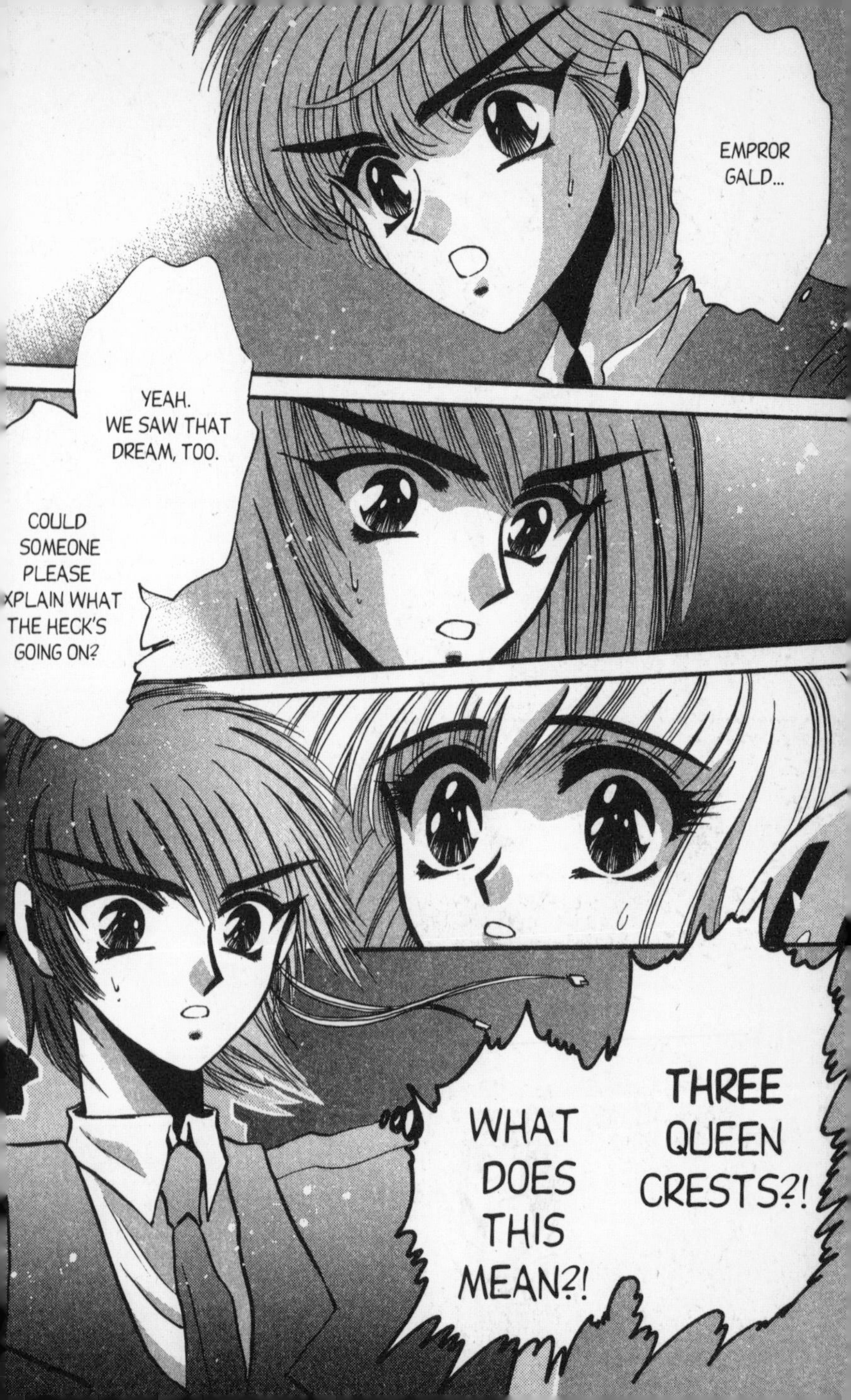
EMPROR GALD...
YEAH. WE SAW THAT DREAM, TOO.
COULD SOMEONE PLEASE XPLAIN WHAT THE HECK'S GOING ON?
THREE QUEEN CRESTS?!
WHAT DOES THIS MEAN?!

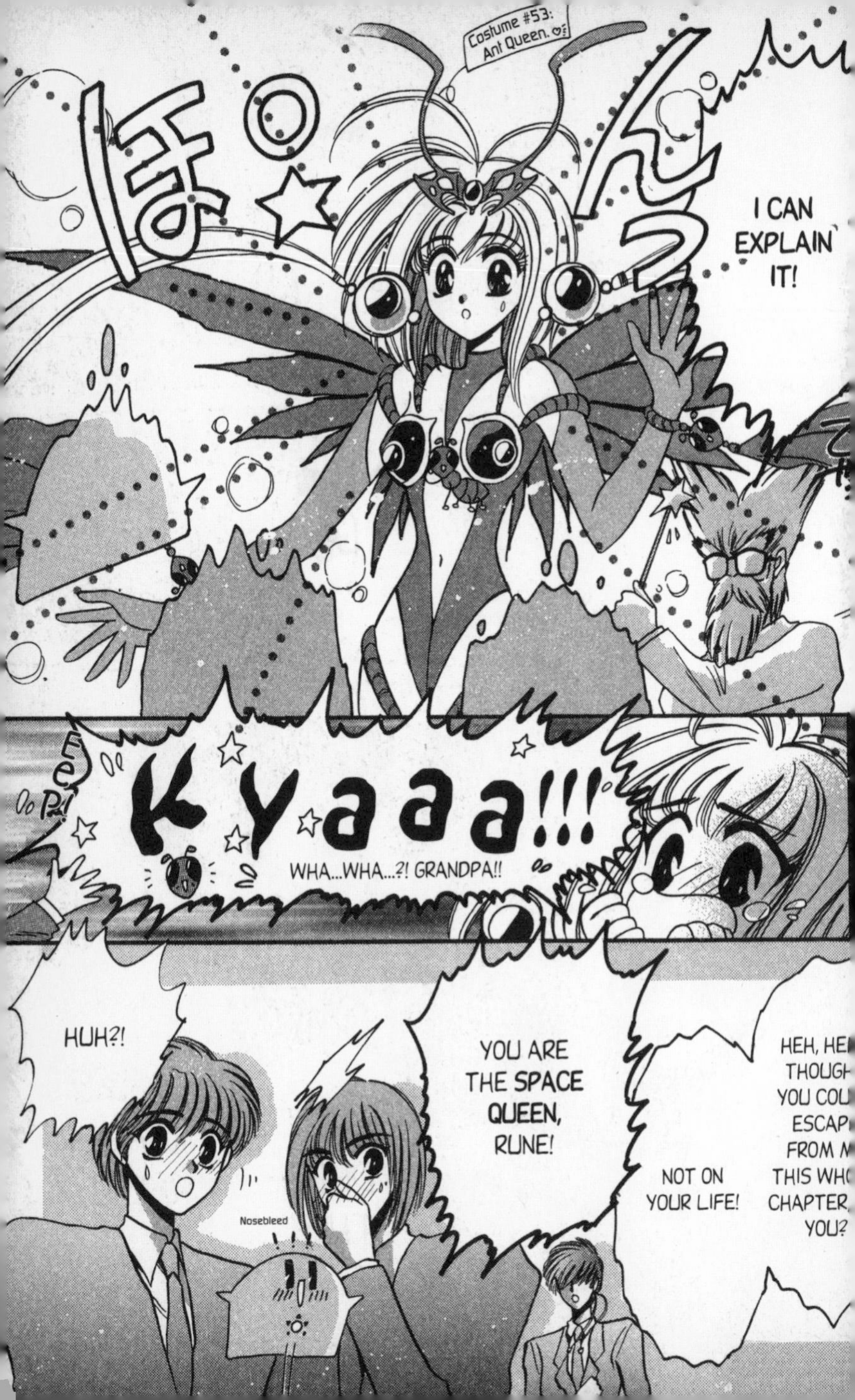

Costume #53: Ant Queen. ♡
I CAN EXPLAIN IT!
ぽん
Kyaaa!!!
Eeep!
WHA...WHA...?! GRANDPA!!
HEH, HE
THOUGH
YOU COU
ESCAP
FROM M
THIS WHO
CHAPTER,
YOU?
NOT ON YOUR LIFE!
YOU ARE THE SPACE QUEEN, RUNE!
HUH?!
Nosebleed

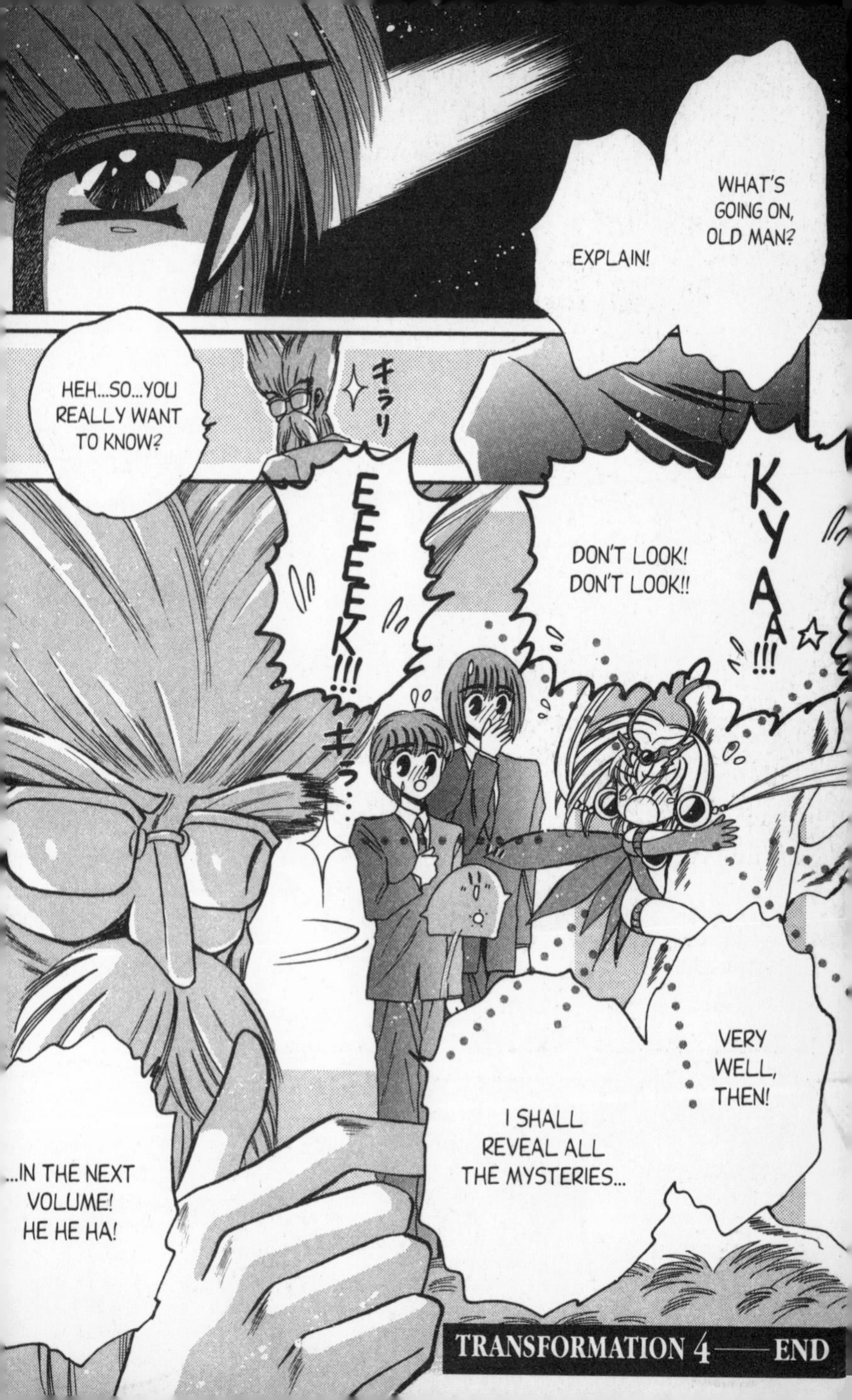
WHAT'S GOING ON, OLD MAN?
EXPLAIN!
キラリ
HEH...SO...YOU REALLY WANT TO KNOW?
KYAA☆!!!
DON'T LOOK! DON'T LOOK!!
EEEEK!!!
キラ...
VERY WELL, THEN!
I SHALL REVEAL ALL THE MYSTERIES...
...IN THE NEXT VOLUME! HE HE HA!
TRANSFORMATION 4 — END

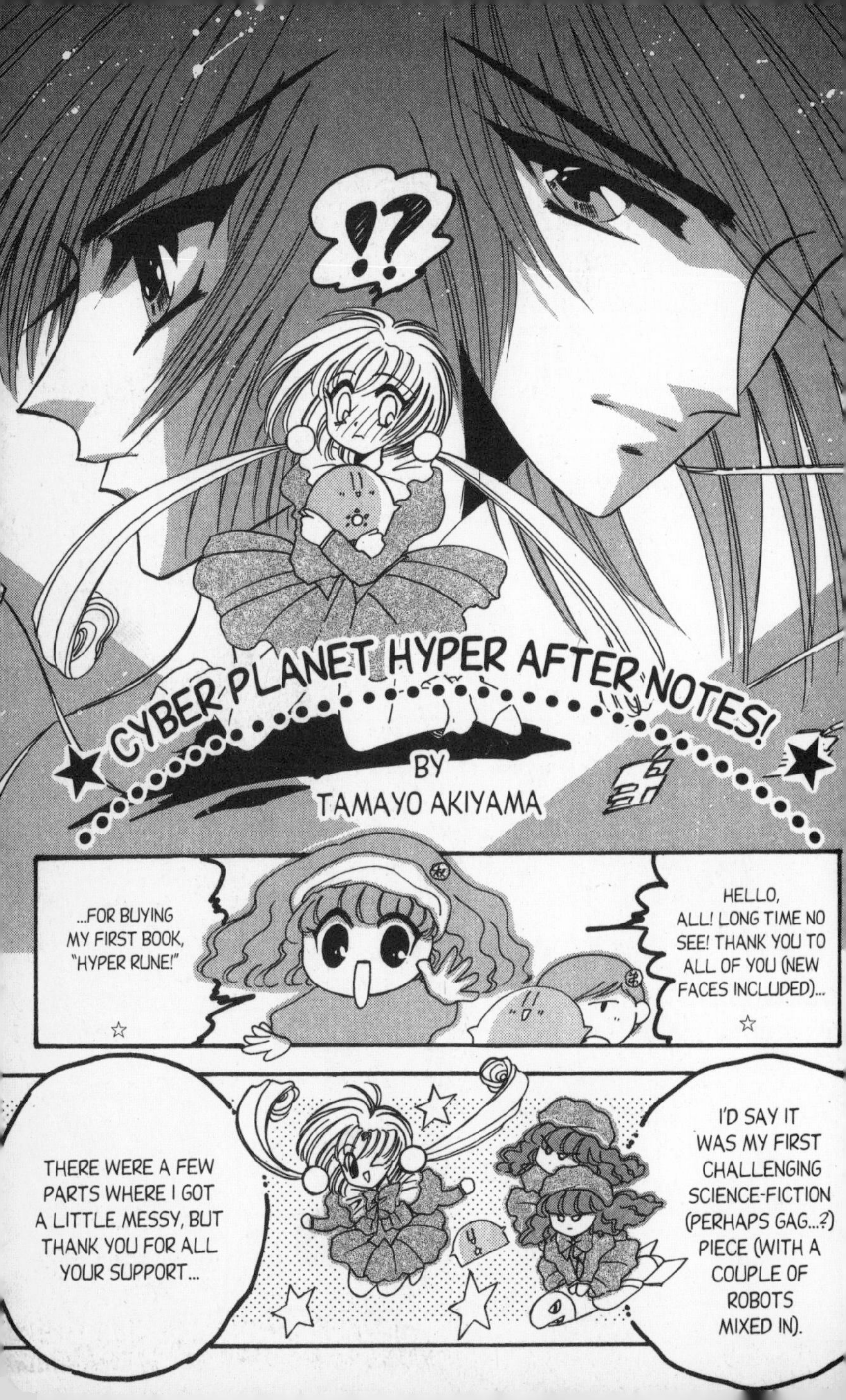
!?
CYBER PLANET HYPER AFTER NOTES!
BY
TAMAYO AKIYAMA
HELLO, ALL! LONG TIME NO SEE! THANK YOU TO ALL OF YOU (NEW FACES INCLUDED)...
...FOR BUYING MY FIRST BOOK, "HYPER RUNE!"
I'D SAY IT WAS MY FIRST CHALLENGING SCIENCE-FICTION (PERHAPS GAG...?) PIECE (WITH A COUPLE OF ROBOTS MIXED IN).
THERE WERE A FEW PARTS WHERE I GOT A LITTLE MESSY, BUT THANK YOU FOR ALL YOUR SUPPORT...

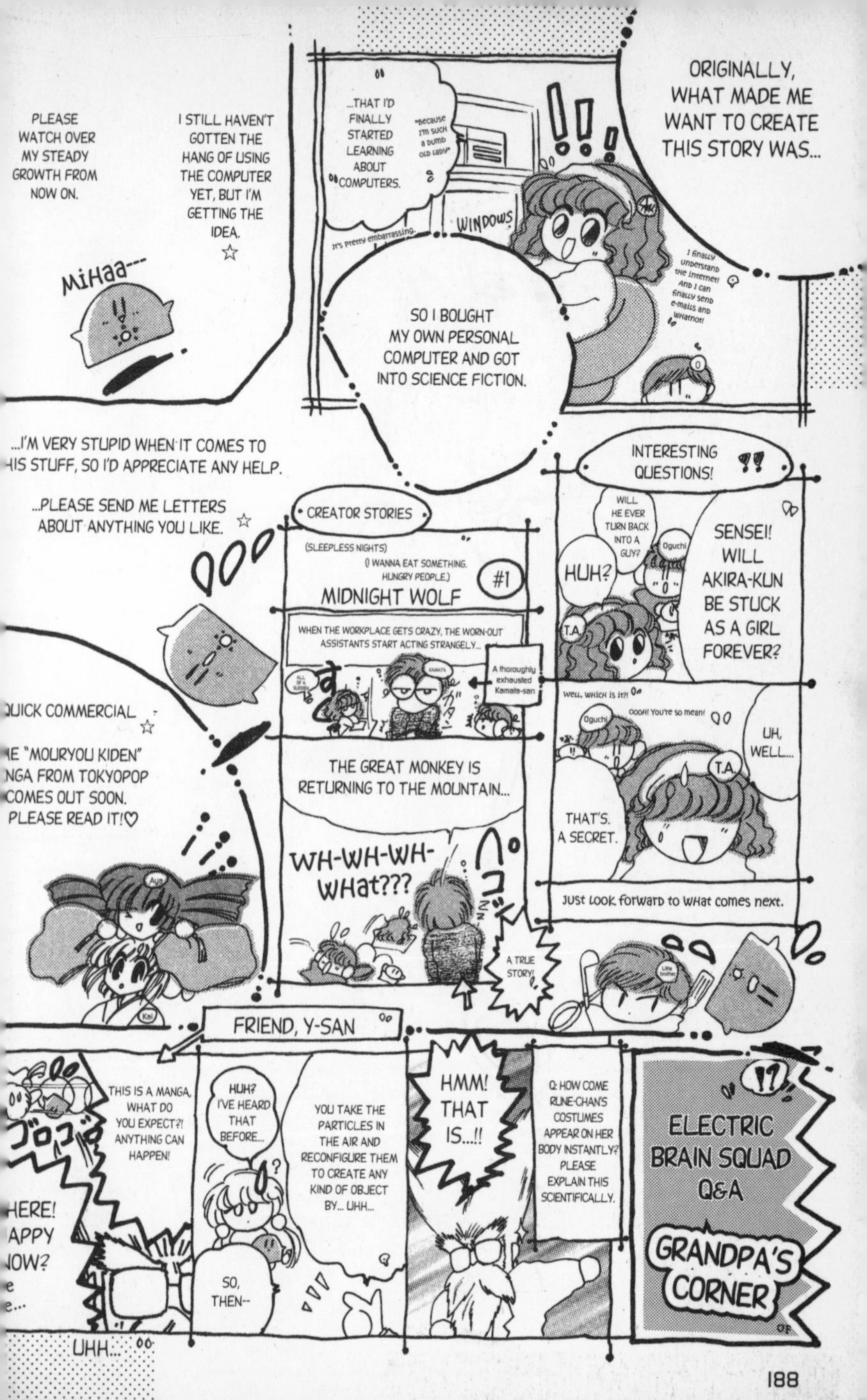
ORIGINALLY, WHAT MADE ME WANT TO CREATE THIS STORY WAS...
I finally understand the internet!! And I can finally send e-mails and whatnot!
...THAT I'D FINALLY STARTED LEARNING ABOUT COMPUTERS.
Because I'm such a dumb old lady
WINDOWS
It's pretty embarrassing.
SO I BOUGHT MY OWN PERSONAL COMPUTER AND GOT INTO SCIENCE FICTION.
I STILL HAVEN'T GOTTEN THE HANG OF USING THE COMPUTER YET, BUT I'M GETTING THE IDEA. ☆
PLEASE WATCH OVER MY STEADY GROWTH FROM NOW ON.
MiHaa---
...I'M VERY STUPID WHEN IT COMES TO HIS STUFF, SO I'D APPRECIATE ANY HELP.
...PLEASE SEND ME LETTERS ABOUT ANYTHING YOU LIKE. ☆
INTERESTING QUESTIONS!
SENSEI! WILL AKIRA-KUN BE STUCK AS A GIRL FOREVER?
WILL HE EVER TURN BACK INTO A GUY?
Oguchi
HUH?
T.A.
Well, which is it?!
Oooh! You're so mean!
UH, WELL...
THAT'S. A SECRET.
Just look forward to what comes next.
CREATOR STORIES
(SLEEPLESS NIGHTS)
(I WANNA EAT SOMETHING. HUNGRY PEOPLE.)
#1
MIDNIGHT WOLF
WHEN THE WORKPLACE GETS CRAZY, THE WORN-OUT ASSISTANTS START ACTING STRANGELY...
ALL OF A SUDDEN
KAMATA
A thoroughly exhausted Kamata-san
THE GREAT MONKEY IS RETURNING TO THE MOUNTAIN...
WH-WH-WH-WHat???
A TRUE STORY!
Little brother
UICK COMMERCIAL ☆
E "MOURYOU KIDEN"
NGA FROM TOKYOPOP
COMES OUT SOON.
PLEASE READ IT!♡
Aya
Kai
FRIEND, Y-SAN
ELECTRIC BRAIN SQUAD Q&A
GRANDPA'S CORNER
Q: HOW COME RUNE-CHAN'S COSTUMES APPEAR ON HER BODY INSTANTLY? PLEASE EXPLAIN THIS SCIENTIFICALLY.
HMM! THAT IS...!!
YOU TAKE THE PARTICLES IN THE AIR AND RECONFIGURE THEM TO CREATE ANY KIND OF OBJECT BY... UHH...
HUH? I'VE HEARD THAT BEFORE...
SO, THEN--
THIS IS A MANGA, WHAT DO YOU EXPECT?! ANYTHING CAN HAPPEN!
HERE!
APPY
NOW?
UHH...

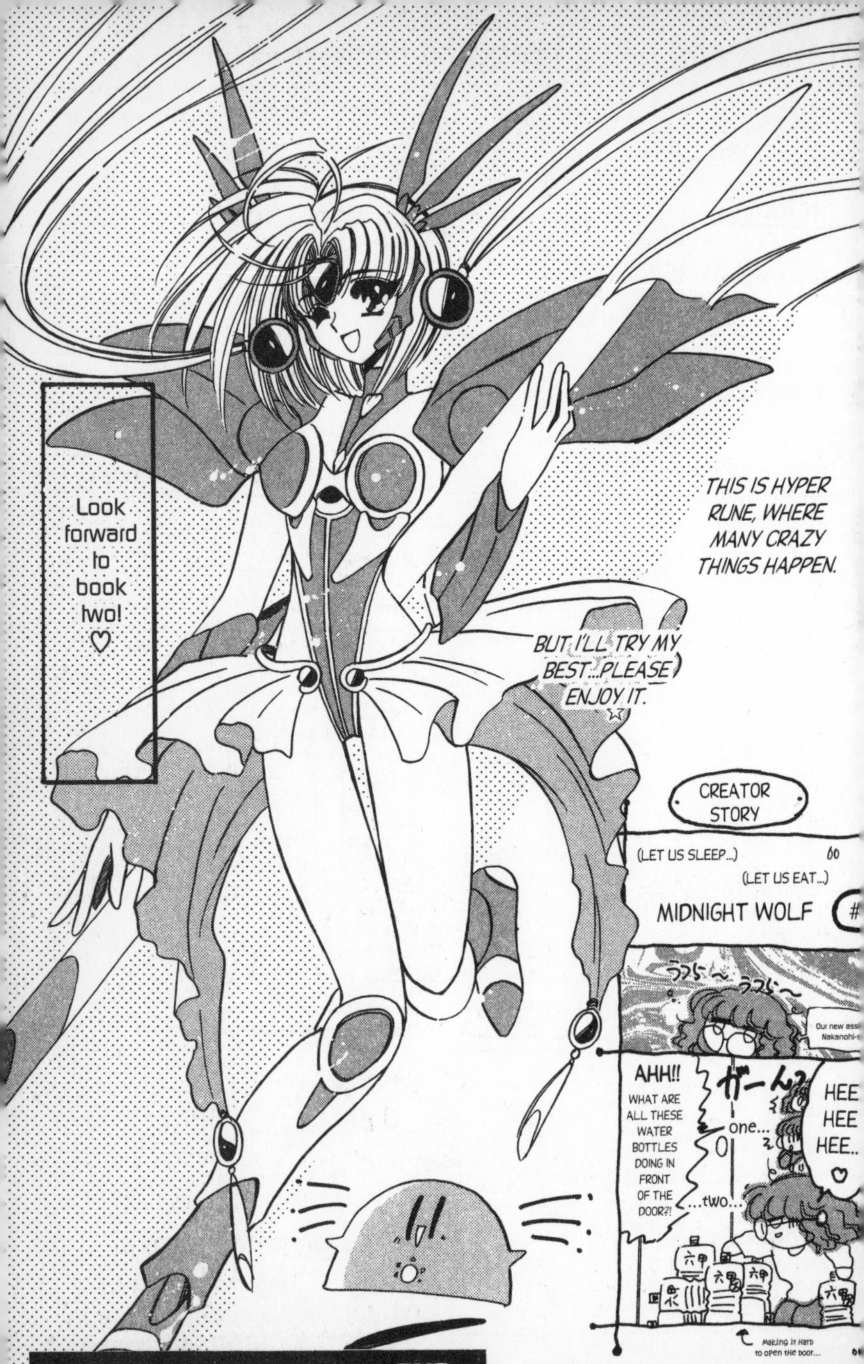
THIS IS HYPER RUNE, WHERE MANY CRAZY THINGS HAPPEN.
BUT I'LL TRY MY BEST...PLEASE ENJOY IT. ☆
Look forward to book two! ♡
CREATOR STORY
(LET US SLEEP...)
(LET US EAT...)
MIDNIGHT WOLF
うつら〜 うつら〜
HEE HEE HEE.. ♡
ガーン
one...
two...
AHH!! WHAT ARE ALL THESE WATER BOTTLES DOING IN FRONT OF THE DOOR?!
Making it Hard to open the door...

★ Cyber Planet Hyper After Notes* ★ END

ALSO AVAILABLE FROM TOKYOPOP

ALSO AVAILABLE FROM

MANGA

.HACK//LEGEND OF THE TWILIGHT
@LARGE
ABENOBASHI: MAGICAL SHOPPING ARCADE
A.I. LOVE YOU
AI YORI AOSHI
ALICHINO
ANGELIC LAYER
ARM OF KANNON
BABY BIRTH
BATTLE ROYALE
BATTLE VIXENS
BOYS BE...
BRAIN POWERED
BRIGADOON
B'TX
CANDIDATE FOR GODDESS, THE
CARDCAPTOR SAKURA
CARDCAPTOR SAKURA - MASTER OF THE CLOW
CHOBITS
CHRONICLES OF THE CURSED SWORD
CLAMP SCHOOL DETECTIVES
CLOVER
COMIC PARTY
CONFIDENTIAL CONFESSIONS
CORRECTOR YUI
COWBOY BEBOP
COWBOY BEBOP: SHOOTING STAR
CRAZY LOVE STORY
CRESCENT MOON
CROSS
CULDCEPT
CYBORG 009
D•N•ANGEL
DEARS
DEMON DIARY
DEMON ORORON, THE
DEUS VITAE
DIGIMON
DIGIMON TAMERS
DIGIMON ZERO TWO
DOLL
DRAGON HUNTER
DRAGON KNIGHTS
DRAGON VOICE
DREAM SAGA
DUKLYON: CLAMP SCHOOL DEFENDERS
EERIE QUEERIE!
ERICA SAKURAZAWA: COLLECTED WORKS
ET CETERA
ETERNITY
EVIL'S RETURN
FAERIES' LANDING
FAKE
FLCL
FLOWER OF THE DEEP SLEEP, THE
FORBIDDEN DANCE
FRUITS BASKET

G GUNDAM
GATEKEEPERS
GETBACKERS
GIRL GOT GAME
GRAVITATION
GTO
GUNDAM SEED ASTRAY
GUNDAM WING
GUNDAM WING: BATTLEFIELD OF PACIFISTS
GUNDAM WING: ENDLESS WALTZ
GUNDAM WING: THE LAST OUTPOST (G-UNIT)
HANDS OFF!
HAPPY MANIA
HARLEM BEAT
HYPER RUNE
I.N.V.U.
IMMORTAL RAIN
INITIAL D
INSTANT TEEN: JUST ADD NUTS
ISLAND
JING: KING OF BANDITS
JING: KING OF BANDITS - TWILIGHT TALES
JULINE
KARE KANO
KILL ME, KISS ME
KINDAICHI CASE FILES, THE
KING OF HELL
KODOCHA: SANA'S STAGE
LAMENT OF THE LAMB
LEGAL DRUG
LEGEND OF CHUN HYANG, THE
LES BIJOUX
LOVE HINA
LOVE OR MONEY
LUPIN III
LUPIN III: WORLD'S MOST WANTED
MAGIC KNIGHT RAYEARTH I
MAGIC KNIGHT RAYEARTH II
MAHOROMATIC: AUTOMATIC MAIDEN
MAN OF MANY FACES
MARMALADE BOY
MARS
MARS: HORSE WITH NO NAME
MINK
MIRACLE GIRLS
MIYUKI-CHAN IN WONDERLAND
MODEL
MOURYOU KIDEN: LEGEND OF THE NYMPHS
NECK AND NECK
ONE
ONE I LOVE, THE
PARADISE KISS
PARASYTE
PASSION FRUIT
PEACH GIRL
PEACH GIRL: CHANGE OF HEART
PET SHOP OF HORRORS
PITA-TEN
PLANET LADDER

08.2

STOP!

This is the back of the book.
You wouldn't want to spoil a great ending!

This book is printed "manga-style," in the authentic Japanese right-to-left format. Since none of the artwork has been flipped or altered, readers get to experience the story just as the creator intended. You've been asking for it, so TOKYOPOP® delivered: authentic, hot-off-the-press, and far more fun!

DIRECTIONS

top right panel, numbers. Have fun, and look for more 100% authentic manga from TOKYOPOP®!